English
Sixteenth-Century
Verse

AMORETTI

AND

Epithalamion.

Written not long since
by Edmunde
Spenser.

Printed for William
Ponsonby.1595.

Title page of Edmund Spenser's *Amoretti and Epithalamion*. First edition, 1595. Courtesy of the Folger Shakespeare Library, Washington, D.C.

English Sixteenth-Century Verse

AN ANTHOLOGY

EDITED WITH AN INTRODUCTION AND NOTES BY

RICHARD S. SYLVESTER

W · W · NORTON & COMPANY

New York · London

FOR MY

Mother AND *Father*

First published as a Norton paperback 1984
by arrangement with Doubleday & Company, Inc.

Originally published 1974 under the title
The Anchor Anthology of Sixteenth-Century Verse

Library of Congress Cataloging in Publication Data
Anchor anthology of sixteenth–century verse
English sixteenth–century verse.
Originally published: The Anchor anthology of
sixteenth–century verse. 1st ed. 1974.
Bibliography: p.
Includes index.
1. English poetry—Early modern, 1500–1700.
I. Sylvester, Richard Standish.   II. Title.
PR1205.S78   1984   821'.3'08   84–1091
ISBN 0-393-30206-7 {PBK}

W. W. Norton & Company, Inc.,
500 Fifth Avenue, New York, N.Y. 10110
W. W. Norton & Company Ltd.,
37 Great Russell Street, London WC1B 3NU

CONTENTS

THE SONNETEERS

ACKNOWLEDGMENTS

I am deeply indebted to Professors Louis L. Martz of Yale University and J. Max Patrick of New York University, who first encouraged me in my efforts to interest publishers in the kind of inexpensive, old-spelling texts presented here. Their advice, together with that of Professor William Ringler, Jr., of the University of Chicago, on matters of selection and choice of copy-text, has been invaluable. Specific thanks are due, and are here gratefully rendered, to Professor Richard C. Harrier of New York University (for permission to use his texts of Wyatt), to Professor Charles W. Eckert of Indiana University (for permission to use his text of Surrey), and to Professor Walter R. Davis (for permission to use his text of Campion). Wanda Fiak, Grace Michele, Dorothy Pfuderer, and Ray Banion have given me much help with the preparation of typescripts and the checking of the texts and I am deeply grateful to them. My thanks are recorded here to the Director of the Folger Shakespeare Library, O. B. Hardison, for permission to reproduce the title page of Spenser's *Amoretti and Epithalamion*, which serves as the frontispiece to this volume. William Whitehead and William Strachan of Doubleday's Anchor division have, with the assistance of their staff, more than upheld the fine tradition of scholarly publishing in which I am happy to have participated.

INTRODUCTION

In editing this old-spelling anthology of sixteenth-century verse
I have been guided by two main considerations. First, years of
teaching with both undergraduate and graduate students have
convinced me that the original texts, whether they derive from
manuscripts or printed editions, present fewer difficulties to the
average reader than the typical, "normalized" texts of Chaucer
now employed in many classrooms. On the other hand, the
positive advantages to be gained from studying our early poetry
in its original spelling[1] do not need to be pressed. Making di-
rect contact with the past can be, and often is, an exciting mo-
ment in the development of the critical imagination. One
acquires not only a new historical perspective on poetic lan-
guage as its forms and rhythms were being shaped, but philologi-
cal curiosity is also aroused, with an attendant interest in
semantics and phonetics. In short, the reader, prodded at first
by an archaic idiom or puzzled by an odd-seeming contraction,
focuses more sharply on the text before him. This heightening
of attention, particularly when it is skillfully guided, is always
the primary critical act. To read exactly, with historical ac-
curacy, is the proper threshold of true literary appreciation.

Secondly, and again I believe I speak from shared pedagogi-
cal experience, there is a real need for an anthology of six-
teenth-century poetry that includes a reasonable selection of
both major poets and major poems. In the present edition, the
general reader will discover, I trust, many old favorites, but also

---

[1] And to a lesser extent, in the present edition, in its original punctuation.
For the editorial principles adopted here, see below, "A Note on the Texts."

some pleasant surprises. The teacher should now find it practical to plan a course in sixteenth-century verse without resorting either to an agglomeration of book orders (hardbound here, paperback there) or to the assignment of an expensively comprehensive anthology. With each of the poets represented here, I have always given complete poems—*Phyllyp Sparowe*, the *Induction* to *A Mirror for Magistrates*, *The Steele Glas*, *Hero and Leander*. In addition, I have deliberately tried to give the fullest possible selection from the poets who loomed largest in the century—fifty-one poems by Wyatt, twenty-seven by Surrey, all of *Astrophil and Stella*, the *Amoretti* together with the *Epithalamion* and *Prothalamion*, and thirty-three poems by Campion. If one adds Shakespeare's *Sonnets* to the sequences and individual selections given here, it should be possible to achieve a fair overview of the sonnet, that most characteristic sixteenth-century lyrical form.

To emphasize (if not, indeed, to advertise) these advantages will scarcely fail to lessen my own and the reader's awareness of the limitations which I have had to impose on my selections. Every anthologist, and every critic of anthologies, comes in the end to think of all the other possibilities, the missed chances, the "startling omissions," the books that might have been. My deliberate exclusions were not, however, meant as pejorative judgments on either poets or poems. I have omitted lyrics from the early Tudor songbooks, which meant losing gems like the following:

> Benedicite! Whate dremyd I this nyght?
> Methought the worlde was turnyd up so downe,
> The son, the moone, had lost ther force and light;
> The see also drownyd both towre and towne:
> Yett more mervell how that I harde the sownde
> Of onys voice sayying, 'Bere in thy mynd,
> Thi lady hath forgoten to be kynd.'[2]

Nor have I attempted to represent the full development of the miscellany tradition during the century, from Tottel's *Songs*

---

[2] No. 12 in the Fayrfax MS. (British Museum Additional MS. 5465); text as given by John Stevens, *Music and Poetry in the Early Tudor Court* (London, Methuen, 1961), p. 357.

and Sonets (1557) to *England's Helicon* (1600).³ Thus a number of fine lyrics are not to be found here, but it is my hope that the concentrated offerings from Surrey and Wyatt, who formed the heart of Tottel's influential collections, and from Campion, the finest flower of the later lyricism, will provide some compensation.⁴

My other exclusions have been almost as arbitrary if not quite so painful. Verse translations are omitted, which entails the loss of Surrey's blank-verse *Aeneid* and Wyatt's terza rima *Penitential Psalms*. Satiric verse, except for Gascoigne's *The Steele Glas*, is not represented, and thus both the bulk of Skelton's mature work at the beginning of the century and the almost instantaneous satiric reaction to the sonnet vogue at its end are not evident in this volume. Minor poets have inevitably suffered, not merely Googe and Turberville, but also Greene and Nashe. Perhaps a greater loss is my failure to illustrate Sidney's many poetic experiments in both the *Old* and the *New Arcadia* or to show Chapman at work as he refashioned Marlowe's great poem into something new and strange. My hope is that readers of this volume may be led by it to some of the other rich banquets which the poetic traditions of the century so frequently offer. For now, and within the present covers, I trust that enough will be as good as a feast.

At first glance, the sixteenth-century poetic scene might almost be said to have opened on an empty stage. English poetry, it has been somewhat unfairly argued, had been in a state of decline since Chaucer's death one hundred years earlier. The political and social turmoil of the Wars of the Roses, the rapidly changing nature of English pronunciation, the dearth of real poets (or, conversely, the dominance of John Lydgate)—all of these factors have been adduced by

³ For a general survey of the miscellanies, see Franklin Dickey, "Collections of Songs and Sonnets," in *Elizabethan Poetry* (Stratford-Upon-Avon Studies 2, London, Edward Arnold, 1960), pp. 30–51.
⁴ I have, however, tried to illustrate Tottel's treatment of Wyatt's text by giving, in three instances (Wyatt nos. 2, 15, and 29), his 1557 "modernization" of the poet's original.

critics who tend to view the fifteenth century as, so far as poetry goes, a vast desert, imaginatively sterile however glittering the rays which were at times emitted from its "aureate language."[5] Yet a century that could produce the miracle plays as well as a strong series of vernacular romances and allegorical poems,[6] a century in which the popular ballads, as we know them, were written down, and which strongly nourished a late medieval lyrical tradition in both secular and religious verse, can scarcely be dismissed as the most barren period of our literature. By the end of the century, Caxton, who had established his press at Westminster in 1477, had printed Malory and most of Chaucer.[7] If no great poetry was being written in the 1490s, the means for its wide and rapid dissemination was already at hand.

The figure of John Skelton (c. 1460–1529) illustrates one aspect of the problems that the early Tudor poets in this volume are so often trying to define and solve. Skelton is the only cleric among the poets presented here, a fact that suggests his many links with the middle ages as well as the peculiar difficulties which, as poet-priest, he was so often to confront in his verse. *The Bowge of Courte* (1498) is a curiously uneasy poem: its allegorical pattern (the ship of state, the personified uncertainties of court life) looks backward, but its tone and the dramatic concreteness of its dialogue emphasize the individual voice that speaks through it. In *Phyllyp Sparowe*, writing now in his own meter—the Skeltonic—the poet is less insecure, more convinced of the power and value of his fictions even though they are threatened, in the second part of the poem, by those literal-minded readers who could imagine that

---

[5] For an excellent survey of Lydgate in terms of his century, and for a deft corrective to the view described above, see Derek Pearsall, *John Lydgate* (Charlottesville, The University of Virginia Press, 1970).
[6] The best of the latter are collected in W. W. Skeat's "Chaucerian and Other Pieces," Vol. 7 of his edition of Chaucer's *Works* (Oxford, Clarendon Press, 1894–97). Another useful collection is E. P. Hammond's *English Verse between Chaucer and Surrey* (Durham, N.C., Duke University Press, 1927).
[7] For the development of the book trade in this period, see H. S. Bennett, *English Books and Readers 1475 to 1557* (Cambridge, Cambridge University Press, 1952).

all was not morally sound in such trivial writing.[8] Skelton spent most of his career trying to reconcile his moral earnestness with his desire to play, his dislike for the new humanistic learning with his real love for language and all its effects. His problem—where does the poet stand in relation to his medium and to his audience?—becomes a central question for the later century.

The vernacular poetry of Skelton's contemporary Sir Thomas More forms a slender, but significant, body of verse. More was, in fact, far better as a Latin poet than he was as an English one.[9] When he writes in a popular meter, as in *A Mery Gest*, he has no touble at all with the keeping of accent:

> Yet or this daye
> I have herde saye,
>   That many a man certesse,
> Hath with good cast
> Be ryche at last,
>   That hath begon with lesse.

But when More turns to rhyme royal, the courtly stanza that had enjoyed tremendous popularity since Chaucer used it in the *Troilus*, his touch is less sure:

> Whoso ne knoweth the strength, power and myght,
> Of Venus and me her lytle sonne Cupyde . . .

---

8 Perhaps typical of the contemporary attitude are the following lines by Alexander Barclay:

> Holde me excusyd: for why my wyll is gode
> Men to induce unto vertue and goodnes,
> I wryte no jest ne tale of Robyn hode
> Nor sawe no sparcles ne sede of vyciousnes.
> Wyse men love vertue, wylde people wantones;
> It longeth nat to my scyence nor cunnynge
> For Phylyp the Sparowe the Dirge to synge.

(*The Ship of Fools*, ed. T. H. Jamieson [Edinburgh, William Paterson, 1874], 2, 331.)
9 See *The Latin Epigrams of Thomas More*, edited and translated by L. Bradner and C. A. Lynch (Chicago, Chicago University Press, 1953). More's *Utopia* (1516), one of the great books of Western civilization, was written in Latin, not in English.

The limping effect here, deriving mainly from the poet's failure to reconcile word accent with metrical accent, is characteristic of much of the verse written in the first half of the century. More himself could, on occasion, do better, never more finely than in the haunting refrain of his *A Rueful Lamentation:* "Farewell and pray for me, for lo now here I ly."

The metrical problem was not to be finally and fully coped with until Sidney, seventy-five years later, showed firmly how voice and verse could be made to combine and clash in restless harmony. In the meantime, one finds poet after poet, each working off the varied traditions that had come down to him, trying to achieve a regular iambic meter which would replace the four- or five-stress line of the fifteenth century. "Poulter's measure,"[10] alternating lines of iambic hexameter and septameter, was a convenient answer for the poets of the middle century. Its metronomic beat, painfully tedious to modern ears, perhaps provided just that emphatic degree of syllabic and accentual regularity that, to the poets (Surrey and Gascoigne especially) employing it, had been lacking in earlier verse. The difficulty with poulter's was that once one succumbed to its hypnotic patterns—"In youth I lived with love, she had my lustye dayes,/In age I thought with lingering life to stay my wandering wais,"[11]—there seemed to be no way to escape. If John Thompson is correct,[12] release came only with the experiments in classical meters undertaken by Spenser, Sidney, and others in the late seventies and early eighties.

Wyatt's metrics, over which so much critical discussion has occurred, pose the problem in an acute form, though it should be noted that the situation has been somewhat exaggerated. A

---

[10] For Gascoigne, in his *Certayne notes of Instruction* (1575, printed here in the selection from Gascoigne), poulter's was "the commonest sort of verse which we use now adayes." The form, which was used in the Sternhold and Hopkins Psalm translations, later became known as "common meter."

[11] Gascoigne, "The Divorce of a Lover," ll. 3–4.

[12] *The Founding of English Metre* (New York, Columbia University Press, 1961). For the classical experiments, represented here only by some of Campion's poems (nos. 30–32), see W. L. Ringler's introduction and notes to his edition of Sidney's *Poems* (Oxford, Clarendon Press, 1962) and G. D. Willcock, "Passing Pitefull Hexameters," *Modern Language Review*, 29 (1934), 1–19.

line like "For hetherto though I have lost all my tyme" (no. 5) is not irregular at all if one makes the normal contraction of the speaking voice to read "I've" for "I have." Moreover, when Wyatt writes in the native song tradition in his best plain style, he is as syllabically correct as Campion is later. The difficulties come in some of the sonnets, where Wyatt may be trying to reproduce the effect of Italian weak endings, and in a few of his relatively rare rhyme royal stanzas. Whatever the technical explanation for these irregularities may be, it is hard not to believe that they were deliberate in this subtle, austere poet. There may be no "correct" way to scan "Besely seking with a continuell chaunge" (no. 15), but here meter and meaning harmonize so perfectly that the problem seems almost irrelevant.

With Surrey, metrical difficulties are infrequent and syllabic regularity is the norm. This fact, combined with an effort to see Wyatt as a kind of "proto-John Donne," has led to the modern downgrading of the younger poet in reference to his older contemporary. Tottel in his *Miscellany* and the Elizabethans saw things otherwise. For George Puttenham, writing in 1588, Wyatt and Surrey were the two leaders of "a new company of courtly makers" who, drawing upon Italian poetry, "greatly pollished our rude & homely maner of vulgar Poesie from that it had bene before, and for that cause may justly be sayd the first reformers of our English meetre and style."[13] For Tottel, Surrey's style was "honorable," and he went on to speak of "the weightinesse of the depewitted sir Thomas Wyatt."[14] The Elizabethans saw the two poets as complementary, in much the same way as the eighteenth century was later to look back at the dual example of Waller and Denham. They found sources of strength in each poet's achievement—and they were right.

To praise Surrey again now need involve no detraction from Wyatt's achievement. There are many things in Wyatt that are

---

[13] *The Arte of English Poesie*, in G. G. Smith, *Elizabethan Critical Essays* (Oxford, Oxford University Press, 1904), 2, 62–63.
[14] *Tottel's Miscellany*, ed. H. E. Rollins (Cambridge, Mass., Harvard University Press, 1928–29), 1, 2.

simply beyond Surrey; the older poet's "deep wittedness" leads
him, in his best poems, to a delicately nuanced interiority; he
cannot stomach the higher flights of Petrarchanism; his love is
earthly, self-centered, at times ironic, and often bitterly venge-
ful:

> Perchaunce the[e] lye wethered and old,
> The wynter nyght that are so cold,
>   Playnyng in vain unto the mone;
> Thy wisshes then dare not be told,
>   Care then who lyst, for I have done.[15]

Wyatt's sturdy manliness can be very attractive, never more so
than in "Myne owne John Poyntz" (no. 49), the best of his
satires; but he can also fall victim to a kind of hesitant,
clichéed self-pity, an attitude easy enough to sympathize with
when we reflect on the pressures to which he was subject in the
court of Henry VIII.[16]

   Surrey, on the other hand, is a much more public poet.
When he does look into his heart and write, as in "So crewell
prison, howe could betyde, alas" (no. 17), he seeks not so
much to analyze himself as to portray his relationships with
others. Where Wyatt relishes the internal psychological tensions
of Petrarch's *Canzoniere*, Surrey catches something of the
other side of Petrarch's genius, that willingness to reach out
into the natural world and to see his love reflected in it:

> Alas so all thinges nowe doe holde their peace.
>   (no. 12)

Or,

> Set me wheras the sonne dothe perche the grene,
> Or whear his beames may not dissolve the Ise.
>   (no. 9)

Surrey's best efforts come when he attempts a semi-narrative or
semi-dramatic mode, writing an invective against the citizens of

---

[15] "My lute, awake!" (no. 26)
[16] The thinness of Wyatt's emotional (not metrical) range is evident in
the way in which he fails to employ natural imagery.

London (no. 18) or richly commemorating the lusts of a
Sardanapalus:

> The dent of swordes from kysses semed straunge,
> And harder then hys ladyes syde his targe;
> From glotton feastes to sowldyers fare a chaunge,
> His helmet, far above a garlandes charge.
>
> (no. 8)

This kind of powerful eloquence was as far beyond Wyatt's
capacities as a penetrating phrase like "lustes negligence"[17] was
beyond Surrey's. It shows to even better advantage when Surrey
produces his poetry of praise, to a young lady,

> From Tuscan cam my ladies worthi race,
>
> (no. 1)

to a youthful retainer,

> Norfolk sprang thee, Lambeth holds thee dead,
>
> (no. 14)

or, best of all, to the memory of Wyatt himself,

> Wyat resteth here, that quicke coulde never rest.
>
> (no. 23)

This last poem, perhaps Surrey's finest, gets the relationship be-
tween Wyatt and Surrey just right. Wyatt had, for Surrey, "A
Hand that taught what *might* be saide in rime"; Wyatt is the
innovator, the poet who suggested new possibilities, but he left
much for his successors to develop and explore.

The third quarter of the century, or, more precisely, the
years (1557–79) between the publication of *Tottel's Miscellany*
and Spenser's *The Shepheardes Calendar*, can best be viewed as
a period of experimentation which, however tentative and in-
secure it may at times appear to be, was nevertheless a necessary
prelude to the great achievements of 1580–1600. The *Calendar*,
a great landmark in the history of English verse, is itself one
poet's record of his own experiments with a variety of new and

---

[17] Wyatt, no. 2, l. 6. Both Wyatt and Surrey translated this sonnet of
Petrarch (*Rime*, cxl). Surrey's weaker equivalent is "hote desire" (no. 4).
The Italian line reads "E vòl che 'l gran desio, l'accesa spene."

xxiv *Introduction*

old forms. But the more typical poets of this seedbed time were Thomas Sackville and George Gascoigne.

Almost all of Sackville's verse is contained in *A Mirror for Magistrates*,[18] that vast storehouse of historical exempla which went through edition after edition between 1559 and 1610. Whether or not Sackville's *Induction* was designed to introduce all the poems in the 1563 edition of the *Mirror* or merely his own "Complaint of Buckingham" remains debatable, but there can be little doubt that his visionary stanzas establish a mood and atmosphere singularly appropriate to the "tragedies" that follow. Sackville's intention was not so much to make something new as to bring the dead to life, a theme which he develops both literally and dramatically through the tale of his dreamer's descent into hell. This kind of revitalizing looks back to Chaucer quite strongly, but it also looks ahead, as the meter and archaizing diction of the *Induction* show, to Spenser. The *Induction*, in fact, is the only poetry written in the sixteenth century before Spenser that sounds and feels very much like him.

"Experiment," in the ordinary sense of the word, is more properly applicable to the works of George Gascoigne, dramatist, courtier, poet, journalist, literary critic. In *The Posies*, Gascoigne essays most of the current lyrical forms,[19] sometimes straightforwardly, sometimes with a winning tongue-in-cheek irony which ought to remind us that even the journeymen among sixteenth-century poets are usually quite critical of the borrowed or inherited forms they adopt. Gascoigne gives us the first sonnet sequence in English[20] as well as the first long poem in original blank verse (*The Steele Glas*). He is, however,

---

[18] His dedicatory sonnet to Hoby's *Courtier* and his contribution to the tragedy *Gorboduc* are the only exceptions. In addition to the *Induction*, Sackville contributed "The Complaint of Henry, Duke of Buckingham" to the *Mirror*.

[19] To these should be added the dozen or so poems interspersed through the narrative of *The Adventures of Master F. J.*, Gascoigne's prose novella (1573).

[20] Professor William K. Ringler, Jr., informs me that his *Check-List of Sixteenth-Century English Verse* (in progress) will show that hundreds of sonnets, many of them still in manuscript, were being written in the third quarter of the century.

essentially a plain style man, the prime representative of the
school of native lyricism which includes Raleigh and Greville
later.[21] "Gascoigne's Woodmanship," with its wryly reflective
self-criticism, is certainly one of the best poems this tradition
was to produce. With it should be compared the verse epistle
to Bartholomew Withipoll, "Mine owne good *Bat*," a poem
that, for all its echoes of Wyatt's "Myne owne John Poyntz,"
has been relatively ignored in most discussions of Gascoigne
and his predecessors.

Gascoigne died in 1577. Within three years, the advent of
Spenser and Sidney on the literary scene makes much of the
verse written earlier in the century seem amateurish if not
naïf. Here at last were two great poets, men alert to all the
possibilities inherent in the rapidly expanding language. In this
anthology we meet Sidney only in his role as Astrophil, the
"star-crossed lover" of Stella, but that is sufficient. Here, for the
first time, something of the full weight of the Petrarchan tradi-
tion comes through into English poetry. Nor is this just a matter
of Sidney being the first poet to produce a full-length sonnet
sequence in the vernacular.[22] Astrophil, a poet-lover who can
be scornful of poetry but not of love, who finds his role as
conventional lover all too real in moments of crisis, must, in the
end, revert to the unfulfilling oscillations so well delineated in
the Petrarchan paradoxes:

> So strangely (alas) thy [Stella's] works in me prevaile,
> That in my woes for thee thou art my joy,
> And in my joyes for thee my only annoy.
>
> (no. 108)

Along the way we have been given not only a rich emotional
gamut of experience but also an at times dazzling display of
poetic ability. Sidney can use the sonnet for apostrophe ("With

[21] For Ivor Winters' seminal essays on the plain style in sixteenth-century
poetry, see the Bibliography. C. S. Lewis' discussion of "Drab Age Verse"
is another approach to these poets (*English Literature in the Sixteenth
Century* [Oxford, Clarendon Press, 1954], pp. 222–71).
[22] Just how important this precedent was is clear from the several dozen
sequences that came out within a few years of *Astrophil and Stella,* first
published in 1591.

how sad steps, o Moone, thou climb'st the skies," no. 31),
for playful encounters with Cupid (no. 11), or for direct
address to his beloved; he can be intimately colloquial ("Deare,
why make you more of a dog then me?", no. 59) within the
constraints of his fourteen-line form, or he can dramatize his
feelings poignantly in the songs he situates at key points in his
sequence:

> Graunt, o deere, on knees I pray,
> (Knees on ground he then did stay)
> That not I but since I love you
> Time and place for me may move you.
>
> Never season was more fit,
> Never roome more apt for it;
> Smiling ayre allowes my reason
> These birds sing; now use the season.
>
> • • •
>
> Trust me while I thee deny,
> In my selfe the smart I try,
> Tyran honor doth thus use thee,
> Stellas selfe might not refuse thee.
>
> (Eighth Song,
> ll. 49–56, 93–96)

Here, right down to the stage directions, is the tragedy that
Thomas Nashe saw in *Astrophil and Stella* when he first intro-
duced it to English readers: "The argument cruell chastitie, the
Prologue hope, the Epilogue dispaire; *videte, queso, et linguis
animisque fauete.*"[23]

Set beside Sidney's *Astrophil and Stella,* Spenser's *Amoretti*
appears a much cooler, more reserved register of experience.
This is perhaps as it should be, for of all the Elizabethan sonnet
sequences only Spenser's achieves a happy ending in its narra-
tive outline.[24] Spenser's title seems almost to allude to the

---

[23] *The Works of Thomas Nashe,* ed. R. B. McKerrow, 5 vols., revised ed.
(Oxford, Blackwell, 1958), 3, 329. Nash alludes to Ovid, *Amores,* III, ii,
43: "Behold, I beg you, and let your tongues and hearts applaud."
[24] A parallel, but infinitely weaker, outcome also occurs in William Habing-
ton's *Castara* (1634).

poems which he links together to tell the story of his love for
Elizabeth Boyle—"pretty little tokens of love,"[25] the "pretty
rooms" (*stanze*) that Donne would later, in "The Canoniza-
tion," find most convenient for the celebration of an ideal
amour. Although Spenser will, with quiet humor, refer to the
"huge massacres" made by his mistress' eyes (no. X), he is
never a mere victim of love's onslaughts; his lady may be "stub-
borne" (no. XXIX), but he makes us feel, quite early in the
sequence, that she will not hold out forever. The only real
enemy in the *Amoretti* is not the "sweet warrior" of the
Petrarchan tradition but Time itself, which controls the "weary
yeares" (no. LXII) of life, washes away names written in the
sand (no. LXXV), and brings both sorrow and joy to mortal
man. Perhaps, Spenser has his Elizabeth say, it is vain "A
mortall thing so to immortalize" (no. LXXV), but he proceeds
nevertheless to end his sequence with the magnificent *Epi-
thalamion*, the climax of his story that both relates his personal
love to the world in which it must live and shows us how
poetry itself can become "for short time an endlesse moni-
ment."

Among the poets who chose, with Spenser, to grapple with
the problem of time in the 1590s, Shakespeare stands supreme.
His sonnet sequence again and again confronts the inexorable
destroyer:

> Not marble nor the guilded monument . . .
> (no. 55)[26]
> When I doe count the clock that tels the time . . .
> (no. 12)
> Against that time (if ever that time come) . . .
> (no. 49)
> No! Time, thou shalt not bost that I doe change . . .
> (no. 123)

---

[25] I owe this phrase, and much else in this paragraph, to Professor L. L.
Martz. See his essay "The *Amoretti*: 'Most Goodly Temperature,'" in
*Form and Convention in the Poetry of Edmund Spenser: Selected Papers
from the English Institute*, ed. W. Nelson (New York, Columbia Univer-
sity Press, 1961), pp. 146–68.
[26] All the Shakespeare quotations are from *Shakespeare's Poems, A Facsim-
ile of the Earliest Editions* (New Haven, Yale University Press, 1964).

The *Sonnets*, published in 1609 but composed in the 1590s, are the best of all the Elizabethan sequences not merely because they contain more sonnets (154) than any other sequence,[27] but because they probe more deeply, more incisively, into the eternal questions that poetry, at its best, is always asking of itself. Shall the simile be risked? "Shall I compare thee to a Summers day?" (no. 18). I have nothing to write about, but "How can my Muse want subject to invent?" (no. 38). Is the beloved indescribable? "What is your substance, whereof are you made?" (no. 53). Or, at the last, the one question all the Elizabethan sonneteers were constantly asking of themselves, "Yet who knows not conscience is borne of love?"[28]

When measured against perfection, all poets may seem faulty. Yet the achievement of the sonneteers, all of them pricked on by the example of Sidney, writing in the 1590s should not be underrated. It is true that we confront a welter of "Ideas," "Delias," "Diellas," and "Dianas," but, for the most part, the poets know now what they are about. The passion may not be mortal, as it was in Spenser (and possibly in Sidney), but the exercise is more than worth the effort:

> In tyme the strong and statelie turrets fall . . .
> > (Fletcher, no. 2)
> I have not spent the Aprill of my time . . .
> > (Griffin, no. 3)
> Let others sing of Knights and Palladines . . .
> > (Daniel, no. 7)

Even anonymity can confer grace, and thus the author of *Zepheria* comes up with a meditation on "those voyd houres of intermission" that lifts the commonplace "absence makes the

---

[27] Not a negligible factor by any means. Shakespeare's staying power becomes evident when it is recalled that the 100 sonnets of the puny Watson's *Hekatompathia* or the even more dismal 300-odd of H. Lok's *Sonnets of the Christian Passion* (1597) are his only competitors—except for Sidney, whose *Astrophil and Stella* runs to 108 sonnets.
[28] No. 151. The word "conscience" in this charged context refers not only to moral responsibility (so often forgotten by other sonneteers), but also to self-consciousness, the awareness that writing about love fosters.

heart grow fonder" out of the clichéd tradition in which it originated. Coupled with these moments (admittedly rare) of smooth creativity come the alert reflections on form and mode:

> If Musique and sweet Poetrie agree . . .
> (Barnfield, no. 1)
> Into these Loves, who but for Passion lookes,
> At this first sight, here let him lay them by.
> (Drayton, no. 1)

It is a rare age when even a "William Smith" can offer "A few sad sonnets, which my muse hath framed" to Colin Clout[29] without apologizing too much for them. The sonnet, like any fad, would pass,[30] but, even in the hands of minor poets, it had its memorable accomplishments:

> Since ther's no helpe, Come let us kisse and part,
> (Drayton, no. 10)
> Care-charmer Sleepe, sonne of the sable night,
> (Daniel, no. 6)
> O false and treacherous Probability,
> (Greville, no. 7)

Amid the vogue of sonneteering in the 1590s other spirits were casting a slightly jaundiced eye on love and the proper way to write about it. In many ways, Marlowe's *Hero and Leander* climaxes the non-dramatic poetry of the sixteenth century. Here is the new couplet, freed from the mid-century problems of meter and accent, bouncing and yet flexible, a fit vehicle for anything an aspiring poet might wish to say. Marlowe's sophistication, when weighed against the earlier examples of Wyatt and Gascoigne, is remarkable. The jeweled diction of his splendid poem is balanced, in his narrator, by a worldly wisdom that carefully preserves its distance from the scene he describes: "Who ever lov'd, that lov'd not at first sight?" (l. 176). He must admit, and the poem, as we have it in the first

---

[29] Spenser's pseudonym, firmly attached to him since the publication of *The Shepheardes Calendar* in 1579.
[30] Not very easily. In the seventeenth century the form would be put to new uses by Donne, Milton, and others. The new possibilities are already suggested in Greville's *Caelica*.

edition, proves, that "Love makes the world go round," but the story, to this narrator, is an old one. He sympathizes with the lovers, but will not give himself to them completely; granting beauty and youth all their rights, he still leaves us with an awareness that this is not the whole story. The plea had been made before ("Come live with mee, and be my love") and it would be made again. No matter now, in the 1590s, for English poetry had come of age and it would be a long time before it forgot how to ask the questions.

A NOTE ON THE TEXTS

In accordance with the principles adopted in the Anchor Seventeenth-Century Series, to which this volume is both complementary and companion,[1] the texts presented here are given in the original spelling. Long "ſ" has been rendered as s, and u and v, i and j have been normalized to conform with modern usage. Abbreviations in the original texts have been expanded. A few obvious printers' errors in spelling have been silently corrected but substantive emendations of the early editions or manuscripts are made only on rare occasions. The sources for the texts are indicated in the Commentary section for each poet.

Punctuation and capitalization in sixteenth-century texts have presented special problems. In the cases of authors whose works were printed relatively carefully during their lifetime or shortly after their death (More, Sackville, Spenser, Sidney, Marlowe, and the sonneteers), I have followed the original punctuation and capitalization, emending only in cases of obvious error. Where texts are based on manuscripts or on poorly printed early editions (Skelton, Wyatt, Surrey, Raleigh, and Campion), modern punctuation and capitalization have been supplied. Gascoigne has proven to be a special case. His lyrics and the prose texts of his *Dedicatory Epistle* and *Certayne Notes of Instruction* are given as in the first editions (1575 and 1576); in *The Steele Glas*, however, almost every line is broken by a medial comma which quite destroys the movement of the meter. These caesural stops have been removed from the text presented here, except where they are required by modern standards of punctuation.

---

[1]See Louis L. Martz, ed., *English Seventeenth-Century Verse*, Vol. I (W. W. Norton, New York, 1973), originally *The Anchor Anthology of Seventeenth-Century Verse*, Vol. I.

JOHN SKELTON

1460?–1529

1.

The Bowge of Courte

In Autumpne, whan the sonne in vyrgyne
By radyante hete enryped hath our corne,
Whan Luna, full of mutabylyte,
As Emperes the dyademe hath worne
Of our pole artyke, smylynge halfe in scorne   5
At our foly and our unstedfastnesse,
The tyme whan Mars to werre hym dyde dres,

I, callynge to mynde the great auctoryte
Of poetes olde, whyche full craftely
Under as coverte termes as coude be,   10
Can touche a troughte and cloke it subtylly
Wyth fresshe utteraunce full sentencyously,
Dyverse in style, some spared not vyce to wrythe,
Some of moralyte nobly dyde endyte,

Title: "Bowge of Courte" means literally "the mouth (French *bouche*) of court," i.e., the rations or rewards which the court gives to its retainers.
1. *vyrgyne:* the astrological sign of Virgo (August 22–September 21)
2. *enryped:* ripened; *corne:* grain
3. *Luna:* the harvest moon, which is now beginning to wane
5. *pole artyke:* Arcturus, part of the Corona Borealis
7. *to werre . . . dres:* began to get ready for war
11. *troughte:* truth
13. *wrythe:* write (i.e., describe satirically)
14. *endyte:* compose

Wherby I rede theyr renome and theyr fame   15
Maye never dye bute evermore endure.
I was sore moved to a force the same,
But Ignoraunce full soone dyde me dyscure
And shewed that in this arte I was not sure,
For to illumyne she sayde I was to dulle,   20
Avysynge me my penne awaye to pulle

And not to wrythe, for he so wyll atteyne,
Excedynge ferther than his connynge is,
His hede maye be harde, but feble is his brayne!
Yet have I knowen suche er this;   25
But of reproche surely he maye not mys
That clymmeth hyer than he may fotynge have;
What and he slyde downe, who shall hym save?

Thus up and down my mynde was drawen and cast
That I ne wyste what to do was beste;   30
Soo sore enwered that I was, at the laste,
Enforsed to slepe and for to take some reste,
And to lye downe as soone as I me dreste.
At Harwyche Porte, slumbrynge as I laye
In myne hostes house, called Powers Keye,   35

Me thoughte I sawe a shyppe, goodly of sayle,
Come saylyng forth into that haven brood,
Her takelynge ryche and of hye apparayle;

---

15. *rede:* understand (through reading); *renome:* renown
17. *a force:* try
18. *dyde me dyscure:* revealed to me the truth of my situation
21. *pulle:* pull back
22. *he so:* whoever
23. *connynge:* knowledge
28. *and:* if
30. *ne wyste:* didn't know
31. *enwered:* tired out
33. *me dreste:* was ready
38. *of hye apparayle:* her rigging fine

She kyste an anker and there she laye at rode.
Marchauntes her borded to see what she had lode.   40
Therein they founde Royall marchaundyse,
Fraghted with plesure of what ye coude devyse.

But than I thoughte I wolde not dwell behynde,
Amonge all other I put myselfe in prece.
Than there coude I none aquentaunce fynde;   45
There was moche noyse, anone one cryed, cese!
Sharpely commaundynge eche man holde hys pece.
Maysters, he sayde, the shyp that ye here see,
The Bowge of Courte it hyghte for certeynte;

The awnner thereof is lady of estate,   50
Whoos name to tell is Dame Saunce Pere.
Her marchaundyse is ryche and fortunate,
But who wyll have it muste paye therfore dere;
This royall chaffre that is shypped here
Is called favore-to-stonde-in-her-good-grace.   55
Than sholde ye see there pressynge in a pace

Of one and other that wolde this lady see,
Whiche sat behynde a traves of sylke fyne,
Of golde of tessew the fynest that myghte be,
In a trone whiche fer clerer dyde shyne   60
Than Phebus in his spere celestyne,
Whoos beaute, honoure, goodly porte,
I have to lytyll connynge to reporte.

---

39. *kyste:* cast; *at rode:* in the harbor
40. *lode:* loaded (in her cargo)
44. *prece:* the throng
49. *hyghte:* is called
50. *awnner:* owner
51. *Saunce Pere:* without equal
54. *chaffre:* merchandise
58. *traves:* screen
59. *gold of tessew:* cloth woven with gold
61. *Phebus . . . celestyne:* the sun in his celestial sphere
62. *porte:* bearing
63. *connynge:* knowledge

But of eche thynge there as I toke hede,
Among all other was wrytten in her trone   65
In golde letters, this worde, whiche I dyde rede:
Garder le fortune que est mauelz et bone.
And as I stode redynge this verse myselfe allone,
Her chyef gentylwoman, daunger by her name,
Gave me a taunte, and sayde I was to blame   70

To be so perte to prese so proudly uppe.
She sayde she trowed that I had eten sause;
She asked yf ever I dranke of saucys cuppe.
And I than softly answered to that clause,
That, so to saye, I had gyven her no cause.   75
Than asked she me, Syr, so God the spede,
What is thy name? and I sayde it was Drede.

What movyd the, quod she, hydder to come?
Forsoth, quod I, to bye some of youre ware.
And with that worde on me she gave a glome   80
With browes bente and gan on me to stare
Full daynnously, and fro me she dyde fare,
Levynge me stondynge as a mased man,
To whome there came another gentylwoman.

Desyre her name was, and so she me tolde,   85
Sayenge to me, Broder, be of good chere,
Abasshe you not, but hardely be bolde,
Avaunce your selfe to aproche and come nere.
What though our chaffer be never so dere,
Yet I avyse you to speke for ony drede;   90
Who spareth to speke, in fayth, he spareth to spede.

---

67. "Beware of fortune which is both bad and good"
69. *daunger:* disdain
72. *had:* omitted in *1499; eten sause:* become bold
77. *Drede:* Dread, Fear
80. *glome:* sour look
82. *daynnously:* disdainfully
83. *mased:* amazed
87. *hardely:* strongly
90. *for ony drede:* no matter what you fear
91. *spede:* achieve success

Maystres, quod I, I have none aquentaunce
That wyll for me be medyatoure and mene;
And this an other, I have but smale substaunce.
Pece, quod Desyre, ye speke not worth a bene! 95
Yf ye have not, in fayth, I wyll you lene
A precyous jewell, no rycher in this londe:
Bone aventure have here now in your honde.

Shyfte now therwith, let see, as ye can,
In Bowge of Courte chevysaunce to make; 100
For I dare saye that there nys erthly man
But, and he can *Bone aventure* take,
There can no favour nor frendshyp hym forsake.
Bone aventure may brynge you in suche case
That ye shall stonde in favoure and in grace. 105

But of one thynge I werne you er I goo:
She that styreth the shyp, make her your frende.
Maystres, quod I, I praye you tell me why soo,
And how I maye that waye and meanes fynde.
Forsothe, quod she, how ever blowe the wynde, 110
Fortune gydeth and ruleth all oure shyppe.
Whome she hateth shall over the see boorde skyp.

Whome she loveth, of all plesyre is ryche
Whyles she laugheth and hath luste for to playe,
Whome she hateth she casteth in the dyche, 115
For whan she fronneth, she thynketh to make a fray;
She cheryssheth him, and hym she casseth awaye.

---

93. *mene:* go-between
94. *this an other:* besides
95. *bene:* bean
96. *lene:* lend
98. *Bone aventure:* Good luck
100. *chevysaunce to make:* to do some business
101. *nys:* is no
107. *styreth:* steers
112. *see boorde:* side of the ship
114. *laugheth:* 1499 reads *laughed: hath luste:* desires
116. *fronneth:* frowns; *make a fray:* cause a fight
117. *casseth:* casts

6

Alas, quod I, how myghte I have her sure?
In fayth, quod she, by *bone aventure.*

Thus in a rowe of martchauntes a grete route   120
Suwed to Fortune that she would be theyre frynde.
They thronge in fast and flocked her aboute,
And I with them prayed her to have in mynde.
She promysed to us all she wolde be kynde;
Of Bowge of Court she asketh what we wold have,   125
And we asked favoure, and favour she us gave.

       Thus endeth the prologue; and begynneth
       the Bowge of Courte brevely compyled.

DREDE

THE sayle is up, Fortune ruleth our helme,
We wante no wynde to passe now over all;
Favoure we have toughther than ony elme,
That wyll abyde and never frome us fall.   130
But under hony ofte tyme lyeth bytter gall,
For as me thoughte in our shyppe I dyde see
Full subtyll persones in nombre foure and thre.

The fyrste was Favell, full of flatery,
Wyth fables false, that well coude fayne a tale;   135
The seconde was Suspecte whiche that dayly
Mysdempte eche man, with face deedly and pale;
And Harvy Hafter, that well coude picke a male;
With other foure of theyr affynyte:
Dysdayne, Ryotte, Dyssymuler, Subtylte.   140

---

120. *route:* crowd
129. *toughther:* tougher
134. *Favell:* Flattery
136. *Suspecte:* Suspicion
137. *Mysdempte:* Misjudged
138. *Hafter:* the Deceiver; *male:* piece of baggage

Fortune theyr frende with whome oft she dyde daunce:
They coude not faile, thei thought, they were so sure.
And oftentymes I wolde myselfe avaunce
With them to make solace and pleasure;
But my dysporte they coude not well endure;   145
They sayde they hated for to dele with Drede.
Than Favell gan wyth fayre speche me to fede.

FAVELL

Noo thynge erthely that I wonder so sore
As of your connynge that is so excellent;
Deynte to have with us suche one in store,   150
So vertuously that hath his dayes spente.
Fortune to you gyftes of grace hath lente:
Loo, what it is a man to have connynge!
All erthly tresoure it is surmountynge.

Ye be an apte man, as ony can be founde,   155
To dwell with us and serve my ladyes grace.
Ye be to her, yea, worth a thousande pounde;
I herde her speke of you within shorte space,
Whan there were dyverse that sore dyde you manace.
And though I say it I was myselfe your frende,   160
For here be dyverse to you that be unkynde.

But this one thynge ye maye be sure of me,
For by that lorde that bought dere all mankynde,
I can not flater, I muste be playne to the.
And ye nede ought, man, shewe to me your mynde,   165
For ye have me whome faythfull ye shall fynde;
Whyles I have ought, by God, thou shalt not lacke,
And yf nede be, a bolde worde I dare cracke.

---

148. *sore:* seriously
150. *Deynte:* A delight
154. *All . . . surmountynge:* It surpasses all earthly treasure
158. *within . . . space:* a little while ago
163. *bought dere:* redeemed at a great price
165. *And . . . ought:* If you need anything
168. *cracke:* utter

Nay, naye, be sure, whyles I am on your syde
Ye maye not fall, truste me, ye maye not fayle.   170
Ye stonde in favoure and Fortune is your gyde,
And as she wyll so shall our grete shyppe sayle.
Thyse lewde cok wattes shall nevermore prevayle
Ageynste you hardely; therefore be not afrayde,
Farewell tyll soone, but no worde that I sayde.   175

DREDE

Than thanked I hym for his grete gentylnes,
But as me thoughte he ware on hym a cloke
That lyned was with doubtfull doublenes.
Me thoughte of wordes that he had full a poke,
His stomak stuffed ofte tymes dyde reboke.   180
Suspycyon, me thoughte, mette hym at a brayde,
And I drewe nere to herke what they two sayde.

In fayth, quod Suspecte, spake Drede no worde of me?
Why, what than? wylte thou lete men to speke?
He sayth he can not well accorde with the.   185
Twyst, quod Suspecte, goo playe, hym I ne reke!
By Cryste, quod Favell, Drede is soleyne freke.
What, lete us holde him up, man, for a whyle.
Ye, soo, quod Suspecte, he maye us bothe begyle.

And whan he came walkynge soberly,   190
Wyth 'Whom' and 'Ha' and with a croked loke,
Me thoughte his hede was full of gelousy,
His eyen rollynge, his hondes faste they quoke;
And to mewarde the strayte waye he toke.

---

173. *cok wattes:* cuckolds
175. *that:* of what
179. *full a poke:* a full bag
180. *reboke:* belch
181. *at a brayde:* in a quick exchange
184. *lete . . . speke:* keep men from speaking
186. *Twyst:* The hell with it; *hym . . . reke:* I don't care about him
187. *soleyne freke:* a sullen person
193. *quoke:* shook

God spede, broder, to me quod he than,   195
And thus to talke with me he began:

SUSPYCYON

Ye remembre the gentylman ryghte nowe
That commaunde with you, me thought, a praty space?
Beware of him, for I make God avowe,
He wyll begyle you and speke fayre to your face.   200
Ye never dwelte in suche an other place,
For here is none that dare well other truste;
But I wolde telle you a thynge, and I durste.

Spake he, a fayth, no worde to you of me?
I wote and he dyde ye wolde me telle.   205
I have a favoure to you, wherof it be
That I muste shewe you moche of my counselle;
But I wonder what the devyll of helle
He sayde of me, whan he with you dyde talke;
By myne avyse use not with him to walke.   210

The soveraynst thynge that ony man maye have
Is lytyll to saye and moche to here and see;
For but I trusted you so God me save,
I wolde noo thynge so playne be.
To you oonly, me thynke, I durste shryve me,   215
For now am I plenarely dysposed
To shewe you thynges that may not be disclosed.

DREDE

Than I assured hym my fydelyte,
His counseyle secrete never to dyscure,

198. *commaunde:* conversed; *praty:* pretty
204. *a fayth:* truly
205. *wote . . . dyde:* wonder if he did
215. *shryve me:* make my confession
216. *plenarely:* fully
219. *dyscure:* reveal

Yf he coude fynde in herte to truste me.   220
Els I prayed hym with all my besy cure
To kepe it hymselfe, for than he myghte be sure
That noo man erthly coude hym bewreye.
Whyles of his mynde it were lockte with the keye.

By God, quod he, this and thus it is,   225
And of his mynde he shewed me all and some.
Fare well, quod he, we wyll talke more of this.
Soo he departed there he wolde be come.
I dare not speke, I promysed to be dome.
But as I stode musynge in my mynde,   230
Harvy Hafter came lepynge, lyghte as lynde.

Upon his breste he bare a versynge boxe;
His throte was clere and lustely coude fayne;
Me thoughte his gowne was all furred wyth foxe;
And ever he sange, Sythe I am no thynge playne.   235
To kepe him frome pykynge, it was a grete payne;
He gased on me with his gotyshe berde;
Whan I loked on hym, my purse was half aferde.

HERVY HAFTER

Syr, God you save, why loke you so sadde?
What thynge is that I maye do for you?   240
A wonder thynge that ye waxe not madde.
For and I studye sholde as ye doo nowe,
My wytte wolde waste, I make God avowe.
Tell me your mynde, me thynke ye make a verse,
I coude it skan and ye wolde it reherse.   245

---

221. *cure: care*
223. *bewreye:* betray
228. *there . . . come:* even when he wished he were present
229. *dome:* silent
231. *lynde:* linden leaf
232. *versynge boxe:* box for dice
236. *pykynge:* playing the pickpocket
242. *and:* if

But to the poynte shortely to procede,
Where hathe your dwellynge ben, er ye cam here?
For as I trowe, I have sene you in dede
Er this, whan that ye made me royall chere.
Holde up the helme, loke up and lete God stere: 250
I wolde be mery that wynde that ever blowe,
Heve and how, rombelow, Row the bote, Norman, rowe!

Prynces of youghte can ye synge by rote?
Or Shall I sayle wyth you a felashyp assaye?
For on the booke I can not synge a note,   255
Wolde to God it wolde please you some daye
A balade boke before me for to laye,
And lerne me to synge *Re my fa sol!*
And whan I fayle bobbe me on the noll.

Loo, what is to you a pleasure grete   260
To have that connynge and wayes that ye have;
By Goddis soule, I wonder how ye gete
Soo greate pleasyre or who to you it gave.
Syr, pardone me, I am an homely knave
To be with you thus perte and thus bolde;   265
But ye be welcome to our housholde.

And I dare saye there is no man hereinne
But wolde be glad of your company:
I wyste never man that so soone coude wynne
The favoure that ye have with my lady.   270
I praye to God that it maye never dy;
It is your fortune for to have that grace,
As I be saved, it is a wonder case.

---

251. *that . . . ever:* whatsoever wind that
252. Harvey utters two refrains from popular songs. "Princes of youth"
in the next line is a similar tag.
253. *by rote:* from memory
254. *Shall . . . assaye?:* can you sing "Shall I sail with you" with me?
255. *For . . . note: i.e.,* Harvey cannot read music; *I:* omitted 1499
259. *bobbe:* hit; *noll:* head
269. *wyste never:* never knew a

12

For as for me, I served here many a daye,
And yet unneth I can have my lyvynge—   275
But I requyre you no worde that I saye.
For, and I knowe ony erthly thynge
That is agayne you, ye shall have wetynge;
And ye be welcome, syr, so God me save,
I hope here after a frende of you to have.   280

DREDE

Wyth that, as he departed soo fro me,
Anone ther mette with him, as me thoughte,
A man, but wonderly besene was he:
He loked hawte, he sette eche man at noughte,
His gawdy garment with scornnys was all wrought;   285
With Indygnacyon lyned was his hode;
He frowned as he wolde swere by Cockes blode.

He bote the lyppe, he loked passynge coye,
His face was belymmed as byes had him stounge;
It was no tyme with him to jape nor toye.   290
Envye hathe wasted his lyver and his lounge,
Hatred by the herte so had hym wrounge
That he loked pale as asshes to my syghte;
Dysdayne, I wene, this comerous carkes hyghte.

To Hervy Hafter than he spake of me,   295
And I drewe nere to harke what they two sayde.

---

275. *unneth . . . lyvynge:* I scarcely make a living
276. *But . . . saye:* But don't repeat anything I say
278. *wetynge:* knowledge of it
282. *Anone:* At once; *me thoughte:* it seemed to me
283. *wonderly besene:* marvelous to behold
284. *hawte:* proud
285. *scornnys:* 1499 misprints *storunys:* scornful ornamentation
287. *Cockes:* a euphemism for "God's."
288. *bote:* bit
289. *belymmed:* swollen, marred; *byes:* bees
294. *comerous . . . hyghte:* tiresome body was called

Now, quod Dysdayne, as I shall saved be,
I have grete scorne and am ryghte evyll apayed.
Than, quod Hervy, why arte thou so dysmayde?
By Cryste, quod he, for it is shame to saye,   300
To see Johan Dawes that came but yesterdaye

How he is now taken in conceyte,
This Doctour Dawcocke, Drede, I wene he hyghte.
By Goddis bones, but yf we have som sleyte,
It is lyke he wyll stonde in our lyghte.   305
By God, quod Hervy, and it so happen myghte.
Lete us therfore shortely at a worde
Fynde some mene to caste him over the borde.

By him that me boughte, than quod Dysdayne,
I wonder sore he is in suche cenceyte.   310
Turde, quod Hafter, I wyll the nothynge layne,
There muste for hym be layde some prety beyte.
We tweyne, I trowe, be not withoute dysceyte:
Fyrste pycke a quarell and fall oute with hym then,
And soo outface hym with a carde of ten.   315

Forthwith he made on me a prowde assawte,
With scornfull loke meuyd all in moode.
He wente aboute to take me in a fawte;
He frounde, he stared, he stampped where he stoode.
I loked on hym, I wende he had be woode.   320
He set the arme proudly under the syde,
And in this wyse he gan with me to chyde.

---

298. *evyll apayed:* poorly rewarded
301. *Johan Dawes:* i.e., "John Doe," or "Drede"
302. *taken in conceyte:* fancied
303. *Doctour Dawcocke:* stupid fellow; *wene he hyghte:* think he is called
304. *sleyte:* tricky plan
309. *him . . . boughte:* i.e., Christ
311. *layne:* 1499 reads *sayne:* blame on you
315. *carde of ten:* bluff
317. *meuyd . . . moode:* moved all in anger
320. *wende . . . woode:* thought he was mad

DISDAYNE

Remembrest thou what thou sayd yesternyght?
Wylt thou abyde by the wordes agayne?
By God, I have of the now grete dyspyte;   325
I shall the angre ones in every vayne.
It is greate scorne to see suche an hayne
As thou arte, one that cam but yesterdaye,
With us olde servauntes such maysters to playe.

I tell the I am of countenaunce;   330
What weneste I were? I trowe thou knowe not me.
By Goddis woundes but for dysplesaunce
Of my querell soone wolde I venged be.
But, no force, I shall ones mete with the;
Come whan it wyll, oppose the I shall,
Whatsomever aventure therof fall.   335

Trowest thou, drevyll, I saye, thou gawdy knave,
That I have deynte to see the cherysshed thus?
By Goddis syde, my sworde thy berde shall shave!
Well, ones thou shalte be chermed, I wus.   340
Naye, strawe for tales, thou shalte not rule us,
We be thy betters and so thou shalte us take,
Or we shall the oute of thy clothes shake!

DREDE

Wyth that came Ryotte russhynge all at ones,
A rusty gallande, to ragged and to rente,   345

---

327. *hayne:* wretch
329. *maysters:* masteries, tricks
330. *of countenaunce:* someone to be noticed
332–33. *but . . . querell:* except for the fact that my quarrel displeases me
337. *drevyll:* drudge
338. *have deynte:* take any pleasure
340. *I wus:* to be sure
341. *strawe for:* the hell with
345. *gallande:* gallant; *to ragged and to rente:* all torn and bedraggled

And on the borde he whyrled a payre of bones;
Quater treye dews, he clatered as he wente:
Now have at all, by Saynte Thomas of Kente.
And ever he threwe, and kyst I wote nere what,
His here was growen thorowe oute his hat.   350

Thenne I behelde how he dysgysed was,
His hede was hevy for watchynge overnyghte,
His eyen blereed, his face shone lyke a glas,
His gowne so shorte that it ne cover myghte
His rumpe, he wente so all for somer lyghte;   355
His hose was garded wyth a lyste of grene,
Yet at the knee they were broken, I wene.

His cote was checked with patches rede and blewe,
Of Kyrkeby Kendall was his shorte demye;
And ay he sange, In fayth, Decon, thou crewe.   360
His elbowe bare, he ware his gere so nye,
His nose a-droppynge, his lyppes were full drye,
And by his syde his whynarde and his pouche,
The Devyll myghte daunce therin for ony crowche.

Counter he coude (*O lux*) upon a potte,   365
An eestryche fedder of a capons tayle
He set up fresshely upon his hat alofte;
What, revell route, quod he, and gan to rayle
How ofte he hadde hit Jenet on the tayle,

---

347. *Quater . . . dews:* Four, three, deuce
348. *have . . . Kente:* risk it all, by St. Thomas of Canterbury
349. *kyst . . . what:* I don't know how the dice fell
353. *blereed:* bleared, blurry
356. *garded . . . lyste:* trimmed with a strip
359. *Kyrkeby Kendall:* poor-grade cloth; *demye:* short gown
360. *In . . . crewe:* a line from a popular song
363. *whynarde:* dagger
364. *for ony crowche:* because there was no "crouche" (coin with a cross on it) in it
365. *Counter:* Accompany himself; *O lux:* "O light," first words of a hymn
366. *eestryche:* ostrich. Just how the feather came out of a capon's tail, only Riot could decide.
369. *Jenet:* a horse

Of Felyce fetewse and lytell prety Cate,   370
How ofte he knocked at her klycked gate.

What sholde I tell more of his rebaudrye?
I was ashamed so to here hym prate,
He had no pleasure but in harlotrye.
Ay, quod he, in the devylles date,   375
What arte thou? I sawe the nowe but late.
Forsothe, quod I, in this courte I dwell nowe.
Welcome, quod Ryote, I make God avowe.

RYOTE

And, syr, in fayth, why comste not us amonge
To make the mery, as other felowes done?   380
Thou muste swere and stare, man, aldaye longe,
And wake all nyghte and slepe tyll it be none;
Thou mayste not studye or muse on the mone.
This worlde is nothynge but ete, drynke and slepe,
And thus with us good company to kepe.   385

Plucke up thyne herte upon a mery pyne,
And lete us laugh a placke or tweyne at nale;
What the devyll, man, myrthe was never one.
What, loo, man, see here of dyce a bale;
A brydelynge caste for that is in thy male!   390
Now have at all that lyeth upon the burde,
Fye on this dyce, they be not worth a turde!

---

370. *Felyce fetewse:* well-built Felicia
371. *klycked:* locked
372. *rebaudrye:* ribaldry
375. *date:* name
382. *none:* noon
386. *pyne:* pin, i.e., be merry
387. *placke . . . nale:* for a drink or two at the alehouse
388. *one:* alone
389. *bale:* set
390. *A . . . male:* I'll roll you, one last chance for what is in your bag
391. *burde:* table

Have at the hasarde or at the dosen browne,
Or els I pas a peny to a pounde;
Now wolde to God thou wolde leye money downe!   395
Lorde, how that I wolde caste it full rounde!
Ay, in my pouche a buckell I have founde,
The armes of Calyce, I have no coyne nor crosse,
I am not happy, I renne ay on the losse!

Now renne muste I to the stewys syde,   400
To wete yf Malkyn, my lemman, have gete oughte:
I lete her to hyre that men maye on her ryde,
Her harnes easy ferre and nere is soughte.
By Goddis sydes, syns I her thyder broughte,
She hath gote me more money with her tayle   405
Than hath some shyppe that into Bordews sayle.

Had I as good an hors as she is a mare,
I durste aventure to journey thorugh Fraunce;
Who rydeth on her, he nedeth not to care,
For she is trussed for to breke a launce.   410
It is a curtel that well can wynche and praunce;
To her wyll I nowe all my poverte lege.
And tyll I come have, here is myne hat to plege.

DREDE

Gone is this knave, this rybaude foule and leude;
He ran as fast as ever that he myghte.   415

---

393. *dosen browne:* full dozen, possibly a game of chance
394. *pas:* give you odds
398. *armes of Calyce:* possibly, a coin made in Calais; *crosse:* coin with a cross on it
399. *renne . . . losse:* am always on the lose
400. *stewys:* brothel's
401. *wete:* see
403. *harnes easy:* 1499 reads *harmes; harnes* means "sexual organs"; *ferre:* far
406. *shyppe:* ships; *Bordews:* Bordeaux
411. *curtel:* curtal, horse with a docked tail
412. *lege:* attribute

Unthryftynes in hym may well be shewed,
For whome Tyborne groneth both daye and nyghte.
And as I stode and kyste asyde my syghte,
Dysdaync I sawe with Dyssymulacyon,
Standynge in sadde communicacion.   420

But there was poyntynge and noddynge with the hede,
And many wordes sayde in secrete wyse;
They wandred ay and stode styll in no stede.
Me thoughte, alwaye Dyscymular dyde devyse;
Me, passynge sore, myne herte than gan aryse,   425
I dempte and drede theyr talkynge was not good.
Anone Dyscymular came where I stode.

Than in his hode I sawe there faces tweyne,
That one was lene and lyke a pyned goost,
That other loked as he wolde me have slayne.   430
And to mewarde as he gan for to coost,
Whan that he was even at me almoost,
I sawe a knyfe hyd in his one sleve,
Wheron was wryten this worde, *myscheve.*

And in his other sleve, me thought I sawe   435
A spone of golde, full of hony swete,
To fede a fole, and for to preye a dawe.
And on that sleve these wordes were wrete,
A *false abstracte cometh from a fals concrete.*
His hode was syde, his cope was roset graye,   440
Thyse were the wordes he to me dyde saye:

---

417. *Tyborne:* i.e., the gallows
418. *kyste:* cast
420. *sadde:* serious
423. *ay:* always; *stede:* place
424. *Dyscymular:* the dissimulating figure
426. *dempte and drede:* judged and feared
434. *myscheve:* evil
437. *preye a dawe:* catch a fool
440. *syde:* long; *roset:* russet

DYSSYMULATION

How do ye, mayster? Ye loke so soberly,
As I be saved at the dredefull daye,
It is a perylous vyce, this envy.
Alas, a connynge man ne dwelle maye   445
In no place well, but foles with hym fraye.
But as for that, connynge hath no foo
Save hym that nought can: scrypture sayth soo.

I knowe your vertu and your lytterkture
By that lytel connynge that I have;   450
Ye be malygned sore, I you ensure
But ye have crafte your selfe alwaye to save.
It is grete scorne to se a mysproude knave
With a clerke that connynge is to prate:
Lete theym go lowse theym, in the devylles date.   455

For allbeit that this longe not to me,
Yet on my backe I bere suche lewde delynge;
Ryghte now I spake with one, I trowe, I see—
But, what, a strawe! I maye not tell all thynge.
By God, I saye, there is grete herte brennynge   460
Betwene the persone ye wote of, you—
Alas, I coude not dele so with a Jew!

I wolde eche man were as playne as I,
It is a worlde, I saye, to here of some;

---

443. *dredefull:* judgment
445. *connynge:* learned
446. *with hym fraye:* quarrel or fight with him
448. *nought can:* knows nothing
449. *lytterkture:* knowledge of letters
452. *But:* Unless
453–54. *mysproude . . . prate:* arrogant knave prattle with a learned man
455. *lowse theym:* get lost; *date:* name
456. *longe . . . me:* doesn't concern me
457. *lewde:* stupid
460. *herte brennynge:* heart burning, envious grudging

I hate this faynynge, fye upon it, fye!   465
A man can not wote where to become;
Iwys I coude tell—but humlery, home,
I dare not speke, we be so layde awayte,
For all our courte is full of dysceyte.

Now, by Saynte Fraunceys, that holy man and frere,   470
I hate this wayes agayne you that they take!
Were I as you, I wolde ryde them full nere,
And by my trouthe but yf an ende they make,
Yet wyll I saye some wordes for your sake
That shall them angre, I holde thereon a grote,   475
For some shall wene be hanged by the throte.

I have a stoppyng oyster in my poke,
Truste me and yf it come to a nede;
But I am lothe for to reyse a smoke,
Yf ye coude be otherwyse agrede;   480
And so I wolde it were, so God me spede,
For this maye brede to a confusyon,
Withoute God make a good conclusyon.

Naye, see where yonder stondeth the teder man,
A flaterynge knave and false he is, God wote;   485
The drevyll stondeth to herken and he can.
It were more thryft he boughte him a newe cote;
It wyll not be, his purse is not on flote.
All that he wereth it is borowed ware,
His wytte is thynne, his hode is threde-bare.   490

---

467. *humlery, home:* hum, hum
468. *layde awayte:* suspiciously watched
470. *frere:* friar
475. *I . . . grote:* I'll bet a small coin (groat) upon it
476. *wene . . . throte:* think their throats have really been shut up
477. *stoppyng:* blocking (the throat); *poke:* bag
479. *reyse:* raise
484. *teder:* other, i.e., Disceyte
486. *drevyll:* drudge; *and:* if
488. *on flote:* afloat (with money)

More coude I saye, but what this is ynowe;
Adewe tyll soone, we shall speke more of this.
Ye muste be ruled as I shall tell you howe,
Amendis maye be of that is now amys.
And I am your, syr, so have I blys,   495
In every poynte that I can do or saye.
Gyve me your honde, fare well and have good daye.

DREDE

Sodaynly, as he departed me fro,
Came pressynge in one in a wonder araye;
Er I was ware, behynde me he sayde Bo!   500
Thenne I, astonyed of that sodeyne fraye,
Sterte all at ones. I lyked no thynge his playe,
For yf I had not quyckely fledde the touche,
He had plucte oute the nobles of my pouche.

He was trussed in a garmente strayte   505
(I have not sene suche anothers page)
For he coude well upon a casket wayte,
His hode all pounsed and garded lyke a cage.
Lyghte lyme fynger, he toke none other wage.
Harken, quod he, loo here myne honde in thyne,   510
To us welcome thou arte, by Saynte Quyntyne.

DISCEYTE

But by that Lorde that is one, two and thre,
I have an errande to rounde in your ere.

---

491. *ynowe:* enough
495. *your:* yours
499. *wonder araye:* marvelous outfit
501. *fraye:* attack
504. *nobles:* gold coins
505. *strayte:* tight
508. *pounsed and garded:* perforated and trimmed
509. *lyme:* i.e., sticky
511. *Quyntyne:* Quentin

He tolde me so, by God, ye maye truste me.
Parde, remembre whan ye were there,   515
There I wynked on you, wote ye not where?
In (A) *loco*, I mene *juxta* (B),
Woo is hym that is blynde and maye not see!

But to here the subtylte and the crafte,
As I shall tell you, yf ye wyll harke agayne: 520
And whan I sawe the horsons wolde you hafte,
To holde myne honde, by God, I had grete payne;
For forthwyth there I had him slayne,
But that I drede mordre wolde come oute;
Who deleth with shrewes hath nede to loke aboute.   525

DREDE

And as he rounded thus in myne ere
Of false collusyon confetryd by assente,
Me thoughte I see lewde felawes here and there
Came for to slee me of mortall entente.
And as they came, the shypborde faste I hente,   530
And thoughte to lepe, and even with that woke,
Caughte penne and ynke, and wroth this lytyll boke.

I wolde therwith no man were myscontente,
Besechynge you that shall it see or rede,
In every poynte to be indyfferente,   535
Syth all in substaunce of slumbrynge doth procede.
I wyll not saye it is mater in dede,
But yet oftyme suche dremes be founde trewe;
Now constrewe ye what is the resydewe.

---

517. (A) . . . (B): i.e., in such and such a place, near
521. *horsons*: whoresons; *hafte*: rob
525. *shrewes*: evil fellows
527. *confetryd*: confederate
530. *hente*: grasped
532. *wroth*: wrote
535. *indyfferente*: impartial
537. *mater in dede*: really true

2.

Phyllyp Sparowe

Pla ce bo,
Who is there, who?
Di le xi,
Dame Margery;
Fa, re, my, my,   5
Wherfore and why, why?
For the sowle of Philip Sparowe,
That was late slayn at Carowe,
Among the Nones Blake,
For that swete soules sake,   10
And for all sparowes soules,
Set in our bederolles,
Pater noster qui,
With an *Ave Mari,*
And with the corner of a Crede,   15
The more shalbe your mede.
   Whan I remembre agayn
How mi Philyp was slayn,

Title: "Phyllyp Sparowe" is usually dated 1505–7. It humorously com-
memorates the death of Jane Scrope's pet sparrow. Part I (ll. 1–844)
echoes phrases from the Office for the Dead; Part II (ll. 845–1268)
follows the Commendations service; Part III (ll. 1269–1382) is Skelton's
"Addition," written in response to an attack on the poem made by the poet
Alexander Barclay.
1. *Pla ce bo:* "I shall please," Psalm 114:9. References to the Psalms are
to the Vulgate numbering.
3. *Di le xi:* "I have loved," Psalm 114:1
4. *Margery:* possibly the senior nun at Carrow Abbey, where Jane's mother
died in 1505
9. *Nones Blake:* i.e., Benedictines
12. *bederolles:* lists of souls for whom "beads" (the rosary) were offered
13. *Pater . . . qui:* "Our Father who"
14. *Ave Mari:* "Hail Mary"
16. *mede:* reward

Never halfe the payne
Was betwene you twayne,   20
Pyramus and Thesbe,
As than befell to me:
I wept and I wayled,
The tearys downe hayled;
But nothynge it avayled   25
To call Phylyp agayne,
Whom Gyb our cat hath slayne.
    Gib, I saye, our cat
Worrowyd her on that
Which I loved best: 30
It can not be exprest
My sorowfull hevynesse,
But all without redresse;
For within that stounde,
Halfe slumbrynge, in a sounde   35
I fell downe to the grounde.
    Unneth I kest myne eyes
Towarde the cloudy skyes:
But whan I dyd beholde
My sparow dead and colde,   40
No creature but that wolde
Have rewed upon me,
To behold and se
What hevynesse dyd me pange;
Wherewith my handes I wrange,   45
That my senaws cracked,
As though I had ben racked,
So payned and so strayned,
That no lyfe wellnye remayned.
    I syghed and I sobbed,   50
For that I was robbed

---

21. *Pyramus:* see Ovid, *Metamorphoses,* IV, 55ff., for the story
29. *Worrowyd her:* "Worried," bit and pulled
34. *stounde:* moment
35. *sounde:* faint
37. *Unneth:* Hardly had
46. *senaws:* sinews

Of my sparowes lyfe.
O mayden, wydow, and wyfe,
Of what estate ye be,
Of hye or lowe degre,   55
Great sorowe than ye myght se,
And lerne to wepe at me!
Such paynes dyd me frete,
That myne hert dyd bete,
My vysage pale and dead,   60
Wanne, and blewe as lead;
The panges of hatefull death
Wellnye had stopped my breath.
   Heu, heu, me,
That I am wo for the!   65
Ad Dominum, cum tribularer, clamavi:
Of God nothynge els crave I
But Phyllypes soule to kepe
From the marees deepe
Of Acherontes well,   70
That is a flode of hell;
And from the great Pluto,
The prynce of endles wo;
And from foule Alecto,
With vysage blacke and blo;   75
And from Medusa, that mare,
That lyke a fende doth stare;
And from Megeras edders,
For rufflynge of Phillips fethers,
And from her fyry sparklynges,   80
For burnynge of his wynges;

---

57. *at:* from
64. *Heu, heu, me:* "Alas, alas, O me," Psalm 119:5
66. *Ad . . . clamavi:* "I cried out to the Lord when I suffered," Psalm 119:1
69. *marees:* marsh
70. *Acherontes well:* the spring of Acheron, one of the four rivers of hell
74. *Alecto:* one of the Furies
75. *blo:* blue
76. *Medusa:* monstrous woman of classical myth; *mare:* specter
78. *Megeras edders:* the adders of Megaera, one of the Furies
79. *For:* i.e., to prevent the

26

And from the smokes sowre
Of Proserpinas bowre;
And from the dennes darke,
Wher Cerberus doth barke,   85
Whom Theseus dyd afraye,
Whom Hercules dyd outraye,
As famous poetes say;
From that hell hounde,
That lyeth in cheynes bounde,   90
With gastly hedes thre,
To Jupyter pray we
That Phyllyp preserved may be!
Amen, say ye with me!
  Do mi nus,   95
Helpe nowe, swete Jesus!
Levavi oculos meos in montes:
Wolde God I had Zenophontes,
Or Socrates the wyse,
To shew me their devyse,   100
Moderatly to take
This sorow that I make
For Phyllip Sparowes sake!
So fervently I shake,
I fele my body quake;   105
So urgently I am brought
Into carefull thought.
Like Andromach, Hectors wyfe,
Was wery of her lyfe,
Whan she had lost her joye,   110
Noble Hector of Troye;

---

83. *Proserpinas:* daughter of Ceres, carried off to the underworld by Pluto
85. *Cerberus:* the three-headed dog of hell
86. *Theseus:* Greek hero, who frightened ("dyd afraye") Cerberus when he
went down to hell. Hercules dragged Cerberus from hell on one of his labors (line 87).
87. *outraye:* conquer
95. *Do mi nus:* "Lord," Psalm 120:5
97. *Levavi . . . montes:* "I lifted my eyes to the mountains," Psalm 120:1
98. *Zenophontes:* Xenophon
108. *Andromach:* Andromache (*Iliad*, xxiv, 725ff.)

In lyke maner also
Encreaseth my dedly wo,
For my sparowe is go.
   It was so prety a fole,   115
It wold syt on a stole,
And lerned after my scole
For to kepe his cut,
With, Phyllyp, kepe your cut!
   It had a velvet cap,   120
And wold syt upon my lap,
And seke after small wormes,
And somtyme white bred crommes;
And many tymes and ofte
Betwene my brestes softe   125
It wolde lye and rest;
It was propre and prest.
   Somtyme he wolde gaspe
Whan he sawe a waspe;
A fly or a gnat,   130
He wolde flye at that;
And prytely he wold pant
Whan he saw an ant;
Lord, how he wolde pry
After the butterfly!   135
Lorde, how he wolde hop
After the gressop!
And whan I sayd, Phyp, Phyp,
Than he wold lepe and skyp,
And take me by the lyp.   140
Alas, it wyll me slo,
That Phillyp is gone me fro!
   Si in i qui ta tes,
Alas, I was evyll at ease!

---

114. *go:* gone
118. *kepe his cut:* mind his manners
127. *prest:* deftly quick
134. *pry:* search
137. *gressop:* grasshopper
141. *slo:* slay
143. *Si in i qui ta tes:* "If iniquities," Psalm 129:3
144. *evyll:* ill

De pro fun dis cla ma vi,   145
Whan I sawe my sparowe dye!
  Nowe, after my dome,
Dame Sulpicia at Rome,
Whose name regystred was
For ever in tables of bras,   150
Because that she dyd pas
In poesy to endyte,
And eloquently to wryte,
Though she wolde pretende
My sparowe to commende,   155
I trowe she coude not amende
Reportynge the vertues all
Of my sparowe royall.
  For it wold come and go,
And fly so to and fro;   160
And on me it wolde lepe
Whan I was aslepe,
And his fethers shake,
Wherewith he wolde make
Me often for to wake,   165
And for to take him in
Upon my naked skyn;
God wot, we thought no syn:
What though he crept so lowe?
It was no hurt, I trowe,   170
He dyd nothynge perde
But syt upon my kne:
Phyllyp, though he were nyse,
In him it was no vyse;

---

145. *De pro fun dis cla ma vi:* "Out of the depths I have cried," Psalm 129:1
147. *dome:* judgment
148. *Sulpicia:* Skelton seems to have confused two poetesses of this name, both of classical Rome
150. *tables:* tablets
151. *pas:* excel
171. *perde:* indeed
173. *nyse:* wanton
174. *vyse:* vice

Phyllyp had leve to go   175
To pyke my lytell too;
Phillip myght be bolde
And do what he wolde;
Phillip wolde seke and take
All the flees blake   180
That he coulde there espye
With his wanton eye.
    O *pe ra,*
La, soll, fa, fa,
Confitebor tibi, Domine, in toto corde meo.   185
Alas, I wold ryde and go
A thousand myle of grounde!
If any such might be found,
It were worth an hundreth pound
Of kynge Cresus golde,   190
Or of Attalus the olde,
The ryche prynce of Pargame,
Who so lyst the story to se.
Cadmus, that his syster sought,
And he shold be bought   195
For golde and fee,
He shuld over the see,
To wete if he coulde brynge
Any of the ofsprynge,
Or any of the blode.   200
But whoso understode
Of Medeas arte,
I wolde I had a parte

---

176. *pyke:* peck; *too:* toe
183. O *pe ra:* "Works (of your hands, Lord, do not despise)," Psalm 137:8
185. *Confitebor . . . meo:* "I shall confess, Lord, with all my heart," Psalm 137:1
190. *Cresus:* Croesus, the fabulously wealthy Lydian king
191. *Attalus:* Attalus I (d. 197 B.C.), king of Pergamum
193. *lyst:* desires
194. *Cadmus:* his father Agenor made him search for Europa and threatened him with exile (Ovid, *Metamorphoses,* III, 1ff.)
198. *wete:* find out
202. *Medeas:* she restored Jason's youth with her magic

Of her crafty magyke!
My sparowe than shuld be quycke 205
With a charme or twayne,
And playe with me agayne.
But all this is in vayne
Thus for to complayne.
    I toke my sampler ones, 210
Of purpose, for the nones,
To sowe with stytchis of sylke
My sparow whyte as mylke,
That by representacyon
Of his image and facyon, 215
To me it myght importe
Some pleasure and comforte
For my solas and sporte:
But whan I was sowing his beke,
Methought, my sparow did speke, 220
And opened his prety byll,
Saynge, Mayd, ye are in wyll
Agayne me for to kyll,
Ye prycke me in the head!
With that my nedle waxed red, 225
Methought, of Phyllyps blode;
Myne hear ryght upstode,
And was in suche a fray,
My speche was taken away.
I kest downe that there was, 230
And sayd, Alas, alas,
How commeth this to pas?
My fyngers, dead and colde,
Coude not my sampler holde;

205. *quycke:* alive
211. *for the nones:* for the occasion
215. *facyon:* fashion, form
216. *importe:* bring
219. *sowing his beke:* sewing his beak (in her embroidery)
222. *are in wyll:* intend
228. *fray:* fright

My nedle and threde   235
I threwe away for drede.
The best now that I maye,
Is for his soule to pray:
A *porta inferi,*
Good Lorde, have mercy   240
Upon my sparowes soule,
Wryten in my bederoule!
   Au di vi vo cem,
Japhet, Cam, and Sem,
Mag gni fi cat,   245
Shewe me the ryght path
To the hylles of Armony,
Wherfore the bordes yet cry
Of your fathers bote,
That was sometyme aflote,   250
And nowe they lye and rote;
Let some poetes wryte
Deucalyons flode it hyght:
But as verely as ye be
The naturall sonnes thre   255
Of Noe the patryarke,
That made that great arke,
Wherin he had apes and owles,
Beestes, byrdes, and foules,
That if ye can fynde   260
Any of my sparowes kynde,
God sende the soule good rest!
I wolde have yet a nest
As pretty and as prest

239. A . . . *inferi:* "From the gates of hell." Skelton here changes the
proper antiphon response, "Deliver their souls."
243. *Au di vi vo cem:* "I heard your voice," Revelation 14:13
244. *Japhet . . . Sem:* the sons of Noah
245. *Mag gni fi cat:* "(My soul) magnifies (the Lord)." The Magnificat.
247. *Armony:* Armenia, where Noah's ark is said to have come to rest on
Mount Ararat
248. *bordes:* some early editions read *birdes*
251. *rote:* rot
253. *Deucalyons:* the classical Noah
264. *prest:* neat

As my sparowe was.   265
But my sparowe dyd pas
All sparowes of the wode
That were syns Noes flode,
Was never none so good;
Kynge Phylyp of Macedony   270
Had no such Phylyp as I,
No, no, syr, hardely.
    That vengeaunce I aske and crye,
By way of exclamacyon,
On all the hole nacyon   275
Of cattes wylde and tame;
God send them sorowe and shame!
That cat specyally
That slew so cruelly
My lytell prety sparowe   280
That I brought up at Carowe.
    O cat of carlyshe kynde,
The fynde was in thy mynde
Whan thou my byrde untwynde!
I wold thou haddest ben blynde!   285
The leopardes savage,
The lyons in theyr rage,
Myght catche the in theyr pawes,
And gnawe the in theyr jawes!
The serpentes of Lybany   290
Myght stynge the venymously!
The dragones with their tonges
Might poyson thy lyver and longes!
The mantycors of the montaynes
Myght fede them on thy braynes!   295

---

270. *Phylyp:* father of Alexander the Great
282. *carlyshe:* brutal
283. *fynde:* fiend
284. *untwynde:* destroyed
288. *the:* thee
290. *Lybany:* Libia. African serpents were considered particularly venomous.
294. *mantycors:* legendary monsters with three rows of teeth

Melanchates, that hounde
That plucked Acteon to the grounde,
Gave hym his mortall wounde,
Chaunged to a dere,
The story doth appere, 300
Was chaunged to an harte:
So thou, foule cat that thou arte,
The selfe same hounde
Myght the confounde,
That his owne lord bote, 305
Myght byte asondre thy throte!
Of Inde the gredy grypes
Myght tere out all thy trypes!
Of Arcady the beares
Might plucke awaye thyne eares! 310
The wylde wolfe Lycaon
Byte asondre thy backe bone!
Of Ethna the brennynge hyll,
That day and night brenneth styl,
Set in thy tayle a blase, 315
That all the world may gase
And wonder upon the,
From Occyan the greate se
Unto the Iles of Orchady,
From Tyllbery fery 320
To the playne of Salysbery!
So trayterously my byrde to kyll
That never ought the evyll wyll!

---

296. *Melanchates:* one of Actaeon's hounds, who turned on his master after
the latter was changed into a stag
300. *story:* as told by Ovid (*Metamorphoses*, III, 232ff.)
305. *bote:* bit
307. *grypes:* griffins
311. *Lycaon:* king of Arcadia, transformed into a wolf (Ovid, *Metamorphoses*, I, 163ff.)
313. *Ethna:* Etna; *brennynge:* burning
318. *Occyan:* Ocean
319. *Orchady:* Orkney Islands
320. *Tyllbery:* Tilbury ferry, twenty-five miles east of London
321. *Salysbery:* Salisbury, eighty miles west of London
323. *ought the:* showed thee

    Was never byrde in cage
More gentle of corage   325
In doynge his homage
Unto his soverayne.
Alas, I say agayne,
Deth hath departed us twayne!
The false cat hath the slayne: 330
Farewell, Phyllyp, adew!
Our Lorde thy soule reskew!
Farewell without restore,
Farewell for evermore!
    And it were a Jewe,   335
It wolde make one rew,
To se my sorow new.
These vylanous false cattes
Were made for myse and rattes,
And not for byrdes smale.   340
Alas, my face waxeth pale,
Tellynge this pyteyus tale,
How my byrde so fayre,
That was wont to repayre,
And go in at my spayre,   345
And crepe in at my gore
Of my gowne before,
Flyckerynge with his wynges!
Alas, my hert it stynges,
Remembrynge prety thynges!   350
Alas, myne hert is sleth
My Phyllyppes dolefull deth,
Whan I remembre it,
How pretely it wolde syt,
Many tymes and ofte,   355
Upon my fynger aloft!
I played with him tyttell tattyll,
And fed him with my spattyl,

---

325. *corage:* heart
345. *spayre:* opening in a gown
346. *gore:* skirt
358. *spattyl:* spittle

With his byll betwene my lippes;
It was my prety Phyppes! 360
Many a prety kusse
Had I of his swete musse;
And now the cause is thus,
That he is slayne me fro,
To my great payne and wo. 365
　Of fortune this the chaunce
Standeth on varyaunce:
Oft tyme after pleasaunce
Trouble and grevaunce;
No man can be sure 370
Allway to have pleasure:
As well perceyve ye maye
How my dysport and play
From me was taken away
By Gyb, our cat savage, 375
That in a furyous rage
Caught Phyllyp by the head,
And slew him there starke dead.
　　Kyrie, eleison,
　　Christe, eleison, 380
　　Kyrie, eleison!
For Phylyp Sparowes soule,
Set in our bederolle,
Let us now whysper
A *Pater noster.* 385
　Lauda, anima mea, Dominum!
To wepe with me loke that ye come,
All maner of byrdes in your kynd;
Se none be left behynde.
To mornynge loke that ye fall 390
With dolorous songes funerall,

---

362. *musse:* mouth
379–81. *Kyrie . . . eleison:* "Lord have mercy, Christ have mercy, etc."
The Our Father was to be recited silently (line 384) after the Kyrie.
386. *Lauda . . . Dominum:* "Praise the Lord, my soul," Psalm 145:1.
Skelton now stops echoing the Vespers service and begins a medieval bird
mass, as Jane summons every type of fowl to the ritual.

Some to synge, and some to say,
Some to wepe, and some to pray,
Every byrde in his laye.
The goldfynche, the wagtayle;   395
The janglynge jay to rayle,
The fleckyd pye to chatter
Of this dolorous mater;
And robyn redbrest,
He shall be the preest   400
The requiem masse to synge,
Softly warbelynge,
With helpe of the red sparow,
And the chattrynge swallow,
This herse for to halow;   405
The larke with his longe to;
The spynke, and the martynet also;
The shovelar with his brode bek;
The doterell, that folyshe pek,
And also the mad coote,   410
With a balde face to toote;
The feldefare, and the snyte;
The crowe, and the kyte;
The ravyn, called Rolfe,
His playne songe to solfe;   415
The partryche, the quayle;
The plover with us to wayle;
The woodhacke, that syngeth chur
Horsly, as he had the mur;

---

392. *say:* talk
394. *laye:* own voice
397. *fleckyd pye:* spotted magpie
406. *to:* toe
407. *spynke:* chaffinch; *martynet:* martin
408. *shovelar:* spoonbill
409. *doterell:* plover; *pek:* silly bird
411. *toote:* peer
412. *feldefare:* thrush; *snyte:* snipe
415. *solfe:* sing (from the notes "sol" and "fa")
418. *woodhacke:* woodpecker, who makes a "churring" noise
419. *the mur:* a severe cold

The lusty chauntyng nyghtyngale;   420
The popyngay to tell her tale,
That toteth oft in a glasse,
Shal rede the Gospell at masse;
The mavys with her whystell
Shal rede there the pystell.   425
But with a large and a longe
To kepe just playne songe,
Our chaunters shalbe the cuckoue,
The culver, the stockedowve,
With puwyt the lapwyng,   430
The versycles shall syng.
    The bitter with his bumpe,
The crane with his trumpe,
The swan of Menander,
The gose and the gander,   435
The ducke and the drake,
Shall watche at this wake;
The pecocke so prowde,
Bycause his voyce is lowde,
And hath a glorious tayle,   440
He shall syng the grayle;
The owle, that is so foule,
Must helpe us to houle;
The heron so gaunce,
And the cormoraunce,   445
With the fesaunte,
And the gaglynge gaunte,

---

421. *popyngay:* parrot
424. *mavys:* song-thrush
425. *pystell:* epistle
426. *large . . . longe:* a large note was equal to two or three long notes
430. *puwyt:* peewit, the sound the lapwing makes
431. *versycles:* short prayers said by the priest
432. *bitter:* bittern, whose cry goes "bumpe"
434. *Menander:* Skelton's error for "Maeander," a classical river
441. *grayle:* gradual, which came just before the gospel of the mass
444. *gaunce:* gaunt
447. *gaunte:* kind of goose

38

And the churlysshe chowgh;
The knoute and the rowgh;
The barnacle, the bussarde,   450
With the wylde mallarde;
The dyvendop to slepe;
The water hen to wepe;
The puffyn and the tele
Money they shall dele   455
To poore folke at large,
That shall be theyr charge;
The semewe and the tytmose;
The wodcocke with the longe nose;
The threstyl with her warblyng;   460
The starlyng with her brablyng;
The roke, with the ospraye
That putteth fysshes to a fraye;
And the denty curlewe,
With the turtyll most trew.   465
    At this *Placebo*
We may not well forgo
The countrynge of the coe:
The storke also,
That maketh his nest   470
In chymneyes to rest;
Within those walles
No broken galles

448. *churlysshe chowgh:* rough jack daw
449. *knoute:* red-breasted sandpiper; *rowgh:* ruff, male sandpiper
450. *barnacle:* kind of wild goose
452. *dyvendop:* small water bird
454. *puffyn:* large sea bird; *tele:* small duck
455. *dele:* distribute (as alms at the service)
458. *semewe:* sea mew; *tytmose:* a little, quick bird
460. *threstyl:* song-thrush
462. *roke:* rook; *ospraye:* osprey
463. *to a fraye:* in a fright
464. *denty:* dainty
465. *turtyll:* turtledove
466. *Placebo:* see above, line 1
468. *countrynge . . . coe:* accompaniment of the jackdaw
473. *galles:* sores. The stork protects the house against cuckoldry (line 475).

May there abyde
Of cokoldry syde,   475
Or els phylosophy
Maketh a great lye.
   The estryge, that wyll eate
An horshowe so great,
In the stede of meate,   480
Such fervent heat
His stomake doth freat;
He can not well fly,
Nor synge tunably,
Yet at a brayde   485
He hath well assayde
To solfe above ela,
Fa, lorell, fa, fa;
Ne quando   490
Male cantando,
The best that we can,
To make hym our belman,
And let hym ryng the bellys;
He can do nothyng ellys.
   Chaunteclere, our coke,   495
Must tell what is of the clocke
By the astrology
That he hath naturally
Conceyved and cought,
And was never tought   500
By Albumazer
The astronomer,
Nor by Ptholomy
Prince of astronomy,

478. *estryge*: ostrich
479. *horshowe*: horseshoe
482. *freat*: consume
485. *at a brayde*: in a sudden outburst
487. *solfe . . . ela*: sing above the highest note
488. *lorell*: worthless bird
489–90. *Ne . . . cantando*: "Lest by singing badly"
499. *cought*: acquired
501. *Albumazer*: Arabian astronomer (d. 885)
503. *Ptholomy*: Ptolemy, second-century astronomer

40

Nor yet by Haly;   505
And yet he croweth dayly
And nyghtly the tydes
That no man abydes,
With Partlot his hen,
Whom now and then   510
Hee plucketh by the hede
Whan he doth her trede.
  The byrde of Araby,
That potencyally
May never dye,   515
And yet there is none
But one alone;
A phenex it is
This herse that must blys
With armatycke gummes   520
That cost great sumes,
The way of thurifycation
To make a fumigation,
Swete of reflayre,
And redolent of eyre,   525
This corse for to sence
With greate reverence,
As patryarke or pope
In a blacke cope;
Whyles he senseth the herse,   530
He shall synge the verse,
Libera me,
In de, la, soll, re,

---

505. *Haly:* Haly Aben Ragel (d. 1008)
507–8. *tydes . . . abydes:* times that wait for no man
512. *her trede:* copulate with her
513. A new service, the "absolution over the tomb," begins here with the entrance of the phoenix.
519. *blys:* bless
520. *armatycke:* aromatic
522. *thurifycation:* burning of incense
524. *reflayre:* smell
526. *This . . . sence:* To incense this body
532. *Libera me:* "Free me," the first words of the response in the service

Softly bemole
For my sparowes soule.   535
Plinni sheweth all
In his story naturall,
What he doth fynde
Of the phenyx kynde;
Of whose incyneracyon   540
There ryseth a new creacyon
Of the same facyon
Without alteracyon,
Savyng that olde age
Is turned into corage   545
Of fresshe youth agayne;
This matter trew and playne,
Playne matter indede,
Who so lyst to rede.
But for the egle doth flye   550
Hyest in the skye,
He shall be the sedeane,
The quere to demeane,
As provost pryncypall,
To teach them theyr ordynall;   555
Also the noble fawcon,
With the gerfawcon,
The tarsell gentyll,
They shall morne soft and styll
In theyr amysse of gray;   560
The sacre with them shall say

---

534. *bemole:* sing the appropriate note
537. *story naturall:* the *Historia Naturalis* of Pliny the Elder
542. *facyon:* fashion
545. *corage:* heartiness
550. *for:* since
552. *sedeane:* sub-dean
553. *The . . . demeane:* To govern the choir
555. *ordynall:* service book
558. *tarsell:* a kind of male falcon
560. *amysse:* amice, clerical robe
561. *sacre:* large falcon

Dirige for Phyllyppes soule;
The goshauke shall have a role
The queresters to controll;
The lanners and the marlyons   565
Shall stand in their morning gounes;
The hobby and the muskette
The sensers and the crosse shall fet;
The kestrell in all this warke
Shall be holy water clarke.   570
    And now the darke cloudy nyght
Chaseth away Phebus bryght,
Taking his course toward the west,
God sende my sparoes sole good rest!
Requiem æternam dona eis, Domine!   575
Fa, fa, fa, my, re,
A por ta in fe ri,
Fa, fa, fa, my, my.
    Credo videre bona Domini,
I pray God, Phillip to heven may fly!   580
Domine, exaudi orationem meam!
To heven he shall, from heven he cam!
    Do mi nus vo bis cum!
Of al good praiers God send him sum!
        Oremus.   585
Deus, cui proprium est misereri et parcere,
On Phillips soule have pyte!

---

562. *Dirige:* service for the dead
564. *queresters:* choir singers
565. *lanners:* falcons; *marlyons:* merlins
567. *hobby:* small falcon; *muskette:* male sparrow hawk
568. *sensers:* containers for incense; *fet:* fetch
569. *kestrell:* hawk
574. *sole:* soul. Skelton now returns to the Vespers service for the dead.
575. *Requiem . . . Domine:* "Lord, grant them eternal rest"
577. *A por ta in fe ri:* "From the gates of hell"
579. *Credo . . . Domini:* "I trust that I shall see the good things of the Lord"
581. *Domine . . . meam:* "Lord, hear my prayer"
583. *Do mi nus vo bis cum:* "The Lord be with you"
585–86. *Oremus . . . parcere:* "Let us pray. O God, who alone can pity and spare."

For he was a prety cocke,
And came of a gentyll stocke,
And wrapt in a maidenes smocke, 590
And cherysshed full dayntely,
Tyll cruell fate made him to dy:
Alas, for dolefull desteny!
But whereto shuld I
Lenger morne or crye? 595
To Jupyter I call,
Of heven emperyall,
That Phyllyp may fly
Above the starry sky,
To treade the prety wren, 600
That is our Ladyes hen:
Amen, amen, amen!
   Yet one thynge is behynde,
That now commeth to mynde;
An epytaphe I wold have 605
For Phyllyppes grave:
But for I am a mayde,
Tymerous, halfe afrayde,
That never yet asayde
Of Elyconys well, 610
Where the Muses dwell;
Though I can rede and spell,
Recounte, reporte, and tell
Of the Tales of Caunterbury,
Some sad storyes, some mery; 615
As Palamon and Arcet,
Duke Theseus, and Partelet;
And of the Wyfe of Bath,
That worketh moch scath
Whan her tale is tolde 620
Amonge huswyves bolde,

---

610. *Elyconys well:* the Greek fountain of Helicon, seat of the Muses
614–27. Jane reviews Chaucer's *Canterbury Tales*, mentioning the Knight's Tale, the Nun's Priest's Tale, and the Wife of Bath's Tale.
619. *scath:* harm

44

How she controlde
Her husbandes as she wolde,
And them to despyse
In the homylyest wyse,   625
Brynge other wyves in thought
Their husbandes to set at nought:
And though that rede have I
Of Gawen and syr Guy,
And tell can a great pece   630
Of the Golden Flece,
How Jason it wan,
Lyke a valyaunt man;
Of Arturs rounde table,
With his knightes commendable,   635
And dame Gaynour, his quene,
Was somwhat wanton, I wene;
How syr Launcelote de Lake
Many a spere brake
For his ladyes sake;   640
Of Trystram, and kynge Marke,
And al the hole warke
Of Bele Isold his wyfe,
For whom was moch stryfe;
Some say she was lyght,   645
And made her husband knyght
Of the comyne hall,
That cuckoldes men call;
And of syr Lybius,
Named Dysconius;   650

---

629. *Gawen . . . Guy:* i.e., romances dealing with Sir Gawain and Sir Guy
of Warwick. Most of the literature Jane mentions was available in printed
form by 1505.
634. *Arturs:* alluding to Malory's *Morte d'Arthur*
636. *Gaynour:* Guinevere
645. *lyght:* wanton
647. *comyne:* common
649–50. *Lybius . . . Dysconius: Libeaus Desconus,* a romance dealing with
Gawain's son

Of Quater Fylz Amund,
And how they were sommonde
To Rome, to Charlemayne,
Upon a great payne,
And how they rode eche one   655
On Bayarde Mountalbon;
Men se hym now and than
In the forest of Arden:
What though I can frame
The storyes by name   660
Of Judas Machabeus,
And of Cesar Julious;
And of the love betwene
Paris and Vyene;
And of the duke Hannyball,   665
What made the Romaynes all
Fordrede and to quake;
How Scipion dyd wake
The cytye of Cartage,
Which by his mercyfull rage   670
He bete downe to the grounde:
And though I can expounde
Of Hector of Troye,
That was all theyr joye,
Whom Achylles slew,   675
Wherfore all Troy dyd rew;
And of the love so hote
That made Troylus to dote
Upon fayre Cressyde,
And what they wrote and sayd,   680
And of theyr wanton wylles
Pandaer bare the bylles

---

651. *Quater Fylz Amund: The Four Sons of Aymon,* another popular romance
656. *Bayarde Mountalbon:* the horse named Mountalbon
661–62. *Judas . . . Julious:* two of the medieval "Nine Worthies"
667. *Fordrede:* Fear
682. *bylles:* letters

46

From one to the other;
His maisters love to further,
Somtyme a presyous thyng,   685
An ouche, or els a ryng;
From her to hym agayn
Sometyme a prety chayn,
Or a bracelet of her here,
Prayd Troylus for to were   690
That token for her sake;
How hartely he dyd it take,
And moche therof dyd make;
And all that was in vayne,
For she dyd but fayne;   695
The story telleth playne,
He coulde not optayne,
Though his father were a kyng,
Yet there was a thyng
That made the male to wryng;   700
She made hym to syng
The song of lovers lay;
Musyng nyght and day,
Mournyng all alone,
Comfort had he none,   705
For she was quyte gone;
Thus in conclusyon,
She brought him in abusyon;
In ernest and in game
She was moch to blame;   710
Disparaged is her fame,
And blemysshed is her name,
In maner half with shame;
Troylus also hath lost
On her moch love and cost,   715
And now must kys the post;

---

686. *ouche:* brooch
700. *made . . . wryng:* brought about trouble
716. *kys the post:* get nothing for his effort

Pandara, that went betwene,
Hath won nothing, I wene,
But lyght for somer grene;
Yet for a speciall laud   720
He is named Troylus baud,
Of that name he is sure
Whyles the world shall dure:
  Though I remembre the fable
Of Penelope most stable,   725
To her husband most trew,
Yet long tyme she ne knew
Whether he were on lyve or ded;
Her wyt stood her in sted,
That she was true and just   730
For any bodely lust
To Ulixes her make,
And never wold him forsake:
  Of Marcus Marcellus
A proces I could tell us;   735
And of Anteocus;
And of Josephus
De Antiquitatibus;
And of Mardocheus,
And of great Assuerus,   740
And of Vesca his queene,
Whom he forsoke with teene,
And of Hester his other wyfe,
With whom he ledd a pleasaunt life;

---

719. *But . . . grene:* i.e., light clothing for summer, or "very little at all"
723. *dure:* last
728. *on lyve:* alive
732. *make:* husband
734. *Marcellus:* Roman consul, d. 207 B.C. Jane returns to Hannibal and to Roman history.
735. *proces:* story
736. *Anteocus:* Antioch, king of Syria, in whose court Hannibal sought refuge after his defeat by the Romans
737. *Josephus:* His *Jewish Antiquities* was completed about A.D. 94
739–44. *Mardocheus . . . life:* the story of the Book of Esther (Hester), dealing with Mordecai, Ahasuerus, and Vashti
742. *teene:* anger

48

Of kyng Alexander;   745
And of kyng Evander;
And of Porcena the great,
That made the Romayns to sweat:
　　Though I have enrold
A thousand new and old   750
Of these historious tales,
To fyll bougets and males
With bokes that I have red,
Yet I am nothyng sped,
And can but lytell skyll   755
Of Ovyd or Virgyll,
Or of Plutharke,
Or Frauncys Petrarke,
Alcheus or Sapho,
Or such other poetes mo,   760
As Linus and Homerus,
Euphorion and Theocritus,
Anacreon and Arion,
Sophocles and Philemon,
Pyndarus and Symonides,   765
Philistion and Phorocides;
These poetes of auncyente,
They ar to diffuse for me:
　　For, as I tofore have sayd,
I am but a yong mayd,   770
And cannot in effect
My style as yet direct
With Englysh wordes elect:

---

746. *Evander:* Aeneas' friend (*Aeneid,* VIII, 126ff.). Porsena (line 747) is also mentioned in the *Aeneid.*
748. *sweat:* the early editions read *smart*
752. *bougets and males:* bag and baggage
754. *nothyng sped:* not very advanced
759–66. *Alcheus . . . Phorocides:* Jane runs through a list of Greek poets: Alcaeus, Sappho, Linus, Homer . . . Pindar, Simonides, Philistion, and Pherecydes
768. *diffuse:* hard to understand
769. *tofore:* before
772–73. *My . . . elect:* Cannot as yet control my style with choice English words. Jane then proceeds to lament over the poor state of the language, not her own ability to use it.

Our naturall tong is rude,
And hard to be enneude   775
With pullysshed termes lusty;
Our language is so rusty,
So cankered, and so full
Of frowardes, and so dull,
That if I wolde apply   780
To wryte ornatly,
I wot not where to fynd
Termes to serve my mynde.
    Gowers Englysh is olde,
And of no value told;   785
His mater is worth gold,
And worthy to be enrold.
    In Chauser I am sped,
His tales I have red:
His mater is delectable,   790
Solacious, and commendable;
His Englysh well alowed,
So as it is enprowed,
For as it is enployd,
There is no Englysh voyd,   795
At those dayes moch commended;
And now men wold have amended
His Englysh, whereat they barke,
And mar all they warke:
Chaucer, that famus clerke,   800
His termes were not darke,
But plesaunt, easy, and playne;
Ne worde he wrote in vayne.
    Also Johnn Lydgate
Wryteth after an hyer rate;   805

779. *frowardes*: poorly formed words
775. *enneude*: revived
780. *apply*: endeavor
784. *Gowers*: John Gower, Chaucer's contemporary
791. *Solacious*: Pleasurable
793. *So . . . enprowed*: As long as it is used to advantage
799. *warke*: write
803. *Ne*: Not a
804. *Lydgate*: fifteenth-century poet, Chaucer's follower, who produced a
huge number of lines

It is dyffuse to fynde
The sentence of his mynde,
Yet wryteth he in his kynd,
No man that can amend
Those maters that he hath pende;   810
Yet some men fynde a faute,
And say he wryteth to haute.
    Wherfore hold me excused
If I have not well perused
Myne Englyssh halfe abused;   815
Though it be refused,
In worth I shall it take,
And fewer wordes make.
    But, for my sparowes sake,
Yet as a woman may,   820
My wyt I shall assay
An epytaphe to wryght
In Latyne playne and lyght,
Wherof the elegy
Foloweth by and by: 825
Flos volucrum formose, vale!
Philippe, sub isto
Marmore jam recubas,
Qui mihi carus eras.
Semper erunt nitido   830
Radiantia sidera cœlo;

---

806. *dyffuse:* extremely difficult
807. *sentence:* meaning
812. *to haute:* in too high a style
817. *In . . . take:* I shall take it in good part
826–43. *Flos . . . sapit:* The first section of this "elegy" (lines 826–33) constitutes Jane's epitaph for Philip. The poet Skelton then asserts his authorship of Part I and prepares to praise Jane herself in the Commendations that follow. "O flower of birds, fair one, farewell. Philip, you lie now under this marble, you who were dear to me. The brilliant stars will always be in the bright sky, and you will always be remembered in my heart. By me, Skelton, the laurel-crowned British poet, it is permitted to have sung these things, composed under a feigned likeness of the girl whose bird you will be, a maiden with a lovely body: Nais was fair, but this Jane is more beautiful; Corinna was learned, but Jane is wiser." "eris" (line 838) in the early editions may be an error for "eras" (were).

Impressusque meo
Pectore semper eris.
Per me laurigerum
Britonum Skeltonida vatem   835
Hæc cecinisse licet
Ficta sub imagine texta.
Cujus eris volucris,
Præstanti corpore virgo:
Candida Nais erat,   840
Formosior ista Joanna est;
Docta Corinna fuit,
Sed magis ista sapit.
   Bien m'en souvient.

     THE COMMENDACIONS.
  Beati im ma cu la ti in via,   845
O gloriosa fœmina!
Now myne hole imaginacion
And studyous medytacion
Is to take this commendacyon
In this consyderacion;   850
And under pacyent tolleracyon
Of that most goodly mayd
That *Placebo* hath sayd,
And for her sparow prayd
In lamentable wyse,   855
Now wyll I enterpryse,
Thorow the grace dyvyne
Of the Muses nyne,
Her beautye to commende,
If Arethusa wyll send   860
Me enfluence to endyte,
And with my pen to wryte;

---

844. *Bien m'en souvient:* "I remember it well," a motto that Skelton
used elsewhere in his poetry
845–46. *Beati . . . fœmina:* "Blessed are the pure in the way (of this life),
O glorious woman." The Latin phrases in the second part of the poem
echo, with variations, the Order of Commendations, which followed the
service for the dead.
860. *Arethusa:* a celebrated fountain in Sicily, named after one of
Diana's nymphs

If Apollo wyll promyse
Melodyously it to devyse
His tunable harpe stryngges 865
With armony that synges
Of princes and of kynges
And of all pleasaunt thynges,
Of lust and of delyght,
Thorow his godly myght; 870
To whom be the laude ascrybed
That my pen hath enbybed
With the aureat droppes,
As verely my hope is,
Of Thagus, that golden flod, 875
That passeth all erthly good;
And as that flode doth pas
Al floodes that ever was
With his golden sandes,
Who so that understandes 880
Cosmography, and the stremys
And the floodes in straunge remes,
Ryght so she doth excede
All other of whom we rede,
Whose fame by me shall sprede 885
Into Perce and Mede,
From Brytons Albion
To the Towre of Babilon.
    I trust it is no shame,
And no man wyll me blame, 890
Though I regester her name
In the courte of Fame;
For this most goodly floure,
This blossome of fresshe coulour,
So Jupiter me socour, 895

872. *enbybed*: imbibed
875. *Thagus*: Tagus, the Spanish river with its golden sands
882. *remes*: realms
886. *Perce and Mede*: Persia and Media
893–97. *For . . . vertew*: these lines become a refrain throughout the second part

She floryssheth new and new
In bewte and vertew:
Hac claritate gemina
O gloriosa fœmina,
Retribue servo tuo, vivifica mel 900
Labia mea laudabunt te.
But enforsed am I
Openly to askry,
And to make an outcri
Against odyous Envi, 905
That evermore wil ly,
And say cursedly;
With his ledder ey,
And chekes dry;
With vysage wan, 910
As swarte as tan;
His bones crake,
Leane as a rake;
His gummes rusty
Are full unlusty; 915
Hys herte withall
Bytter as gall;
His lyver, his longe
With anger is wronge;
His serpentes tonge 920
That many one hath stonge;
He frowneth ever;
He laugheth never,
Even nor morow,
But other mennes sorow 925
Causeth him to gryn
And rejoyce therin;

898–901. *Hac . . . te:* "With this twin brightness, O glorious woman, deal
bountifully with your servant, give me life, my lips will praise you,"
Psalm 62:3
903. *askry:* cry out against
908. *ledder:* leather
912. *crake:* creak
915. *unlusty:* without vigor

No slepe can him catch,
But ever doth watch,
He is so bete   930
With malyce, and frete
With angre and yre,
His foule desyre
Wyll suffre no slepe
In his hed to crepe;   935
His foule semblaunt
All displeasaunte;
Whan other ar glad,
Than is he sad;
Frantyke and mad;   940
His tong never styll
For to say yll,
Wrythyng and wringyng,
Bytyng and styngyng;
And thus this elf   945
Consumeth himself,
Hymself doth slo
Wyth payne and wo.
This fals Envy
Sayth that I   950
Use great folly
For to endyte,
And for to wryte,
And spend my tyme
In prose and ryme,   955
For to expres
The noblenes
Of my maistres,
That causeth me
Studious to be   960

---

930. *bete:* agitated
931. *frete:* eroded
936. *foule semblaunt:* ugly appearance
945. *elf:* wretch
947. *slo:* slay

To make a relation
Of her commendation;
And there agayne
Envy doth complayne,
And hath disdayne;   965
But yet certayne
I wyll be playne,
And my style dres
To this prosses.
  Now Phebus me ken   970
To sharpe my pen,
And lede my fyst
As hym best lyst,
That I may say
Honour alway   975
Of womankynd!
Trouth doth me bynd
And loyalte
Ever to be
Their true bedell,   980
To wryte and tell
How women excell
In noblenes;
As my maistres,
Of whom I thynk   985
With pen and ynk
For to compyle
Some goodly style;
For this most goodly floure,
This blossome of fresh coloure,   990
So Jupyter me socoure,
She flourissheth new and new
In beaute and vertew:

---

963. *agayne:* against
968. *dres:* address
969. *prosses:* account, theme
970. *ken:* teach
980. *bedell:* herald

56

Hac claritate gemina
O gloriosa fœmina,   995
Legem pone mihi, domina, in viam justificationum tuarum!
Quemadmodum desiderat cervus ad fontes aquarum.
　　How shall I report
All the goodly sort
Of her fetures clere,   1000
That hath non erthly pere?
Her favour of her face
Ennewed all with grace,
Confort, pleasure, and solace,
Myne hert doth so enbrace,   1005
And so hath ravyshed me
Her to behold and se,
That in wordes playne
I cannot me refrayne
To loke on her agayne: 1010
Alas, what shuld I fayne?
It wer a pleasaunt payne
With her aye to remayne.
　　Her eyen gray and stepe
Causeth myne hert to lepe;   1015
With her browes bent
She may well represent
Fayre Lucres, as I wene,
Or els fayre Polexene,
Or els Caliope,   1020
Or els Penolope;

996–97. *Legem . . . aquarum:* "Teach me the law, O Lady, the way of
your statutes; as the deer pants after the water brooks," Psalm 41:2. Skelton
here, and in later passages (lines 1061, 1114), changes the biblical
"lord" (*domine*) to "lady" (*domina*).
999. *sort:* set
1002. *Her favour:* The fair appearance
1003. *Ennewed:* Vivified
1013. *aye:* forever
1014. *stepe:* arched
1018. *Lucres:* the chaste Roman matron Lucrece, raped by Tarquin
1019. *Polexene:* Polyxena, one of Priam's daughters
1020. *Caliope:* the Muse of epic poetry, said to be the mother of Orpheus

For this most goodly floure,
This blossome of fresshe coloure,
So Jupiter me socoure,
She florisheth new and new   1025
In beautye and vertew:
Hac claritate gemina
O gloriosa fœmina,
Memor esto verbi tui servo tuo!
Servus tuus sum ego.   1030
   The Indy saphyre blew
Her vaynes doth ennew;
The orient perle so clere,
The whytnesse of her lere;
The lusty ruby ruddes   1035
Resemble the rose buddes;
Her lyppes soft and mery
Emblomed lyke the chery,
It were an hevenly blysse
Her sugred mouth to kysse.   1040
   Her beautye to augment,
Dame Nature hath her lent
A warte upon her cheke,
Who so lyst to seke
In her vysage a skar,   1045
That semyth from afar
Lyke to the radyant star,
All with favour fret,
So properly it is set:
She is the vyolet,   1050
The daysy delectable,
The calumbyn commendable,
The jelofer amyable;

1029–30. *Memor . . . ego:* "Remember thy word to your servant, I am
your servant," Psalm 118:49 and 125
1031. *Indy:* azure (from India)
1032. *ennew:* ornament, enliven
1034. *lere:* face
1035. *lusty . . . ruddes:* pleasant red hues of her complexion
1048. *favour fret:* beauty adorned
1052. *calumbyn:* columbine
1053. *jelofer:* gillyflower

For this most goodly floure,
This blossom of fressh colour,   1055
So Jupiter me succour,
She florysheth new and new
In beaute and vertew:
Hac claritate gemina
O gloriosa fœmina,   1060
Bonitatem fecisti cum servo tuo, domina,
Et ex praecordiis sonant praeconia!
   And whan I perceyved
Her wart and conceyved,
It cannot be denayd   1065
But it was well convayd,
And set so womanly,
And nothynge wantonly,
But ryght convenyently,
And full congruently,   1070
As Nature cold devyse,
In most goodly wyse;
Who so lyst beholde,
It makethe lovers bolde
To her to sewe for grace,
Her favoure to purchase;   1075
The sker upon her chyn,
Enhached on her fayre skyn,
Whyter than the swan,
It wold make any man   1080
To forget deadly syn
Her favour to wyn;
For this most godly floure,
This blossom of fressh coloure,
So Jupiter me socoure,   1085

1061–62. *Bonitatem . . . praeconia:* "Thou hast dealt bountifully with thy
servant, O Lady, and from the heart praises sound," Psalm 118
1065. *denayd:* denied
1069. *convenyently:* fittingly
1076. *sker:* scar
1077. *Enhached:* Inlaid

She flouryssheth new and new
In beaute and vertew:
Hac claritate gemina
O gloriosa fœmina,
Defecit in salutatione tua anima mea;   1090
Quid petis filio, mater dulcissima? babae!
   Soft, and make no dyn,
For now I wyll begyn
To heve in remembraunce
Her goodly dalyaunce,   1095
And her goodly pastaunce:
So sad and so demure,
Behavynge her so sure,
With wordes of pleasure
She wold make to the lure   1100
And any man convert
To gyve her his hole hert.
She made me sore amased
Upon her whan I gased,
Me thought min hert was crased,   1105
My eyne were so dased;
For this most goodly flour,
This blossom of fressh colour,
So Jupyter me socour,
She flouryssheth new and new   1110
In beauty and vertew:
Hac claritate gemina
O gloriosa fœmina,
Quomodo dilexi legem tuam, domina!
Recedant vetera, nova sint omnia.   1115

1090–91. *Defecit . . . babae:* "My soul faints as it greets you; what do you ask for your son, sweetest mother?" Psalm 118:81
1094. *heve:* raise
1096. *pastaunce:* pastime
1097. *sad:* serious
1100. *make . . . lure:* draw to her, like a falcon diving for the lure
1105. *crased:* crushed
1106. *dased:* dazzled
1114–15. *Quomodo . . . omnia:* "How I loved thy law, O Lady; old things pass away, everything is new," Psalm 118:97 and II Corinthians 5:17

And to amende her tale,
Whan she lyst to avale,
And with her fyngers smale,
And handes soft as sylke,
Whyter than the mylke,   1120
That are so quyckely vayned,
Wherwyth my hand she strayned,
Lorde, how I was payned!
Unneth I me refrayned,
How she me had reclaymed,   1125
And me to her retayned,
Enbrasynge therwithall
Her godly myddell small
With sydes longe and streyte;
To tell you what conceyte   1130
I had than in a tryce,
The matter were to nyse,
And yet there was no vyce,
Nor yet no villany,
But only fantasy;   1135
For this most goodly floure,
This blossom of fressh coloure,
So Jupiter me succoure,
She floryssheth new and new
In beaute and vertew: 1140
Hac claritate gemina
O gloriosa fœmina,
Iniquos odio habui!
Non calumnientur me superbi.

1116. *amende her tale:* make up her list of perfections
1117. *lyst to avale:* it pleased her to avail herself (of them)
1121. *quyckely:* lively
1124. *Unneth . . . refrayned:* I could scarcely hold myself back
1125. *reclaymed:* tamed
1129. *sydes:* loins; *streyte:* slender
1130. *conceyte:* an idea
1132. *nyse:* delicate
1143–44. *Iniquos . . . superbi:* "I hate vain thoughts; let not the proud oppress me," Psalm 118:113 and 122.

But whereto shulde I note   1145
How often dyd I tote
Upon her prety fote?
It raysed myne hert rote
To se her treade the grounde
With heles short and rounde.   1150
She is playnly expresse
Egeria, the goddesse,
And lyke to her image,
Emportured with corage,
A lovers pylgrimage;   1155
Ther is no beest savage,
Ne no tyger so wood,
But she wolde chaunge his mood,
Such relucent grace
Is formed in her face;   1160
For this most goodly floure,
This blossome of fresshe coloure,
So Jupiter me succour,
She flouryssheth new and new
In beaute and vertew: 1165
Hac claritate gemina
O gloriosa fœmina,
Mirabilia testimonia tua!
Sicut novellæ plantationes in juventute sua.
So goodly as she dresses,   1170
So properly she presses
The bryght golden tresses
Of her heer so fyne,
Lyke Phebus beames shyne.

1146. *tote:* peer
1148. *hert rote:* the root of my heart
1152. *Egeria:* in Roman mythology, the nymph who was Numa's wife and teacher. See Ovid, *Metamorphoses,* XV, 482ff.
1154. *Emportured:* probably a misprint for "importuned"
1157. *wood:* furious
1159. *relucent:* refulgent
1168–69. *Mirabilia . . . sua:* "Wonderful are thy testimonies; that our sons may be as plants grown up in their youth," Psalms 118:129 and 143:12
1174. *Phebus . . . shyne:* the shine of the sun's beams

Wherto shuld I disclose   1175
The garterynge of her hose?
It is for to suppose
How that she can were
Gorgiously her gere;
Her fresshe habylementes   1180
With other implementes
To serve for all ententes,
Lyke dame Flora, quene
Of lusty somer grene;
For this most goodly floure,   1185
This blossom of fressh coloure,
So Jupiter me socoure,
She florisheth new and new
In beautye and vertew:
Hac claritate gemina   1190
O gloriosa fœmina,
Clamavi in toto corde, exaudi me!
Misericordia tua magna est super me.
  Her kyrtell so goodly lased,
And under that is brased   1195
Such plasures that I may
Neyther wryte nor say;
Yet though I wryte not with ynke,
No man can let me thynke,
For thought hath lyberte,   1200
Thought is franke and fre;
To thynke a mery thought
It cost me lytell nor nought.
Wolde God myne homely style
Were pullysshed with the fyle   1205
Of Ciceros eloquence,
To prase her excellence!

1179. *gere:* clothes
1180. *habylementes:* apparel
1192–93. *Clamavi . . . me:* "I have cried with all my heart, hear me; great is thy mercy toward me," Psalms 118:145 and 85:13
1195. *brased:* supported
1199. *let me thynke:* keep me from thinking
1205. *pullysshed:* polished

For this most goodly floure,
This blossome of fressh coloure,
So Jupiter me succoure,   1210
She flouryssheth new and new
In beaute and vertew:
Hac claritate gemina
O gloriosa fœmina,
Principes persecuti sunt me gratis!   1215
Omnibus consideratis,
Paradisus voluptatis
Hæc virgo est dulcissima.
    My pen it is unable,
My hand it is unstable,   1220
My reson rude and dull
To prayse her at the full;
Goodly maystres Jane,
Sobre, demure Dyane;
Jane this maystres hyght   1225
The lode star of delyght,
Dame Venus of all pleasure,
The well of worldly treasure;
She doth excede and pas
In prudence dame Pallas;   1230
For this most goodly floure,
This blossome of fresshe colour,
So Jupiter me socoure,
She florysseth new and new
In beaute and vertew: 1235
Hac claritate gemina
O gloriosa fœmina!
    Requiem æternam dona eis, Domine!
With this psalme, *Domine, probasti me,*
Shall sayle over the see,   1240
With *Tibi, Domine, commendamus,*

1215–18. *Principes . . . dulcissima:* "Princes have persecuted me unjustly
[Psalm 118:161]; all things considered, this girl is the sweetest of heavenly
pleasures"
1225. *hyght:* is called
1238. *Requiem . . . Domine:* "Grant them eternal rest, O Lord"
1239. *Domine . . . me:* "Lord, you have tested me"
1241. *Tibi . . . commendamus:* "We commend ourselves to thee, O Lord"

64

On pylgrimage to saynt Jamys,
For shrympes, and for pranys,
And for stalkynge cranys;
And where my pen hath offendyd,   1245
I pray you it may be amendyd
By discrete consyderacyon
Of your wyse reformacyon;
I have not offended, I trust,
If it be sadly dyscust.   1250
It were no gentle gyse
This treatyse to despyse
Because I have wrytten and sayd
Honour of this fayre mayd;
Wherefore shulde I be blamed,   1255
That I Jane have named,
And famously proclamed?
She is worthy to be enrolde
With letters of golde.
       Car elle vault.   1260
Per me laurigerum Britonum Skeltonida vatem
Laudibus eximiis merito hæc redimita puella est:
Formosam cecini, qua non formosior ulla est;
Formosam potius quam commendaret Homerus.
Sic juvat interdum rigidos recreare labores,   1265
Nec minus hoc titulo tersa Minerva mea est.
       Rien que playsere.

1242. *Jamys:* i.e., the shrine of St. James of Compostella
1243. *pranys:* prawns. Skelton is perhaps hinting that his poem will be used for paper to wrap shrimp and prawns in; *stalkynge cranys* in the next line remains unexplained.
1250. *sadly:* seriously
1251. *gyse:* fashion
1260. *Car elle vault:* "Because she is worthy"
1261–66. *Per . . . est:* A rough translation of these lines might run as follows: "Through me, Skelton, the laureate British poet, this girl is deservedly honored with praise. I have called her beautiful, than whom no one is more beautiful. There is no lovely one whom Homer would rather praise. Thus it delights me now and then to refresh myself after stern toil. Nor is my art less pure than this title [i.e., the motto in the next line]."
1267. *Rien que playsere:* "Nothing but to please"

*Thus endeth the boke of Philip Sparow, and here foloweth
an adicyon made by maister Skelton.*

    The gyse now a dayes
Of some janglynge jayes
Is to discommende   1270
That they cannot amend,
Though they wold spend
All the wyttes they have.
    What ayle them to deprave
Phillip Sparowes grave?   1275
His *Dirige,* her Commendacyon
Can be no derogacyon,
But myrth and consolacyon
Made by protestacyon,
No man to myscontent   1280
With Phillyppes enterement.
    Alas, that goodly mayd,
Why shuld she be afrayde?
Why shuld she take shame
That her goodly name,   1285
Honorably reported,
Sholde be set and sorted,
To be matriculate
With ladyes of estate?
    I conjure the, Phillip Sparow,   1290
By Hercules that hell dyd harow,
And with a venemous arow
Slew of the Epidaures
One of the Centaures,
Or Onocentaures,   1295
Or Hipocentaures;

1268ff. Skelton's "adicyon" to his poem was first published in the *Garland of Laurel* (1523), from which text a few readings are accepted here.
1274. *deprave:* vilify
1276. *His . . . Commendacyon:* i.e., the first two parts of the poem
1281. *enterement:* burial
1289. *estate:* dignity
1291. *harow:* lay waste
1293. *Epidaures:* apparently, the inhabitants of Epidaurus
1295. *Onocentaures:* half human, half asses
1296. *Hipocentaures:* half human, half horses

By whose myght and mayne
An hart was slayne
With hornes twayne
Of glytteryng gold;   1300
And the appels of gold
Of Hesperides withhold,
And with a dragon kept
That never more slept,
By marcyall strength   1305
He wan at length;
And slew Gerion
With thre bodyes in one;
With myghty corage
Adauntid the rage   1310
Of a lyon savage;
Of Dyomedes stable
He brought out a rable
Of coursers and rounses
With leapes and bounses;   1315
And with mighty luggyng,
Wrestlyng and tuggyng,
He plucked the bull
By the horned skull,
And offred to Cornucopia;   1320
And so forth *per cetera:*
    Also by Ecates bower
In Plutos gastly tower;
    By the ugly Eumenides,
That never have rest nor ease;   1325

1302. *Of . . . withhold:* Withheld by the Hesperides. Skelton is running
through the various labors of Hercules.
1310. *Adauntid:* Baffled
1314. *rounses:* hackney horses
1318. *bull:* Achelous, who assumed this shape in his battle with Hercules.
See Ovid, *Metamorphoses,* IX, 85ff.
1321. *per cetera:* "through the rest"
1322. *Ecates:* Hecate's
1324. *Eumenides:* the Furies

By the venemous serpent,
That in hell is never brent,
In Lerna the Grekes fen,
That was engendred then;
   By Chemeras flames,   1330
And all the dedly names
Of infernall posty,
Where soules frye and rousty;
   By the Stygyall flood,
And the streames wood   1335
Of Cocitus botumles well;
   By the feryman of hell,
Caron with his beerd hore,
That roweth with a rude ore
And with his frownsid fore top   1340
Gydeth his bote with a prop:
   I conjure Phylyp, and call
In the name of kyng Saul;
Primo Regum expresse,
He bad the Phitonesse   1345
To wytchcraft her to dresse,
And by her abusyons,
And dampnable illusyons
Of marveylus conclusyons,
And by her supersticyons   1350
Of wonderfull condityons,

1327. *brent:* burnt
1328. *Lerna:* alluding to the monstrous Hydra of Lerna
1330. *Chemeras:* Chimera's
1332. *posty:* power
1333. *rousty:* roast
1335. *wood:* wild
1338. *Caron . . . hore:* Charon with his hoary beard
1340. *frownsid . . . top:* wrinkled forehead
1344. *Primo Regum:* the First Book of Kings (1 Samuel in the Authorized Version), which tells the story in Chapter 28
1345. *Phitonesse:* Pythoness, witch
1346. *dresse:* apply
1351. *condityons:* qualities

She raysed up in that stede
Samuell that was dede;
But whether it were so,
He were *idem in numero*,   1355
The selfe same Samuell,
How be it to Saull dyd he tell
The Philistinis shuld hym ascry,
And the next day he shuld dye,
I wyll my selfe dyscharge   1360
To lettred men at large:
    But, Phylyp, I conjure thee
Now by these names thre,
Diana in the woodes grene,
Luna that so bryght doth shene,   1365
Procerpina in hell,
That thou shortly tell,
And shew now unto me
What the cause may be
Of this perplexite!   1370

Inferias, Philippe, tuas Scroupe pulchra Joanna
Instanter petiit: cur nostri carminis illam
Nunc pudet? est sero; minor est infamia vero.

    Than suche as have disdayned
And of this worke complayned,   1375
I pray God they be payned
No worse than is contayned
In verses two or thre
That folowe as you may se.

1352. *stede:* place
1355. *idem in numero:* "in the same body." The apparition may or may not
have been Samuel.
1358. *ascry:* assail
1360. *my . . . dyscharge:* open my mind
1361. *lettred:* educated
1365. *shene:* shine
1371–73. *Inferias . . . vero:* "Philip, the fair Joanna Scrope ardently
desired your obsequies. Why is she now ashamed of our song? It is too
late. Shame is less than truth."

Luride, cur, livor, volucris pia funera damnas?   1380
Talia te rapiant rapiunt quæ fata volucrem!
Est tamen invidia mors tibi continua.

3.

The Tunnyng of Elynour Rummyng

TELL you I chyll,
If that ye wyll
A whyle be styll,
Of a comely gyll
That dwelt on a hyll;   5
But she is not gryll,
For she is somwhat sage
And well worne in age,
For her vysage
It woldt aswage   10
A mannes courage.
  Her lothely lere
Is nothynge clere,
But ugly of chere,
Droupy and drowsy,   15
Scurvy and lowsy;
Her face all bowsy,

1380–82. *Luride . . . continua:* a final curse against the detractors of the
poem: "Why, ghostly Envy, do you condemn the sacred funeral rites of the
bird? May the fate which seized him now overtake you. Yet your malice is
a perpetual death to you."
Title: Tunnyng: pouring of ale into tuns (casks), brewing. A real
"Alianora Romyng" has been identified as living at Leatherhead, Surrey,
in 1525. Skelton's poem probably dates from about 1517.
1. *chyll:* shall
4. *gyll:* jill, girl
6. *gryll:* fierce
12. *lere:* face
17. *bowsy:* boozy

Comely crynklyd,
Woundersly wrynklyd,
Lyke a rost pygges eare   20
Brystled with here.
  Her lewde lyppes twayne,
They slaver, men sayne,
Lyke a ropy rayne,
A gummy glayre.   25
She is ugly fayre:
Her nose somdele hoked
And camously croked,
Never stoppynge
But ever droppynge;   30
Her skynne lose and slacke,
Greuyned lyke a sacke;
With a croked backe.
  Her eyen gowndy
Are full unsowndy,   35
For they are blered;
And she gray-hered,
Jawed lyke a jetty;
A man wolde have pytty
To se howe she is gumbed,   40
Fyngered and thumbed,
Gently joynted,
Gresed and anoynted
Up to the knockles;
The bones of her huckels   45
Lyke as they were with buckels
Togyder made fast.
Her youth is farre past;

---

24. *ropy rayne*: rain coming down in long streams (ropes)
25. *glayre*: beaten egg whites
28. *camously*: concavely
32. *Greuyned*: Grained
34. *gowndy*: bleary
38. *jetty*: pier
40. *gumbed*: gummed
45. *huckels*: hips

Foted lyke a plane,
Legged lyke a crane;   50
And yet she wyll jet
Lyke a joyly fet
In her furred flocket
And graye russet rocket,
With symper the cocket.   55
Her huke of Lyncole grene,
It had ben hers, I wene,
More then fourty yere;
And so doth it apere,
For the grene bare thredes   60
Loke lyke sere wedes,
Wyddered lyke hay,
The woll worne away.
And yet I dare saye
She thynketh herselfe gaye   65
Upon the holy daye,
Whan she doth her aray,
And gyrdeth in her gytes
Stytched and pranked with pletes;
Her kyrtell Brystowe red,   70
With clothes upon her hed
That wey a sowe of led,
Wrythen in wonder wyse
After the Sarasyns gyse,

---

49. *Foted . . . plane:* With feet like trowels
52. *joyly fet:* jolly, fat woman
53. *flocket:* long-sleeved garment
54. *rocket:* smock
55. *symper the cocket:* in an affected way
56. *huke:* hooded cape; *Lyncole:* Lincoln, a bright green
61. *sere:* dried-out
67. *her:* herself
68. *gytes:* skirts
69. *pranked:* ornamented
70. *kyrtell:* outer petticoat; *Brystowe:* Bristol
72. *sowe:* huge lump
73. *Wrythen:* Wound
74. *Sarasyns gyse:* Turkish fashion

With a whym-wham 75
Knyt with a trym-tram
Upon her brayne-pan,
Lyke an Egypcyan
Lapped about.
Whan she goeth out 80
Herselfe for to shewe,
She dryveth downe the dewe
With a payre of heles
As brode as two wheles;
She hobles as she gose 85
With her blanket hose
Over the falowe,
Her shone smered wyth talowe,
Gresed upon dyrt
That baudeth her skyrt. 90

PRIMUS PASSUS

And this comely dame,
I understande, her name
Is Elynour Rummynge,
At home in her wonnynge;
And as men say, 95
She dwelt in Sothray
In a certayne stede
Bysyde Lederhede.
She is a tonnysh gyb,
The devyll and she be syb. 100

78. *Egypcyan:* gypsy
86. *blanket:* woolen
88. *shone:* shoes
90. *baudeth:* befouls
91. *Primus passus:* "First Fit" or section
94. *wonnynge:* dwelling
96. *Sothray:* Surrey
97. *stede:* place
99. *tonnysh gyb:* fat old cat
100. *syb:* kin

But to make up my tale,
She breweth noppy ale,
And maketh thereof port sale
To travellars, to tynkers,
To sweters, to swynkers   105
And all good ale drynkers,
That wyll nothynge spare,
But drynke tyll they stare
And brynge themselve bare,
With, Now away the mare,   110
And let us sley care!
As wyse as an hare!
    Come whoso wyll
To Elynoure on the hyll,
With, Fyll the cup, fyll!   115
And syt there by styll,
Erly and late:
Thyther cometh Kate,
Cysly and Sare,
With theyr legges bare,   120
And also theyr fete
Hardely full unswete;
With theyr heles dagged,
Theyr kyrtelles all to-jagged,
Theyr smockes all to-ragged,   125
With tytters and tatters,
Brynge dysshes and platters,
With all theyr myght runnynge
To Elynour Rummynge
To have of her tunnynge;   130

---

102. *noppy:* nappy. The ale was made from malt barley, sweet and fermented, without hops.
103. *port:* public
105. *sweters:* sweaters, laborers
110. *Now . . . mare:* "Let's be merry"
116. *syt . . . styll:* remain there constantly
119. *Cysly and Sare:* Cecily and Sarah
122. *Hardely full unswete:* Not very sweet at all
123. *dagged:* slashed

She leneth them on the same,
And thus begynneth the game.
   Some wenches come unlased,
Some huswyves come unbrased,
With theyr naked pappes,   135
That flyppes and flappes,
It wygges and it wagges
Lyke tawny saffron bagges—
A sorte of foule drabbes
All scurvy with scabbes.   140
Some be flybytten,
Some skewed as a kytten;
Some with a sho clout
Bynde theyr heddes about;
Some have no herelace,   145
Theyr lockes aboute theyr face,
Theyr tresses untrust,
All full of unlust;
Some loke strawry,
Some cawry mawry;   150
Full untydy tegges,
Lyke rotten egges:
Such a lewde sorte
To Elynour resorte
From tyde to tyde.   155
Abyde, abyde,
And to you shall be tolde
Howe hyr ale is solde
To mawte and to molde.

---

131. *leneth them:* makes loans to them
142. *skewed:* walking sideways
143. *sho clout:* shoe rag
145. *herelace:* headband
147. *untrust:* not tied up
148. *unlust:* repulsiveness
149. *strawry:* coarse, like straw
150. *cawry mawry:* like a rough cloth
151. *tegges:* unshorn sheep
155. *tyde:* time
159. *mawte:* i.e., turn to malt

SECUNDUS PASSUS

Some have no mony 160
That thyder commy,
For theyr ale to pay—
That is a shreud aray!
Elynour swered, Nay,
Ye shall not bere awaye 165
Myne ale for nought,
By hym that me bought!
   With, Hey, dogge, hay,
Have these hogges away!
With, Get me a staffe, 170
The swyne eate my draffe!
Stryke the hogges with a clubbe,
They have dronke up my swyllyng tubbe!
For be there never so moche prese,
These swyne go to the hye dese; 175
The sowe with her pygges,
The bore his tayle wrygges,
His rumpe also he frygges
Agaynst the hye benche.
With, Fo, ther is a stenche! 180
Gather up, thou wenche;
Seest thou not what is fall?
Take up dyrt and all
And bere out of the hall!
God gyve it yll prevynge, 185
Clenly as yvell chevynge!

---

163. *shreud aray:* wretched business
167. *hym . . . bought:* i.e., Christ
171. *draffe:* refuse
174. *moche prese:* great a crowd
175. *hye dese:* high dais, upper platform
177. *wrygges:* wriggles
178. *frygges:* rubs
185. *God . . . prevynge:* May God make it turn out badly
186. *yvell chevynge:* bad luck

But let us turne playne
There we lefte agayne.
For as yll a patch as that,
The hennes ron in the mashfat;   190
For they go to roust
Streyght over the ale joust,
And donge, whan it commes,
In the ale tunnes.
Than Elynour taketh   195
The mashe bolle and shaketh
The hennes donge awaye,
And skommeth it into a tray
Whereas the yeest is,
With her maungy fystis.   200
And somtyme she blennes
The donge of her hennes
And the ale togyder,
And sayth, gossyp, come hyder,
This ale shal be thycker   205
And floure the more quycker;
For, I may tell you,
I lerned it of a Jewe
Whan I began to brewe,
And I have found it trew.   210
Drinke now whyle it is new;
And ye may it broke,
It shall make you loke
Yonger than ye be
Yeres two or thre,   215
For ye may prove it by me.
Behold, she sayd, and se
How bright I am of ble!

---

189. *yll:* poor; *patch:* patch of ground (?)
190. *mashfat:* vat for mash
192. *joust:* large pot
196. *bolle:* bowl
198. *skommeth:* skims
201. *blennes:* blends
204. *gossyp:* good friend
206. *floure:* froth
212. *broke:* brook (i.e., if you can stand it)
218. *ble:* complexion

Ich am not cast away,
That can my husband say, 220
Whan we kys and play
In lust and in lykyng.
He calleth me his whytyng,
His mullyng and his mytyng,
His nobbes and his conny, 225
His swetyng and his honny,
With, bas, my prety bonny,
Thou art worth good and monny.
This make I my falyre fonny,
Tyll that he dreme and dronny, 230
For after all our sport,
Than wyll he rout and snort;
Thus swete togither we ly,
As two pygges in a sty.
 To cease me semeth best, 235
And of this tale to rest,
And for to leve this letter
Bicause it is no better;
And bicause it is no swetter,
We wyll no farther ryme 240
Of it at this tyme,
But we wyll turne playne
Where we left agayne.

TERTIUS PASSUS

 In stede of coyne and monny,
Some brought her a conny, 245
And some a pot with honny,

---

224. *mytyng:* dear little thing
225. *nobbes:* darling; *conny:* rabbit
227. *bas:* kiss
228. *monny:* many
229. *falyre fonny:* dear husband dote
230. *dronny:* doze
232. *rout:* snore
233. *Thus swete:* 1545 reads *than swetely*
239. *swetter:* sweeter

Some a salt, and some a spone,
Some their hose, some their shone;
Some ranne a good trot
With a skellet or a pot;   250
Some fyll theyr pot full
Of good Lemster woll:
An huswyfe of trust,
Whan she is athrust,
Suche a webbe can spyn   255
Her thryfte is full thyn.
　　Some go streyght thyder,
Be it slaty or slyder,
They holde the hye waye
They care not what men saye.   260
Be that as be maye,
Some lothe to be espyde,
Some start in at the backe syde,
Over the hedge and pale,
And all for the good ale.   265
　　Some renne tyll they swete,
Brynge with them malte or whete,
And Dame Elynour entrete
To byrle them of the best.
　　Than cometh another gest,   270
She swereth by the Rode of Rest,
Her lyppes are so drye
Without drynke she must dye;
Therefore fyll it by and by
And have here a pecke of ry.   275
　　Anone cometh another,
As drye as the other,

---

247. *salt:* salt shaker
252. *Lemster:* a fine grade of wool
254. *athrust:* thirsty
258. *slaty or slyder:* slate-like or slippery
264. *pale:* fence
266. *renne:* run
268. *entrete:* entreat
269. *byrle:* pour
271. *Rode of Rest:* Christ's cross

And with her doth brynge
Mele, salte, or other thynge,
Her hernest gyrdle, her weddynge rynge,   280
To pay for her scot
As cometh to her lot.
Some bryngeth her husbandis hood
Bycause the ale is good;
Another brought her his cap   285
To offer to the ale tap,
With flaxe and with towe,
And some brought sowre dowe;
With, Hey and with howe,
Syt we downe arowe   290
And drynke tyll we blowe
And pype tyrly-tyrlowe!
  Some layde to pledge
Theyr hatchet and theyr wedge,
Theyr hekell and theyr rele,   295
Theyr rocke, theyr spynnyng whele;
And some went so narrowe
They layde to pledge theyr wharrowe,
Theyr rybskyn and theyr spyndell,
Theyr nedell and theyr thymbell;   300
Here was scant thryft
Whan they made suche shyft.
  Theyr thrust was so great
They asked never for mete
But, Drynke, still drynke,   305
And let the cat wynke!
Let us wasshe our gommes
From the drye crommes!

---

279. *Mele:* Meal
280. *hernest:* ornamented
288. *dowe:* dough
291. *blowe:* belch
295. *hekell:* tool for combing flax; *rele:* reel to wind thread on
296. *rocke:* distaff
298. *wharrowe:* pulley in spinning wheel
299. *rybskyn:* leather apron

Some for very nede
Layde downe a skeyne of threde   310
And some a skeyne of yarne;
Some brought from the barne
Both benes and pease:
Small chaffer doth ease
Sometyme, now and than.   315
Another there was that ran
With a good brasse pan,
Her colour was full wan,
She ran in all the hast
Unbrased and unlast,   320
Tawny, swart and sallowe
Lyke a cake of tallowe;
I swere by all hallowe
It was a stale to take
The devyll in a brake.   325
    And than come haltyng Jone
And brought a gambone
Of bakon that was resty,
But, Lord, that she was testy,
Angry as a waspy;   330
She began to yane and gaspy
And bad Elynour go bet,
And fyll in good met:
It was dere that was far fet.

---

314. *chaffer:* merchandise
323. *all hallowe:* all that's holy
324. *stale:* lure
325. *brake:* trap
327. *gambone:* gammon
328. *resty:* rancid
331. *yane:* yawn
332. *bad:* bade; *bet:* on
333. *met:* measure
334. *far fet:* fetched from a distance

Another brought a spycke 335
Of a bacon flycke,
Her tonge was very quycke,
But she spake somwhat thycke.
Her felowe dyd stammer and stut,
But she was a foule slut 340
For her mouth fomyd
And her bely groned:
Jone sayde she had eten a fyest.
By Chryst, sayde she, thou lyest;
I have as swete a breth 345
As thou, with shamefull deth!
　　Than Elynour sayde, Ye calettes,
I shall breke your palettes,
Wythout ye now cease,
And so was made the peace. 350
　　Than thydder came dronken Ales
And she was full of tales,
Of tydynges in Wales
And Saynte James in Gales,
And of the Portyngales. 355
With, Lo, gossyp, i wys,
Thus and thus it is,
There hath ben greate war
Betwene Temple Bar
And the Crosse in Chepe, 360
And thyder came an hepe
Of mylstones in a route.
She spake this in her snout,

---

335. *spycke:* fat piece
336. *flycke:* flitch
343. *fyest:* fart
347. *calettes:* sluts
351. *Ales:* Alice. Cf. Chaucer's Wife of Bath.
353. *tydynges:* news
354. *Gales:* Galicia
355. *Portyngales:* Portuguese
356. *i wys:* indeed
358–60. *war . . . Chepe:* possibly a reference to the May Day riots in London in 1517

Snevelyng in her nose
As though she had the pose.   365
Lo, here is an olde typpet,
And ye wyll gyve me a syppet
Of your stale ale,
God sende you good sale!
And as she was drynkynge,   370
She fell in a wynkynge
With a barly hood—
She pyst where she stood.
Than began she to wepe,
And forthwith fell on slepe.   375
Elynour toke her up,
And blessed her with a cup
Of newe ale in cornes;
Ales founde therin no thornes,
But supped it up at ones,   380
She founde therein no bones.

QUINTUS PASSUS

Nowe in cometh another rabell:
First one with a ladell,
Another with a cradell
And with a syde sadell;   385
And there began a fabell,
A clatterynge and a babell
Of a foles fylly
That had a fole with Wylly,
With, Jast you, and gup, gylly,   390
She coulde not lye stylly.

---

365. *the pose:* a cold
366. *typpet:* scarf
371. *in a wynkynge:* as quickly as you could wink
372. *barly hood:* fit of drunkenness
375. *on:* to
378. *in cornes:* i.e., just drawn
386. *fabell:* foolish tale
388. *foles:* foolish, foal's

Then came in a genet,
And sware by Saynt Benet,
I dranke not this sennet
A draught to my pay.   395
Elynour, I the pray,
Of thyne ale let us assaye,
And have here a pylche of graye;
I were skynnes of conny
That causeth I loke so donny.   400
Another than dyd hyche her,
And brought a pottell pycher,
A tonnell, and a bottell;
But she had lost the stoppell—
She cut of her sho-sole   405
And stopped therewith the hole.
    Amonge all the blommer,
Another brought a skommer,
A fryenge pan and a slyce;
Elynour made the pryce   410
For god ale eche whyt.
    Than sterte in mad Kyt,
That had lytell wyt;
She semed somdele seke,
And brought a peny cheke   415
To Dame Elynour
For a draught of her lycour.

---

392. *genet:* jennet (contemptuously for "woman")
394. *sennet:* week
395. *pay:* satisfaction
398. *pylche of graye:* gray outer garment
399. *were:* wear
400. *donny:* drab
402. *pottell pycher:* large pitcher
403. *tonnell:* barrel
407. *blommer:* confusion
408. *skommer:* skimmer
409. *slyce:* kitchen knife
411. *god:* good; *whyt:* bit, piece
415. *peny cheke:* chick worth a penny

Than Margery Mylke-Ducke
Her kyrtell she dyd uptucke
An ynche above her kne,   420
Her legges that ye myght se;
But they were sturdy and stubbed,
Myghty pestels and clubbed,
As fayre and as whyte
As the fote of a kyte.   425
She was somwhat foule,
Croke nebbed lyke an oule,
And yet she brought her fees,
A cantell of Essex chese
Was well a fote thycke,   430
Full of magottes quycke;
It was huge and greate,
And myghty stronge meate
For the devyll to eate;
It was tart and punyete.   435
Another sorte of sluttes:
Some brought walnuttes,
Some apples, some peres,
Some brought theyr clyppyng sheres,
Some brought this and that,   440
Some brought I wote nere what,
Some brought theyr husbands hat,
Some podynges and lynkes,
Some trypes that stynkes.
But of all this thronge   445
One came them amonge,
She semed halfe a leche,
And began to preche

---

427. *Croke nebbed:* with a crooked beak; *1545* reads *Croke necked*
429. *cantell:* thick piece; *Essex cheese:* made from sheep's milk
435. *punyete:* pungent
441. *wote nere:* don't know
443. *podynges and lynkes:* meat puddings and links of sausage
447. *leche:* doctor

Of the Tewsday in the weke
Whan the mare doth keke,   450
Of the vertue of an unset leke
And of her husbandes breke.
With the feders of a quayle
She could to Burdews sayle;
And with good ale barme   455
She could make a charme
To helpe withall a stytch:
She seemed to be a wytch.
Another brought two goslynges
That were noughty froslynges;   460
She brought them in a wallet—
She was a cumly callet.
The goslenges were untyde;
Elynor began to chyde,
They be wretchockes thou hast brought,   465
They are shyre shakyng nought.

   Maude Ruggy thyther skypped:
She was ugly hypped,
And ugly thycke-lypped,
Like an onyon syded,   470
Lyke tan ledder hyded.
She had her so guyded
Betwene the cup and the wall
That she was there withall
Into a palsey fall;   475

---

450. *keke:* kick
451. *unset leke:* maiden's leek
452. *breke:* breeches
454. *Burdews:* Bourdeaux
455. *barme:* froth
460. *noughty froslynges:* worthless things, stunted by frost
461. *wallet:* bag
465. *wretchockes:* weak fowls
466. *shyre . . . nought:* completely without value

With that her hed shaked,
And her handes quaked;
Ones hed wold have aked
To se her naked;
She dranke so of the dregges   480
The dropsy was in her legges,
Her face glystryng lyke glas,
All foggy fat she was.
She had also the gout
In all her joyntes about;   485
Her breth was soure and stale
And smelled all of ale:
Such a bedfellaw
Wold make one cast his craw;
But yet for all that   490
She dranke on the mash fat.
　　There came an old rybybe:
She halted of a kybe,
And had broken her shyn
At the threshold comyng in,   495
And fell so wyde open
That one might se her token,
The devyll thereon be wroken!
What nede all this be spoken?
She yelled lyke a calfe.   500
Ryse up, on Gods halfe,
Sayd Elynour Rummyng,
I beshrew the for thy cummyng.
And as she at her dyd pluck,
Quake, quake, sayd the duck   505

483. *foggy:* flabby
489. *cast his craw:* vomit
492. *rybybe:* hag
493. *halted:* limped; *kybe:* chilblain
497. *token:* sexual organs
498. *wroken:* avenged

In that lampatrams lap.
With, fy, cover thy shap
With sum flyp-flap,
God gyve it yll hap!
Sayd Elynour, for shame! 510
Lyke an honest dame.
Up she stert, halfe lame,
And skantly could go
For payne and for wo.
   In came another dant, 515
With a gose and a gant;
She had a wyde wesant,
She was nothynge plesant:
Necked lyke an olyfant;
It was a bullyfant, 520
A gredy cormerant.
Another brought her garlyke heddes;
Another brought her bedes
Of jet or of cole
To offer to the ale-pole; 525
Some brought a wymble,
Some brought a thymble,
Some brought a sylke lace,
Some brought a pyncase,
Some her husbandes gowne, 530
Some a pyllowe of downe,
Some of the napery;
And all this shyfte they make
For the good ale sake.

---

506. *lampatrams:* lamprey's
515. *dant:* slut
516. *gant:* gander
517. *wesant:* throat
519. *olyfant:* elephant
520. *bullyfant:* apparently a nonce word, modeled on "olyfant"
526. *wymble:* gimlet

A strawe, sayde Bele, stande utter,   535
For we have egges and butter,
And of pygeons a payre.
    Than sterte forth a fysgygge
And she brought a bore pygge;
The flesshe thereof was ranke,   540
And her brethe strongely stanke;
Yet or she went, she dranke,
And gat her great thanke
Of Elynour for her ware
That she thyder bare   545
To pay for her share.
Nowe truly, to my thynkynge,
This is a solempne drynkynge.

                    SEPTIMUS PASSUS

    Soft, quod one hyght Sybbyll,
And let me with you bybyll.   550
She sat downe in the place,
With a sory face
Whey wormed about;
Garnysshed was her snout
With here and there a puscull,   555
Lyke a scabbyd muscull.
This ale, sayd she, is noppy;
Let us syppe and soppy
And not spyll a droppy,
For so mote I hoppy,   560
It coleth well my croppy.
    Dame Elynour, sayde she,
Have here is for me,

---

535. *Bele:* Belle; *utter:* aside
538. *fysgygge:* gadabout
549. *hyght:* called
550. *bybyll:* tipple
553. *Whey wormed:* Pimpled
555. *puscull:* pustule
556. *scabbyd muscull:* diseased mussel
560. *mote I hoppy:* may I have good luck

A clout of London pynnes.
And with that she begynnes   565
The pot to her plucke,
And dranke a good lucke—
She swynged up a quarte
At ones for her parte—
Her paunche was so puffed   570
And so with ale stuffed,
Had she not hyed apace,
She had defoyled the place.
    Than began the sporte
Amonge that dronken sorte: 575
Dame Elynour, sayde they,
Lende here a cocke of hey
To make all thynge cleane,
Ye wote well what we meane.
    But, syr, amonge all   580
That sate in that hall,
There was a prycke me denty
Sat lyke a seynty
And began to paynty
As though she wolde faynty.   585
She made it as koye
As a lege moy;
She was not halfe so wyse
As she was pevysshe nyse.
She sayde never a worde,   590
But rose from the borde
And called for our dame,
Elynour by name.
We supposed, iwys,
That she rose to pys;   595

---

564. *clout:* pack
573. *defoyled:* befouled
582. *prycke me denty:* an overly dainty one
584. *paynty:* pant
587. *lege moy:* a kind of dance?
589. *nyse:* fastidious

But the very grounde
Was for to compound
With Elynour in the spence
To paye for her expence.
I have no penny or grote   600
To paye, sayde she, God wote,
For wasshyng of my throte
But my bedes of amber;
Bere them to your chamber.
    Than Elynour dyd them hyde   605
Within her beddes syde.
But some than sate ryght sad
That nothynge had
There of their awne,
Neyther gelt nor pawne.   610
Suche were there menny
That had not penny;
But whan they shulde walke,
Were fayne with a chalke
To score on the balke   615
Or score on the tayle.
God gyve it yll hayle,
For my fyngers ytche!
I have wrytten to mytche
Of this mad mummynge   620
Of Elynour Rummynge.
Thus endeth the gest
Of this worthy fest.

---

596. *very grounde:* true reason
598. *spence:* separate part of the room
601. *wote:* knows
610. *gelt:* money
615. *balke:* crossbeam
616. *tayle:* tally, notched stick
617. *hayle:* greeting
622. *gest:* story

LAUREATI SKELTONIDIS IN DESPECTU MALIGNANTIUM DISTICHON.

Quamvis insanis, quamvis marcescis inanis,   625
   Invide, cantamus: hæc loca plena jocis.
        Bien m'en souvient.

*Omnes fœminas, quae vel nimis bibulae sunt, vel quae
sordida labe squaloris, aut qua spurca fœditatis macula, aut
verbosa loquacitate notantur, poeta invitat ad audiendum*   630
hunc libellum, &c.
   Ebria, squalida, sordida fœmina, prodiga verbis,
   Huc currat, properet, veniat! Sua gesta libellus
   Iste volutabit: Pæan sua plectra sonando
   Materiam risus cantabit carmine rauco.   635
        Finis.
             QUOD SKELTON, LAUREAT.

4.

Uppon a deedmans hed, that was sent to hym from an
honorable jentyllwoman for a token, devysyd this gostly
medytacyon in Englysh, covenable in sentence, comendable,
lamentable, lacrymable, profytable for the soule.

YOURE ugly tokyn
My mynd hath brokyn
From worldly lust;
For I have dyscust
We ar but dust,   5
And dy we must.

624–35. *LAUREATI . . . rauco:* These lines may be translated as follows:
"The distich of the poet laureate Skelton in scorn of evil speakers. How-
ever mad you may be, however much you languish in your inanity, envious
one, we sing: these places are full of jests. All women, who are either too
drunken or dirty or squalid, or are distinguished by a filthy blot of foulness,
or by wordy loquacity, the poet bids listen to this little book, etc. The
drunken, squalid, dirty woman, prodigal of words, let her run hither, let
her hasten, let her come. This little book will tell its own tale. The hymn
of praise, singing its own music, will set forth the stuff of laughter with a
harsh note."
Title: convenable in sentence: suitable in meaning; *lacrymable:* causing tears

It is generall
To be mortall:
I have well espyde
No man may hym hyde   10
From Deth holow eyed,
With synnews wyderyd,
With bonys shyderyd,
With hys worme etyn maw,
And his gastly jaw   15
Gaspyng asyde,
Nakyd of hyde,
Neyther flesh nor fell.
    Then, by my councell,
Loke that ye spell   20
Well thys gospell:
For wher so we dwell
Deth wyll us qwell,
And with us mell.
    For all oure pamperde paunchys,   25
Ther may no fraunchys,
Nor worldly blys,
Redeme us from this:
Oure days be datyd,
To be chekmatyd   30
With drawttys of deth,
Stoppyng oure breth;
Oure eyen synkyng,
Oure bodys stynkyng,
Oure gummys grynnyng,   35
Oure soulys brynnyng.

---

13. *shyderyd:* shattered
14. *maw:* throat
18. *fell:* skin
24. *mell:* interfere
26. *fraunchys:* immunity
31. *drawttys:* draughts, chessmen
36. *brynnyng:* burning

To whom, then, shall we sew,
For to have rescew,
But to swete Jesu,
On us then for to rew? 40
  O goodly chyld
Of Mary mylde,
Then be oure shylde!
That we be not exylyd
To the dyne dale 45
Of boteles bale,
Nor to the lake
Of fendys blake.
  But graunt us grace
To se thy face, 50
And to purchace
Thyne hevenly place,
And thy palace,
Full of solace,
Above the sky, 55
That is so hy;
Eternally
To beholde and se
The Trynyte!
  Amen. 60
Myrres vous y.

5.

WOMANHOD, wanton, ye want;
Youre medelyng, mastres, is manerles;
Plente of yll, of goodnes skant,
Ye rayll at ryot, recheles:
To prayse youre porte it is nedeles; 5

---

37. *sew:* sue, petition
45. *dyne:* gloomy
46. *boteles bale:* pain without remedy
61. *Myrres vous y:* "See yourself therein"
2. *mastres:* mistress
4. *recheles:* heedlessly

94

For all your draffe yet and youre dreggys,
As well borne as ye full oft tyme beggys.

Why so koy and full of skorne?
Myne horse is sold, I wene, you say;
My new furryd gowne, when it is worne,   10
Put up youre purs, ye shall non pay.
By crede, I trust to se the day,
As proud a pohen as ye sprede,
Of me and other ye may have nede.

Though angelyk be youre smylyng,   15
Yet is youre tong an adders tayle,
Full lyke a scorpyon styngyng
All those by whom ye have avayle:
Good mastres Anne, there ye do shayle:
What prate ye, praty pyggysny?   20
I truste to quyte you or I dy.

Youre key is mete for every lok,
Youre key is commen and hangyth owte;
Youre key is redy, we nede not knok,
Nor stand long wrestyng there aboute;   25
Of youre doregate ye have no doute:
But one thyng is, that ye be lewde:
Holde youre tong now, all beshrewde!

To mastres Anne, that farly swete,
That wonnes at the Key in Temmys strete.   30

---

6. *draffe:* refuse fed to pigs
9. *wene:* think
12. *crede:* the Creed
13. *pohen:* female peacock
19. *shayle:* blunder
20. *praty pyggysny:* pretty pigseye (a flower)
21. *quyte:* revenge myself on; *or:* before
22. *mete:* fit. Skelton puns on the many meanings of "key."
29. *farly swete:* wonderful sweetheart
30. *wonnes:* dwells

6.

WITH, Lullay, lullay, lyke a chylde,
Thou slepyst to long, thou art begylde.

My darlyng dere, my daysy floure,
Let me, quod he, ly in your lap.
Ly styll, quod she, my paramoure,   5
Ly styll hardely, and take a nap.
Hys hed was hevy, such was his hap,
All drowsy dremyng, dround in slepe,
That of hys love he toke no kepe,
        With, Hey, lullay, &c.   10

With ba, ba, ba, and bas, bas, bas,
She cheryshed hym both cheke and chyn,
That he wyst never where he was;
He had forgoten all dedely syn.
He wantyd wyt her love to wyn;   15
He trusted her payment, and lost all hys pray:
She left hym slepyng, and stale away,
        Wyth, Hey, lullay, &c.

The ryvers rowth, the waters wan;
She sparyd not to wete her fete;   20
She wadyd over, she found a man
That halsyd her hartely and kyst her swete:
Thus after her cold she cought a hete.

1–2. The refrain parodies those of medieval carols in which the Virgin sings
to her child.
6. *Ly styll hardely:* Just lie still
9. *kepe:* regard
13. *wyst:* knew
15. *wantyd:* lacked
17. *stale:* stole
19. *rowth:* rough
22. *halsyd:* embraced

My lefe, she sayd, rowtyth in hys bed;
I wys he hath an hevy hed,   25
   Wyth, Hey, lullay, &c.

What dremyst thou, drunchard, drousy pate!
Thy lust and lykyng is from the gone;
Thou blynkerd blowboll, thou wakyst to late,
Behold, thou lyeste, luggard, alone!   30
Well may thou sygh, well may thou grone,
To dele wyth her so cowardly:
I wys, powle hachet, she bleryd thyne I.

7.

THE auncient acquaintance, madam, betwen us twayn,
The famylyaryte, the formar dalyaunce,
Causyth me that I can not myself refrayne
But that I must wryte for my plesaunt pastaunce:
Remembryng your passyng goodly countenaunce,   5
Your goodly port, your bewteous visage,
Ye may be countyd comfort of all corage.

Of all your feturs favorable to make tru discripcion,
I am insuffycyent to make such enterpryse;
For thus dare I say, without tradiccyon,   10
That dame Menolope was never half so wyse:
Yet so it is that a rumer begynnyth for to ryse,
How in good horsmen ye set your hole delyght,
And have forgoten your old trew lovyng knyght.

---

24. *lefe:* dear one; *rowtyth:* snores
25. *I wys:* Indeed
29. *blowboll:* drunkard
33. *powle hachet:* ? Kinsman conjectures that this means one who frequents
an alehouse, with its sign on a pole; *bleryd thyne I:* made a fool of you
4. *pastaunce:* pastime
7. *all corage:* every heart
10. *tradiccyon:* slander
11. *Menolope:* a martial queen of the Amazons

Wyth bound and rebound, bounsyngly take up   15
Hys jentyll curtoyl, and set nowght by small naggys!
Spur up at the hynder gyrth, with, Gup, morell, gup!
With, Jayst ye, jenet of Spayne, for your tayll waggys!
Ye cast all your corage uppon such courtly haggys.
Have in sergeaunt ferrour, myne horse behynde is bare;   20
He rydeth well the horse, but he rydeth better the mare.

Ware, ware, the mare wynsyth wyth her wanton hele!
She kykyth with her kalkyns and keylyth with a clench;
She goyth wyde behynde, and hewyth never a dele:
Ware gallyng in the widders, ware of that wrenche!   25
It is perlous for a horseman to dyg in the trenche.
Thys grevyth your husband, that ryght jentyll knyght,
And so with youre servantys he fersly doth fyght.

So fersly he fytyth, hys mynde is so fell,
That he dryvyth them doune with dyntes on ther day wach;   30
He bresyth theyr braynpannys and makyth them to swell,
Theyre browys all to-brokyn, such clappys they cach;
Whose jalawsy malycyous makyth them to lepe the hach;
By theyr conusaunce knowing how they serve a wily py:
Ask all your neybours whether that I ly.   35

It can be no counsell that is cryed at the cros:
For your jentyll husband sorowfull am I;
How be it, he is not furst hath had a los:

---

16. *curtoyl:* horse with a docked tail
17. *morell:* dark-colored horse
18. *Jayst:* "Jump"; *jenet:* jennet
20. *sergeaunt ferrour:* i.e., a veterinarian
23. *kalkyns:* ends of horseshoes; *keylyth . . . clench:* kills with a kick (or an embrace)
24. *wyde behynde:* with her legs spread apart; *hewyth . . . dele:* never keeps them close together
25. *widders:* withers; *wrenche:* sudden twist
29. *fell:* cruel
30. *day wach:* daytime duties
31. *bresyth:* bruises
33. *hach:* lower half of a double door
34. *conusaunce:* cognizance, heraldic badge; *py:* magpie
36. *counsell:* secret; *at the cros:* i.e., in public

Advertysyng you, madame, to warke more secretly,
Let not all the world make an owtcry;   40
Play fayre play, madame, and loke ye play clene,
Or ells with gret shame your game wylbe sene.

8.

KNOLEGE, aquayntance, resort, favour with grace;
Delyte, desyre, respyte wyth lyberte;
Corage wyth lust, convenient tyme and space;
Dysdayns, dystres, exylyd cruelte;
Wordys well set with good habylyte;   5
Demure demenaunce, womanly of porte;
Transendyng plesure, surmountyng all dysporte;

Allectuary arrectyd to redres
These feverous axys, the dedely wo and payne
Of thoughtfull hertys plungyd in dystres;   10
Refresshyng myndys the Aprell shoure of rayne;
Condute of comforte, and well most soverayne;
Herber enverduryd, contynuall fressh and grene;
Of lusty somer the passyng goodly quene;

The topas rych and precyouse in vertew;   15
Your ruddys wyth ruddy rubys may compare;
Saphyre of sadnes, envayned wyth indy blew;
The pullyshed perle youre whytenes doth declare;
Dyamand poyntyd to rase oute hartly care;

---

39. *Advertysyng:* Warning
1. *Knolege:* the first letters of the first words in each stanza spell out the name "Kateryn"
5. *habylyte:* ability
6. *demenaunce:* demeanor
8. *Allectuary arrectyd:* Medicine designed
9. *axys:* attacks (of fever)
12. *well:* spring
13. *Herber:* Arbor
16. *ruddys:* rosy complexion
17. *indy blew:* a deep violet blue
19. *rase:* erase

Geyne surfetous suspecte the emeraud comendable;   20
Relucent smaragd, objecte imcomperable;

Encleryd myrroure and perspectyve most bryght,
Illumynyd wyth feturys far passyng my reporte;
Radyent Esperus, star of the clowdy nyght,
Lode star to lyght these lovers to theyr porte,   25
Gayne dangerous stormys theyr anker of supporte,
Theyr sayll of solace most comfortably clad,
Whych to behold makyth hevy hartys glad:

Remorse have I of youre most goodlyhod,
Of youre behavoure curtes and benynge,   30
Of your bownte and of youre womanhod,
Which makyth my hart oft to lepe and sprynge,
And to remember many a praty thynge;
But absens, alas, wyth tremelyng fere and drede
Abashyth me, albeit I have no nede.   35

You I assure, absens is my fo,
My dedely wo, my paynfull hevynes;
And if ye lyst to know the cause why so,
Open myne hart, beholde my mynde expres:
I wold ye coud! then shuld ye se, mastres,   40
How there nys thynge that I covet so fayne
As to enbrace you in myne armys twayne.

Nothynge yerthly to me more desyrous
Than to beholde youre bewteouse countenaunce:
But, hatefull absens, to me so envyous,   45
Though thou withdraw me from her by long dystaunce,
Yet shall she never oute of remembraunce;

---

20. *Geyne . . . suspecte:* Against immoderate suspicion
21. *Relucent smaragd:* Bright smaragdine
22. *Encleryd:* Shining
24. *Esperus:* Hesperus, the evening star
25. *Lode:* Magnetic
29. *Remorse:* Regretful remembrance
30. *curtes and benynge:* courteous and benign
33. *praty:* pleasant
41. *nys thynge:* isn't anything
43. *yerthly:* earthly

For I have gravyd her wythin the secret wall
Of my trew hart, to love her best of all!

9.

Manerly Margery Mylk and Ale

Ay, besherewe yow, be my fay,
This wanton clarkes be nyse all way;
Avent, avent, my popagay!
What, will ye do no thyng but play?
Tully valy, strawe, let be, I say!   5
Gup, Cristian Clowte, gup, Jak of the vale!
With, manerly Margery mylk and ale.

Be Gad, ye be a prety pode,
And I love you an hole cart lode.
Strawe, Jamys foder, ye play the fode,   10
I am no hakney for your rode;
Go watch a bole, your bak is brode:
Gup, Cristian Clowte, gup, Jak of the vale!
With, manerly Margery mylk and ale.

I wiss ye dele uncurtesly;   15
What wolde ye frompill me? now, fy, fy!
What, and ye shalbe my piggesnye?
Be Crist, ye shal not, no, no, hardely;
I will not be japed bodely:

---

48. *gravyd:* engraved
1. *fay:* faith
2. *This:* These; *nyse:* too scrupulous
3. *Avent:* "Get out"; *popagay:* parrot
8. *prety pode:* pleasing sausage
10. *foder:* fodder, ragweed (useless stuff); *fode:* one who beguiles with gay words
11. *rode:* riding
12. *bole:* bull
15. *I wiss:* Indeed
16. *frompill:* rumple
18. *Be:* By
19. *be . . . bodely:* have any tricks played with my body

Gup, Cristian Clowte, gup, Jake of the vale!   20
With, manerly Margery mylk and ale.

Walke forth your way, ye cost me nought;
Now have I fownd that I have sought,
The best chepe flessh that evyr I bought.
Yet, for His love that all hath wrought,   25
Wed me, or els I dye for thought!
Gup, Cristian Clowte, your breth is stale!
With, manerly Margery Mylk and Ale!
Gup, Cristian Clowte, gup, Jak of the vale!
With, manerly Margery mylk and ale.   30

10.

To maystres Jane Blenner-Haiset

   What though my penne wax faynt,
And hath smale lust to paint?
Yet shall there no restraynt
Cause me to cese,
Amonge this prese,   5
For to encrese
Yowre goodly name.
   I wyll my selfe applye,
Trust me, ententifly,
Yow for to stellyfye;   10

Title: This poem and the two which follow it are part of a series of ten lyrics that Skelton wove into his long *Garland of Laurel*, published in 1523. Parts of the poem, including the lyrics, were written earlier, perhaps in the 1490s. Jane Blennerhasset was probably the wife of Ralph Blennerhasset; she died in 1501, aged ninety-seven. Isabel Pennell was the daughter of John Paynell and related, through her mother, to the Countess of Surrey. Margaret Hussey has not been identified with certainty.
2. *lust:* desire
5. *prese:* band (of ladies to whom the lyrics are directed)
9. *ententifly:* carefully
10. *stellyfye:* set among the stars

And so observe
That ye ne swarve
For to deserve
Inmortall fame.
Sith mistres Jane Haiset   15
Smale flowres helpt to sett
In my goodly chapelet,
Therefore I render of her the memory
Unto the legend of fare Laodomi.

11.

To maystres Isabell Pennell

By saynt Mary, my lady,
Your mammy and your dady
Brought forth a godely babi!
My mayden Isabell,
Reflaring rosabell,   5
The flagrant camamell;
The ruddy rosary,
The soverayne rosemary,
The praty strawbery;
The columbyne, the nepte,   10
The jeloffer well set,
The propre vyolet;
Enuwyd your colowre
Is lyke the dasy flowre
After the Aprill showre;   15

---

12. *ne swarve:* swerve not
17. *chapelet:* crown, garland
19. *Laodomi:* Laodamia, who followed her husband Protesilaus down to
the underworld
3. *godely:* goodly
5. *Reflaring rosabell:* Odorous, beautiful rose
6. *flagrant camamell:* fragrant camomile
7. *rosary:* rosebush
9. *praty:* pretty
10. *nepte:* cats mint
11. *jeloffer:* gillyflower
13. *Enuwyd:* Freshened

Sterre of the morow gray,
The blossom on the spray,
The fresshest flowre of May;
   Maydenly demure,
Of womanhode the lure;   20
Wherfore I make you sure,
   It were an hevenly helth,
It were an endeles welth,
A lyfe for God hymselfe,
   To here this nightingale,   25
Amonge the byrdes smale,
Warbelynge in the vale,
Dug, dug,
Jug, jug,
Good yere and good luk,   30
With chuk, chuk, chuk, chuk!

12.

To maystres Margaret Hussey

Mirry Margaret,
As mydsomer flowre,
Jentill as fawcoun
Or hawke of the towre;
   With solace and gladnes,   5
Moche mirthe and no madnes,
All good and no badnes,
So joyously,
So maydenly,
So womanly   10
Her demenyng
In every thynge,
Far, far passynge

---

16. *Sterre:* Star
20. *lure:* pattern, model (which attracts others)
3. *Jentill:* Gentle
4. *of the towre:* which towers in the air
11. *demenyng:* behavior

That I can endyght,
Or suffyce to wryght   15
Of mirry Margarete,
As mydsomer flowre,
Jentyll as fawcoun
Or hawke of the towre;
   As pacient and as styll,   20
And as full of good wyll,
As fayre Isaphill;
Colyaunder,
Swete pomaunder,
Good cassaunder;   25
Stedfast of thought,
Wele made, wele wrought;
Far may be sought
Erst that ye can fynde
So corteise, so kynde   30
As mirry Margarete,
This midsomer flowre,
Ientyll as fawcoun
Or hawke of the towre.

---

22. *Isaphill:* Hypsipyle, queen of Lemnos, noted for her endurance
23. *Colyaunder:* Coriander
24. *pomaunder:* perfume ball
25. *cassaunder:* Cassandra, another steadfast heroine
29. *Erst:* Before
30. *corteise:* courteous

SIR THOMAS MORE

1477–1535

1.

A mery gest
how a sergeaunt wolde
lerne to be a frere

Wyse men alwaye,
Afferme & say,
  That best is for a man:
Dylygently,
For to apply,   5
  The besynes that he can,
And in no wyse,
To enterpryse,
  An other faculte,
For he that wyll,   10
And can no skyll,
  Is never lyke to the.
He that hath lafte,
The hosiers crafte,
  & falleth to makynge shone,   15
The smythe that shall,
To payntynge fall,
  His thryfte is wel nygh done.

---

6. *besynes:* business, occupation
7. *wyse:* way
9. *faculte:* trade, skill
11. *can no skyll:* has no knowledge
12. *the:* prosper
13. *lafte:* left
15. *shone:* shoes
18. *thryfte:* prosperity

A blacke draper,
With wyte paper,
  To go to wrytynge scole,   20
An olde butler,
Becum a cutler,
  I wene shal prove a fole.
An olde trot,   25
That good can not,
  But ever kysse the cup,
With her physyke,
Wyll kepe one seke,
  Tyll she have soused hym up.   30
A man of lawe,
That never sawe,
  The wayes to by and sell,
Wenynge to aryse,
By marchaundyse,   35
  I praye god spede hym well.
A marchaunt eke,
That wyll good seke,
  By all the meanes he maye,
To fall in sute,
Tyll he dyspute,   40
  His monay clene awaye.
Pletynge the lawe,
For every strawe,
  Shall prove a thryfty man,
With bate and stryfe,   45
But by my lyfe,
  I can not tell you whan.

---

24. *wene . . . prove:* think shall turn out to be
25. *trot:* hag
26–27. *That . . . cup:* i.e., the only thing she does well is to kiss the (drinking) cup
28. *physyke:* medicine
29. *seke:* sick
33. *by:* buy
34. *Wenynge:* Thinking
37. *eke:* too
48. *seke:* seek
40. *sute:* a lawsuit
43. *Pletynge:* Pleading
46. *bate:* argument

Whan an hatter
Wyll go smater,   50
   In phylosophy,
Or a pedlar,
Waxe a medlar,
   In theolegy,
All that ensewe,   55
Suche craftes newe,
   They dryve so fere a cast,
That evermore,
They do therfore,
   Beshrewe themselfe at laste.   60
This thynge was tryed
And verefyed,
   Here by a sergeaunt late,
That ryfely was,
Or he coude pas,   65
   Rapped aboute the pate,
Whyle that he wolde
Se how he coude,
   In goddes name play the frere:
Now yf you wyll,   70
Knowe how hyt fyll,
   Take hede & ye shall here.
It happed so,
Not longe ago,
   A thryfty man dyede,   75
An hondred pounde,
Of nobles rounde,
   That had he layde a syde:
His sone he wolde,
Sholde have this golde,   80

---

55. *ensewe:* follow
57. *dryve . . . cast:* are so far off the mark
63. *sergeaunt:* a sergeant of the law
64. *ryfely:* frequently, abundantly
65. *Or:* Before; *pas:* escape
69. *frere:* friar
71. *hyt fyll:* it happened
77. *nobles:* gold coins worth, in More's day, about ten shillings

For to begyne with all:
But to suffyce
His chylde, well thryes,
   That monay were to small.
Yet or this daye   85
I have herde saye,
   That many a man certesse,
Hath with good cast,
Be ryche at last,
   That hath begon with lesse.   90
But this yonge man,
So well began,
   His monaye to imploye,
That certenly,
His policy,   95
   To se hyt was a joye.
For lest sum blaste,
Myght over caste,
   His shyp, or by myschaunce,
Men with some wyle,   100
Myght hym begyle,
   And mynysshe his substaunce,
For to put out,
All manere doubte,
   He made a good purvaye   105
For every whyt,
By his owne wyt,
   And toke an other waye:
Fyrste fayre and wele,
Therof grete dele,   110

---

83. *thryes:* thrice
87. *certesse:* to be sure
88. *cast:* management
89. *Be:* Become
102. *mynysshe his substaunce:* diminish his capital
104. *manere:* kind of
105. *purvaye:* arrangement
106. *whyt:* bit
109. *wele:* well
110. *dele:* deal

He dyghth yt in a pot,
But then hym thought,
That way was nought,
   And there he lefte hyt not.
So was he fayne,   115
Frome thens agayne,
   To put hyt in a cup,
And by and by,
Covetously,
   He supped hyt fayre up.   120
In his owne brest,
He thought hyt best,
   His monaye to enclose,
Then wyst he well,
What ever fell,   125
   He coude hyt never lose.
He borowed than,
Of another man,
   Monaye and marchaundyse:
Never payde hyt,   130
Up he layde hyt,
   In lyke maner wyse.
Yet on the gere,
That he wolde were,
   He rought not what he spente,   135
So hyt were nyce,
As for the pryce,
   Coude hym not myscontente.
With lusty sporte,
And with resorte,   140
   Of joly company,
In myrthe and playe,
Full many a daye,
   He lyved merely.

---

111. *dyghth:* put
133. *gere:* clothing
135. *rought:* cared
136–38. *So . . . myscontente:* As long as it appealed to him, he was never
discontented with the price
144. *merely:* merrily

110

And men had sworne,   145
Some man is borne,
   To have a goodly floure,
And so was he,
For suche degre,
   He gate and suche honoure,   150
That with out doubte,
When he went out,
   A sergaunt well and fayne,
Was redy strayte,
On him to wayte,   155
   As sowne as on the mayre.
But he doubtlesse,
Of his mekenes,
   Hated suche pompe & pryde,
And wolde not go,   160
Companyed so,
   But drewe hym selfe a syde,
To saynt Katheryne,
Streyght as a lyne,
   He gate hym at a tyde,   165
For devocion,
Or promocyon,
   There wolde he nedes abyde.
There spente he fast,
Tyll all was past,   170
   And to hym came there many,
To aske theyr det,
But non coude get,
   The valour of a peny.

---

147. *floure:* flowering
149. *degre:* a position in society
150. *gate:* got
163. *saynt Katheryne:* the convent and hospital of St. Katherine, a well-known sanctuary for thieves and debtors
165. *tyde:* certain time
167. *promocyon:* i.e., because he feared that someone might inform on him if he did not make use of the protection of the hospital
174. *valour:* value

With vysage stoute,   175
He bare hyt oute,
   Even unto the harde hedge,
A moneth or twayne,
Tyll he was fayne,
   To laye his gowne to pledge.   180
Than was he there,
In greter fere,
   Then or that he came thyder,
And wolde as fayne,
Departe agayne,   185
   But that he wyst not whyther.
Than after this,
To a frende of his,
   He went and there abode,
Where as he laye,   190
So syke al waye,
   He myght not come abrode.
Hyt happed than,
A marchaunt man,
   That he ought monaye to,   195
Of an offycere,
Than gan enquyre,
   What hym was best to do.
And he answerde,
Be not a ferde,   200
   Take an accyon therfore,
I you beheste,
I shall hym reste,
   And than care for no more.

---

177. *Even . . . hedge*: Right to the very limit
183. *or*: before; *thyder*: thither
195. *ought*: owed
197. *gan*: began to
200. *a ferde*: afraid
202. *beheste*: promise
203. *reste*: arrest

I fere quod he,   205
Hyt will not be,
  For he wyll not com out.
The sergeaunt sayd,
Be not afrayde,
  Hyt shall be brought aboute.   210
In many a game,
Lyke to the same,
  Have I bene well in ure,
And for your sake,
Let me be bake,   215
  But yf I do this cure.
Thus part they bothe,
And to hym goth,
  A pace this offycere,
And for a daye,   220
All his araye,
  He chaunged with a frere.
So was he dyght,
That no man myght,
  Hym for a frere deny,   225
He dopped and doked,
He spake and loked,
  So relygyously.
Yet in a glasse,
Or he wolde passe,   230
  He toted and he pered,
His herte for pryde,
Lepte in his syde,
  To se how well he frered.

---

213. *in ure:* experienced
215. *bake:* baked
216. *But . . . cure:* If I don't bring this matter off successfully
219. *A pace:* Quickly
223. *dyght:* dressed
226. *dopped and doked:* bowed his head and cringed
231. *toted:* gazed; *pered:* peered
234. *frered:* played the part of a friar

Than forth a pace, 235
Unto the place,
  He goeth in goddes name,
To do this dede,
But nowe take hede,
  For here begynneth the game. 240
He drewe hym nye,
And softely,
  At the dore he knocked:
A damoysell,
That herde hym well, 245
  Came & it unlocked.
The frere sayd,
God spede fayre mayde,
  Here lodgeth such a man,
It is tolde me: 250
Well syr quod she,
  And yf he do what than?
Quod he maystresse,
No harme doubtlesse:
  Hyt longethe for our ordre, 255
To hurte no man,
But as we can,
  Every wyght to fordre:
With hym truely,
Fayne speke wolde I. 260
  Syr quod she by my faye,
He is so syke,
Ye be not lyke,
  To speke with hym to daye.
Quod he fayre maye, 265
Yet I you praye,

---

255. *Hyt . . . for:* It is the duty of
258. *wyght to fordre:* creature to help
261. *faye:* faith
265. *maye:* maiden

This moche at my desyre,
Vouchesafe to do,
As go hym to,
   And saye an austen frere,   270
Wolde with hym speke,
And maters breke,
   For his avayle certyne.
Quod she I wyll,
Stonde ye here styll,
   Tyll I come downe agayne.   275
Up is she go.
And tolde hym so,
   As she was bode to saye,
He mystrystynge,
No maner thynge,   280
   Sayd mayden go thy waye,
And fetche hym hyder,
That we togyder,
   May talke. Adowne she goth,   285
Up she hym brought,
No harme she thought,
   But it made some folke wroth.
But this offycere,
This fayned frere,   290
   Whan he was come alofte,
He dopped than,
And grete this man,
   Relygyously and ofte.
And he agayne,   295
Ryght gladde & fayne,

---

270. *austen:* Augustinian
272. *breke:* discuss
273. *For . . . certyne:* which will assuredly help him
279. *bode:* bidden
280. *mystrystynge:* suspecting
281. *No . . . thynge:* nothing at all
288. *wroth:* angry
293. *grete:* greeted

Toke hym there by the honde,
The frere than sayd,
Ye be dysmayde,
  With trouble I understonde.   300
In dede quod he,
Hyt hath with me,
  Ben better than hyt is.
Syr quod the frere,
Be of good chere,   305
  Yet shall hyt after this,
For crystes sake,
Loke that you take,
  No thought within your brest:
God may tourne all,   310
And so he shall,
  I truste unto the best.
But I wolde now,
Comyn with you,
  In counsell yf you please,   315
Or elles nat,
Of maters that,
  Shall set your herte at ease.
Downe went the mayde,
The marchaunt sayd,   320
  Now say on gentyll frere,
Of all this tydynge,
That ye me brynge,
  I longe full sore to here.
Whan there was none,   325
But they alone,
  The frere with evyll grace,
Sayd I rest the,
Come on with me,
  And out he toke his mace: 330

---

314. *Comyn:* Talk
315. *In counsell:* In private
316. *Or elles nat:* "If you don't want to, we won't"
327. *evyll:* ill
328. *rest the:* arrest thee
330. *mace:* symbol of his office as sergeant

Thou shalte obaye,
Come on thy waye,
   I have the in my cloche,
Thou goest not hense,
For all the pense,
   The mayre hath in his pouche.   335
This marchaunt there,
For wrathe and fere,
   Waxed welnyghe wode,
Sayde horsone thefe,
With a mischefe,   340
   Who hath taught the thy good?
And with his fyste,
Upon the lyste,
   He gave hym suche a blowe,
That bacwarde downe,   345
Almoste in sowne,
   The frere is overthrowe.
Yet was this man,
Well ferder than,
   Lest he the frere had slayne,   350
Tyll with good rappes,
And hevy clappes,
   He dawde hym up agayne.
The frere toke herte,
And up he sterte,   355
   And well he layed aboute,
And so there goth,
Betwene them bothe,
   Many a lusty cloute.   360

---

333. *cloche:* clutch
339. *wode:* mad
340. *horsone:* whoreson
341. *mischefe:* curse upon you
342. *Who . . . good?:* Who's taught you what was good for you?
344. *lyste:* cheek
347. *in sowne:* knocked out
350. *Well . . . than:* Very much afraid then
354. *dawde hym up:* brought him to

They rente and tere,
Eche other here,
   And clave togyder fast,
Tyll with luggynge,
Halynge & tugynge,   365
   They fell doune both at last
Than on the grounde,
Togyder rounde,
   With many a sadde stroke,
They roll and rumble,   370
They tourne & tumble,
   Lyke pygges in a poke.
So longe above,
They heve and shove,
   Togyder that at the last,   375
The mayde and wyfe,
To breke the stryfe,
   Hyed them upwarde faste.
And whan they spye,
The captaynes lye,   380
   Waltrynge on the place,
The freres hode
They pulled a good,
   Adoune aboute his face.
Whyle he was blynde,   385
The wenche behynde,
   Lent hym on the flore,
Many a jolle,
Aboute the nolle,
   With a grete batylldore.   390

---

362. *other here:* other's hair
365. *Halynge:* Dragging
369. *sadde:* heavy
372. *poke:* bag
381. *Waltrynge:* Rolling about
382. *hode:* hood
388. *jolle:* knock
389. *nolle:* head
390. *batylldore:* a wooden bat used for smoothing out clothes after they had been washed

The wyfe came yet,
And with her fete,
   She holpe to kepe hym downe,
And with her rocke,
Many a knocke,   395
   She gave hym on the crowne.
They layde his mace,
Aboute his face,
   That he was wode for payne;
The frere frappe,   400
Gate many a swappe,
   Tyll he was full nyghe slayne.
Up they hym lyfte,
And with evyll thryfte,
   Hedlynge all the stayre,   405
Downe they hym threwe,
And sayd a dewe,
   Commaunde us to the mayre.
The frere arose,
But I suppose,   410
   Amased was his hede,
He shoke his eres,
And frome grete feres,
   He thought hym well a flede.
Quod he now lost,   415
Is all this cost,
   We be never the nere.
Ill mote he the,
That caused me,
   To make my selfe a frere.   420

---

392. *fete:* feet
393. *holpe:* helped
394. *rocke:* distaff
400. *frere frappe:* friar manqué, fake friar
404. *with . . . thryfte:* to his bad luck
405. *Hedlynge:* Headlong
407. *a dewe:* adieu
408. *Commaunde:* Commend
411. *Amased:* Dazed
415. *Quod:* Said
417. *nere:* nearer
418. *Ill . . . the:* May he never prosper

Now maysters all,
And now I shall,
   Ende there I began,
In ony wyse,
I wolde avyse, 425
   And counseyll every man,
His owne craft use,
All newe refuse,
   And utterly let them gone:
Playe not the frere, 430
Now make good chere,
   And welcome everychone.

2.

Pageant Verses

Mayster Thomas More in his youth devysed in hys fathers
house in London, a goodly hangyng of fyne paynted clothe,
with nyne pageauntes, and verses over every of those
pageauntes: which verses expressed and declared, what the
ymages in those pageauntes represented: and also in those 5
pageauntes were paynted, the thynges that the verses over them
dyd (in effecte) declare, whiche verses here folowe.

In the first pageant was painted a boy playing at the top &
squyrge. And over this pageaunt was writen as foloweth.

---

432. *everychone:* everyone. More's "Merry Jest" may well have been de-
signed for recitation at a civic feast.
2. *hangyng:* a wall hanging, designed both to prevent drafts and for orna-
mentation
3. *pageauntes:* pictorial representations; *every:* each
9. *squyrge:* whip, used to make the top spin

CHYLDHOD 10

I am called Chyldhod, in play is all my mynde,
To cast a coyte, a cokstele, and a ball.
A toppe can I set, and dryve it in his kynde.
But would to god these hatefull bookes all,
Were in a fyre brent to pouder small. 15
Than myght I lede my lyfe alwayes in play:
Whiche lyfe god sende me to myne endyng day.

In the second pageaunt was paynted a goodly freshe yonge
man, rydyng uppon a goodly horse, havynge an hawke on his
fyste, and a brase of grayhowndes folowyng hym. And 20
under the horse fete, was paynted the same boy, that in the
fyrst pageaunte was playing at the top & squyrge. And over this
second pageant the wrytyng was thus.

MANHOD

Manhod I am therefore I me delyght, 25
To hunt and hawke, to nourishe up and fede,
The grayhounde to the course, the hawke to the flyght,
And to bestryde a good and lusty stede.
These thynges become a very man in dede,
Yet thynketh this boy his pevishe game swetter, 30
But what no force, his reason is no better.

In the thyrd pagiaunt, was paynted the goodly younge man,
in the seconde pagiaunt lyeng on the grounde. And uppon hym

---

12. *coyte:* quoit; *cokstele:* a stick to throw at a cock. The game was called "cockshying."
13. *dryve . . . kynde:* make it spin as it is supposed to do
15. *brent:* burned; *pouder:* powder, ashes
20. *brase:* brace
21. *horse fete:* horse's feet
27. *course:* pursuit of the quarry
28. *stede:* steed
29. *very:* true
30. *swetter:* sweeter
31. *force:* matter

stode ladye Venus goddes of love, and by her uppon this man
stode the lytle god Cupyde. And over this thyrd pageaunt,   35
this was the wrytyng that foloweth.

Whoso ne knoweth the strength, power and myght,
Of Venus and me her lytle sonne Cupyde,
Thou Manhod shalt a myrour bene a ryght,   40
By us subdued for all thy great pryde,
My fyry dart perceth thy tender syde,
Now thou whiche erst despysedst children small,
Shall waxe a chylde agayne and be my thrall.

In the fourth pageaunt was paynted an olde sage father   45
sittyng in a chayre. And lyeng under his fete was painted the
ymage of Venus & Cupyde, that were in the third pageant. And
over this fourth pageant the scripture was thus.

AGE

Olde Age am I, with lokkes, thynne and hore,   50
Of our short lyfe, the last and best part.
Wyse and discrete: the publike wele therefore,
I help to rule to my labour and smart,
Therefore Cupyde withdrawe thy fyry dart,
Chargeable matters shall of love oppresse,   55
Thy childish game and ydle bysinesse.

In the fyfth pageaunt was paynted an ymage of Death: and
under hys fete lay the olde man in the fourth pageaunte. And
above this fift pageant, this was the saying.

---

43. *erst:* formerly
48. *scripture:* inscription
50. *lokkes:* locks (of hair); *hore:* hoar, gray
52. *wele:* weal
55. *Chargeable:* Responsible; *of love:* to be construed with "game" in the
next line
57. *ymage of Death:* i.e., a skull

DETH   60

Though I be foule, ugly, lene and mysshape,
Yet there is none in all this worlde wyde,
That may my power withstande or escape.
Therefore sage father greatly magnifyed,
Discende from your chayre, set a part your pryde, 65
Witsafe to lende (though it be to your payne)
To me a fole, some of your wise brayne.

In the sixt pageant was painted lady Fame. And under her
fete was the picture of Death that was in the fifth pageant. And
over this sixt pageaunt the writyng was as foloweth. 70

FAME

Fame I am called, marvayle you nothing,
Though with tonges I am compassed all rounde
For in voyce of people is my chiefe livyng.
O cruel death, thy power I confounde. 75
When thou a noble man hast brought to grounde
Maugry thy teeth to lyve cause hym shall I,
Of people in parpetuall memory.

In the seventh pageant was painted the ymage of Tyme, and
under hys fete was lyeng the picture of Fame that was in 80
the sixt pageant. And this was the scripture over this seventh
pageaunt.

---

61. *lene and mysshape:* lean and misshapen
64. *magnifyed:* extolled
66. *Witsafe:* Vouchsafe
73. *compassed:* encircled
77. *Maugry thy teeth:* In spite of anything you can do

TYME

I whom thou seest with horyloge in hande,
Am named tyme, the lord of every howre,   85
I shall in space destroy both see and lande.
O simple fame, how darest thou man honowre,
Promising of his name, an endlesse flowre,
Who may in the world have a name eternall,
When I shall in proces distroy the world and all.   90

   In the eyght pageant was pictured the ymage of lady
Eternitee, sittyng in a chayre under a sumptious clothe of
estate, crowned with an imperial crown. And under her fete lay
the picture of Time, that was in the seventh pageant. And
above this eight pageaunt, was it writen as foloweth.   95

ETERNITEE

Me nedeth not to bost, I am Eternitee,
The very name signifyeth well,
That myne empyre infinite shalbe.
Thou mortall Tyme every man can tell,   100
Art nothyng els but the mobilite
Of sonne and mone chaungyng in every degre;
When they shall leve theyr course thou shalt be brought,
For all thy pride and bostyng into nought.

   In the nynth pageant was painted a Poet sitting in a   105
chayre. And over this pageant were there writen these verses
in latin folowyng.

---

84. *horyloge:* hourglass
88. *flowre:* flowering
90. *proces:* due course
92–93. *clothe of estate:* canopy placed over a royal seat

THE POET

Has fictas quemcunque juvat spectare figuras,
 Sed mira veros quas putat arte homines,   110
Ille potest veris, animum sic pascere rebus,
 Ut pictis oculos poscit imaginibus.
Namque videbit uti fragilis bona lubrica mundi,
 Tam cito non veniunt, quam cito pretereunt,
Gaudia, laus & honor, celeri pede omnia cedunt,   115
 Qui manet excepto semper amore dei.
Ergo homines, levibus jamjam diffidite rebus,
 Nulla recessuro spes adhibenda bono,
Qui dabit eternam nobis pro munere vitam,
 In permansuro ponite vota deo.   120

3.

A Rueful Lamentation

A ruful lamentacion (writen by master Thomas More in his
youth) of the deth of quene Elisabeth mother to king Henry
the eight, wife to king Henry the seventh, & eldest doughter to
king Edward the fourth, which quene Elisabeth dyed in
childbed in February in the yere of our lord .1503. & in the
18. yere of the raigne of king Henry the seventh.

109–20. *Has . . . deo:* More's Latin verses are translated as follows by
L. Bradner and C. A. Lynch (*The Latin Epigrams of Thomas More*
[Chicago, Chicago University Press, 1953], p. 238): "If anyone finds
pleasure in looking at these pictures because he feels that, although they
are products of the imagination, still they represent man truly and with re-
markable skill, then he can delight his soul with the actual truth just as he
feasts his eyes on its painted image. For he will see that the elusive goods
of this perishable world do not come so readily as they pass away. Pleas-
ures, praise, homage, all things quickly disappear—except the love of God,
which endures forever. Therefore, mortals, put no confidence hereafter in
trivialities, no hope in transitory advantage; offer your prayers to the ever-
lasting God, who will grant us the gift of eternal life."

O ye that put your trust and confidence,
In worldly joy and frayle prosperite,
That so lyve here as ye should never hence,
Remember death and loke here uppon me.
Ensaumple I thynke there may no better be.   5
Your selfe wotte well that in this realme was I,
Your quene but late, and lo now here I lye.

Was I not borne of olde worthy linage?
Was not my mother queene my father kyng?
Was I not a kinges fere in marriage?   10
Had I not plenty of every pleasaunt thyng?
Mercifull god this is a straunge reckenyng:
Rychesse, honour, welth, and auncestry
Hath me forsaken and lo now here I ly.

If worship myght have kept me, I had not gone.   15
If wyt myght have me saved, I neded not fere.
If money myght have holpe, I lacked none.
But O good God what vayleth all this gere?
When deth is come thy mighty messangere,
Obey we must, there is no remedy,   20
Me hath he sommoned, and lo now here I ly.

Yet was I late promised otherwyse,
This yere to live in welth and delice.
Lo where to commeth thy blandishyng promyse,
O false astrolagy and devynatrice,   25
Of goddes secretes makyng thy selfe so wyse.
How true is for this yere thy prophecy.
The yere yet lasteth, and lo nowe here I ly.

---

5. *Ensaumple*: Example
6. *wotte*: know
9. *mother*: Elizabeth Woodville, Edward IV's queen
10. *fere*: consort, spouse
13. *Rychesse*: Wealth (riches)
18. *vayleth . . . gere*: use are all these possessions
23. *welth and delice*: happiness and delight
25. *astrolagy and devynatrice*: astrology and divination. A court astrologer, William Parron, who published various prophecies between 1498 and 1503, had predicted, on New Year's Day, 1503, that the queen would live to be eighty. She died on February 11 of that year at the age of thirty-seven.

O bryttill welth, ay full of bitternesse,
Thy single pleasure doubled is with payne.   30
Account my sorow first and my distresse,
In sondry wyse, and recken there agayne
The joy that I have had, and I dare sayne,
For all my honour, endured yet have I,
More wo then welth, and lo now here I ly.   35

Where are our Castels, now where are our Towers,
Goodly Rychmonde sone art thou gone from me,
At westminster that costly worke of yours,
Myne owne dere lorde, now shall I never see.
Almighty god vouchesafe to graunt that ye,   40
For you and your children well may edefy.
My palyce bylded is, and lo now here I ly.

Adew myne owne dere spouse, my worthy lorde,
The faithfull love that dyd us both combyne,
In mariage and peasable concorde,   45
Into your handes here I cleane resyne,
To be bestowed uppon your children and myne.
Erst wer you father, & now must ye supply,
The mothers part also, for lo now here I ly.

Farewell my doughter lady Margarete.   50
God wotte full oft it greved hath my mynde,
That ye should go where we should seldome mete.

---

29. *ay:* ever
31. *Account:* Add up
32. *sondry wyse:* various ways
36. *Where are . . . :* More echoes the *ubi sunt* theme that ran through medieval literature
37. *Rychmonde:* this royal palace was new at the time of the queen's death
38. *westminster:* Henry VII's royal chapel was then being built. The queen was buried there after its completion.
41. *edefy:* build
42. *My palyce:* i.e., the grave
45. *peasable:* peaceful
48. *Erst:* Before (my death)
50. *Margarete:* the queen's second child (1489–1541). She married James IV of Scotland on August 8, 1503. The queen alludes to her coming marriage in line 52.

Now am I gone, and have left you behynde.
O mortall folke that we be very blynde.
That we least feare, full oft it is most nye,   55
From you depart I fyrst, and lo now here I lye.

Farewell Madame my lordes worthy mother,
Comfort your sonne, and be ye of good chere.
Take all a worth, for it will be no nother.
Farewell my doughter Katherine late the fere,   60
To prince Arthur myne owne chyld so dere,
It booteth not for me to wepe or cry,
Pray for my soule, for lo now here I ly.

Adew lord Henry my lovyng sonne adew.
Our lorde encrease your honour and estate,   65
Adew my doughter Mary bright of hew.
God make you vertuous, wyse and fortunate.
Adew swete hart my litle doughter Kate,
Thou shalt swete babe suche is thy desteny,
Thy mother never know, for lo now here I ly.   70

Lady Cicyly, Anne and Katheryne.
Farewell my welbeloved sisters three,
O lady Briget other sister myne,
Lo here the ende of worldly vanitee.
Now well are ye that earthly foly flee,   75

---

54. *that . . . blynde:* how very blind we are
57. *Madame:* Margaret Beaufort (1441–1509), Countess of Richmond and Derby, Henry VII's mother
59. *a worth:* in good part; *nother:* other
60. *Katherine:* Catherine of Aragon (1485–1536), who had married Prince Arthur (1486–1501) on November 14, 1501. Arthur died shortly after the marriage.
62. *booteth:* helps
64. *Henry:* Henry VIII (1491–1547)
66. *Mary:* third daughter of Elizabeth (1496–1533). She married Louis XII of France in 1514 and, after his death in 1515, Charles Brandon, Duke of Suffolk. *hew:* complexion
68. *Kate:* Elizabeth's seventh and last child, born February 2, 1503. She died shortly after her mother's death.
71–73. *Cicyly . . . Briget:* Elizabeth's four sisters: Cecily (1469–1507), Anne (1475–1511), Catherine (1479–1527), and Bridget (1480–1517). Bridget was a Dominican nun (cf. line 75).

And hevenly thynges love and magnify,
Farewell and pray for me, for lo now here I ly.

Adew my lordes, adew my ladies all,
Adew my faithfull servauntes every chone,
Adew my commons whom I never shall,   80
See in this world, wherfore to the alone,
Immortall god verely three and one,
I me commende, thy infinite mercy,
Shew to thy servant, for lo now here I ly.

---

76. *magnify:* praise
79. *every chone:* every one of you
80. *commons:* the people of England
82. *verely:* truly

SIR THOMAS WYATT

1503–42

1.

What vaileth trouth? or by it to take payn?
To stryve by stedfastnes for to be tayne?
  To be juste and true, and fle from dowblenes?
  Sythens all alike, where rueleth craftines,
Rewarded is boeth fals and plain.   5
Sonest he spedeth that moost can fain,
True meanyng hert is had in disdayn.
  Against deceipte and dowblenes,
    What vaileth trouth?

Deceved is he by crafty trayn   10
That meaneth no gile and doeth remayn
  Within the trapp, withoute redresse,
  But for to love, lo, suche a maistres,
Whose crueltie nothing can refrayn,
    What vaileth trouth?   15

No. II in the Muir-Thompson edition (abbreviated hereafter as *MT*).
1. *What . . . trouth?*: Of what use is truth (or trustworthiness)?
2. *tayne*: taken, trapped
4. *Sythens*: Since
5. *plain*: honest, true
13. *maistres*: mistress
14. *refrayn*: control

2.

The longe love, that in my thought doeth harbar
And in myn hert doeth kepe his residence,
Into my face preseth with bolde pretence,
And therin campeth, spreding his baner.
She that me lerneth to love and suffre,   5
And will that my trust and lustes negligence
Be rayned by reason, shame and reverence,
With his hardines taketh displeasur.
Wherewithall, unto the hertes forrest he fleith,
Leving his entreprise with payn and cry,   10
And ther him hideth and not appereth.
What may I do when my maister fereth
But in the feld with him to lyve and dye?
For goode is the liff, ending faithfully.

2a.

The lover for shamefastnesse hideth
his desire within his faithfull hart

The longe love, that in my thought I harber,
And in my hart doth kepe his residence,
Into my face preaseth with bold pretence,
And there campeth, displaying his banner.
She that me learns to love, and to suffer,   5
And willes that my trust, and lustes negligence
Be reined by reason, shame, and reverence,
With his hardinesse takes displeasure.

MT, No. IV. Wyatt's source is Petrarch, *Rime,* cxl. Cf. Surrey's version
of the same original, below, Surrey, no. 4.
4. *baner:* banner, standard
5. *lerneth:* teaches
6. *will:* commands
7. *rayned:* checked
8. *hardines:* boldness
No. 2a. Tottel's 1557 version of no. 2.

Wherwith love to the hartes forest he fleeth,
Leavyng his enterprise with paine and crye,   10
And there him hideth and not appeareth.
What may I do? when my maister feareth,
But in the field with him to live and dye,
For good is the life, endyng faithfully.

3.

Who so list to hount, I knowe where is an hynde,
But as for me, helas, I may no more:
The vayne travaill hath weried me so sore.
I ame of theim that farthest cometh behinde.
Yet may I by no meanes my weried mynde   5
Drawe from the Diere: but as she fleeth afore,
Faynting I folowe. I leve of therefore,
Sins in a nett I seke to hold the wynde.
Who list her hount I put him owte of dowbte,
As well as I may spend his tyme in vain: 10
And, graven with Diamonds, in letters plain
There is written her faier neck rounde abowte:
Noli me tangere, for Cesars I ame,
And wylde for to hold though I seme tame.

4.

Eche man me telleth I chaunge moost my devise,
And on my faith me thinck it goode reason
To chaunge propose like after the season,

MT, No. VII. Wyatt adapts Petrarch, *Rime*, cxc. Many critics believe
this sonnet refers to Anne Boleyn and Henry VIII (Caesar).
1. *list to hount*: would like to hunt; *hynde*: female deer
3. *vayne travaill*: idle labor
6. *afore*: in front of me
7. *of*: off
13–14. Both of these lines are engraved on the deer's collar. *Noli me
tangere*: "Touch me not." Cf. John 20:17 and Matthew 22:21.
MT, No. X.
1. *devise*: device, manner of behavior
3. *To . . . season*: To change my purpose as the seasons do

For in every cas to kepe still oon gyse
Ys mytt for theim that would be taken wyse,   5
And I ame not of suche maner condition,
But treted after a dyvers fasshion,
And therupon my dyvernes doeth rise.
But you that blame this dyvernes moost,
Chaunge you no more but still after oon rate   10
Trete ye me well, and kepe ye in the same state;
And while with me doeth dwell this weried goost,
My wordes nor I shall not be variable,
But alwaies oon, your owne boeth ferme and stable.

5.

Farewell Love and all thy lawes for ever,
Thy bayted hookes shall tangill me no more;
Senec and Plato call me from thy lore,
To perfaict welth my wit for to endever.
In blynde error when I did persever,   5
Thy sherpe repulse that pricketh ay so sore
Hath taught me to sett in tryfels no store
And scape fourth syns libertie is lever.
Therefore farewell, goo trouble yonger hertes
And in me clayme no more authoritie;   10
With idill yeuth goo use thy propertie
And theron spend thy many brittil dertes.
For hetherto though I have lost all my tyme
Me lusteth no lenger rotten boughes to clymbe.

---

4. *gyse:* manner
5. *mytt:* meet, fitting
8. *dyvernes:* diverseness
10. *still:* always; *after oon rate:* in the same way
12. *goost:* spirit
MT, No. XIII.
3. *Senec and Plato:* cited as types of moral wisdom
4. *welth:* happiness
8. *lever:* to be preferred
11. *use thy propertie:* do what you do best
12. *brittil dertes:* probably alluding to Cupid's arrows
14. *Me . . . lenger:* I no longer take any pleasure (in climbing, etc.)

6.

Helpe me to seke for I lost it there,
And if that ye have founde it, ye that be here,
    And seke to convaye it secretely,
    Handell it soft and trete it tenderly,
Or els it will plain and then appere.   5
    But rather restore it mannerly,
    Syns that I do aske it thus honestly;
For to lese it, it sitteth me to neere:
        Helpe me to seke.

Alas, and is there no remedy,   10
But have I thus lost it wilfully?
    I wis it was a thing all to dere
    To be bestowed and wist not where.
It was myn hert. I pray you hertely
        Helpe me to seke.   15

7.

It may be good, like it who list,
    But I do dowbt: who can me blame?
For oft assured yet have I myst,
    And now again I fere the same.
The wyndy wordes, the Ies quaynt game,   5
Of soden chaunge maketh me agast:
For dred to fall I stond not fast.

Alas! I tred an endles maze
    That seketh to accorde two contraries;

MT, No. XVII.
3. *convaye it:* hide it away
5. *plain:* complain; *appere:* pine away
6. *mannerly:* fittingly
8. *lese:* lose; *sitteth:* touches
12. *I wis:* To be sure
13. *wist:* know
MT, No. XXI.
5. *Ies:* eyes'

And hope still and nothing hase,   10
  Imprisoned in libertes;
  As oon unhard and still that cries;
Alwaies thursty and yet nothing I tast;
For dred to fall I stond not fast.

Assured, I dowbt I be not sure,   15
  And should I trust to suche suretie
That oft hath put the prouff in ure
  And never hath founde it trusty?
  Nay, sir, in faith it were great foly.
And yet my liff thus I do wast,   20
For dred to fall I stond not fast.

8.

Resound my voyse, ye wodes that here me plain,
  Boeth hilles and vales causing reflexion;
And Ryvers eke record ye of my pain,
  Which have ye oft forced by compassion
  As judges to here myn exclamation;   5
Emong whome pitie I fynde doeth remayn:
Where I it seke, Alas, there is disdain.

Oft ye Revers, to here my wofull sounde,
  Have stopt your course and, plainly to expresse,
Many a tere by moystour of the grounde   10
  The erth hath wept to here my hevenes;
  Which causeles to suffre without redresse
The howgy okes have rored in the wynde:
Eche thing me thought complayning in their kynde.

---

10. *hase:* has
11. *Imprisoned in libertes:* i.e., because he cannot choose
12. *unhard:* unheard; *and . . . cries:* who continues to cry
15. *dowbt:* fear
17. *put . . . ure:* put the experience to the test
MT, No. XXII.
1. *plain:* complain
3. *eke:* also
13. *howgy:* huge

Why then, helas, doeth not she on me rew?   15
  Or is her hert so herd that no pitie
May in it synke, my joye for to renew?
  O stony hert ho hath thus joyned the?
  So cruell that art, cloked with beaultie,
No grace to me from the there may procede,   20
But as rewarded deth for to be my mede.

9.

I fynde no peace and all my warr is done,
I fere and hope, I burne and freise like yse;
I fley above the wynde yet can I not arrise,
And noght I have and all the worold I seson.
That loseth nor locketh holdeth me in prison   5
And holdeth me not, yet can I scape nowise;
Nor letteth me lyve nor dye at my devise,
And yet of deth it gyveth me occasion.
Withoute Iyen, I se, and withoute tong I plain,
I desire to perisshe, and yet I aske helthe,   10
I love an othre, and thus I hate my self,
I fede me in sorrowe and laughe in all my pain,
Likewise displeaseth me boeth deth and lyffe,
And my delite is causer of this stryff.

10.

My galy charged with forgetfulnes
Thorrough sharpe sees in wynter nyghtes doeth pas

---

18. *ho:* who; *joyned:* enjoined (who has ordered you to act in this way?)
19. *beaultie:* beauty
21. *But . . . mede:* Except insofar as the reward of death is my only reward
MT, No. XXVI. Wyatt's source is Petrarch, *Rime*, cxxxiv.
2. *freise like yse:* freeze like ice
3. *fley:* fly
4. *seson:* grasp, seize on
5. *That loseth:* Something which neither releases
7. *at my devise:* according to my own choice
9. *Iyen:* eyes
MT, No. XXVIII. Wyatt's source is Petrarch, *Rime*, clxxxix.
1. *charged:* laden
2. *Thorrough:* Through

Twene Rock and Rock; and eke myn ennemy, Alas,
That is my lorde, sterith with cruelnes;
And every owre a thought in redines,   5
As tho that deth were light in suche a case.
An endles wynd doeth tere the sayll a pase
Of forced sightes and trusty ferefulnes.
A rayn of teris, a clowde of derk disdain
Hath done the wered cordes great hinderaunce,   10
Wrethed with errour and eke with ignoraunce.
The starres be hid that led me to this pain,
Drowned is reason that should me confort,
And I remain dispering of the port.

11.

How oft have I, my dere and cruell foo,
With those your Iyes for to get peace and truyse,
Profferd you myn hert, but you do not use
Emong so high thinges to cast your mynde so lowe.
Yf any othre loke for it, as ye trowe,   5
There vayn weke hope doeth greatly theim abuse;
And thus I disdain that that ye refuse;
It was ones myn: it can no more be so.
Yf I then it chase, nor it in you can fynde
In this exile no manner of comfort,   10
Nor lyve allone, nor where he is called resort,
He may wander from his naturall kynd.
So shall it be great hurt unto us twayn,
And yours the losse and myn the dedly pain.

---

5. *owre:* hour
6. *light:* easy
7. *a pase:* quickly
8. *sightes:* sighings
10. *wered cordes:* worn (wearied) ropes
14. *dispering:* despairing
MT, No. XXXII. Wyatt's source is Petrarch, *Rime*, xxi
2. *truyse:* truce
3. *do not use:* are not accustomed
5. *trowe:* believe
8. *ones:* once
12. *He . . . kynd:* i.e., the speaker's heart may die

12.

Like to these unmesurable montayns
Is my painfull lyff, the burden of Ire,
For of great height be they, and high is my desire,
And I of teres, and they be full of fontayns.
Under Craggy rockes they have full barren playns,   5
Herd thoughtes in me my wofull mynde doeth tyre;
Small fruyt and many leves their toppes do atyre,
Small effect with great trust in me remayns.
The boyseus wyndes oft their high bowghes do blast,
Hote sighes from me continuelly be shed;   10
Cattell in theim, and in me love is fed;
Immoveable ame I, and they are full stedfast.
Of the restles birdes they have the tone and note,
And I always plaintes that pass thorough my throte.

13.

Madame, withouten many wordes,
   Ons I ame sure ye will or no;
And if ye will, then leve your bordes,
   And use your wit and shew it so.

And with a beck ye shall me call,   5
   And if of oon that burneth alwaye
Ye have any pitie at all,
   Aunswer him faire with yea or nay.

Yf it be yea, I shalbe fayne;
   If it be nay, frendes as before;   10
Ye shall an othre man obtain,
   And I myn owne and yours no more.

MT, No. XXXIII. Wyatt's source is a sonnet by Sannazzaro.
6. *Herd:* Hard
9. *boyseus:* boisterous
MT, No. XXXIV. Wyatt's source is a madrigal by D. Bonifacio (1500–
26).
3. *bordes:* jests

14.

Ye old mule, that thinck your self so fayre,
Leve of with craft your beautie to repaire,
   For it is time withoute any fable
    No man setteth now by riding in your saddell;
To muche travaill so do your train apaire,   5
    Ye old mule!

With fals favoure though you deceve th'ayer,
Who so tast you shall well perceve your layer
   Savoureth som what of a Kappurs stable,
    Ye old mule!   10

Ye must now serve to market and to faire,
All for the burden for pannyers a paire;
   For syns gray heres ben powderd in your sable,
    The thing ye seke for you must yourself enable
To pourchase it by payement and by prayer,   15
    Ye old mule!

15.

They fle from me that sometyme did me seke
With naked fote stalking in my chambre.
I have sene theim gentill tame and meke
That nowe are wyld and do not remembre

MT, No. XXXV. The text of this poem in the Egerton MS. is very difficult to decipher.
4. *setteth . . . riding:* cares any more to ride
5. *To . . . apaire:* i.e., the riding ("train") of you is impaired by the fact that it involves too much work
7. *favoure:* MT read *savours* (perfumes); *th'ayer:* the air
8. *layer:* lair
9. *Kappurs:* colt's (and hence wanton)
12. *All for:* Notwithstanding; *pannyers:* saddlebags
13. *powderd . . . sable:* sprinkled through your sable locks
MT, No. XXXVII.
2. *stalking:* walking softly

That sometyme they put theimself in daunger   5
To take bred at my hand; and nowe they raunge
Besely seking with a continuell chaunge.

Thancked be fortune, it hath ben othrewise
Twenty tymes better; but ons in speciall,
In thyn arraye after a pleasaunt gyse,   10
When her lose gowne from her shoulders did fall,
And she me caught in her armes long and small;
Therewithall swetely did me kysse,
And softely saide, dere hert, howe like you this?

It was no dreme: I lay brode waking.   15
But all is torned thorough my gentilnes
Into a straunge fasshion of forsaking;
And I have leve to goo of her goodenes,
And she also to use new fangilnes.
But syns that I so kyndely ame served,   20
I would fain knowe what she hath deserved.

15a.

The lover sheweth how he is
forsaken of such as he somtime enjoyed.

They flee from me, that somtime did me seke
With naked fote stalkyng within my chamber.
Once have I seen them gentle, tame, and meke,
That now are wild, and do not once remember
That sometyme they have put them selves in danger,   5
To take bread at my hand, and now they range,
Busily sekyng in continuall change.

---

5. *in daunger:* in my power
10. *gyse:* manner
15. *brode waking:* wide awake
19. *new fangilnes:* a new mode of behavior, inconstancy
20. *kyndely:* naturally, but also "kindly"
No. 15a. Tottel's 1557 version of no. 15.

Thanked be fortune, it hath bene otherwise
Twenty tymes better: but once especiall,
In thinne aray, after a pleasant gyse,   10
When her loose gowne did from her shoulders fall,
And she me caught in her armes long and small,
And therwithall, so swetely did me kysse,
And softly sayd: deare hart, how like you this?

It was no dreame: for I lay broade awakyng.   15
But all is turnde now through my gentlenesse,
Into a bitter fashion of forsakyng:
And I have leave to go of her goodnesse,
And she also to use newfanglenesse.
But, sins that I unkindly so am served: 20
How like you this, what hath she now deserved?

16.

There was never nothing more me payned,
   Nor nothing more me moved,
As when my swete hert her complayned
   That ever she me loved.
     Alas the while!   5

With pituous loke she saide and sighed,
   Alas, what aileth me
To love and set my welth so light
   On hym that loveth not me?
     Alas the while!   10

Was I not well voyde of all pain,
   When that nothing me greved?
And nowe with sorrous I must complain
   And cannot be releved.
     Alas the while!   15

---

20. *unkindly:* unnaturally
MT, No. XXXVIII.
6. *pituous:* mournful, deserving pity
8. *welth:* well-being, happiness
14. *sorrous:* sorrows

My restfull nyghtes and joyfull daies
    Syns I began to love
Be take from me, all thing decayes,
    Yet can I not remove.
      Alas the while! 20

She wept and wrong her handes withall,
    The teres fell in my nekke,
She torned her face and let it fall;
    Scarsely therewith coulde speke.
      Alas the while! 25

Her paynes tormented me so sore
    That comfort had I none,
But cursed my fortune more and more
    To se her sobbe and grone.
      Alas the while! 30

17.

Who hath herd of suche crueltye before?
That when my plaint remembred her my woo
That caused it, she cruell more and more
Wisshed eche stitche, as she did sit and soo,
Had prykt myn hert, for to encrese my sore. 5
And, as I thinck, she thought it had ben so:
For as she thought this is his hert in dede,
She pricked herd and made her self to blede.

18.

If fansy would favor
    As my deserving shall,
My love, my paramor,
    Should love me best of all.

MT, No. XLII.
2. *remembred . . . woo:* reminded her of my woe
4. *soo:* sew
8. *herd:* hard
MT, No. XLIII.

But if I cannot attain 5
   The grace that I desire,
Then may I well complain
   My service and my hiere.

Fansy doethe knowe how
   To fourther my trew hert 10
If fansy myght avowe
   With faith to take part.

But fansy is so fraill
   And flitting still so fast,
That faith may not prevaill 15
   To helpe me furst nor last.

For fansy at his lust
   Doeth rule all but by gesse,
Whereto should I then trust
   In trouth or stedfastnes? 20

Yet gladdely would I please
   The fansy of her hert,
That may me onely ease
   And cure my carefull smart.

Therefore, my lady dere, 25
   Set ons your fantasy
To make som hope appere
   Of stedfastnes remedy.

For if he be my frend
   And undertake my woo, 30
My greif is at at ende
   If he continue so.

---

7. *complain:* lament
8. *hiere:* wages, reward
17. *lust:* pleasure
24. *carefull:* sorrowful
26. *ons:* once
28. *stedfastnes remedy:* a remedy for my steadfastness
29. *he:* i.e., fancy

Elles fansy doeth not right,
  As I deserve and shall
To have you daye and nyght,   35
  To love me best of all.

19.

What no, perdy, ye may be sure!
Thinck not to make me to your lure,
  With wordes and chere so contrarieng,
  Swete and sowre contrewaing,
To much it were still to endure.   5
Trouth is tryed where craft is in ure,
But though ye have had my hertes cure,
  Trow ye I dote withoute ending?
    What no, perdy!

Though that with pain I do procure   10
For to forgett that ons was pure
  Within my hert shall still that thing,
  Unstable, unsure, and wavering,
Be in my mynde withoute recure?
    What no, perdye!   15

20.

What wourde is that that chaungeth not,
Though it be tourned and made in twain?
It is myn aunswer, god it wot,

---

34. *As:* For
MT, No. XLV.
2. *make . . . lure:* make me return to your lure, like a falcon or a hawk
4. *contrewaing:* weighing in equal balance
6. *tryed:* put to the test. The Devonshire MS. text of this poem reads *trayed* (betrayed). *in ure:* used
14. *recure:* hope of recovery
MT, No. L. The poem is a riddle, the answer to which is "Anna." If the word is divided in two and the second syllable reversed (line 2) then one gets "An An." Tottel, in 1557, ruined the effect by substituting *Anna* for *aunswer* in line 3. The poem may refer to Anne Boleyn.
3. *god it wot:* God knows it

And eke the causer of my payn.
A love rewardeth with disdain,   5
Yet is it loved. What would ye more?
It is my helth eke and my sore.

21.

Marvaill no more all tho
  The songes I syng do mone,
For othre liff then wo
  I never proved none.
And in my hert also   5
  Is graven with lettres diepe
A thousand sighes and mo,
  A flod of teres to wepe.

How may a man in smart
  Fynde matter to rejoyse?   10
How may a morning hert
  Set fourth a pleasaunt voise?
Play who that can that part,
  Nedes must in me appere
How fortune overthwart   15
  Doeth cause my morning chere.

Perdy, there is no man
  If he never sawe sight
That perfaictly tell can
  The nature of the light.   20
Alas, how should I then,
  That never tasted but sowre,
But do as I began,
  Continuelly to lowre?

---

4. *eke:* also
MT, No. LII.
4. *proved:* experienced
11. *morning:* mourning
15. *overthwart:* perverse
16. *morning chere:* mournful appearance
18. *If . . . sight:* i.e., if he was blind from birth
24. *lowre:* frown, scowl

But yet perchaunce som chaunce   25
   May chaunce to chaunge my tune,
And when suche chaunce doeth chaunce,
   Then shall I thanck fortune.
And if I have suche chaunce,
   Perchaunce ere it be long,   30
For such a pleasaunt chaunce
   To syng som plaisaunt song.

22.

A Robyn
Joly Robyn,
Tell me how thy leman doeth
And thou shall knowe of myn.

My lady is unkynd, perde!   5
   Alack, whi is she so?
She loveth an othre better then me,
   And yet she will say no.

RESPONCE

I fynde no suche doublenes,
   I fynde women true.   10
My lady loveth me dowtles
   And will chaunge for no newe.

LE PLAINTIF

Thou art happy while that doeth last,
   But I say as I fynde,
That womens love is but a blast   15
   And torneth like the wynde.

---

32. *To syng*: i.e., I shall sing
MT, No. LV. Wyatt builds his poem from a popular song; the music for the first three stanzas is extant in a contemporary manuscript.
3. *leman*: lover
8. *yet*: always
13. *Le plaintif*: the "complainant"

RESPONCE

Yf that be trew yett as thov sayst
    That women turn their hart,
Then spek better of them thov mayst
    In hope to han thy partt.   20

LE PLAINTIF

Suche folkes shall take no harme by love
    That can abide their torn,
But I, alas, can no way prove
    In love but lake and morn.

RESPONCE

But if thou will avoyde thy harme   25
    Lerne this lessen of me,
At othre fieres thy self to warme
    And let theim warme with the.

23.

Some tyme I fled the fyre that me brent
By see, by land, by water and by wynd;
And now I folow the coles that be quent
From Dovor to Calais against my mynde.
Lo! how desire is boeth sprong and spent!   5
And he may se that whilome was so blynde;

---

17. *thov:* thou
17–20. These lines, omitted in the Egerton MS., are supplied from the Devonshire text.
20. *han:* have
23–24. *can . . . morn:* can find nothing in love but a sense of loss and sadness
MT, No. LIX. Probably written in October 1532, when Anne Boleyn went to Calais. Wyatt was in her retinue.
1. *brent:* burned
3. *quent:* quenched
4. *against my mynde:* unwillingly
6. *whilome:* once

And all his labor now he laugh to scorne,
Mashed in the breers that erst was all to torne.

24.

He is not ded that somtyme hath a fall,
The sonne retorneth that was under the clowd,
And when fortune hath spitt oute all her gall,
I trust good luck to me shalbe allowd.
For I have sene a shipp into haven fall   5
After the storme hath broke boeth mast and shrowd,
And eke the willowe that stoppeth with the wynde
Doeth ryse again and greater wode doeth bynd.

25.

Ons as me thought fortune me kyst
    And bad me aske what I thought best;
And I should have it as me list,
    Therewith to set my hert in rest.

I asked nought but my dere hert   5
    To have for evermore myn owne:
Then at an ende were all my smert,
    Then should I nede no more to mone.

Yet for all that a stormy blast
    Had overtorned this goodely day;   10
And fortune semed at the last
    That to her primes she saide nay.

---

7. *laugh:* may laugh
8. *Mashed . . . torne:* Even while he is enmeshed in the briars which had
formerly torn him to pieces
MT, No. LX. Wyatt's source is an eight-line poem by Serafino
6. *shrowd:* sail
7. *stoppeth:* stoops, bends
8. *greater . . . bynd:* probably "winds or ties itself around trees that are
larger and stronger than it is"
MT, No. LXV.
2. *bad:* bade
3. *me list:* it pleased me

But like as oon oute of dispere
   To soudden hope revived I;
Now fortune sheweth herself so fayer   15
   That I content me wonderly.

My moost desire my hand may reche,
   My will is alwaye at my hand;
Me nede not long for to beseche
   Her that hath power me to commaund.   20

What erthely thing more can I crave?
   What would I wisshe more at my will?
No thing on erth more would I have,
   Save that I have to have it still.

For fortune hath kept her promes   25
   In graunting me my moost desire:
Of my sufferaunce I have redres,
   And I content me with my hiere.

26.

My lute, awake! perfourme the last
Labour that thou and I shall wast
   And end that I have now begon,
For when this song is song and past,
   My lute be still, for I have done.   5

As to be herd where ere is none,
As lede to grave in marbill stone,
   My song may perse her hert as sone;

16. *wonderly:* wonderfully
24. *still:* always
27. *sufferaunce:* suffering
28. *hiere:* reward
MT, No. LXVI.
2. *wast:* waste
4. *is song:* is sung
6. *ere:* ear
7. *lede to grave:* to engrave lead. It would take as long to do this as to
pierce (line 8) her heart.

Should we then sigh, or syng, or mone?
  No, no, my lute, for I have done. 10

The Rokkes do not so cruelly
Repulse the waves continuelly,
  As she my suyte and affection,
So that I ame past remedy,
  Whereby my lute and I have done. 15

Prowd of the spoyll that thou hast gott
Of simple hertes thorough loves shot,
  By whome, unkynd, thou has theim wone,
Thinck not he haith his bow forgot,
  All tho my lute and I have done. 20

Vengeaunce shall fall on thy disdain,
That makest but game on ernest pain;
  Thinck not alone under the sonne
Unquyt to cause thy lovers plain,
  All tho my lute and I have done. 25

Perchaunce the lye wethered and old,
The wynter nyght that are so cold,
  Playnyng in vain unto the mone;
Thy wisshes then dare not be told,
  Care then who lyst, for I have done. 30

And then may chaunce the to repent
The tyme that thou hast lost and spent
  To cause thy lovers sigh and swoune;
Then shalt thou knowe beaultie but lent
  And wisshe and want as I have done. 35

---

16. *spoyll:* plunder
17. *thorough:* through
19. *he:* Love (Cupid)
24. *Unquyt:* Unrevenged; *plain:* to lament
26. *the:* thee; *wethered:* withered
27. *nyght:* possibly an uninflected plural; other early texts read *nyghtes*
33. *swoune:* swoon, faint
34. *beaultie:* beauty

Now cesse, my lute, this is the last
Labour that thou and I shall wast,
  And ended is that we begon;
Now is this song boeth sung and past,
  My lute be still, for I have done.   40

27.

In eternum I was ons determed
For to have lovid and my mynde affermed
That with my herte it shuld be confermed
    In eternum.

Forthwith I founde the thing that I myght like,   5
And sought with love to warme her hert alike,
For as me thought I shulde not se the like
    In eternum.

To trase this daunse I put my self in prese,
Vayne hope ded lede and bad I should not cese   10
To serve, to suffer, and still to hold my pease
    In eternum.

With this furst rule I fordred me a pase,
That, as me thought, my trowghthe had taken place
With full assurans to stonde in her grace   15
    In eternum.

It was not long or I by proofe had found
That feble bilding is on feble grounde,
For in her herte this worde ded never sounde
    In eternum.   20

MT, No. LXXI.
1. *In eternum:* Eternally; *determed:* determined
9. *trase:* perform; *put . . . prese:* joined the crowd
13. *fordred . . . pase:* quickly made headway
14. *trowghthe:* truth
17. *or:* before; *by proofe:* through experience

In eternum then from my herte I kest
That I had furst determed for the best,
Nowe in the place another thought doeth rest
    In eternum.

28.

To cause accord or to aggre,
Two contraries in oon degre,
And in oon poynct, as semeth me,
To all mans wit it cannot be:
    It is impossible.   5

Of hete and cold when I complain
And say that hete doeth cause my pain,
When cold doeth shake me every vain
And boeth at ons, I say again
    It is impossible.   10

That man that hath his hert away,
If lyff lyveth there as men do say
That he hertles should last on day
Alyve and not to torn to clay,
    It is impossible.   15

Twixt lyff and deth, say what who sayth,
There lyveth no lyff that draweth breth;
They joyne so nere and eke i' feith
To seke for liff by wissh of deth,
    It is impossible.   20

Yet love that all thing doeth subdue,
Whose power ther may no liff eschew,

---

21. *kest:* cast
MT, No. LXXVII.
8. *every vain:* in every vein
11. *that . . . away:* who has lost (or given away) his heart
13. *on:* one
18. *eke i' feith:* also upon my faith

Hath wrought in me that I may rew
These miracles to be so true
    That are impossible.   25

29.

Unstable dreme according to the place
Be stedfast ons, or els at leist be true:
By tasted swetenes make me not to rew
The sudden losse of thy fals fayned grace.
By goode respect in such a daungerous case   5
Thou broughtes not her into this tossing mew,
But madest my sprite lyve my care to renew,
My body in tempest her succor to embrace.
The body dede, the spryt had his desire;
Paynles was thone, thothre in delight.   10
Why then, Alas, did it not kepe it right,
Retorning to lepe into the fire,
And where it was at wysshe it could not remain?
Such mockes of dremes they torne to dedly pain.

29a.

The lover having dreamed enjoying
of his love, complaineth that the dreame
is not either longer or truer.

Unstable dreame, accordyng to the place,
Be stedfast ones, or els at least be true.

MT, No. LXXIX.
1. *according . . . place*: which suits the situation I am in. The speaker is presumably tossing in his bed (*mew*, prison, as he calls it in line 6).
5. *By goode respect*: Through proper consideration (said ironically)
7. *sprite*: spirit
8. *her . . . embrace*: to embrace whatever aid she might offer me
10. *thone, thothre*: the one (the body), the other (the spirit)
11. *it*: the spirit; *kepe it right*: continue in such a satisfactory way
13. *And . . . remain?*: And could not remain in the wishful state which it had achieved
14. *mockes of*: mocking
No. 29a. Tottel's 1557 version of no. 29.

By tasted swetenesse, make me not to rew
The soden losse of thy false fained grace.
By good respect in such a dangerous case 5
Thou broughtest not her into these tossing seas,
But madest my sprite to live my care tencrease,
My body in tempest her delight timbrace.
The body dead, the sprite had his desire.
Painelesse was thone, the other in delight. 10
Why then alas did it not kepe it right,
But thus return to leape in to the fire:
And where it was at wishe, could not remayne?
Such mockes of dreames do turne to deadly payne.

30.

You that in love finde lucke and habundance
And live in lust and joyful jolitie,
Arrise for shame! Do away your sluggardie!
Arise, I say, do May some obseruance!
Let me in bed lye dreming in mischaunce, 5
Let me remember the happs most unhappy
That me betide in May most comonly,
As oon whome love list litil to avaunce.
Sephame saide true that my nativitie
Mischaunced was with the ruler of the May: 10
He gest, I prove, of that the veritie.
In May my welth and eke my liff, I say,
Have stonde so oft in such perplexitie:
Rejoyse! Let me dreme of your felicitie.

---

7. *tencrease:* to increase
MT, No. XCII.
1. *habundance:* abundance, richness
2. *lust:* pleasure
3. *sluggardie:* laziness. Lines 1–4 recall the traditional rites of May.
6. *happs most unhappy:* most unfortunate events
7. *me betide:* happened to me
9. *Sephame:* Edward Sephame, a court astrologer
9–10. *my . . . May:* my birth had bad luck with the planet that dominated during the month of May. Wyatt was imprisoned in May 1534 and again in May 1536.
11. *gest . . . veritie:* guessed, I find, the truth about that
12. *welth:* well-being, or possibly the happiness of love; *eke:* also
13. *stonde:* stood

31.

If waker care, if sodayne pale Coulor,
If many sighes with little speche to playne,
Now joy, now woo, if they my chere distayne,
For hope of smalle, if muche to fere therfore,
To hast, to slak my passe lesse or more, 5
Be signe of love then do I love agayne.
If thow aske whome, sure sins I did refrayne
Brunet that set my welth in such a rore,
Th'unfayned chere of Phillis hath the place
That Brunet had: she hath and ever shal. 10
She from my self now hath me in her grace;
She hath in hand my witt, my will and all,
My hert alone wel worthie she doth staye,
Without whose helpe skant do I live a daye.

32.

Tagus, fare well, that westward with thy stremes
Torns up the grayns off gold alredy tryd:
With spurr and sayle for I go seke the Tems,
Gaynward the sonne that shewth her welthi pryd;

MT, No. XCVII.
1. *waker:* watchful
3. *chere distayne:* face discolor
4. *smalle:* i.e., small reward
5. *passe:* pace
7. *refrayne:* draw back from
8. *Brunet:* possibly Anne Boleyn. Wyatt introduced this change into the
Egerton MS., which originally read "her that did set our country in a rore."
9. *Phillis:* perhaps Elizabeth Darnell, Wyatt's mistress
13. *staye:* support
MT, No. XCIX.
1. *Tagus:* a Spanish river, famed for its golden sands. Wyatt left Spain in
June 1539.
2. *tryd:* tested, experienced (?)
3. *Tems:* Thames
4. *Gaynward:* Facing, Toward; *that:* apparently referring to the Tagus,
which shows her "wealthy pride" by exposing her sands to the sun

And to the town wych Brutus sowght by drems   5
Like bendyd mone doth lend her lusty syd.
My Kyng, my Contry, alone for whome I lyve,
Of myghty love the winges for this me gyve.

33.

What rage is this? what furour of what kynd?
What powre, what plage, doth wery thus my mynd?
Within my bons to rancle is assind
    What poyson, plesant swete?

Lo, se myn iyes swell with contynuall terys;   5
The body still away sleples it weris;
My fode nothing my faintyng strenght reperis,
    Nor doth my lyms sustayne.

In diepe wid wound the dedly strok doth torne
To curid skarre that never shalle retorne.   10
Go to, tryumphe, rejoyse thy goodly torne,
    Thi frend thow dost opresse.

Opresse thou dost, and hast off hym no cure;
Nor yett my plaint no pitie can procure,
Fiers tygre fell, hard rok withowt recure,   15
    Cruell rebell to love!

Ons may thou love, never belovffd agayne;
So love thou still and not thy love obttayne;
So wrathfull love with spites of just disdayne
    May thret thy cruell hert.   20

---

5. *Brutus:* the legendary founder of London. He is said to have been told to
go there by Diana in a dream.
6. *Like . . . syd:* the Thames, like a crescent moon, lends her lusty side to
London
MT, No. CI.
3. *assind:* assigned
6. *weris:* wears
13. *off:* of
15. *fell:* cruel; *recure:* rescue
17. *belovffd:* be loved

156

34.

Ys yt possyble
That so hye debate,
So sharpe, so sore, and off suche rate,
Shuld end so sone and was begone so late?
    Is it possyble?   5

Ys yt possyble
So cruell intent,
So hasty hete and so sone spent,
From love to hate, and thens for to Relent?
    Is it possyble?   10

Ys yt possyble
That eny may fynde
Within on hert so dyverse mynd,
To change or torne as wether and wynde?
    Is it possyble?   15

Is it possyble
To spye yt in an Iye
That tornys as oft as chance on dy?
The trothe whereoff can eny try?
    Is it possyble?   20

It is possyble
For to torne so oft,
To bryng that lowyste that wasse most aloft,
And to fall hyest yet to lyght sofft:
    It is possyble.   25

MT, No. CLXXXIV.
13. *on:* one
18. *dy:* the throw of the dice

All ys possyble,
Who so lyst beleve;
Trust therfore fyrst, and after preve;
As men wedd ladyes by lycence and leve,
All ys possyble.   30

35.

And wylt thow leve me thus?
Say nay, say nay, for shame,
To save the from the Blame
Of all my greffe and grame;
And wylt thow leve me thus?   5
  Say nay, Say nay!

And wylt thow leve me thus,
That hathe lovyd the so long,
In welthe and woo among?
And ys thy hart so strong   10
As for to leve me thus?
  Say nay, Say nay!

And wylt thow leve me thus,
That hathe gevyn the my hart,
Never for to Depart,   15
Nother for payn nor smart;
And wylt thow leve me thus?
  Say nay, Say nay!

And wylt thow leve me thus
And have nomore Pyttye   20
Of hym that lovythe the?
Helas thy cruellte!
And wylt thow leve me thus?
  Say nay, Say nay!

---

28. *after preve:* learn the truth afterward
29. *lycence and leve:* marriage license and the ladies' permission. The men
take everything on trust.
MT, No. CLXXXVI.
4. *grame:* woe
9. *welthe:* happiness
22. *Helas:* Alas

158

36.

Now must I lerne to lyve at rest
  And weyne me of my wyll,
For I repent where I was prest
  My fansy to fullfyll.

I may no lenger more endure   5
  My wontyd lyf to lede,
But I must lerne to put in ure
  The change of womanhede.

I may not se my servys long
  Rewardyd in suche wyse,   10
Nor may I not sustayn suche wrong
  That ye my love dyspyce.

I may not syghe in sorows depe,
  Nor wayle the wante of love,
Nor I may nother cruche nor crepe   15
  Where hyt dothe not behove.

But I of force must nedes forsake
  My faythe so fondly sett,
And frome henceforthe must undertake
  Suche foly to forgett.   20

Now must I seke some otherways
  My self for to withsave,
And as I trust by myn assays
  Some Remedy to have.

MT, No. CCII.
2. *weyne:* wean; *wyll:* desires
6. *wontyd:* accustomed
7. *in ure:* to use
15. *nother cruche:* neither crouch
16. *hyt:* it
22. *withsave:* preserve
23. *assays:* attempts

I aske none other Remedy 25
 To recompence my wronge,
But ons to have the lyberty
 That I have lakt so long.

37.

Forget not yet the tryde entent
Of suche a truthe as I have ment,
My gret travayle so gladly spent
 Forget not yet.

Forget not yet when fyrst began 5
The wery lyffe ye know syns whan,
The sute, the servys none tell can,
 Forgett not yett.

Forget not yet the gret assays,
The cruell wrong, the skornfull ways, 10
The paynfull pacyence in denays,
 Forgett not yet.

Forget not yet, forget not thys,
How long ago hathe ben and ys
The mynd that never ment amys, 15
 Forget not yet.

Forget not then thyn owne aprovyd,
The whyche so long hathe the so lovyd,
Whose stedfast faythe yet never movyd,
 Forget not thys. 20

38.

Blame not my lute for he must sownde
 Of thes or that as liketh me,

MT, No. CCIII.
11. *denays:* denials
MT, No. CCV.
2. *thes:* this

For lake of wytt the lutte is bownde
　　To gyve suche tunes as plesithe me:
Tho my songes be sume what strange,　　　　　　5
And spekes suche wordes as toche thy change,
　　　　Blame not my lutte.

My lutte, alas, doth not ofende,
　　Tho that perforus he must agre
To sownde suche teunes as I entende　　　　　10
　　To sing to them that hereth me;
Then tho my songes be some what plain,
And tochethe some that use to fayn,
　　　　Blame not my lutte.

My lute and strynges may not deny,　　　　　15
　　But as I strike they must obay;
Brake not them than soo wrongfully,
　　But wryeke thy selff some wyser way:
And tho the songes whiche I endight
Do qwytt thy chainge with rightfull spight,　　20
　　　　Blame not my lute.

Spyght askyth spight and changing change,
　　And falsyd faith must nedes be knowne;
The faute so grett, the case so strange,
　　Of right it must abrode be blown:　　　　　25
Then sins that by thyn own desartt
My soinges do tell how trew thou artt,
　　　　Blame not my lute.

Blame but the selffe that hast mysdewn
　　And well desarvid to have blame;　　　　　30

---

3. *lake*: lack
9. *Tho . . . must*: Even though he must needs
13. *use to fayn*: are accustomed to feign
18. *wryeke*: revenge
19. *endight*: compose
20. *qwytt*: requite
29. *the*: thy; *misdewn*: misdone, acted wrongly

Change thou thy way, so evyll bygown,
  And then my lute shall sownde that same:
But if tyll then my fyngeres play
By thy desartt their wontyd way,
    Blame not my lutte.   35

Farwell, unknowne, for tho thow brake
  My strynges in spight with grett desdayn,
Yet have I fownde owtt for thy sake
  Stringes for to strynge my lute agayne;
And yf perchance this folys Rymyme   40
Do make the blushe at any tyme,
    Blame nott my lutte.

39.

Me list no more to sing
Of love nor of suche thing,
Howe sore that yt me wring;
    For what I song or spake
    Men dede my songis mistake.   5

My songes ware to defuse,
Theye made folke to muse;
Therefor, me to excuse,
    Theye shall be song more plaine,
    Nothr of joye nor payne.   10

What vaileth then to skipp
At fructe over the lippe?

. . . .

31. *evyll bygown:* ill begun
34. *By thy desartt:* According to your merits
40. *folys:* fool's, or possibly a scribal error for "folysh"; *Rymyme:* rhyme
MT, No. CCX.
1. *Me list:* It pleases me
5. *dede:* did
6. *defuse:* vague, obscure
10. *Nothr:* Neither
11–12. *What . . . lippe?:* What good is it to pass your lips over fruit without tasting it? A line has been lost after line 12 in the Devonshire MS.

For frute withouten taste
Dothe noght but rott and waste.

What vaileth undre kaye   15
To kepe treasure alwaye
That never shall se daye?
    Yf yt be not usid,
    Yt ys but abusid.

What vayleth the flowre   20
To stond still and whither?
Yf no man yt savour
    Yt servis onlye for sight
    And fadith towardes night.

Therefore fere not tassaye   25
To gadre ye that maye
The flower that this daye
    Is fresher than the next:
    Marke well, I saye, this text.

Let not the frute be lost   30
That is desired moste,
Delight shall quite the coste.
    Yf hit be tane in tyme,
    Small labour is to clyme.

And as for siche treasure   35
That makithe the the richer,
And no dele the porer,
    When it is gyven or lente
    Me thinkes yt ware well spente.

---

15. *kaye*: key
21. *whither*: wither
25. *tassaye*: to attempt
26. *gadre*: gather
32. *quite the coste*: make the effort worthwhile
33. *tane*: taken
37. *no dele*: not a bit

Yf this be undre miste, 40
And not well playnlye wyste,
Undrestonde me who lyste;
  For I reke not a bene,
  I wott what I doo meane.

40.

Lament my losse, my labor, and my payne,
All ye that here mye wofull playnte and crye;
Yf ever man might ons your herte constrayne
To pytie wordes of right, yt shulde bee I,
That sins the tyme that youthe yn me ded rayne 5
My pleasaunte yeris to bondage ded aplye,
Wiche as yt was I pourpose to declare,
Wherebye me frendes hereafter maye be ware.

And if perchaunce some redrs list to muse
What menith me so playnlye for to wright, 10
My good entente the fawte of yt shall skuse,
Wiche meane nothing, but trulye to endyght
The crafte and care, the greef and long abuse
Of lovers lawe and eke her puisshaunte might,
Wiche though that man oft tymes bye paynis doth know, 15
Lyttle theye wot wiche wayes the gylis doth growe.

---

40. *be undre miste*: sounds mysterious
41. *wyste*: comprehended
43. *bene*: bean
44. *wott*: know
MT, No. CCXIV. Petrarch's first sonnet has been suggested as a possible
source. But this poem may not be by Wyatt. If it is, then he perhaps
planned (line 28) to publish a collection of his verse.
4. *wordes of right*: truthful words
5. *ded rayne*: did reign
7. *pourpose*: intend
8. *me*: my
9. *redrs*: readers
11. *skuse*: excuse
14. *puisshaunte*: powerful
16. *wot*: know; *gylis*: guiles, subtle deceits

Yet well ye know yt will renwe my smerte
Thus to rehearse the paynes that I have past;
My hand doth shake, my pen skant dothe his parte,
My boddye quakes, my wyttis begynne to waste;   20
Twixt heate and colde, in fere I fele my herte
Panting for paine, and thus, as all agaste
I do remayne, skant wotting what I wrytt,
Perdon me then, rudelye tho I indyte.

And patientely, O Redre, I the praye,   25
Take in good parte this worke as yt ys mente,
And greve the not with ought that I shall saye,
Sins with good will this boke abrode ys sent
To tell men howe in youthe I ded assaye
What love ded mene and nowe I yt repente: 30
That moving me my frendes might well be ware,
And kepe them fre from all soche payne and care.

41.

Dyvers dothe use as I have hard and kno,
Whan that to chaunge ther ladies do beginne
To morne and waile and never for to lynne,
Hoping therbye to pease ther painefull woo.
And some ther be that when it chansith soo   5
That women change and hate where love hath bene,
Thei call them fals and think with woordes to wynne
The hartes of them wich otherwhere dothe gro.
But as for me though that by chaunse indede
Change hath outworne that favour that I had,   10

---

17. *renwe:* renew
18. *rehearse:* relate
23. *skant wotting:* hardly knowing; *wrytt:* write
27. *ought:* aught
31. *moving:* most editors emend to "musing" (meditating on my condition)
MT, No. CCXVII.
1. *hard:* heard
3. *lynne:* stop
4. *pease:* appease, mitigate

I will not wayle, lament, nor yet be sad,
Nor call her fals that falsley ded me fede,
But let it passe and think it is of kinde
That often chaunge doth plese a womans minde.

42.

Mye love toke skorne my servise to retaine
Wherein me thought she usid crueltie:
Sins with good will I lost my libretye
To followe her wiche causith all my payne.
Might never care cause me for to refrayne   5
But onlye this wiche is extremytie,
Gyving me nought, alas, not to agree
That as I was her man, I might remayne.
But sins that thus ye list to ordre me
That wolde have bene your servaunte true and faste,   10
Displese the not, my doting dayes bee paste,
And with my losse to leve I must agre;
For as there is a certeyne tyme to rage,
So ys there tyme suche madnes to asswage.

43.

Tanglid I was yn loves snare,
Opprest with payne, tormente with care,
Of grefe right sure, of Joye full bare,
      Clene in dispaire bye crueltye;
      But ha, ha, ha, full well is me,   5
      For I am now at libretye.

---

13. *of kinde:* a natural thing
MT, No. CCXXIII.
1. *toke skorne:* scorned; *servise;* i.e., as a lover
7-8. *Gyving . . . remayne:* "She gave me no choice; I was forced to consent to remain as her servant, even though I was not allowed to love her." In the sestet of the sonnet, the speaker declines to accept such an arrangement.
MT, No. CCXXIV. This poem may not be by Wyatt.
2. *tormente:* tortured
4. *bye:* because of

The wofull dayes so full of paine,
The werye night all spent in vayne,
The labor lost for so small gayne,
  To wryt them all yt will not bee;   10
  But ha, ha, ha, full well is me,
  For I am now at libretye.

Everye thing that faire doth sho,
When prof is made yt provithe not soo,
But tournith mirthe to bittre woo,   15
  Wiche in this case full well I see;
  But ha, ha, ha, full well is me,
  For I am now at libretye.

To grete desire was my guide,
And wanton will went bye my syde,   20
Hope rulid still and made me byde
  Of loves craft th'extremitye.
  But ha, ha, ha, full well is me,
  For I am now at libretye.

With faynid wordes which ware but winde   25
To long delayes I was assind,
Her wylye lokes my wyttes ded blinde,
  Thus as she wolde I ded agree.
  But ha, ha, ha, full well is me,
  For I am now at libretye.   30

Was never birde tanglid yn lyme
That brake awaye yn bettre tyme,
Then I that rotten bowes ded clyme,
  And had no hurte but scaped fre.
  Now ha, ha, ha, full well is me,   35
  For I am nowe at libretye.

---

19. *To:* Too
31. *lyme:* sticky sap from the holly tree, used to catch small birds

44.

Luckes, my faire falcon, and your fellowes all,
How well plesaunt yt were your libertie!
Ye not forsake me that faire might ye befall.
But they that somtyme lykt my companye,
Like lyse awaye from ded bodies thei crall: 5
Loe, what a profe in light adversytie!
But ye my birdes I swear by all your belles,
Ye be my fryndes, and so be but few elles.

45.

The piller pearisht is whearto I lent,
The strongest staye of myne unquyet mynde;
The lyke of it no man agayne can fynde,
From East to West, still seking thoughe he went.
To myne unhappe! for happe away hath rent   5
Of all my joye the vearye bark and rynde;
And I (alas) by chaunce am thus assynde
Dearlye to moorne till death do it relent.
But syns that thus it is by destenye,
What can I more but have a wofull hart,   10
My penne in playnt, my voyce in wofull crye,
My mynde in woe, my bodye full of smart,
And I my self my self alwayes to hate,
Till dreadfull death do ease my dolefull state?

MT, No. CCXLI. The poem may have been written during one of Wyatt's
imprisonments.
1. *Luckes:* "Alas, these strokes of ill fortune"; a pun on *lux* (light) is per-
haps intended
5. *lyse:* lice; *crall:* crawl
MT, No. CCXXXVI. Wyatt's source is Petrarch, *Rime,* cclxix. This sonnet
has often been taken to refer to the death of his patron, Thomas Cromwell,
in 1540.
2. *myne . . . mynde:* Wyatt's translation of Plutarch's *De Tranquillitate et
Securitate Animi,* published in 1528, was entitled "The Quyete of Mynde"
5. *myne unhappe:* my severe misfortune; *happe:* chance; *rent:* torn
8. *relent:* ease

46.

Stond who so list upon the Slipper toppe
Of courtes estates, and lett me heare rejoyce;
And use me quyet without lett or stoppe,
Unknowe in courte, that hath suche brackishe joyes:
In hidden place, so lett my dayes forthe passe,   5
That when my yeares be done, withouten noyse,
I may dye aged after the common trace.
For hym death greep'the right hard by the croppe
That is moche knowen of other; and of him self alas,
Doth dye unknowen, dazed with dreadfull face.   10

47.

V. Innocentia
Veritas Viat Fides
Circumdederunt me inimici mei

Who lyst his welthe and eas Retayne,
Hyme selffe let hym unknowne contayne;
   Presse not to fast in at that gatte
Wher the Retorne standes by desdayne:
   For sure, *circa Regna tonat.*   5

MT, No. CCXL. This epigram is translated from Seneca's *Thyestes*, lines
391–403.
1. *who so list:* whoever cares to; *Slipper:* slippery
3. *And . . . lett:* As long as they let me remain in peace, without any
hindrance
4. *Unknowe:* Unknown
7. *trace:* way
8. *greep'the:* grips; *croppe:* throat
MT, No. CLXXVI. This poem was probably written during Wyatt's 1536
imprisonment, when he witnessed, from the Bell Tower (line 16), the exe-
cution of Anne Boleyn. The Latin title adapts Psalm 16, verse 9 (Vulgate):
"My enemies surround my soul." Innocence, Truth, and Faith surround
Wyatt's name in the adaptation.
1. *welthe:* happiness
5. *circa . . . tonat:* "It thunders through the realms." Seneca, *Phaedra*,
line 1140. The first two stanzas of Wyatt's poem paraphrase lines 1125ff.
from this play.

The hye montaynis ar blastyd oft,
When the lowe vaylye ys myld and soft;
   Fortune with helthe stondis at debate;
The fall ys grevous frome Aloffte:
   And sure, *circa Regna tonat.*   10

These blodye dayes have brokyn my hart;
My lust, my youth dyd then departe,
   And blynd desyre of astate;
Who hastis to clyme sekes to reverte:
   Of truthe, *circa Regna tonat.*   15

The bell towre showed me such syght
That in my hed stekys day and nyght;
   Ther dyd I lerne out of a grate,
For all vavore, glory or myght,
   That yet *circa Regna tonat.*   20

By proffe, I say, ther dyd I lerne,
Wyt helpythe not deffence to yerne,
   Of innocence to pled or prate;
Ber low, therffor, geve god the sterne,
   For sure, *circa Regna tonat.*   25

48.

Lyve thowe gladly, yff so thowe may:
   Pyne thou not in loukynge for me;

---

7. *vaylye:* valley
8. *Fortune . . . debate:* Fortune is engaged in a battle with prosperity
12. *lust:* zest for life
13. *of astate:* for an important position in society
17. *stekys:* sticks
18. *grate:* the bars on the prison window
19. *vavore:* favor
21. *proffe:* bitter experience
22. *yerne:* earn
24. *geve . . . sterne:* let God control the ship
MT, No. CXLIX.
1. *thowe:* thou
2. *loukynge:* looking

Syns that dispayr hathe shut thy wey,
Thoue to see me, or I to see the.

Make thoue a vertu of a constreynte;   5
  Deme no faulte wer non ys wourthy;
  Myn ys to muche, what nedes thy playnt?
God he knoythe who ys for me.

Cast apon the Lorde thy cuer,
  Prey ounto hym thy cause to urge;   10
  Belyve, and he shall send recur:
Vayne ys all trust of mans refuge.

49.

Myne owne John Poyntz, sins ye delight to know
  The cawse why that homeward I me drawe,
  And fle the presse of courtes wher soo they goo,
Rather then to lyve thrall under the awe
  Of lordly lookes, wrappid within my cloke,   5
  To will and lust lerning to set a lawe;
It is not for becawsse I skorne or moke
  The power of them to whome fortune hath lent
  Charge over us, of Right, to strike the stroke.
But trew it is that I have allwais ment   10
  Lesse to estime them then the common sort
  Of owtward thinges that juge in their intent

---

6. *Deme:* Judge, Think
8. *knoythe:* knows
9. *cuer:* care
11. *recur:* aid
MT, No. CV. Wyatt's source is the tenth satire of the Italian poet Luigi
Alamanni (1495–1556), first published in 1532–33. The first fifty-two
lines of this poem are omitted in the Egerton MS.; they are supplied here
from the Devonshire and Cambridge MSS.
1. *Poyntz:* little is known of Wyatt's friend (Poyns or Poyntz). He was at
court during the 1520s.
11–12. *then . . . intent:* than do the common people, who tend to judge
courtiers solely on the basis of their outward appearance

Withowt regarde what dothe inwarde resort.
   I grawnt sumtime that of glorye the fyar
   Dothe touche my hart: me lyst not to report   15
Blame by honowr and honour to desyar.
   But how may I this honour now atayne
   That cannot dy the coloure blak a lyer?
My Poyntz, I cannot frame my tonge to fayne,
   To cloke the trothe for praisse, withowt desart,   20
   Of them that lyst all vice for to retayne.
I cannot honour them that settes their part
   With Venus and Baccus all theire lyf long;
   Nor holld my pece of them allthoo I smart.
I cannot crowche nor knelle nor do so grete a wrong,   25
   To worship them lyke gode on erthe alone,
   That ar as wollffes thes sely lambes among.
I cannot with my wordes complayne and mone
   And suffer nought, nor smart wythout complaynt,
   Nor torne the worde that from my mouthe is gone.   30
I cannot speke and loke lyke a saynct,
   Use wiles for witt and make deceyt a plesure,
   And call crafft counsell, for proffet styll to paint.
I cannot wrest the law to fill the coffer,
   With innocent blode to fede my sellff fat,   35
   And doo most hurt where most hellp I offer.
I am not he that can alow the state
   Off highe Cesar and dam Cato to dye,
   That with his dethe dyd skape owt off the gate
From Cesares handes, if Lyvye do not lye,   40
   And wolld not lyve whar lyberty was lost:
   So did his hert the commonn wele aplye.

---

16. *by:* concerning
18. *dy . . . lyer:* i.e., the color black cannot be dyed to another color
20. *withowt desart:* which is undeserved
27. *sely:* innocent
33. *paint:* use make-up
38. *Cato:* Cato of Utica, the uncle of Brutus. He committed suicide in
46 B.C. The story is taken from Livy, *History,* cxiv
42. *So . . . aplye:* His heart was so devoted to the commonwealth

I am not he suche eloquence to boste,
  To make the crow singing as the swane,
  Nor call the lyon of cowarde bestes the moste   45
That cannot take a mows as the cat can:
  And he that diethe for hunger of the golld
  Call him Alessaundre; and say that Pan
Passithe Apollo in musike manyfolld;
  Praysse Syr Thopas for a nobyll tale,   50
  And skorne the story that the knyght tolld.
Praise him for counceill that is droncke of ale;
  Grynne when he laugheth that bereth all the swaye,
  Frowne when he frowneth and grone when he is pale;
On othres lust to hang boeth nyght and daye: 55
  None of these poyntes would ever frame in me;
  My wit is nought, I cannot lerne the waye.
And much the lesse of thinges that greater be,
  That asken helpe of colours of devise
  To joyne the mene with eche extremitie,   60
With the neryst vertue to cloke alwaye the vise:
  And as to pourpose like wise it shall fall,
  To presse the vertue that it may not rise;
As dronkenes good felloweshippe to call;
  The frendly foo with his dowble face   65
  Say he is gentill and courtois therewithall;
And say that Favell hath a goodly grace
  In eloquence, and crueltie to name
  Zele of justice and chaunge in tyme and place;

---

45. *moste:* greatest
48. *Alessaundre:* Alexander the Great
49. *manyfolld:* many times
50. *Syr Thopas:* the humorously inept tale told by Chaucer the Pilgrim in the *Canterbury Tales.* "The Knight's Tale," in contrast, is a "noble" romance.
59. *colours of devise:* deceptions
60. *mene:* means
61. *vise:* vice
62. *as . . . fall:* likewise, as the occasion demands
63. *presse:* oppress
66. *courtois:* courteous
67. *Favell:* Flattery. Cf. the figure in Skelton's *Bowge of Courte.*
68. *name:* call

And he that sufferth offence withoute blame   70
  Call him pitefull; and him true and playn
  That raileth rekles to every mans shame.
Say he is rude that cannot lye and fayn,
  The letcher a lover, and tirannye
  To be the right of a prynces reigne.   75
I cannot, I. No, no, it will not be.
  This is the cause that I could never yet
  Hang on their slevis that way as thou maist se
A chippe of chaunce more then a pownde of witt.
  This maketh me at home to hounte and to hawke   80
  And in fowle weder at my booke to sitt.
In frost and snowe then with my bow to stawke;
  No man doeth marke where so I ride or goo;
  In lusty lees at libertie I walke,
And of these newes I fele nor wele nor woo,   85
  Sauf that a clogg doeth hang yet at my hele:
  No force for that for it is ordered so,
That I may lepe boeth hedge and dike full well.
  I ame not now in Fraunce to judge the wyne,
  With saffry sauce the delicates to fele;   90
Nor yet in Spaigne where oon must him inclyne
  Rather then to be, owtewerdly to seme.
  I meddill not with wittes that be so fyne,
Nor Flaunders chiere letteth not my sight to deme
  Of black and white, nor taketh my wit awaye   95
  With bestlynes, they beestes do so esteme;
Not I ame not where Christe is geven in pray
  For mony, poison and traison at Rome,
  A commune practise used nyght and daie:

---

78. *that way*: who weigh
81. *weder*: weather
84. *lusty lees*: pleasant meadows
85. *wele*: happiness
86. *Sauf*: Except. Wyatt was restricted to his father's estate in Kent.
90. *saffry*: savory; *delicates to fele*: delicacies to taste
94. *chiere letteth*: cheer hinders. The Flemish and Dutch were often stereo-
typed as drunkards.
97. *pray*: prey

But here I ame in Kent and Christendome   100
   Emong the muses where I rede and ryme;
   Where if thou list, my Poynz, for to come,
Thou shalt be judge how I do spend my tyme.

50.

My mothers maydes when they did sowe and spynne,
   They sang sometyme a song of the feld mowse,
   That forbicause her lyvelood was but thynne,
Would nedes goo seke her townysshe systers howse.
   She thought her self endured to much pain,   5
   The stormy blastes her cave so sore did sowse,
That when the forowse swymmed with the rain
   She must lye cold and whete in sorry plight;
   And wours then that, bare meet there did remain
To comfort her when she her howse had dight,   10
   Sometyme a barly corne, sometyme a bene,
   For which she laboured hard boeth daye and nyght
In harvest tyme whilest she myght goo and glyne;
   And when her stoore was stroyed with the flodd,
   Then wellaway! for she undone was clene.   15
Then was she fayne to take in stede of fode
   Slepe if she myght her hounger to begile.
   My syster, quod she, hath a lyving good,

MT, No. CVI. Wyatt's second satire is based on Horace's fable, *Satires*, II, 6.
1. *sowe:* sew
3. *lyvelood:* livelihood
6. *cave:* nest
7. *forowse:* furrows
8. *whete:* wet
9. *bare meet:* hardly enough food
10. *dight:* put in order
13. *glyne:* glean
14. *stoore:* supply of food; *stroyed:* destroyed
15. *wellawaye:* woe to her
18. *quod:* said

And hens from me she dwelleth not a myle.
   In cold and storme she lieth warme and dry,   20
   In bed of downe the dyrt doeth not defile
Her tender fote. She laboureth not as I.
   Richely she fedeth and at the richemans cost,
   And for her meet she nydes not crave nor cry.
By se, by land, of delicates the moost   25
   Her Cater sekes and spareth for no perell;
   She fedeth on boyled bacon, meet and roost,
And hath therof neither charge nor travaill;
   And when she list the licour of the grape
   Doeth glad her hert, till that her belly swell.   30
And at this jorney she maketh but a jape;
   So fourth she goeth trusting of all this welth
   With her syster her part so for to shape
That if she myght kepe her self in helth
   To lyve a Lady while her liff doeth last.   35
   And to the dore now is she come by stelth,
And with her foote anon she scrapeth full fast.
   Th'othre for fere durst not well scarse appere,
   Of every noyse so was the wretche agast.
At last she asked softly who was there,   40
   And in her langage as well as she cowd,
   Pepe, quod the othre, syster I ame here.
Peace, quod the towne mowse, why spekest thou so lowde?
   And by the hand she toke her fayer and well.
   Welcome, quod she, my sister by the Roode.   45
She fested her, that joy it was to tell
   The faere they had: they drancke the wyne so clere.
   And as to pourpose now and then it fell

---

24. *nydes:* needs
26. *Cater:* caterer
27. *boyled . . . roost:* boiled bacon and roasted meat
28. *charge:* expense
31. *at . . . jape:* she (the town mouse) makes a joke about the idea of a journey from my house to hers
45. *Roode:* cross
46. *fested:* feasted
47. *faere:* fare
48. *as to . . . fell:* when the remark seemed to suit the course of their conversation

She chered her with how, syster, what chiere?
 Amyddes this joye befell a sorry chaunce   50
 That well awaye the straunger bought full dere
The fare she had; for as she loked ascaunce,
 Under a stole she spied two stemyng Ise
 In a rownde hed with sherp erys. In Fraunce
Was never mowse so ferd for tho the unwise   55
 Had not Isene suche a beest before,
 Yet had nature taught her after her gyse
To knowe her foo and dred him evermore.
 The towney mowse fled: she knewe whether to goo.
 Th'othre had no shift but wonders sore   60
Ferd of her liff: at home she wyshed her tho,
 And to the dore, alas, as she did skipp,
 Thevyn it would, lo, and eke her chaunce was so,
At the threshold her sely fote did tripp,
 And ere she myght recover it again   65
 The traytor Catt had caught her by the hipp
And made her there against her will remain,
 That had forgotten her poure suretie and rest
 For semyng welth wherin she thought to rayne.
Alas, my Poynz, how men do seke the best,   70
 And fynde the wourst by error as they stray!
 And no marvaill, when sight is so opprest,
And blynde the gyde; anon owte of the way
 Goeth gyde and all in seking quyete liff.
 O wretched myndes, there is no gold that may   75

---

49. *what chiere?*: how are you feeling now?
51. *bought full dere*: paid a high price for
52. *ascaunce*: aside
53. *stole*: stool; *stemyng Ise*: flaming eyes
55. *ferd*: afraid; *unwise*: imprudent mouse
56. *Isene*: seen
57. *after her gyse*: according to her instincts
59. *whether*: whither
60–61. *wonders . . . of*: stands amazed, terribly afraid for
61. *tho*: then
63. *Thevyn it would*: Heaven willed; *eke*: also
64. *sely*: innocent
68. *poure*: poor
69. *rayne*: reign

Graunt that ye seke, no warr, no peace, no stryff,
  No, no, all tho thy hed were howpt with gold,
  Sergeaunt with mace, hawbert, sword nor knyff
Cannot repulse the care that folowe should.
  Eche kynd of lyff hath with hym his disease. 80
  Lyve in delight evyn as thy lust would,
And thou shalt fynde when lust doeth moost the please
  It irketh straite and by it self doth fade.
  A small thing it is that may thy mynde apese.
Non of ye all there is that is so madde 85
  To seke grapes upon brambles or breers,
  Nor none, I trow, that hath his wit so badd
To set his hay for Conys over Ryvers,
  Ne ye set not a dragg net for an hare,
  And yet the thing that moost is your desire 90
Ye do mysseke with more travaill and care.
  Make playn thyn hert that it be not knotted
  With hope or dred, and se thy will be bare
From all affectes whome vice hath ever spotted;
  Thy self content with that is the assigned, 95
  And use it well that is to the allotted.
Then seke no more owte of thy self to fynde
  The thing that thou haist sought so long before,
  For thou shalt fele it sitting in thy mynde.
Madde, if ye list to continue your sore, 100
  Let present passe and gape on tyme to come
  And diepe your self in travaill more and more.

---

77. *howpt:* hooped, encircled
78. *hawbert:* halberd, shafted weapon with an axlike head, a beak, and a spiked top
80. *hym his:* it its
81. *lust would:* desires lead you
83. *straite:* at once
84. *apese:* calm, quiet
88. *hay for Conys:* hunting net for rabbits
94. *affectes whome:* passions which
95. *that . . . the:* what is to thee
101. *gape on:* gaze expectantly upon
102. *diepe:* immerse

Hens fourth, my Poynz, this shalbe all and some:
   These wretched fooles shall have nought els of me
   But to the great god and to his high dome   105
None othre pain pray I for theim to be
   But when the rage doeth led them from the right
   That lowking backward vertue they may se
Evyn as she is so goodly fayre and bright;
   And whilst they claspe their lustes in armes a crosse,   110
   Graunt theim, goode lorde, as thou maist of thy myght,
To frete inward for losing suche a losse.

51.

A spending hand that alway powreth owte
   Had nede to have a bringer in as fast,
   And on the stone that still doeth tourne abowte
There groweth no mosse: these proverbes yet do last.
   Reason hath set theim in so sure a place   5
   That lenght of yeres their force can never wast.
When I remember this and eke the case
   Where in thou stondes I thowght forthwith to write,
   Brian, to the, who knowes how great a grace
In writing is to cownsell man the right.   10
   To the, therefore, that trottes still up and downe,
   And never restes, but runnyng day and nyght
From Reaulme to Reaulme, from cite, strete and towne.
   Why doest thou were thy body to the bones,
   And myghtst at home slepe in thy bed of downe   15

103. *all and some:* the long and short of it
105. *dome:* judgment
MT, No. CVII. Addressed to Sir Francis Bryan (d. 1550), the cousin of
Anne Boleyn and one of Henry VIII's favorite courtiers. He had a consid-
erable reputation for dissoluteness and sycophancy.
1. *powreth:* pours
7. *eke:* also
14. *were:* wear

And drynk goode ale so nappy for the noyns.
    Fede thy self fat and hepe up pownd by pownd?
    Lykist thou not this? No. Why? For swyᵤe so groyns
In stye and chaw the tordes molded on the grownd,
    And dryvell on perilles, the hed still in the maunger,   20
    Then of the harp the Asse to here the sownd.
So sackes of durt be filled up in the cloyster
    That servis for lesse then do thes fatted swyne.
    Tho I seme lene and dry withoute moyster,
Yet woll I serve my prynce, my lord and thyn,   25
    And let theim lyve to fede the panche that list,
    So I may fede to lyve both me and myn.
By god, well sayde! But what and if thou wist
    How to bryng in as fast as thou doest spend?
    That would I lerne. And it shall not be myst   30
To tell the how. Now hark what I intend.
    Thou knowst well first who so can seke to plese
    Shall pourchase frendes where trowght shall but offend
Fle therefore trueth; it is boeth welth and ese.
    For tho that trouth of every man hath prayse,   35
    Full nere that wynd goeth trouth in great misese.
Use vertu as it goeth now a dayes:
    In word alone to make thy langage swete,
    And of the dede yet do not as thou sayse;
Elles be thou sure thou shalt be farr unmyt   40
    To get thy bred, eche thing is now so skant.
    Seke still thy proffet upon thy bare fete.

---

16. *noyns:* nonce
18–27. *No . . . myn:* Bryan speaks these lines, except for "Why?" in line
18. He is also assigned "That . . . lerne" (line 30) and "No . . . best!"
(lines 80–84).
18. *groyns:* grunt
20. *perilles:* pearls
26. *panche:* belly
28. *wist:* knew
30. *myst:* amiss
33. *trowght:* truth
36. *misese:* distress
39. *sayse:* sayest
40. *farr unmyt:* completely unfit

Lend in no wise, for fere that thou do want,
   Onles it be as to a dogge a chese;
   By which retorne be sure to wyn a kant   45
Of half at lest: it is not goode to lese.
   Lerne at Kittson that in a long white cote
   From under the stall withoute landes or feise
Hath lept into the shopp; who knoweth by rote
   This rule that I have told the here before.   50
   Sumtyme also riche age begynneth to dote:
Se thou when there thy gain may be the more.
   Stay him by the arme where so he walke or goo;
   Be nere alway: and if he koggh to sore,
When he hath spit tred owte and please him so.   55
   A diligent knave that pikes his maisters purse
   May please him so that he withouten mo
Executor is: and what is he the wourse?
   But if so chaunce you get nought of the man,
   The wedow may for all thy charge deburse.   60
A ryveld skyn, a stynking breth, what than?
   A tothles mowth shall do thy lips no harme:
   The gold is good and tho she curse or ban,
Yet where the list thou maist ly good and warme;
   Let the old mule byte upon the bridill,   65
   Whilst there do ly a swetter in thyn arme.
In this also se you be not Idell:
   Thy nece, thy cosyn, thy sister or thy doghter,
   If she be faire, if handsom be her myddell,

---

45. *kant:* portion
46. *lese:* lose
47. *at:* from. *Kittson* has not been identified with any certainty.
48. *feise:* fees
53. *Stay:* Support
54. *koggh:* cough
55. *tred owte:* step on it
56. *pikes:* picks
57. *withouten mo:* alone
60. *for . . . deburse:* pay all your expenses. Bryan himself had married a rich widow in 1517.
61. *ryveld:* wrinkled
63. *and tho:* even if
69. *myddell:* waist

Yf thy better hath her love besoght her,   70
   Avaunce his cause and he shall help thy nede.
   It is but love: turne it to a lawghter.
But ware, I say, so gold the helpe and spede,
   That in this case thow be not so unwise
   As Pandare was in suche a like dede;   75
For he the fooll of conscience was so nyse
   That he no gayn would have for all his payne.
   Be next thy self, for frendshipp beres no prise.
Laughst thou at me? Why, do I speke in vayne?
   No, not at the, but at thy thrifty gest.   80
   Wouldest thou I should for any losse or gayne
Chaunge that for gold that I have tan for best,
   Next godly thinges, to have an honest name?
   Should I leve that, then take me for a best!
Nay then, farewell, and if you care for shame,   85
   Content the then with honest povertie,
   With fre tong what the myslikes to blame,
And for thy trouth sumtyme adversitie:
   And therewithall this thing I shall the gyve—
   In this worould now litle prosperite,   90
And coyne to kepe as water in a syve.

---

70. *her . . . her:* asked her for her love
75. *Pandare:* Pandarus, in Chaucer's *Troilus and Criseyde*
76. *nyse:* scrupulous
78. *next:* closest to; *beres no prise:* has no value
80. *gest:* story
82. *tan:* taken
84. *best:* beast
91. *syve:* sieve

HENRY HOWARD, EARL OF SURREY
1517–47

1.

From Tuscan cam my ladies worthi race,
Faire Florence was sometime her auncient seate;
The westorne Ile (whose pleasaunt shore doth face
Wylde Chambares cliffes) did geve her lyvely heate.
Fostred she was with mylke of Irishe brest,   5
Her Syer an erle, hir dame of princes bloud;
From tender yeres in Britaine she doth rest
With a kinges child, where she tastes gostly foode.
Honsdon did furst present her to myn eyen,
Bryght ys her hew and Geraldine shee hight;   10
Hampton me tawght to wishe her furst for myne,
And Wind'sor, alas! doth chace me from her sight.

The lady whom Surrey praises in this sonnet was Elizabeth Fitzgerald, who
was born in Ireland about 1528. In 1542 she married Sir Anthony Browne.
Recent scholarship suggests that Surrey wrote his poem about 1541, when
"Geraldine" was thirteen or fourteen. Shakespeare's Juliet, one recalls, was
only fourteen.
1. *Tuscan:* Tuscany. The Fitzgerald family was related to the Geraldis of
Florence.
3. *westorne Ile:* Ireland
4. *Chambares:* Wales' (Cambria)
6. *princes bloud:* Geraldine's mother was Elizabeth Grey, a first cousin of
Henry VIII
7. *rest:* remain
8. *kinges child:* either Princess Mary or Princess Elizabeth, Henry VIII's
children. Their household moved about frequently and Surrey could well
have seen Geraldine at either Hunsdon (line 9) or Hampton Court (line
11). *tastes gostly foode:* receives religious instruction
12. *Wind'sor:* Surrey was at Windsor in May 1541 (Jones' suggestion)

Bewty of kind, her vertues from above,
Happy ys he that may obtaine her love.

2.

When Windesor walles sustain'd my wearied arme,
My hand my chyn, to ease my restles hedd,
Ech pleasant plot revested green with warm,
The blossom'd bowes, with lustie veare yspred,
The flowred meades, the weddyd bird's so late,　　5
Myne eyes discoverd. Than did to mynd resort
The joily woes, the hateles shorte debate,
The rakhell life that longes to loves disporte.
Wherwith, alas! myne hevy charge of care
Heapt in my brest, brake forth against my will,　　10
And smoky sigh's, that over cast the ayer.
My vapored eyes such drery teares distill
The tender spring to quicken wher thei fall,
And I have bent to throwe me downe withall.

3.

I never saw youe madam laye aparte
Your cornet black, in colde nor yet in heate,
Sythe first ye knew of my desire so greate,
Which other fances chac'd cleane from my harte.

13. *Bewty of kind:* A natural beauty
1. *Windesor:* Jones dates this sonnet 1537, when Surrey was confined to Windsor after he struck Sir Edward Seymour in court
3. *revested . . . warm:* clothed in a warm green
4. *veare:* spring
5. *weddyd . . . late:* birds wedded so recently
7. *joily:* jolly; *hateles . . . debate:* brief, friendly contests
8. *longes:* belongs
9. *charge:* burden
14. *have:* half
No. 3. Translated from Petrarch, *Rime*, xi.
2. *cornet:* headdress with a veil
3. *Sythe:* Since
4. *fances:* fancies

Whiles to my self I did the thought reserve   5
That so unware did wounde my wofull brest,
Pytie I saw within your hart dyd rest;
But since ye knew I did youe love and serve
Your golden treese was clad alway in blacke,
Your smilyng lokes that hid thus evermore,   10
All that withdrawne that I did crave so sore.
So doth this comet governe me, a lacke,
In someres sone, in winters breath of frost,
Of your faire eies whereby the light is lost.

4.

Love that doth raine and live within my thought,
And buylt his seat within my captyve brest,
Clad in the armes wherein with me he fowght
Oft in my face he doth his banner rest.
But she that tawght me love and suffre paine,   5
My doubtfull hope and eke my hote desire
With shamfast clooke to shadoo and refrayne,
Her smyling grace convertyth streight to yre.
And cowarde love then to the hart apace
Taketh his flight, where he doth lorke and playne   10
His purpose lost, and dare not shew his face.
For my lordes gylt thus fawtles byde I payine;
Yet from my Lorde shall not foote remove:
Sweet is the death that taketh end by love.

---

10. *lokes:* looks; *that:* i.e., the trees of line 9
14. *Of . . . lost:* Whereby the light of your fair eyes is lost
No. 4. Note Wyatt's version (no. 2 in this edition) of the same Petrarchan
sonnet. (*Rime,* cxl).
1. *raine:* reign
6. *eke:* also
7. *clooke:* cloak
9. *apace:* at once
10. *lorke and playne:* lurk and lament
12. *byde I payine:* I suffer pain

5.

In Cipres springes (wheras dame Venus dwelt)
A well so hote that who so tastes the same,
Were he of stone, as thawed yse shuld melt,
And kindled fynd his brest with secret flame;
Whose moist poison dissolved hath my hate.   5
This creping fier my cold lymes so oprest
That, in the hart that harbred fredom late,
Endles dispaire long thraldom hath imprest.
One, eke so cold in froson snow is found,
Whose chilling venume of repugnant kind   10
The fervent heat doth quenche of Cupides wound,
And with the spote of change infectes the mynd;
Where of my deer hath tasted to my payne.
My service thus is growne into disdayne.

6.

The greate Macedon that out of Persy chased
Darius, of whose huge powre all Asia range,
In the riche arke yf Hommers rymes he placed,
Who fayned gestes of heathen princes sange;
What holie grave, what worthye sepulture,   5
To Wyates Psalmes should Christians than purchace?

No. 5. Jones suggests a probable source for this sonnet in Ariosto (*Orlando Furioso*, I, 78).
1. *Cipres:* Cyprus, where Venus had a shrine
2. *well:* spring, fountain
6. *lymes:* limbs
7. *harbred:* harbored
9. *froson:* frozen
13. *deer:* dear, loved one
1. *Macedon:* Alexander, who carried Homer's poems in a coffer which he obtained after defeating Darius. The story is told by Plutarch and was widely known. *Persy:* Persia
2. *range:* rang
4. *fayned gestes:* fictional stories
6. *Wyates Psalmes:* Wyatt's translations of the penitential Psalms

Where he doth painte the lively fayth and pure,
The stedfast hope, the sweet returne to grace,
Of just David by perfect penitence;
Where rulers may see in a myrrour clere,   10
The bytter frute of false concupicence,
How Jurye bowght Uryas death full deere.
In princes hartes godes scourge yprinted deepe
Mowght them awake out of their synfull sleepe.

7.

In the rude age when scyence was not so rife,
If Jove in Crete, and other where they taught
Artes to reverte to profyte of our lyfe,
Wan after deathe to have their temples sought;
If vertue yet in no unthankfull tyme,   5
Fayled of some to blast her endles fame:
A goodlie meane bothe to deter from cryme
And to her steppes our sequell to enflame;
In dayes of treuthe, if Wyattes frendes then waile
(The onelye debte that ded of quycke may clayme)   10
That rare wit spent, employde to our avayle
Where Christe is tought, deserve they monnis blame?

---

12. *Jurye:* Jewry; *Uryas:* Uriah's
14. *Mowght:* Might
1. *scyence:* knowledge
2. *Jove:* Jupiter's birthplace was uncertain and thus various countries claimed him. *other where:* elsewhere
3. *reverte:* return
4. *Wan:* Managed. The syntax of lines 2–4 is very confused: "Jove, who was of doubtful origin, taught arts to men . . . In return, he and others who did the same thing were worshiped in temples after their death."
6. *blast:* spread abroad
7. *meane:* means
8. *to . . . enflame:* to enflame us so that we might follow her (Virtue's) footsteps
9. *dayes of treuthe:* contrasted here with the heathen days of lines 1–4
10. *quycke:* those who remain alive
11–12. *That . . . blame?:* a reference to Wyatt's translation of the penitential Psalms
12. *tought:* taught; *monnis:* man's

His livelie face thy brest how did it freate,
Whose Cynders yet with envye doo the eate.

8.

Thassyryans king, in peas with fowle desyre
And filthye lustes that staynd his regall harte,
In warr that should sett pryncelye hertes a fyre
Vaynquyshd dyd yelde for want of marcyall arte.
The dent of swordes from kysses semed straunge,   5
And harder then hys ladyes syde his targe;
From glotton feastes to sowldyers fare a chaunge,
His helmet, far above a garlandes charge.
Who scace the name of manhode dyd retayne,
Drenched in slouthe and womanishe delight;   10
Feble of sprete, unpacyent of payne,
When he hadd lost his honour and hys right—
Prowde tyme of welthe, in stormes appawld with drede—
Murdred hymself to shew some manfull dede.

9.

Set me wheras the sonne dothe perche the grene,
Or whear his beames may not dissolve the Ise,
In temprat heat wheare he is felt and sene;
With prowde people, in presence sad and wyse;

---

13. *thy:* possibly an allusion to Edmund Bonner, later Bishop of London. His accusations caused Wyatt to be imprisoned in 1541. *freate:* fret, irritate
14. *Whose . . . eate:* Even his ashes consume thee with envy
1. *Thassyryans king:* Sardanapalus, often viewed as a type of royal degeneration. "It is tempting, but not necessary, to see in this poem a covert allusion to Henry VIII" (Jones).
5. *dent:* dint; *from:* after
6. *targe:* shield
8. *far . . . charge:* a far heavier burden than a garland
9. *scace:* hardly, barely
11. *sprete:* spirit; *unpacyent:* impatient
14. *dede:* deed. Sardanapalus committed suicide by throwing himself into a fire in which he had burned up his treasure.
No. 9. Surrey's source is Petrarch, *Rime,* cxlv.
1. *perche:* parch
4. *sad:* sober

Set me in base, or yet in highe degree,   5
In the long night or in the shortyst day,
In clere weather or whear mysts thikest be,
In lusty yowthe, or when my heares be grey;
Set me in earthe, in heaven, or yet in hell,
In hill, in dale, or in the fowming floode;   10
Thrawle, or at large, alive whersoo I dwell,
Sike, or in healthe, in yll fame or in good:
Yours will I be, and with that onely thought
Comfort my self when that my hape is nowght.

10.

Dyvers thy death doo dyverslye bemone.
Some that in presence of that livelye hedd
Lurked, whose brestes envye with hate had sowne,
Yeld Cesars teres uppon Pompeius hedd.
Some, that watched with the murdrers knyfe,   5
With egre thurst to drynke thy guyltles blood,
Whose practyse brake by happye end of lyfe,
Weape envyous teares to here thy fame so good.
But I that knewe what harbourd in that hedd,
What vertues rare were tempred in that brest,   10
Honour the place that such a jewell bredd,
And kysse the ground where as thy coorse doth rest
With vaporde eyes; from whence suche streames avayle
As Pyramus did on Thisbes brest bewayle.

---

5. *base:* low
11. *Thrawle . . . large:* Slave or free man
13. *onely thought:* thought alone
14. *hape is nowght:* fortune is reduced to naught
1. *thy death:* Wyatt died in October 1542
2. *Some:* perhaps alluding to Edmund Bonner and Simon Heynes, Wyatt's accusers. See no. 7, line 13 n.
4. *Cesars teres:* hypocritical tears, like those which Caesar shed after Pompey's death
6. *egre:* eager
7. *practyse:* political plotting (which was broken up by Wyatt's timely death)
10. *tempred:* balanced
12. *coorse:* body
13. *vaporde:* tearful
14. *Pyramus:* Thisbe slew herself, thinking her lover Pyramus was dead. He then committed suicide.

11.

The soote season, that bud and blome furth bringes,
With grene hath clad the hill and eke the vale:
The nightingale with fethers new she singes:
The turtle to her make hath tolde her tale:
Somer is come, for every spray nowe springes,   5
The hart hath hong his olde hed on the pale:
The buck in brake his winter cote he flings:
The fishes flote with newe repaired scale:
The adder all her sloughe awaye she slinges:
The swift swallow pursueth the flyes smale: 10
The busy bee her honye now she minges:
Winter is worne that was the flowers bale:
And thus I see among these pleasant thinges
Eche care decayes, and yet my sorow springes.

12.

Alas so all thinges nowe doe holde their peace.
Heaven and earth disturbed in nothing:
The beastes, the ayer, the birdes their song doe cease:
The nightes chare the starres aboute dothe bring:
Calme is the Sea, the waves worke lesse and lesse: 5
So am not I, whom love alas doth wring,
Bringing before my face the great encrease
Of my desires, whereat I wepe and syng
In joye and wo as in a doubtful ease.

No. 11. Surrey adopts Petrarch (*Rime*, ccx) to the English scene. The punctuation given here and in nos. 12 and 13 is that of Tottel's text (1557).
1. *soote:* sweet
4. *turtle:* turtledove; *make:* mate
6. *his olde hed:* i.e., his antlers; *pale:* fence, paling
7. *brake:* the bushes
9. *sloughe:* skin
11. *minges:* remembers
12. *bale:* evil
No. 12. Surrey's source is Petrarch, *Rime*, clxiv.
3. *ayer:* wind
4. *nightes chare:* Ursa major, the Great Bear

For my swete thoughtes sometyme doe pleasure bring: 10
But by and by the cause of my disease
Geves me a pang, that inwardly dothe sting,
When that I thinke what griefe it is againe,
To live and lacke the thing should ridde my paine.

13.

The golden gift that nature did thee geve,
To fasten frendes, and fede them at thy wyll,
With fourme and favour, taught me to beleve
How thou art made to shew her greatest skill.
Whose hidden vertues are not so unknowen,   5
But lively domes might gather at the first
Where beautye so her perfect seede hath sowen,
Of other graces folow nedes there must.
Now certesse Ladie, sins all this is true,
That from above thy gyftes are thus elect: 10
Do not deface them than with fansies newe,
Nor chaunge of mindes let not thy minde infect:
But mercy him thy frende, that doth thee serve,
Who seekes alway thine honour to preserve.

14.

Norfolk sprang thee, Lambeth holds thee dead,
Clere of the County of Cleremont though hight.

---

11. *by and by:* immediately
14. *should:* which should
2. *fasten frendes:* bind friends to you
4. *her:* Nature's
6. *lively domes:* discerning judgments
10. *elect:* chosen
13. *mercy:* show mercy to
1. *Norfolk:* Thomas Clere (d. 1545), Surrey's squire, was born at Ormesby, Norfolk. He died from a wound he received while saving Surrey's life at the siege of Montreuil (*Muttrell*, line 9), and was buried in the Howard chapel at Lambeth Palace.
2. *Cleremont:* Thomas was descended from the De Cleremont family; *hight:* named. Surrey, throughout the poem, makes every effort to draw Clere into the Howard family.

Within the womb of Ormondes race thou bread,
And sawest thy cosin crowned in thy sight.
Shelton for love, Surrey for Lord, thou chase: 5
Aye me! while life did last that league was tender.
Tracing whose steps thou sawest Kelsall blaze,
Laundersey burnt, and battered Bullen render.
At Muttrell gates, hopeles of all recure,
Thine Earle halfe dead, gave in thy hand his will;   10
Which cause did thee this pining death procure,
Ere summers four times seven thou couldest fulfill.
Ah, Clere! if love had booted, care, or cost,
Heaven had not wonn, nor earth so timely lost.

15.

Brittle beautie, that nature made so fraile,
Wherof the gift is small, and short the season,
Flowring to-day, to morowe apt to faile,
Tickell treasure abhorred of reason,
Daungerous to dele with, vaine, of none availe,   5
Costly in keping, past not worthe two peason,
Slipper in sliding as is an eles taile,
Harde to attaine, once gotten not geason,
Jewel of jeopardie that perill doth assaile,
False and untrue, enticed oft to treason,   10

---

3. *bread:* was bred
4. *cosin:* Anne Boleyn, a descendant of the house of Ormonde, who was crowned in 1533
5. *Shelton:* Mary Shelton, Anne's cousin; *chase:* follow
7. *Tracing:* Following; *whose:* i.e., Surrey's; *Kelsall:* a Scottish town burned in the 1542 campaign
8. *Laundersey:* Landrecy, besieged in October 1543; *Bullen:* Boulogne, which fell to Henry VIII's army in September 1544; *render:* surrender
9. *recure:* recovery
13. *booted:* availed
14. *timely:* early
No. 15. This poem, traditionally assigned to Surrey, is almost certainly by Thomas Lord Vaux (1510–56).
4. *Tickell:* Treacherous
6. *peason:* peas
7. *Slipper:* Slippery; *eles:* eel's
8. *geason:* held permanently

Enmy to youth: that most may I bewaile.
Ah, bitter swete! infecting as the poyson,
Thou farest as frute that with the frost is taken:
To-day redy ripe, to morowe all to shaken.

16.

The sonne hath twyse brought forthe the tender grene,
And cladd the yerthe in lively lustynes;
Ones have the wyndes the trees dispoyled clene,
And now agayne begynnes their cruelnes;
Sins I have hidd under my brest the harme   5
That never shall recover helthfulnes.
The wynters hurt recovers with the warme;
The perched grene restored is with shade.
What warmth, alas! may sarve for to disarme
The froosyn hart, that my inflame hath made?   10
What colde agayne is hable to restore
My freshe grene yeres that wither thus and faade?
Alas! I see nothinge to hurt so sore
But tyme somtyme reduceth a retourne;
Yet tyme my harme increseth more and more,   15
And semes to have my cure allwayes in skorne.
Straunge kynd of death, in lief that I doo trye:
At hand to melt, farr of in flame to bourne;
And like as time list to my cure aply,
So doth eche place my comfort cleane refuse.   20
Eche thing alive that sees the heaven with eye,
With cloke of night maye cover and excuse

---

11. *Enmy:* Enemy
14. *to shaken:* shaken to pieces
2. *yerthe:* earth
3. *Ones:* Once; *dispoyled clene:* completely stripped
8. *perched:* parched
9. *sarve:* serve
10. *inflame:* inflammation
14. *reduceth:* brings back
17. *lief:* life; *trye:* experience
18. *of:* off; *bourne:* burn
19. *list . . . aply:* cares to devote itself to my recovery

Him self from travaile of the dayes unrest,
Save I, alas! against all others use,
That then sturres upp the torment of my brest,   25
To curse eche starr as cawser of my faat.
And when the sonne hath eke the darke represt
And brought the daie, it doth nothing abaat
The travaile of my endles smart and payne.
For then, as one that hath the light in haat,   30
I wishe for night, more covertlye to playne,
And me withdrawe from everie haunted place,
Lest in my chere my chaunce should pere to playne;
And with my mynd I measure, paas by paas,
To seke that place where I my self hadd lost,   35
That daye that I was tangled in that laase,
In seming slacke that knytteth ever most.
But never yet the trayvaile of my thought
Of better state could catche a cawse to bost,
For yf I fynde somtyme that I have sought,   40
Those starres by whome I trusted of the port,
My sayles do fall, and I advaunce right nought,
As anchord fast; my sprites do all resort
To stand a gaas, and sucke in more and more:
The deadlye harme which she doth take in sport.   45
Loo, yf I seke, how I do fynd my sore!
And yf I flye, I carrey with me still,
The venymd shaft which dothe his force restore
By hast of flight. And I maye playne my fill
Unto my self, oneles this carefull song   50
Prynt in your hert some parcell of my will.
For I, alas! in sylence all to long,

---

24. *use:* normal course
26. *faat:* fate
30. *haat:* hate
32. *haunted:* frequented
33. *chere:* face; *pere to playne:* appear too plainly
34. *paas:* step
36. *laase:* net, snare
40. *that:* that which
44. *a gaas:* aghast
50. *oneles:* unless; *carefull:* sorrowful
51. *parcell:* portion

Of myne old hurt yet fele the wound but grene.
Rue on me, lief, or elles your crewell wrong
Shall well appeare, and by my deth be sene.   55

<h1 style="text-align:center">17.</h1>

So crewell prison, howe could betyde, alas,
As prowde Wyndsour, where I in lust and joye
With a kinges soon my childishe yeres did passe,
In greater feast then Priams sonnes of Troye;

Where eche swete place retournes a tast full sowre.   5
The large grene courtes, where we wer wont to hove,
With eyes cast upp unto the maydens towre,
And easye sighes, such as folke drawe in love.

The statelye sales, the Ladyes bright of hewe,
The daunces short, long tales of great delight,   10
With wordes and lookes that Tygers could but rewe,
Where eche of us did plead the others right.

The palme playe, where, dispoyled for the game,
With dased eyes oft we by gleames of love
Have mist the ball and got sight of our dame   15
To bayte her eyes which kept the leddes above.

The graveld ground, with sleves tyed on the helme,
On fomynge horse, with swordes and frendlye hertes,
With chere, as thoughe the one should overwhelme,
Where we have fought and chased oft with dartes.   20

---

54. *Rue . . . lief:* Take pity on me, dear
1. *betyde:* it happen
2. *Wyndsour:* Surrey was imprisoned at Windsor in 1537. See no. 2, line
1 n. *lust:* pleasure
3. *soon:* the Earl of Richmond, Henry Fitzroy (1519–36), bastard son of
Henry VIII. He married Surrey's sister in 1533. *childishe:* youthful
6. *wont to hove:* accustomed to linger
9. *sales:* halls; *hewe:* complexion
13. *palme playe:* a game like tennis in which the hand was used instead of a
racket; *dispoyled:* undressed
16. *bayte:* allure; *which . . . leddes:* who was on the roof
17. *graveld ground:* tiltyard; *sleves:* ladies' favors
19. *chere:* friendly dispositions

With sylver dropps the meades yet spredd for rewthe,
In active games of nymblenes and strengthe
Where we dyd strayne, trayled by swarmes of youthe,
Our tender lymes, that yet shott upp in lengthe.

The secret groves, which oft we made resound   25
Of pleasaunt playnt and of our ladyes prayes,
Recording soft what grace eche one had found,
What hope of spede, what dred of long delayes.

The wyld forest, the clothed holtes with grene,
With raynes avald and swift ybrethed horse,   30
With crye of houndes and merey blastes bitwen,
Where we did chace the fearfull hart a force.

The voyd walles eke, that harbourde us eche night;
Wherwith, alas, revive within my brest
The swete accord, such slepes as yet delight,   35
The pleasaunt dreames, the quyet bedd of rest,

The secret thoughtes imparted with such trust,
The wanton talke, the dyvers chaung of playe,
The frendshipp sworne, eche promyse kept so just,
Wherwith we past the winter nightes awaye.   40

And with this thought the blood forsakes my face,
The teares berayne my chekes of dedlye hewe;
The which, as sone as sobbing sighes, alas,
Upsupped have, thus I my playnt renewe:

O place of blys! renewer of my woos!   45
Geve me accompt wher is my noble fere,

---

21. *rewthe:* ruth, pity
26. *prayes:* praise
28. *spede:* success
29. *holtes:* woods
30. *raynes avald:* reins slackened; *ybrethed:* exercised
32. *a force:* to run it down
33. *voyd:* empty; *eke:* also
44. *Upsupped:* Absorbed
46. *Geve me accompt:* Tell me; *fere:* companion (the Earl of Richmond)

Whome in thy walles thow didest eche night enclose,
To other lief, but unto me most dere.

Each wall, alas, that dothe my sorowe rewe,
Retournes therto a hollowe sound of playnt. 50
Thus I, alone, where all my fredome grew,
In pryson pyne with bondage and restraynt,

And with remembraunce of the greater greif,
To bannishe the lesse, I fynde my chief releif.

18.

London, hast thow accused me
Of breche of lawes, the roote of stryfe?
Within whose brest did boyle to see,
(So fervent hotte) thy dissolute lief,
That even the hate of synnes, that groo 5
Within thy wicked walles so rife,
For to breake forthe did convert soo
That terrour colde it not represse.
The which, by wordes, syns prechers knoo
What hope is left for to redresse, 10
By unknowne meanes it liked me
My hydden burden to expresse,
Wherby yt might appere to the
That secret synn hath secret spight;
From Justice rodd no fault is free; 15

---

48. *lief*: beloved
No. 18. Surrey's satire was perhaps occasioned by an escape in April 1543, when he was accused of breaking windows at night in the city of London with his bow. Thomas Wyatt, the son of the poet, was with him at the time. Both were imprisoned for a short while.
3. *whose*: i.e., my own
4. *lief*: life
5. *groo:* grow
6. *rife*: abundantly
7. *convert:* i.e., convert me (into a reformer)
8. *colde:* could
15. *Justice:* Justice's

But that all such as wourkes unright
In most quyet ar next ill rest.
In secret sylence of the night
This made me, with a reckles brest,
To wake thy sluggardes with my bowe;   20
A fygure of the lordes behest,
Whose scourge for synn the scryptures shew.
That, as the fearfull thonder clapp
By soddayne flame at hand we knowe,
Of peoble stones the sowndles rapp,   25
The dredfull plage might mak the see
Of goddes wrath, that doth the enwrapp;
That pryde might know, from conscyence free,
How loftye workes may her defend;
And envye fynd, as he hath sought,   30
How other seke hym to offend;
And wrath tast of eche crewell thought
The just shapp hyer in the end;
And ydell slouthe, that never wrought,
To heven hys spirite lift may begyn;   35
And gredye lucre lyve in drede
To see what haate ill gott goodes wynn;
The lechers, ye that lustes do feed,
Perceve what secrecye is in synne;
And gluttons hartes for sorow blede,   40
Awaked when their faulte they fynd.
In lothsome vyce, eche dronken wight
To styrr to godd, this was my mynd.
Thy wyndowes had don me no spight;
But prowd people that drede no fall,   45
Clothed with falshed and unright

16. *wourkes unright:* performs an unjust deed
17. *next:* nearest to
20. *To . . . bowe:* echoing Jeremiah 1:9, 14, 29
21. *A . . . behest:* cf. Isaiah 47:11; *behest:* promise
28–41. *pryde . . . fynd:* Surrey now accuses the London citizens of the
seven capital sins: pride, envy, anger, laziness, avarice, lechery, and gluttony
33. *just shapp hyer:* justly appointed judgment
37. *haate:* hate
42. *wight:* creature

Bred in the closures of thy wall,
But wrested to wrathe in fervent zeale
Thow hast to strief my secret call.
Endured hartes no warning feale.   50
Oh shamles hore! is dred then gone
By suche thy foes as ment thy weale?
Oh membre of false Babylon!
The shopp of craft! the denne of ire!
Thy dredfull dome drawes fast uppon;   55
Thy martyres blood, by swoord and fyre,
In heaven and earth for Justice call.
The lord shall here their just desyre;
The flame of wrath shall on the fall;
With famyne and pest lamentablie   60
Stricken shalbe thie lecheres all;
Thy prowd towers and turretes hye,
Enmyes to god, beat stone from stone;
Thyne Idolles burnt that wrought iniquitie.
When none thy ruyne shall bemone,   65
But render unto the right wise lord,
That so hath judged Babylon,
Imortall praise with one accord.

19.

Suche waywarde wais hath love, that moste parte in discorde
Our willes do stand, wherby our hartes but seldom dooth
    accorde.
Disceyte is his delight, and to begyle and mocke
The symple hertes which he doth stryke with froward dyvers
    stroke.

---

49. *Thow . . . call:* i.e., Thou hast my secret call to strife (conflict, trouble). Jones suggests that *hast* should perhaps be emended to *hearst*.
50. *Endured:* Hardened
51. *hore:* whore. Surrey ironically accuses London as the whore of Babylon, a favorite phrase in the Protestant attack on Rome.
52. *By suche:* From such of; *weale:* happiness
55. *dome:* doom
58. *here:* hear. Lines 56–64 echo both Revelation 18:24 and Ezekiel 5:12–17, 6:11–14. Surrey, the rowdy boy, assumes the position of an Old Testament prophet.

He cawseth hertes to rage with golden burninge darte,   5
And doth alaye with ledden cold agayne the tothers harte.
Hot gleames of burning fyre and easye sparkes of flame,
In balaunce of unegall weight he pondereth by ame.
From easye fourde, where I might wade and passe full well,
He me withdrawes and doth me drive into the darke, diep
    well;   10
And me withholdes where I am cald and offerd place,
And wooll that still my mortall foo I do beseche of grace.
He lettes me to pursue a conquest well nere woon,
To follow where my paynes wer spilt or that my sute begune.
Lo, by these rules I know how sone a hart can turne   15
From warr to peace, from trewce to stryf, and so again returne.
I knowe how to convert my will in others lust;
Of litle stuff unto my self to weyve a webb of trust;
And how to hide my harme with soft dissembled chere,
When in my face the paynted thoughtes wolde owtwardlye
    appere.   20
I know how that the blood for sakes the faas for dredd,
And how by shame it staynes agayne the chekes with flaming
    redd.
I knowe under the grene, the serpent how he lurckes;
The hamer of the restles forge, I know eke how yt workes.
I know, and can be roote, the tale that I wold tell,   25
But ofte the wordes come forth a wrye of hym that loveth well.
I know in heat and cold the lover how he shakes,
In singinge how he can complayne, in sleaping how he wakes,

---

6. *ledden cold:* cold lead
7. *easye:* slight
8. *unegall:* unequal; *ame:* guess
9. *fourde:* ford, crossing
12. *wooll:* wills, desires
13. *lettes:* hinders; *well . . . woon:* almost won
14. *spilt or that:* were wasted before
17. *in . . . lust:* so that it may serve others' pleasures
18. *weyve:* weave
20. *paynted:* disguised
21. *faas for dredd:* face when one is afraid
25. *can be roote:* know by heart

To languishe without ache, sickles for to consume,
A thousand thinges for to devyse resolving all in fumc.   30
   And thoughe he lyke to see his ladies face full sore,
Suche pleasure as delightes his eye doth not his health restore.
   I know to seke the tracke of my desyred foo,
And feare to fynd that I do seke; but chefelye this I know,
   That lovers must transforme into the thing beloved,   35
And live—alas (who colde beleve)—with spryte from lief
      removed.
   I know in hartye sighes and lawghters of the splene
At ones to chaunge my state, my will, and eke my colour clene.
   I know how to disceyve myself withouten helpp,
And how the lyon chastysed is by beating of the whelpp.   40
   In standing nere my fyer, I know how that I frese;
Farr of, to burn; in both to wast, and so my lief to lese.
   I know how love doth rage uppon the yeldon mynd,
How small a nett may take and mashe a hart of gentle kynd;
   Which seldome tasted swete, to seasoned heaps of gall,   45
Revyved with a glyns of grace olde sorowes to let fall.
   The hidden traynes I know, and secret snares of love;
How sone a loke may prynt a thought that never will remove.
   That slipper state I know, those sodayne tournes from
      welthe,
That doutfull hope, that certayne woo, and sure dispaire of
      helthe.   50

---

30. *A . . . fume:* Able to devise a thousand things through which he will be able to allay his anguish
33. *desyred foo:* enemy whom I love
36. *spryte:* spirit
37. *lawghters . . . splene:* "forced, melancholy laughter" (Jones). The spleen was considered to be the seat of both mirth and melancholy.
38. *clene:* completely
40. *lyon . . . whelpp:* i.e., the lion will learn to obey by watching a puppy being punished. The Howard coat of arms contained a lion.
42. *of:* off; *lief to lese:* life to lose
43. *yeldon:* submissive
44. *kynd:* nature
46. *glyns:* glimpse; *let fall:* relate
47. *traynes:* seductions
48. *prynt:* imprint
49. *slipper state:* uncertain condition; *welthe:* happiness

20.

When sommer toke in hand the winter to assail
With force of might & vertue gret, his stormy blasts to quail,
   And when he clothed faire the earth about with grene,
And every tree new garmented, that pleasure was to sene,
   Mine hart gan new revive, and changed blood dyd stur   5
Me to withdraw my winter woe, that kept within the dore.
   Abrode, quod my desire, assay to set thy fote,
Where thou shalt finde the savour swete, for sprong is every
     rote;
   And to thy health, if thou were sick in any case,
Nothing more good than in the spring the aire to fele a
     space.   10
   There shalt thou here and se all kindes of birdes ywrought,
Well tune their voice with warble smal, as nature hath them
     tought.
   Thus pricked me my lust the sluggish house to leave,
And for my health I thought it best suche counsail to receave.
   So on a morrow furth, unwist of any wight,   15
I went to prove how well it would my heavy burden light.
   And when I felt the aire so pleasant round about,
Lorde, to my self how glad I was that I had gotten out.
   There might I see how Ver had every blossom hent,
And eke the new betrothed birdes ycoupled how they went.   20
   And in their songes me thought they thanked nature much
That by her lycence all that yere to love, their happe was such,

---

2. *quail:* subdue
4. *sene:* see
8. *sprong . . . rote:* every root has begun to grow
10. *the aire . . . space:* to feel the air a little bit
11. *ywrought:* produced for the occasion
13. *lust:* desire
15. *unwist . . . wight:* without anyone knowing it
16. *prove:* see; *light:* lighten
19. *Ver:* spring; *hent:* seized upon
20. *new betrothed:* birds chose their mates, so it was said, in February. Cf.
Chaucer, *Parliament of Fowls. ycoupled:* linked
22. *happe:* good fortune

Right as they could devise to chose them feres throughout.
With much rejoysing to their Lord thus flew they all about.
　Which when I gan resolve, and in my head conceave,　25
What pleasant life, what heapes of joy, these litle birdes receve,
　And sawe in what estate I, wery man, was brought,
By want of that they had at will, and I reject at nought,
　Lorde, how I gan in wrath unwisely me demeane.
I curssed love, and him defined; I thought to turne the
　　streame.　　30
　But whan I well behelde he had me under awe,
I asked mercie for my fault that so transgrest his law.
　Thou blinded god, quod I, forgeve me this offense;
Unwillingly I went about to malice thy pretense.
　Wherewith he gave a beck, and thus me thought he
　　swore:　　35
Thy sorow ought suffice to purge thy faulte, if it were more.
　The vertue of which sounde mine hart did so revive
That I me thought was made as hole as any man alive.
　But here ye may perceive mine errour all and some,
For that I thought that so it was, yet was it still undone;　40
　And all that was no more but mine empressed mynde,
That fayne woulde have some good relefe of Cupide wel
　　assinde.
　I turned home forthwith, and might perceive it well,
That he agreved was right sore with me for my rebell.
　My harmes have ever since increased more and more,　45
And I remaine, without his help, undone for ever more.
　A miror let me be unto ye lovers all:
Strive not with love, for if ye do, it will ye thus befall.

---

23. *feres:* mates
25. *gan resolve:* began to think about. The correct reading here may be *revolve,* i.e., turn over in my mind.
28. *at will:* when they wanted it; *reject at nought:* despised
29. *gan:* began; *me demeane:* to behave myself
34. *Unwillingly:* some editors emend to *Unwittingly. malice thy pretense:* cast aspersions on your authority
35. *beck:* nod
36. *if . . . more:* even if it were greater
37. *vertue:* strength, solace
40. *For:* Despite the fact; *undone:* not performed
41. *empressed:* depressed
44. *he . . . sore:* Cupid was very disturbed; *rebell:* revolt
45. *harmes:* pains, sorrows

21.

In winters just returne, when Boreas gan his raigne,
And every tree unclothed fast, as nature taught them plaine,
  In misty morning darke, as sheepe are then in holde,
I hyed me fast, it sat me on, my sheepe for to unfolde.
  And as it is a thing that lovers have by fittes,   5
Under a palm I heard one crye as he had lost hys wittes.
  Whose voice did ring so shrill, in uttering of his plaint,
That I amazed was to hear how love could hym attaint.
  Ah wretched man, quod he, come death, and ridde thys wo;
A just reward, a happy end, if it may chaunce thee so.   10
  Thy pleasures past have wrought thy wo without redresse;
If thou hadst never felt no joy, thy smart had bene the lesse.
  And retchlesse of his life, he gan both sighe and grone;
A rufull thing me thought it was to hear him make such mone.
  Thou cursed pen, sayd he, wo worth the bird thee bare;   15
The man, the knife, and all that made thee, wo be to their
      share.
  Wo worth the time, and place, where I so could endite,
And wo be it yet once agayne, the pen that so can write.
  Unhappy hand, it had ben happy time for me
If, when to write thou learned first, unjoynted hadst thou
      be.   20
  Thus cursed he himself, and every other wight,
Save her alone whom love him bound to serve both day and
      night.

---

1. *Boreas:* the North Wind
2. *unclothed:* lost its leaves
3. *as:* when; *holde:* their pen
4. *it . . . on:* it was urgent
6. *palm:* willow
8. *attaint:* affect
13. *retchlesse:* careless
15. *wo worth:* may woe befall; *bird:* because the pen was made from its quill

Which when I heard, and saw, how he himself fordid,
Against the ground, with bloudy strokes, himself even therc to
    rid,
Had ben my heart of flint, it must have melted tho, 25
For in my life I never saw a man so full of wo.
With teares, for his redresse, I rashly to him ran
And in my arms I caught him fast, and thus I spake hym than:
    What wofull wight art thou, that in such heavy case
Tormentes thy selfe with such despite, here in this desert
    place? 30
Wherewith, as all agast, fulfild wyth ire and dred,
He cast on me a staring loke, with colour pale and ded.
    Nay, what art thou, quod he, that in this heavy plight
Doest finde me here, most wofull wretch, that life hath in
    despight?
I am, quoth I, but poore, and simple in degre; 35
A shepardes charge I have in hand, unworthy though I be.
    With that he gave a sighe, as though the skye should fall,
And lowd, alas! he shryked oft, and Shepard gan he call,
    Come, hie the fast at ones, and print it in thy hart;
So thou shalt know, and I shall tell the, giltlesse how I
    smart." 40
His backe against the tree, sore febled all with faint,
With weary sprite hee stretcht him up, and thus hee told his
    plaint.
Ones in my hart, quoth he, it chanced me to love
Such one, in whom hath nature wrought her cunning for to
    prove.
And sure I can not say, but many yeres were spent 45
With such good will so recompenst, as both we were content.

---

23. *fordid:* destroyed
24. *rid:* kill
25. *tho:* then
27. *rashly:* quickly
31. *fulfild:* filled full
38. *shryked:* shrieked
44. *cunning:* masterly knowledge

Wherto then I me bound, and she likewise also,
The sonne should runne his course awry, ere we this faith forgo.
Who joied then, but I, who had this worldes blisse?
Who might compare a life to mine, that never thought on
    this? 50
But dwelling in thys truth, amid my greatest joy,
Is me befallen a greater losse than Priam had of Troy:
She is reversed clene, and beareth me in hand
That my desertes have given her cause to break thys faithful
    band.
And for my just excuse availeth no defense. 55
Now knowest thou all, I can no more. But shepard hye the
    hense
And give him leave to die that may no lenger live.
Whose record, lo, I claime to have, my death, I doe forgive.
And eke, when I am gone, be bolde to speake it plain:
Thou hast seen dye the truest man that ever love did pain. 60
Wherwith he turned him round, and gasping oft for breath,
Into his armes a tree he raught, and sayd, Welcome my death,
    Welcome a thousand fold, now dearer unto me
Than should, without her love to live, an emperour to be.
Thus, in this wofull state, he yelded up the ghost, 65
And little knoweth his lady, what a lover she hath lost.
Whose death when I beheld, no marvail was it, right
For pitie though my heart did blede, to see so piteous sight.
My blood from heat to colde oft changed wonders sore;
A thousand troubles there I found I never knew before. 70
Twene dread and dolour so my sprites were brought in feare,
That long it was ere I could call to minde what I did there.
But, as eche thing hath end, so had these paynes of mine:
The furies past, and I my wits restord by length of time.

---

53. *beareth . . . hand:* claims
54. *desertes:* deeds (deserving of punishment); *band:* bond
58. *record:* witness, testimony (of the shepherd); *claime:* ask
62. *raught:* grasped
67. *right:* right then, at once
69. *wonders:* wondrous
71. *Twene:* Between

Then, as I could devise, to seke I thought it best   75
Where I might finde some worthy place for such a corse to rest.
    And in my mind it came, from thence not farre away,
Where Chreseids love, king Priams sonne, ye worthy Troilus
        lay.
    By him I made his tomb, in token he was treew,
And as to him belonged well, I covered it with bleew.   80
    Whose soule, by Angels power, departed not so sone
But to the heavens, lo, it fled, for to receive his dome.

22.

O Happie dames, that may embrace
The frewte of your delight,
Helpp to bewayle the wofull case
And eke the heavie plight
Of me, that wonted to rejoyce   5
The fortune of my pleasaunt choyce.
Good Ladies, helpp to fill my mourning voyce.

In a ship, fraught with rememberaunce
Of wordes and pleasures past,
He sayles that hath in governaunce   10
My lyf, whyle it will last;
With scyalding sighes, for lack of gaile,
Furthering his hope, that is his sail,
Towarde me, the sweete port of his availe.

---

76. *corse:* corpse
78. *Troilus:* cf. Chaucer, *Troilus and Criseyde*
79. *treew:* true
80. *bleew:* blue symbolized steadfastness
81–82. *soule . . . fled:* i.e., as soon as his soul departed, it fled, by angels'
power, at once to the heavens. *dome:* judgment
No. 22. Probably written for Surrey's wife. He was separated from her while
he served in France during the 1540s.
7. *helpp . . . voyce:* join me in my lament
14. *availe:* help

Alas! how oft in dreames I see   15
Those eyes that were my foode,
Whiche somtyme so rejoyced me
That yet they do me good;
Whearwith I wake with his retourne,
Whose absente flame did make me bourne.   20
But when I fynde the lack, Lord how I mourne!

When other lovers, in armes acrosse,
Rejoyce their chief delight,
Drowned in teares, to mourne my losse,
I stand the bitter night   25
In my windowe, wheare I may se
Before the wyndes how the clowds flye.
Lo, what a maryner Love hath made me!

And in green waves, when the salt floodd
Dothe rise by rage of wynde,   30
A thousand fancyes in that moode
Assayles my restlesse mynde.
Now feare I drenchith my swete foe,
That with spoyle of my hert did goe,
And left me; but, alas, whye did he so?   35

And when the seas wexe calme agayne,
To chace from me anoye,
My doubtful hope dothe cause me playne;
So dread cutts of my joye.
Thus ys my wealth myngled with woe,   40
And of each thought a doubt doth groe:
Now he comes, will he come? alas, no, no!

23.

Wyat resteth here, that quicke coulde never rest;
Whose hevenly gyftes encreased by dysdayne

---

22. *in . . . acrosse:* embracing
33. *drenchith . . . foe:* that my "sweet enemy" is drowned
No. 23. This poem was published in 1542, shortly after Wyatt's death.
1. *quicke:* while he was alive
2. *by dysdayne:* probably the disdain of others, not Wyatt's disdain for
them

And vertue sanke the deper in his brest:
Suche profyte he of envy could optayne.

A Head, where wysdom mysteries dyd frame;   5
Whose hammers beat styll in that lyvely brayne
As on a styth, where some worke of Fame
Was dayly wrought, to turn to Brytayns gayne.

A Vysage, sterne and mylde; where both dyd groo,
Vyce to contempne, in vertues to rejoyce;   10
Amyd great stormes whom grace assured soo
To lyve uprighte and smyle at fortunes choyse.

A Hand that taught what might be saide in rime;
That refte Chaucer the glorye of his wytte;
A marke the whiche (unperfited, for tyme)—   15
Some may approche, but never none shall hyt.

A Tonge that served in foraine realmes his king;
Whose curtoise talke to vertue dyd enflame
Eche noble harte, a worthy guyde to brynge
Our Englysshe youth, by travayle unto fame.   20

An eye whose judgement no affect coulde blind,
Frendes to allure, and foes to reconcyle;
Whose pearcynge looke dyd represent a mynde
With vertue fraught, reposed, voyde of gyle.

A Harte where drede yet never so imprest   25
To hide the thought that might the trouth avaunce;
In neyther fortune lyfte, nor so represt,
To swell in wealth, or yelde unto mischaunce.

---

5. *mysteries:* hidden meanings
7. *styth:* anvil
9. *both:* sternness and mildness; *groo:* grow
14. *refte:* took from
18. *curtoise:* courteous
21. *affect:* passion
25. *drede:* fear
27. *neyther fortune:* neither in happiness (*wealth,* line 28) nor in misfor-
tune (*mischance*); *lyfte:* elated

A valiaunt Corps, where force and beautye met,
Happy, alas! to happy, but for foos,   30
Lyved, and ran the race that nature set;
Of manhodes shape, where she the mold did loos.

But to the heavens that symple soule is fleed;
Which lefte with such, as covet Christ to knowe
Witnes of faith that never shalbe deade: 35
Sent for our welth, but not received so.

Thus, for our gylt, this jewell have we lost;
The earth his bones, the heavens possesse his goost.
AMEN.

24.

When ragyng love with extreme payne,
Most cruelly distrains my hart;
When that my teares, as floudes of rayne,
Beare witnes to my wofull smart;
When sighes have wasted so my breath   5
That I lye at the poynte of death:

I call to minde the navye greate
That the Grekes brought to Troye towne,
And how the boysteous windes did beate
Their shyps, and rente their sayles adowne,   10
Till Agamemnons daughters bloode
Appeasde the goddes that them withstode.

And how that in those ten yeres warre,
Full many a bloudye dede was done,

---

29. *Corps:* body
30. *to:* too; *but for foos:* if it were not for his enemies
32. *loos:* lose
33. *fleed:* fled
35. *Witnes:* Wyatt's translation of the penitential Psalms
2. *distrains:* pains, torments
9. *boysteous:* boisterous
11. *Agamemnons daughters:* Iphigenia's. She was sacrificed by the Greeks.

And many a lord, that came full farre,   15
There caught his bane (alas) to sone,
And many a good knight overronne;
Before the Grekes had Helene wonne.

Then thinke I thus: sithe suche repayre,
So longe time warre of valiant men,   20
Was all to winne a ladye fayre,
Shall I not learne to suffer then,
And thinke my life well spent to be
Servyng a worthier wight than she?

Therfore I never will repent,   25
But paynes, contented, stil endure:
For like as when, rough winter spent,
The pleasant spring straight draweth in ure,
So after ragyng stormes of care,
Joyful at length may be my fare.   30

25.

Geve place, ye lovers, here before
That spent your bostes and bragges in vaine;
My Ladies beawtie passeth more
The best of yours, I dare well sayen,
Than doth the sonne the candle light,   5
Or brightest day the darkest night.

And thereto-hath a trothe as just
As had Penelope the fayre,
For what she saith, ye may it trust
As it by writing sealed were;   10
And vertues hath she many moe
Than I with pen have skill to showe.

---

16. *bane:* death
19. *repayre:* a large host
28. *draweth in ure:* comes into existence
7. *trothe:* truth
8. *Penelope:* Ulysses' wife in the *Odyssey*
11. *moe:* more

I could rehearse, if that I wolde,
The whole effect of natures plaint
When she had lost the perfit mold,   15
The like to whom she could not paint;
With wringyng handes howe she dyd cry,
And what she said, I know it, I.

I knowe she swore with ragyng mynd,
Her kingdom onely set apart,   20
There was no losse, by lawe of kind,
That could have gone so nere her hart.
And this was chiefly all her payne,
She coulde not make the lyke agayne.

Sith nature thus gave her the prayse   25
To be the chiefest worke she wrought,
In faith, me thinke some better waies
On your behalfe might well be sought,
Then to compare (as ye have done)
To matche the candle with the sonne.   30

26.

Though I regarded not
The promise made by me,
Or passed not to spot
My faith and honeste,
Yet were my fancie strange   5
And wilful will to wite,
If I sought now to change
A falkon for a kite.

All men might well dispraise
My wit and enterprise,   10

---

21. *lawe of kind:* natural law
2. *by:* concerning
3. *passed:* cared; *spot:* stain
6. *wite:* blame

If I estemed a pese
Above a perle in price,
Or judged the oule in sight
The sparehauke to excell,
Which flieth but in the night,   15
As all men know right well.

Or if I sought to saile
In the brittle port
Where anker hold doth faile,
To such as doe resort,   20
And leave the haven sure
Where blowes no blustring winde,
Nor fickelnesse in ure,
So farforth as I finde.

No, thinke me not so light   25
Nor of so chorlish kinde,
Though it lay in my might
My bondage to unbinde,
That I would leve the hinde
To hunt the ganders fo.   30
No, no! I have no minde
To make exchanges so,

Nor yet to change at all.
For think it may not be
That I should seke to fall   35
From my felicite,
Desyrous for to win,
And loth for to forgo,
Or new change to begin.
How may all this be so?   40

---

12. *pese:* pea
14. *sparehauke:* sparrow hawk
20. *resort:* land there
23. *Nor . . . ure:* Where fickleness isn't practiced
26. *chorlish:* churlish, peasantlike
29. *hinde:* deer (with the usual pun on "dear")
30. *ganders fo:* presumably, the fox

The fire it can not freze,
For it is not his kinde,
Nor true love cannot lese
The constance of the minde;
Yet as sone shall the fire   45
Want heat to blaze and burn,
As I in such desire
Have once a thought to turne.

27.

My Ratclif, when thy retchlesse youth offendes:
Receve thy scourge by others chastisement.
For such callyng, when it workes none amendes:
Then plages are sent without advertisement.
Yet Salomon sayd, the wronged shall recure: 5
But Wiat said true, the skarre doth aye endure.

---

42. *his kinde:* its nature
43. *lese:* lose
44. *constance:* constancy
46. *Want:* Lack
1. *Ratclif:* probably Thomas Radcliffe, third Earl of Essex; *retchlesse:* heedless
3. *callyng:* summoning; *none:* no
4. *advertisement:* warning
5. *Salomon:* probably an allusion to Ecclesiasticus. This apocryphal book was popularly attributed to Solomon, though it was written by Jesus, son of Sirach. *recure:* recover, be compensated
6. *Wiat:* alluding to Wyatt's "Syghes ar my foode, drynke are my teares," No. CCXLIV in the Muir-Thompson edition. The eighth and last line of this epigram reads: "But yet, alas, the scarre shall styll remayne."

THOMAS SACKVILLE, EARL OF DORSET

1536–1608

A MIRROR FOR MAGISTRATES

To the Reader

When I had read this, one sayd it was very darke, and
hard to be understood: excepte it were diligently and
very leasurely considered. I like it the better (quote an
other). For that shal cause it to be the oftener reade,
and the better remembred. Considering also that it is   5
written for the learned (for such all Magistrates are or
should be) it can not be to hard, so long as it is sound
and learnedly wrytten. Then sayd the reader: The next
here whom I finde miserable are king Edwards two
sonnes, cruelly murdered in the tower of London: Have   10
you theyr tragedy? No surely (quoth I) The Lord
Vaulz undertooke to penne it, but what he hath done
therein I am not certayne, & therfore I let it passe til
I knowe farder. I have here the duke of Buckingham,
king Richardes chyefe instrument, wrytten by mayster   15

TO THE READER: One of the prose links placed between the tragedies of
the *Mirror* by William Baldwin, the general editor.
1. *this:* "The Tragedy of the Lord Hastings," by John Dolman, which im-
mediately precedes this passage in the 1563 edition
9–10. *Edwards two sonnes:* Edward V (1470–83) and Richard, Duke of
York (1473–83)
11–12. *Lord Vaulz:* Thomas Lord Vaux (1510–56) who contributed sev-
eral poems to *Tottel's Miscellany* (1557)
14. *Buckingham:* Henry, second Duke of Buckingham (1454–83)
15. *instrument:* supporter, accomplice

Thomas Sackville. Read it we pray you sayd they: with a good wyl (quoth I) but fyrst you shal heare his preface or Induction. Hath he made a preface? (quoth one) What meaneth he thereby, seeing none other hath used the like order? I wyl tell you the cause thereof (quoth 20 I) which is thys: After that he understoode that some of the counsayle would not suffer the booke to be printed in suche order as we had agreed and determined, he purposed with him selfe to have gotten at my handes, al the tragedies that were before the duke 25 of Buckinghams, which he would have preserved in one volume. And from that time backeward even to the time of William the conquerour, he determined to continue and perfect all the story him selfe, in such order as Lydgate (folowing Bocchas) had already used. 30 And therfore to make a meete induction into the matter, he devised this poesye: which in my judgement is so wel penned, that I would not have any verse therof left out of our volume. Nowe that you knowe the cause and meanyng of his doing, you shal also heare what 35 he hath done. His Induccion beginneth thus.

1.

A MIRROR FOR MAGISTRATES

The Induction

The wrathfull winter prochinge on a pace,
With blustring blastes had al ybared the treen,

19–20. *seeing . . . order:* since no other author has introduced his tragedy in this way
21–22. *some of the counsayle:* plans for printing the *Mirror* were made early in Mary's reign; but the first (1555) edition was suppressed, presumably because it used anti-Catholic material from Halle's *Chronicle*
30. *Lydgate:* whose translation of Boccaccio's *De Casibus, The Fall of Princes,* had been published in 1554
31. *meete:* suitable
1. *prochinge . . . pace:* approaching quickly
2. *ybared the treen:* stripped the trees bare

And olde Saturnus with his frosty face
With chilling colde had pearst the tender green:
The mantels rent, wherein enwrapped been   5
The gladsom groves that nowe laye overthrowen,
The tapets torne, and every blome downe blowen.

The soyle that earst so seemely was to seen
Was all despoyled of her beauties hewe:
And soot freshe flowers (wherwith the sommers queen   10
Had clad the earth) now Boreas blastes downe blewe.
And small fowles flocking, in theyr song did rewe
The winters wrath, wherwith eche thing defaste
In woful wise bewayld the sommer past.

Hawthorne had lost his motley lyverye,   15
The naked twigges were shivering all for colde:
And dropping downe the teares abundantly,
Eche thing (me thought) with weping eye me tolde
The cruell season, bidding me withholde
My selfe within, for I was gotten out   20
Into the fields where as I walkte about.

When loe the night with mistie mantels spred
Gan darke the daye, and dim the azure skyes,
And Venus in her message Hermes sped
To bluddy Mars, to wyl him not to ryse,   25
While she her selfe approcht in speedy wise:
And Virgo hiding her disdaineful brest
With Thetis nowe had layd her downe to rest.

---

7. *tapets:* foliage (lit. tapestries); *blome:* blossom
8. *seen:* be seen
10. *soot:* sweet
11. *Boreas:* the North Wind's
12. *fowles:* birds
13. *defaste:* defaced
15. *motley:* parti-colored
23. *Gan darke:* Began to darken
24–49. Sackville sets his scene in terms of the planetary (and astrological)
configurations that prevail during the winter months. This convention goes
back at least to Chaucer.
24. *in . . . sped:* sent Mercury with her message

Whiles Scorpio dreading Sagittarius dart,
Whose bowe prest bent in sight, the string had slypt,   30
Downe slyd into the Ocean flud aparte,
The Beare that in the Iryshe seas had dipt
His griesly feete, with spede from thence he whypt:
For Thetis hasting from the Virgines bed,
Pursued the Bear, that ear she came was fled.   35

And Phaeton nowe, neare reaching to his race
With glistering beames, gold streamynge where they bent,
Was prest to enter in his resting place.
Erythius that in the cart fyrste went
Had even nowe attaynde his journeyes stent.   40
And fast declining hid away his head,
While Titan couched him in his purple bed.

And pale Cinthea with her borowed light
Beginning to supply her brothers place,
Was past the Noonesteede syxe degrees in sight   45
When sparklyng starres amyd the heavens face
With twinkling light shoen on the earth apace,
That whyle they brought about the nightes chare,
The darke had dimmed the daye ear I was ware.

And sorowing I to see the sommer flowers,   50
The lively greene, the lusty leas forlorne,
The sturdy trees so shattered with the showers,
The fieldes so fade that floorisht so beforne,

---

30. *prest:* ready
32. *The Beare:* Ursa Major
33. *griesly:* gruesome, horrible
35. *ear:* before
36. *Phaeton:* the sun; *neare . . . race:* reaching the end of his daily course
39. *Erythius:* Erythraeus, one of the four horses of the sun's chariot ("cart")
40. *stent:* end
43. *Cinthea:* the moon
45. *Noonesteede:* position of the sun at noon
47. *shoen:* shone; *apace:* directly
48. *nightes chare:* the Big Dipper
51. *lusty leas:* pleasant meadows
53. *fade:* faded; *beforne:* before

It taught me wel all earthly thinges be borne
To dye the death, for nought long time may last.   55
The sommers beauty yeeldes to winters blast.

Then looking upward to the heavens leames
With nightes starres thicke powdred every where,
Which erst so glistened with the golden streames
That chearefull Phebus spred downe from his sphere,   60
Beholding darke oppressing day so neare:
The sodayne sight reduced to my minde,
The sundry chaunges that in earth we fynde.

That musing on this worldly wealth in thought,
Which comes and goes more faster than we see   65
The flyckering flame that with the fyer is wrought,
My busie minde presented unto me
Such fall of pieres as in this realme had be:
That ofte I wisht some would their woes descryve.
To warne the rest whom fortune left alive.   70

And strayt forth stalking with redoubled pace
For that I sawe the night drewe on so fast,
In blacke all clad there fell before my face
A piteous wight, whom woe had al forwaste,
Furth from her iyen the cristall teares outbrast,   75
And syghing sore her handes she wrong and folde,
Tare al her heare that ruth was to beholde.

Her body small forwithered and forespent,
As is the stalke that sommers drought opprest,

---

57. *leames:* rays of light
58. *powdred:* sprinkled
59. *erst:* before
60. *Phebus:* Apollo, the sun
62. *reduced:* recalled
68. *pieres:* peers, noblemen
69. *descryve:* describe
74. *piteous wight:* pitiful creature; *al forwaste:* completely wasted away
75. *iyen:* eyes; *outbrast:* burst forth
76. *wrong and folde:* wrung and folded
77. *Tare . . . heare:* Tore . . . hair
78. *forwithered and forespent:* totally withered and worn out

Her wealked face with woful teares besprent,   80
Her colour pale, and (as it seemed her best)
In woe and playnt reposed was her rest.
And as the stone that droppes of water weares,
So dented were her cheekes with fall of teares.

Her iyes swollen with flowing streames aflote,   85
Wherewith her lookes throwen up full piteouslye,
Her forceles handes together ofte she smote,
With dolefull shrikes, that eckoed in the skye:
Whose playnt such sighes dyd strayt accompany,
That in my doome was never man did see   90
A wight but halfe so woe begon as she.

I stoode agast beholding all her plight,
Tweene dread and dolour so distreynd in hart
That while my heares upstarted with the sight,
The teares out streamde for sorowe of her smart: 95
But when I sawe no ende that could aparte
The deadly dewle, which she so sore dyd make,
With dolefull voice then thus to her I spake.

Unwrap thy woes what ever wight thou be
And stint betime to spill thy selfe wyth playnt,   100
Tell what thou art, and whence, for well I see
Thou canst not dure wyth sorowe thus attaynt.
And with that worde, of sorrowe all forfaynt,
She looked up, and prostrate as she laye
With piteous sound loe thus she gan to saye.   105

---

80. *wealked:* dried-up; *besprent:* sprinkled
87. *forceles:* feeble
88. *shrikes:* shrieks
90. *doome:* judgment
93. *distreynd:* torn apart
96. *aparte:* separate, cause to cease
97. *dewle:* lamentation
100. *stint . . . selfe:* stop, right now, this effort to kill yourself
102. *dure:* last; *attaynt:* afflicted
103. *forfaynt:* exhausted

Alas, I wretche whom thus thou seest distreyned
With wasting woes that never shall aslake,
Sorrowe I am, in endeles tormentes payned,
Among the furies in the infernall lake:
Where Pluto god of Hel so griesly blacke   110
Doth holde his throne and *Letheus* deadly taste
Doth rieve remembraunce of eche thyng forepast.

Whence come I am, the drery destinie
And luckeles lot for to bemone of those,
Whom Fortune in this maze of miserie   115
Of wretched chaunce most wofull myrrours chose
That when thou seest how lightly they did lose
Theyr pompe, theyr power, & that they thought most sure,
Thou mayest soone deeme no earthly joye may dure.

Whose rufull voyce no sooner had out brayed   120
Those wofull wordes, wherewith she sorrowed so,
But out alas she shryght and never stayed,
Fell downe, and all to dasht her selfe for woe.
The colde pale dread my lyms gan overgo,
And I so sorrowed at her sorowes eft,   125
That what with griefe and feare my wittes were reft.

I strecht my selfe, and strayt my hart revives,
That dread and dolour erst did so appale,
Lyke him that with the fervent fever stryves
When sickenes seekes his castell health to skale: 130

---

107. *aslake:* diminish
111. *Letheus:* the river Lethe
112. *rieve remembraunce:* take away the memory
117. *lightly:* easily
120. *out brayed:* breathed out
122. *out . . . shryght:* "Out, alas!," she shrieked; *never stayed:* i.e., instantly
123. *all . . . selfe:* dashed herself all to pieces
125. *eft:* in turn
126. *reft:* taken from me
128. *erst:* formerly; *appale:* make pale, appall
130. *his . . . health:* the castle of his health

With gathered spirites so forst I feare to avale.
And rearing her with anguishe all fordone,
My spirits returnd, and then I thus begonne.

O Sorrowe, alas, sith Sorrowe is thy name,
And that to thee this drere doth well pertayne,   135
In vayne it were to seeke to ceas the same:
But as a man hym selfe with sorrowe slayne,
So I alas do comfort thee in payne,
That here in sorrowe art forsonke so depe
That at thy sight I can but sigh and wepe.   140

I had no sooner spoken of a syke
But that the storme so rumbled in her brest,
As Eolus could never roare the like,
And showers downe rayned from her iyen so fast,
That all bedreynt the place, till at the last   145
Well eased they the dolour of her minde,
As rage of rayne doth swage the stormy wynde.

For furth she paced in her fearfull tale:
Cum, cum, (quod she) and see what I shall shewe,
Cum heare the playning, and the bytter bale   150
Of worthy men, by Fortune overthrowe.
Cum thou and see them rewing al in rowe.
They were but shades that erst in minde thou rolde.
Cum, cum with me, thine iyes shall them beholde.

---

131. *avale:* yield
132. *all fordone:* i.e., she was completely exhausted
134. *sith:* since
135. *drere:* gloom
139. *forsonke:* plunged
141. *syke:* sigh
143. *Eolus:* Aeolus, the god of the winds
145. *all . . . place:* the ground was soaked
147. *swage:* assuage
150. *bale:* pain, woe
152. *rewing:* regretting bitterly
153. *They . . . rolde:* When you first saw them in your mind's eye, they were only shadows

What could these wordes but make me more agast?   155
To heare her tell whereon I musde while eare?
So was I mazed therewyth, tyll at the last,
Musing upon her wurdes, and what they were,
All sodaynly well lessoned was my feare:
For to my minde returned howe she telde   160
Both what she was, and where her wun she helde.

Whereby I knewe that she a Goddesse was,
And therewithall resorted to my minde
My thought that late presented me the glas
Of brittle state, of cares that here we finde,   165
Of thousand woes to silly men assynde:
And howe she nowe byd me come and beholde,
To see with iye that erst in thought I rolde.

Flat downe I fell, and with al reverence
Adored her, perceyving nowe that she   170
A Goddesse sent by godly providence,
In earthly shape thus showed her selfe to me,
To wayle and rue this worldes uncertayntye:
And while I honourd thus her godheds might,
With playning voyce these wurdes to me she shryght.   175

I shal the guyde first to the griesly lake,
And thence unto the blisfull place of rest.
Where thou shalt see and heare the playnt they make,
That whilom here bare swinge among the best.
This shalt thou see, but great is the unrest   180
That thou must byde before thou canst attayne
Unto the dreadfull place where these remayne.

---

156. *while eare:* formerly. Cf. above, lines 68–70.
157. *mazed:* amazed
160. *telde:* told
161. *wun:* dwelling
163. *resorted:* came back
166. *silly:* innocent
179. *whilom:* once; *swinge:* full sway

224

And with these wurdes as I upraysed stood,
And gan to folowe her that strayght furth paced,
Eare I was ware, into a desert wood   185
We nowe were cum: where hand in hand imbraced,
She led the way, and through the thicke so traced,
As, but I had bene guyded by her might,
It was no waye for any mortall wight.

But loe, while thus amid the desert darke,   190
We passed on with steppes and pace unmete:
A rumbling roar confusde with howle and barke
Of Dogs, shoke all the ground under our feete,
And stroke the din within our eares so deepe,
As halfe distraught unto the ground I fell,   195
Besought retourne, and not to visite hell.

But she forthwith uplifting me apace
Removed my dread, and with a stedfast minde
Bad me come on, for here was now the place,
The place where we our travayle ende should finde.   200
Wherewith I arose, and to the place assynde
Astoynde I stalke, when strayt we approched nere
The dredfull place, that you wil dread to here.

An hydeous hole al vaste, withouten shape,
Of endles depth, orewhelmde with ragged stone,   205
Wyth ougly mouth, and grisly Jawes doth gape,
And to our sight confounds it selfe in one.
Here entred we, and yeding forth, anone
An horrible lothly lake we might discerne
As blacke as pitche, that cleped is Averne.   210

183. *upraysed stood:* raised myself up
187. *She led the way:* Sackville's Sorrow plays the part of the Cumaean sibyl who led Virgil's Aeneas down to the underworld (*Aeneid,* VI); *thicke:* thickest part of the woods
188. *but:* unless
190. *desert:* i.e., wilderness
191. *unmete:* unevenly matched
194. *stroke:* struck
202. *Astoynde:* Stunned; *stalke:* walk softly
208. *yeding:* going (one of Sackville's pseudo-archaisms)
210. *cleped is Averne:* is called Avernus

A deadly gulfe where nought but rubbishe growes,
With fowle blacke swelth in thickned lumpes that lyes,
Which up in the ayer such stinking vapors throwes
That over there may flye no fowle but dyes,
Choakt with the pestilent savours that aryse.   215
Hither we cum, whence forth we still dyd pace,
In dreadful feare amid the dreadfull place.

And first within the portche and jawes of Hell
Sate diepe Remorse of conscience, al besprent
With teares: and to her selfe oft would she tell   220
Her wretchednes, and cursing never stent
To sob and sigh: but ever thus lament,
With thoughtful care, as she that all in vayne
Would weare and waste continually in payne.

Her iyes unstedfast rolling here and there,   225
Whurld on eche place, as place that vengeaunce brought,
So was her minde continually in feare,
Tossed and tormented with the tedious thought
Of those detested crymes which she had wrought:
With dreadful cheare and lookes throwen to the skye,   230
Wyshyng for death, and yet she could not dye.

Next sawe we Dread al tremblyng how he shooke,
With foote uncertayne profered here and there:
Benumde of speache, and with a gastly looke
Searcht every place al pale and dead for feare,   235
His cap borne up with staring of his heare,
Stoynde and amazde at his owne shade for dreed,
And fearing greater daungers than was nede.

---

212. *swelth:* foul water
214. *there:* i.e., it
219. *besprent:* drenched
221. *stent:* cease
228. *tedious:* painful
230. *cheare:* countenance
236. *staring . . . heare:* his hair standing on end
237. *shade:* shadow

226

And next within the entry of this lake
Sate fell Revenge gnashing her teeth for yre,   240
Devising meanes howe she may vengeaunce take,
Never in rest tyll she have her desire:
But frets within so farforth with the fyer
Of wreaking flames, that nowe determines she,
To dye by death, or vengde by death to be.   245

When fell Revenge with bloudy foule pretence
Had showed her selfe as next in order set,
With trembling limmes we softly parted thence,
Tyll in our iyes another sight we met:
When fro my hart a sigh forthwith I fet   250
Rewing alas upon the wofull plight
Of Miserie, that next appered in sight.

His face was leane, and sumdeale pyned away,
And eke his handes consumed to the bone,
But what his body was I can not say,   255
For on his carkas, rayment had he none
Save cloutes & patches pieced one by one.
With staffe in hand, and skrip on shoulders cast,
His chiefe defence agaynst the winters blast.

His foode for most, was wylde fruytes of the tree,   260
Unles sumtime sum crummes fell to his share:
Which in his wallet, long God wote kept he.
As on the which full dayntlye would he fare.
His drinke the running streame: his cup the bare
Of his palme closed, his bed the hard colde grounde.   265
To this poore life was Miserie ybound.

---

240. *fell*: cruel
244. *wreaking*: avenging
250. *fet*: fetched
256. *rayment*: garments
257. *cloutes*: pieces of cloth
258. *skrip*: bag, wallet
260. *most*: the most part
262. *wote*: knows

Whose wretched state when we had well behelde
With tender ruth on him and on his feres,
In thoughtful cares, furth then our pace we helde.
And by and by, an other shape apperes   270
Of Greedy care, stil brushing up the breres,
His knuckles knobd, his fleshe deepe dented in,
With tawed handes, and hard ytanned skyn.

The morrowe graye no sooner hath begunne
To spreade his light even peping in our iyes,   275
When he is up and to his worke yrunne,
But let the nightes blacke mistye mantels rise,
And with fowle darke never so much disguyse
The fayre bright day, yet ceasseth he no whyle,
But hath his candels to prolong his toyle.   280

By him lay Heavy slepe the cosin of death
Flat on the ground, and stil as any stone,
A very corps, save yelding forth a breath.
Small kepe tooke he whom Fortune frowned on
Or whom she lifted up into the trone   285
Of high renowne, but as a living death,
So dead alyve, of lyef he drewe the breath.

The bodyes rest, the quyete of the hart,
The travayles ease, the still nightes feer was he.
And of our life in earth the better parte,   290
Rever of sight, and yet in whom we see
Thinges oft that tide, and ofte that never bee.
Without respect esteming equally
Kyng Cresus pompe, and Irus povertie.

---

268. *feres:* companions
271. *breres:* briars
273. *tawed:* lacerated
284. *kepe:* heed
285. *trone:* throne
291. *Rever:* Stealer
292. *tide:* happen
294. *Cresus:* Croesus, the Lydian king (d. 546 B.C.), noted for his great
wealth; *Irus:* the Ithacan beggar in Homer's *Odyssey*

And next in order sad Olde age we found   295
His beard al hoare, his iyes hollow and blynde,
With drouping chere still poring on the ground,
As on the place where nature him assinde
To rest, when that the sisters had untwynde
His vitall threde, and ended with theyr knyfe   300
The fleting course of fast declining life.

There heard we him with broken and hollow playnt
Rewe with him selfe his ende approching fast,
And all for nought his wretched minde torment.
With swete remembraunce of his pleasures past,   305
And freshe delites of lusty youth forwaste.
Recounting which, how would he sob & shrike?
And to be yong againe of Jove beseke.

But and the cruell fates so fixed be
That time forepast can not retourne agayne,   310
This one request of Jove yet prayed he:
That in such withered plight, and wretched paine,
As elde (accompanied with his lothsom trayne.)
Had brought on him, all were it woe and griefe.
He myght a while yet linger forth his lief,   315

And not so soone descend into the pit:
Where death, when he the mortall corps hath slayne,
With retcheles hande in grave doth cover it,
Thereafter never to enjoye agayne
The gladsome light, but in the ground ylayne,   320

---

297. *chere:* face
299. *sisters:* Fates
306. *forwaste:* completely wasted away
309. *and:* if
313. *elde:* old age
318. *retcheles:* careless

In depth of darkenes waste and weare to nought,
As he had never into the world been brought.

But who had seene him sobbing, howe he stoode
Unto him selfe and howe he would bemone
His youth forepast, as though it wrought hym good   325
To talke of youth, al wer his youth foregone,
He would have mused, & mervayld muche whereon
This wretched age should life desyre so fayne,
And knowes ful wel life doth but length his payne.

Crookebackt he was, toothshaken, and blere iyed,   330
Went on three feete, and sometime crept on fower,
With olde lame bones, that ratled by his syde,
His skalpe all pilde, & he with elde forlore:
His withered fist stil knocking at deathes dore,
Fumbling and driveling as he drawes his breth,   335
For briefe the shape and messenger of death.

And fast by him pale Maladie was plaste,
Sore sicke in bed, her colour al forgone,
Bereft of stomake, savor, and of taste,
Ne could she brooke no meat but brothes alone.   340
Her breath corrupt, her kepers every one
Abhorring her, her sickenes past recure,
Detesting phisicke, and all phisickes cure.

But oh the doleful sight that then we see,
We turnde our looke and on the other side   345
A griesly shape of Famine mought we see,
With greedy lookes, and gaping mouth that cryed,
And roard for meat as she should there have dyed,

---

322. *As:* As if
324. *Unto him selfe:* i.e., alone
329. *length:* lengthen
330. *Crookebackt:* Hunchbacked; *toothshaken:* with loose teeth; *blere:* bleary
331. *three:* i.e., with a cane
333. *pilde:* bald; *forlore:* totally lost. Sackville's description here recalls Chaucer's Old Man in "The Pardoner's Tale."
336. *For:* In
337. *plaste:* placed
342. *recure:* recovery
343. *phisicke:* medical treatment
346. *mought:* might

Her body thin and bare as any bone,
Wherto was left nought but the case alone.　　　　350

And that alas was knawen on every where,
All full of holes, that I ne mought refrayne
From teares, to se how she her armes could teare
And with her teeth gnashe on the bones in vayne:
When all for nought she fayne would so sustayne　　355
Her starven corps, that rather seemde a shade,
Then any substaunce of a creature made.

Great was her force whom stonewall could not stay,
Her tearyng nayles snatching at all she sawe:
With gaping Jawes that by no meanes ymay　　　　360
Be satisfyed from hunger of her mawe,
But eates her selfe as she that hath no lawe:
Gnawyng alas her carkas all in vayne,
Where you may count eche sinow, bone, and vayne.

On her while we thus firmely fixt our iyes,　　　　365
That bled for ruth of such a drery sight,
Loe sodaynelye she shryght in so huge wyse,
As made hell gates to shyver with the myght.
Wherewith a darte we sawe howe it did lyght,
Ryght on her brest, and therewithal pale death　　370
Enthryllyng it to reve her of her breath.

And by and by a dum dead corps we sawe,
Heavy and colde, the shape of death aryght,
That dauntes all earthly creatures to his lawe:
Agaynst whose force in vayne it is to fyght　　　　375
Ne piers, ne princes, nor no mortall wyght,

---

350. *case:* shell
351. *knawen:* gnawn
360. *ymay:* may
361. *mawe:* belly
369. *lyght:* stick
371. *Enthryllyng . . . reve:* Piercing her with it to deprive
374. *dauntes:* holds in subjection
376. *piers:* peers, noblemen

No townes, ne realmes, cities, ne strongest tower,
But al perforce must yeeld unto his power.

His Dart anon out of the corps he tooke,
And in his hand (a dreadfull sight to see)   380
With great tryumphe eftsones the same he shooke,
That most of all my feares affrayed me:
His bodie dight with nought but bones perdye
The naked shape of man there sawe I playne,
All save the fleshe, the synowe, and the vayne.   385

Lastly stoode Warre in glitteryng armes yclad.
With visage grym, sterne lookes, and blackely hewed,
In his right hand a naked sworde he had,
That to the hiltes was al with blud embrewed:
And in his left (that kinges and kingdomes rewed)   390
Famine and fyer he held, and therewythall
He razed townes, and threwe downe towers and all.

Cities he sakt, and realmes that whilom flowred,
In honor, glory, and rule above the best,
He overwhelmde, and all theyr fame devowred,   395
Consumed, destroyed, wasted, and never ceast,
Tyll he theyr wealth, theyr name, and all opprest.
His face forhewed with woundes, and by his side,
There hunge his targe with gashes depe and wyde.

In mids of which, depaynted there we founde   400
Deadly debate, al ful of snaky heare,
That with a blouddy fillet was ybound,
Outbrething nought but discord every where.
And round about were portrayd here and there

---

381. *eftsones:* again
382. *affrayed:* frightened
383. *dight:* adorned; *perdye:* pardi, in truth
398. *forhewed:* all gashed
399. *targe:* shield
400. *depaynted:* depicted
401. *debate:* strife
402. *fillet:* headband

The hugie hostes, Darius and his power,   405
His kynges, prynces, his pieres, and all his flower.

Whom great Macedo vanquisht there in sight,
With diepe slaughter, dispoylyng all his pryde,
Pearst through his realmes, and daunted all his might.
Duke Hanniball beheld I there beside,   410
In Cannas field, victor howe he did ride,
And woful Romaynes that in vayne withstoode
And Consull Paulus covered all in blood.

Yet sawe I more the fight at Trasimene.
And Trebey field, and eke when Hanniball   415
And worthy Scipio last in armes were seene
Before Carthago gate, to trye for all
The worldes empyre, to whom it should befal.
There sawe I Pompeye, and Cesar clad in armes,
Theyr hostes alyed and al theyr civil harmes.   420

With conquerours hands forbathde in their owne blood,
And Cesar weping over Pompeyes head.
Yet sawe I Scilla and Marius where they stoode,
Theyr great crueltie, and the diepe bludshed

---

405. *hugie:* immense; *Darius:* king of Persia (d. 330 B.C.), conquered by
Alexander the Great (*Macedo,* line 407)
410. *Hanniball:* Carthaginian leader (247–183 B.C.), who defeated the
Romans at Cannae (216 B.C.). The consul Lucius Paulus had advised
against the battle, but died in it.
414–15. *Trasimene And Trebey:* battles at the Trebbia River (218 B.C.)
and Lake Trasimeno (217 B.C.), both won by Hannibal
415. *eke:* also
416. *Scipio:* Scipio Africanus, who defeated Hannibal in the battle of
Zama (202 B.C.)
419. *Pompeye:* Gnaeus Pompeius Magnus (106–48 B.C.), Caesar's partner,
with Crassus, in the first triumvirate. He later broke with Caesar and was
defeated by him in the battle of Pharsalus (48 B.C.).
420. *alyed:* allied
422. *head:* Pompey, who had fled to Egypt, was murdered there by
Ptolemy's orders and his head sent to Caesar
423. *Scilla and Marius:* Lucius Cornelius Sulla (138–78 B.C.), Roman
dictator; Gaius Marius (155–86 B.C.) or his adopted son of the same name
(109–82 B.C.), both of whom opposed Sulla

Of frendes: Cyrus I sawe and his host dead,   425
And howe the Queene with great despyte hath flonge
His head in bloud of them she overcome.

Xerxes the Percian kyng yet sawe I there
With his huge host that dranke the rivers drye,
Dismounted hilles, and made the vales uprere,   430
His hoste and all yet sawe I slayne perdye.
Thebes I sawe all razde howe it dyd lye
In heapes of stones, and Tyrus put to spoyle,
With walles and towers flat evened with the soyle.

But Troy alas (me thought) above them all,   435
It made myne iyes in very teares consume:
When I beheld the wofull werd befall,
That by the wrathfull wyl of Gods was come:
And Joves unmooved sentence and foredoome
On Priam kyng, and on his towne so bent.   440
I could not lyn, but I must there lament.

And that the more sith destinie was so sterne
As force perforce, there might no force avayle,
But she must fall: and by her fall we learne,
That cities, towres, wealth, world, and al shall quayle.   445
No manhoode, might, nor nothing mought prevayle,
Al were there prest ful many a prynce and piere
And many a knight that solde his death full deere.

---

425. *Cyrus:* Cyrus the Great (d. 529 B.C.). The Scythian queen Tomyris, who had defeated him, threw his head in a bath full of blood.
428. *Xerxes:* Xerxes the Great (519–465 B.C.). Defeated by the Greeks at Plataea (479 B.C.).
430. *Dismounted:* Leveled
432. *Thebes:* destroyed by Philip II of Macedon (382–336 B.C.), the father of Alexander the Great (356–323 B.C.)
433. *Tyrus:* Tyre was sacked by Alexander the Great
437. *werd:* "weird," fate, destiny
439. *foredoome:* judgment meted out beforehand
440. *bent:* directed
441. *lyn:* cease
443. *force perforce:* i.e., in spite of the force exerted by the Trojans
447. *prest:* ready to fight

Not wurthy Hector wurthyest of them all,
Her hope, her joye, his force is nowe for nought.   450
O Troy, Troy, there is no boote but bale,
The hugie horse within thy walles is brought:
Thy turrets fall, thy knightes that whilom fought
In armes amyd the fyeld, are slayne in bed,
Thy Gods defylde, and all thy honour dead.   455

The flames upspring, and cruelly they crepe
From wall to roofe, til all to cindres waste,
Some fyer the houses where the wretches slepe,
Sum rushe in here, sum run in there as fast.
In every where or sworde or fyer they taste.   460
The walles are torne, the towers whurld to the ground,
There is no mischiefe but may there be found.

Cassandra yet there sawe I howe they haled
From Pallas house, with spercled tresse undone,
Her wristes fast bound, and with Greeks rout empaled: 465
And Priam eke in vayne howe he did runne
To armes, whom Pyrrhus with despite hath done
To cruel death, and bathed him in the bayne
Of his sonnes blud before the altare slayne.

But howe can I descryve the doleful sight,   470
That in the shylde so livelike fayer did shyne?
Sith in this world I thinke was never wyght
Could have set furth the halfe, not halfe so fyne.
I can no more but tell howe there is seene

449–76. Sackville follows Virgil's narrative in Book II of the *Aeneid*.
451. *boote but bale:* remedy but sorrow
462. *mischiefe:* disaster
463. *haled:* dragged
464. *Pallas:* the goddess Pallas Athene, whom Cassandra served; *spercled:* disheveled
465. *Greeks rout empaled:* surrounded by a host of Greeks
467. *Pyrrhus:* Neoptolemus, Achilles' son
468. *bayne:* bath
469. *sonnes:* Polites', slain by Pyrrhus at Priam's feet

Faycr Ilium fal in burning red gledes downe,   475
And from the soyle great Troy, Neptunus towne.

Herefrom when scarce I could mine iyes withdrawe
That fylde with teares as doeth the spryngyng well,
We passed on so far furth tyl we sawe
Rude Acheron, a lothsome lake to tell   480
That boyles and bubs up swelth as blacke as hell.
Where grisly Charon at theyr fixed tide
Stil ferreies ghostes unto the farder side,

The aged God no sooner sorowe spyed,
But hasting strayt unto the banke apace   485
With hollow call unto the rout he cryed,
To swarve apart, and geve the Goddesse place.
Strayt it was done, when to the shoar we pace,
Where hand in hand as we then linked fast,
Within the boate we are together plaste.   490

And furth we launch ful fraughted to the brinke,
Whan with the unwonted weyght, the rustye keele
Began to cracke as if the same should sinke.
We hoyse up mast and sayle, that in a whyle
We fet the shore, where scarcely we had while   495
For to arryve, but that we heard anone
A thre sound barke confounded al in one.

We had not long forth past, but that we sawe,
Blacke Cerberus the hydeous hound of hell,

---

475. *gledes:* coals
476. *soyle:* site
481. *bubs:* bubbles
482. *fixed tide:* appointed time
491. *fraughted:* loaded
492. *unwonted:* unaccustomed. Charon usually ferried ghosts, not live people.
494. *hoyse:* hoist; *that:* so that
495. *fet:* fetched, reached. The 1563 edition reads *set. while:* time

With bristles reard, and with a thre mouthed Jawe,   500
Foredinning the ayer with his horrible yel,
Out of the diepe darke cave where he did dwell.
The Goddesse strayt he knewe, and by and by
He peaste and couched, while that we passed by.

Thence cum we to the horrour and the hel,   505
The large great kyngdomes, and the dreadful raygne
Of Pluto in his trone where he dyd dwell,
The wyde waste places, and the hugye playne:
The waylinges, shrykes, and sundry sortes of payne,
The syghes, the sobbes, the diepe and deadly groane,   510
Earth, ayer, and all resounding playnt and moane.

Here pewled the babes, and here the maydes unwed
With folded handes theyr sory chaunce bewayled,
Here wept the gyltles slayne, and lovers dead,
That slewe them selves when nothyng els avayled;   515
A thousand sortes of sorrowes here that wayled
With sighes and teares, sobs, shrykes, and all yfere,
That (oh alas) it was a hel to heare.

We stayed us strayt, and wyth a rufull feare,
Beheld this heavy sight, while from mine eyes,   520
The vapored teares downstilled here and there,
And Sorowe eke in far more woful wyse.
Tooke on with playnt, up heaving to the skyes
Her wretched handes, that with her crye the rout
Gan all in heapes to swarme us round about.   525

Loe here (quoth Sorowe) Prynces of renowne,
That whilom sat on top of Fortunes wheele

501. *Foredinning the ayer:* Filling all the air with noise
503. *by and by:* at once
504. *peaste and couched:* became silent and lay down
509. *shrykes:* shrieks
512. *pewled:* puled, whimpered
517. *yfere:* together
521. *downstilled:* ran down
527. *whilom:* formerly

Nowe layed ful lowe, like wretches whurled downe,
Even with one frowne, that stayed but with a smyle.
And nowe behold the thing that thou erewhile,   530
Saw only in thought, and what thou now shalt heare
Recompt the same to Kesar, King, and Pier.

Then first came Henry duke of Buckingham,
His cloke of blacke al pilde and quite forworne,
Wringing his handes, and Fortune ofte doth blame,   535
Which of a duke hath made him nowe her skorne.
With gastly lookes as one in maner lorne,
Oft spred his armes, stretcht handes he joynes as fast,
With ruful chere, and vapored eyes upcast.

His cloke he rent, his manly breast he beat,   540
His heare al torne about the place it laye,
My hart so molte to see his griefe so great,
As felingly me thought it dropt awaye:
His iyes they whurled about withouten staye,
With stormy syghes the place dyd so complayne,   545
As if his hart at eche had burst in twayne.

Thryse he began to tell his doleful tale,
And thrise the sighes did swalowe up his voyce,
At eche of which he shryked so wythal
As though the heavens rived with the noyse: 550
Tyll at the last recovering his voyce,
Supping the teares that all his brest beraynde
On cruel Fortune weping thus he playnde.

---

529. *Even . . . smyle:* i.e., their fall or rise depended on Fortune's frown or smile
532. *Recompt:* Relate; *Kesar:* Caesar, emperor
533. *Henry:* the subject of Sackville's tragedy. See above, "To the Reader," line 14 n.
534. *pilde:* bare; *forworne:* worn out
537. *lorne:* lost
542. *molte:* melted
546. *at eche:* i.e., at each sigh
550. *rived:* split
552. *beraynde:* rained down on
553. *playnde:* complained, lamented

2.

Thomas Sackevyll in Commendation of the Worke
To the Reader

These royall kinges, that reare up to the skye
Their Palaice tops and decke them all with gold:
With rare and curious woorkes they feed the eye:
And showe what riches here great princes hold.
A rarer worke, and richer far in worth,   5
Castilio's hand presenteth here to the,
No proud ne golden court doth he set forth
But what in Court a Courtier ought to be.
The Prince he raiseth houge and mightie walles,
Castilio frames a wight of noble fame: 10
The King with gorgeous Tyssue claddes his halles,
The Court with golden vertue deckes the same,
Whos passing skill lo Hobbies pen displaise
To Brittain folk, a work of worthy praise.

Title: First published in 1561, this sonnet commends Sir Thomas Hoby
(pronounced "Hobby"), 1530–66, on his translation of Baldassare Casti-
glione's *Il Cortegiano* (1528).
3. *curious:* artful
6. *the:* thee
10. *wight:* man
11. *Tyssue:* fabrics woven with silver and gold; *claddes:* adorns
13. *passing:* surpassing; *displaise:* displays

GEORGE GASCOIGNE

1539–77

Dedicatory Epistle to The Posies *(1575)*

To al yong Gentlemen, and generally to the youth of Eng-
land, George Gascoigne Esquire by birth, and Souldiour by
profession, wisheth increase of knowledge in all vertuous
exercises.

Gallant Gentlemen, and lustie youthes of this my na-
tive Countrey, I have here (as you see) published in
print suche Posies and rymes as I used in my youth, the
which for the barbarousnesse of the stile may seeme
worthlesse, and yet for the doubtfulnesse of some darke   5
places they have also seemed (heretofore) daungerous.
So that men may justly both condemne me of rash-
nesse, and wonder at my simplicitie in suffering or pro-
curing the same to be imprinted.

    A yong man well borne, tenderly fostered, and deli-   10
cately accompanied, shall hardly passe over his youth
without falling into some snares of the Divell, and
temptations of the flesh. But a man of middle yeares,
who hath to his cost experimented the vanities of
youth, and to his perill passed them: who hath bought   15
repentance deare, and yet gone through with the bar-
gaine: who seeth before his face the tyme past lost, and

Title: This is the second of three dedicatory prefaces which Gascoigne
used to introduce *The Posies*. The first was directed "To the Reverende
Divines" and the third "To the Readers Generally."
6. *heretofore:* i.e., in the 1573 edition of *A Hundreth Sundrie Flowres*

the rest passing away in post: Such a man had more
neede to be well advised in his doings, and resolute in
his determinations. For with more ease and greater   20
favour may we answere for tenne madde follies com-
mitted in grene youth, than one sober oversight es-
caped in yeares of discretion. *Lycurgus* the good
princely Philosopher, ordeyned that if an olde man per-
ceiving a yong man to commit any dishonestie, did not   25
rebuke but suffer him: the aged shoulde be chastised,
and the yong man should be absolved.

All this rehearsed and considered, you may (as I say)
growe in some doubt, whether I were worse occupied
in first devising, or at last in publishing these toies &   30
pamphlets: and much the rather, for that it is a thing
commonly seene, that (nowe adayes) fewe or no things
are so well handled, but they shall bee carped at by
curious Readers, nor almost any thing so well ment, but
may bee muche misconstrued.   35

And heerewithall I assure my selfe, that I shall bee
generally condemned as a man verie lightly bent, and
rather desyrous to continue in the freshe remembraunce
of my follyes, than content too cancell them in oblivion
by discontinuance: especially since in a house where   40
many yong children are, it hath bene thought better
pollicie quite to quench out the fire, than to leave any
loose cole in the imbers, wherewith Babes may play and
put the whole edifice in daunger.

But my lustie youthes, and gallant Gentlemen, I had   45
an intent farre contrarie untoo all these supposes, when
I fyrst permitted the publication heereof. And bycause
the greatest offence that hath beene taken thereat is
least your mindes might heereby become envenomed
with vanities, therefore unto you I will addresse my   50
tale, for the better satisfying of common judgements.
And unto you I will explane, that which being before

---

18. *in post:* speedily
23. *Lycurgus:* see below, no. 12, line 272 n.
34. *curious:* fastidious
37. *lightly bent:* easily swayed
49. *least:* lest

mistically covered, and commonly misconstrued, might
be no lesse perillous in seducing you, than greevous
evidence for to prove mee guiltie of condemnation. 55
    Then to come unto the matter, there are three sortes
of men which (beeing wonderfully offended at this
booke) have founde therein three maner of matters
(say they) verie reprehensible. The men are these: curi-
ous Carpers, ignorant Readers, and grave Philosophers. 60
The faults they finde are, *Judicare* in the Creede:
Chalke for Cheese: and the common infection of Love.
Of these three sorts of men and matters, I do but very
little esteeme the two first. But I deeply regarde the
thirde. For of a verie troth, there are one kinde of people 65
nowadayes which will mislyke any thing, being bred (as
I thinke) of the spawne of a Crab or Crevish, which in
all streames and waters will swimme eyther sidewayes,
or flat backwards: and when they can indeede finde
none other fault, will yet thinke *Judicare* verie un- 70
towardlye placed in the Creede. Or (beeing a simple
Sowter) will finde fault at the shape of the legge: or if
they be not there stopped, they wil not spare to step up
higher, and say that *Apelles* paynted Dame *Venus* verie
deformed or evill favoured. 75
    Of this sort I make small accounte, bycause indeede
they seeke a knotte in the Rushe, and woulde seeme to
see verie farre in a Mylstone.
    There are also certaine others, who (having no skill
at all) will yet be verie busie in reading all that may 80
bee read, and thinke it sufficient if (Parrot like) they
can rehearse things without booke: when within booke
they understande neyther the meaning of the Authour,
nor the sense of the figurative speeches, I will forbeare
to recyte examples by any of mine owne doings. Since 85
all comparisons are odious, I will not say how much the

---

61. *Judicare*: "to judge." Gascoigne is concerned here, as he explains in
the following lines, with those who will quibble over matters of no
importance.
67. *Crevish*: crayfish
72. *Sowter*: cobbler
74. *Apelles*: renowned Greek painter of the fourth century B.C.

areignment and divorce of a Lover (being written in jeast) have bene mistaken in sad earnest. It shall suffice that the contentions passed in verse long sithence, betwene maister *Churchyard* and *Camell*, were (by a 90 blockheaded reader) construed to be indeed a quarell betwene two neighbors. Of whom that one having a Camell in keping, and that other having charge of the Churchyard, it was supposed they had grown to debate bicause the Camell came into the Churchyarde. Laugh 95 not at this (lustie yonkers) since the pleasant dittie of the noble Erle of Surrey (beginning thus: *In winters just returne*) was also construed to be made indeed by a Shepeherd. What shoulde I stande much in rehersall how the *L. Vaux* his dittie (beginning thus: *I loth that 100 I did love*) was thought by some to be made upon his death bed? and that the Soulknill of M. Edwards was also written in extremitie of sicknesse? Of a truth (my good gallants) there are such as having only lerned to read English, do interpret Latin, Greke, French and 105 Italian phrases or metaphors, even according to their owne motherly conception and childish skill. The which (bicause they take Chalke for Cheese) shall never trouble me, whatsoever fault they finde in my doings. 110

But the third sort (beeing grave Philosophers, and finding just fault in my doings at the common infection of love) I must needes alledge suche juste excuse as may countervayle their juste complaynts. For else I shoulde remayne woorthie of a severe punishment. 115 They wysely considering that wee are all in youth more

90. *Churchyard:* Thomas Churchyard (1520?–1604), minor, but immensely productive, Elizabethan poet
96. *yonkers:* young men
97. *Surrey:* see Surrey, no. 21
100. *L. Vaux:* for Vaux, see note to Surrey, no. 15
103. *Soulknill:* soul knell, the knell tolled after a person's death. Gascoigne uses the word figuratively, probably referring to the poem "O lorde that ruleste bothe lande and sea," by Richard Edwards (1524–67), Master of the Children of the Chapel Royal. See L. Bradner, *The Life and Poems of Richard Edwards* (New Haven, Yale University Press, 1927), pp. 98, 105–8.

apt to delight in harmefull pleasures, than to disgest
wholesome and sounde advice, have thought meete to
forbid the publishing of any ryming tryfles which may
serve as whetstones to sharpen youth unto vanities.   120
    And for this cause, finding by experience also, how
the first Copie of these my Posies hath beene verie
much inquired for by the yonger sort: and hearing like-
wise that (in the same) the greater part hath beene
written in pursute of amorous enterpryses, they have   125
justly conceyved that the continuance thereof hath
beene more likely to stirre in all yong Readers a venem-
ous desire of vanitie, than to serve as a common
myrrour of greene and youthfull imperfections. Where-
unto I must confesse, that as the industrious Bee may   130
gather honie out of the most stinking weede, so the
malicious Spider may also gather poyson out of the
fayrest floure that growes.
    And yet in all this discourse I see not proved, that
either that Gardener is too blame which planteth his   135
Garden full of fragrant floures: neyther that planter to
be dispraysed, which soweth all his beddes with seedes
of wholesome herbes: neyther is that Orchard unfruit-
full, which (under shew of sundrie weedes) hath me-
dicinable playsters for all infirmities. But if the Chirur-   140
gian which should seeke Sorrell to rypen an Ulcer, will
take Rewe which may more inflame the Impostume,
then is hee more to blame that mistooke his gathering,
than the Gardener which planted aright and presented
store and choyse to be taken. Or if the Phisition will   145
gather hote Perceley in stead of cold Endive, shall he
not worthily beare the burthen of his owne blame?
    To speake English, it is your using (my lustie Gal-
lants) or misusing of these Posies that may make me
praysed or dispraysed for publishing of the same. For if   150
you (where you may learne to avoyd the subtile sandes

---

117. *disgest:* digest
140. *playsters:* dressings
140–41. *Chirurgian:* surgeon
142. *Impostume:* sore
146. *Perceley:* parsley

of wanton desire) will runne upon the rockes of unlaw-
full lust, then great is your folly, and greater will growe
my rebuke. If you (where you might gather wholesome
hearbes to cure your sundrie infirmities) will spende the   155
whole day in gathering of sweete smelling Posies, much
will be the time that you shal mispende, and much
more the harme that you shall heape upon my heade.
Or if you will rather beblister your handes with a Net-
tle, than comfort your senses by smelling to the pleas-   160
ant Marjoram, then wanton is your pastime, and small
will be your profite.

I have here presented you with three sundrie sortes
of Posies: *Floures, Hearbes,* and *Weedes.* In which di-
vision I have not ment that onely the Floures are to be   165
smelled unto, nor that onely the Weedes are to be re-
jected. I terme some Floures, bycause being indeed in-
vented upon a verie light occasion, they have yet in
them (in my judgement) some rare invention and
Methode before not commonly used. And therefore   170
(beeing more pleasant than profitable) I have named
them Floures.

The seconde (being indeede morall discourses, and
reformed inventions, and therefore more profitable than
pleasant) I have named Hearbes.   175

The third (being Weedes) might seeme to some
judgements, neither pleasant nor yet profitable, and
therefore meete to bee cast away. But as many weedes
are right medicinable, so may you find in this none so
vile or stinking, but that it hath in it some vertue if it   180
be rightly handled. Mary, you must take heede how you
use them. For if you delight to put Hemlocke in your
fellowes pottage, you may chaunce both to poyson him,
and bring your selfe in perill. But if you take example
by the harmes of others who have eaten it before you,   185
then may you chaunce to become so warie, that you
will looke advisedly on all the Perceley that you gather,
least amongst the same one braunch of Hemlock might
anoy you.

I assure you, my yong blouds, I have not published   190

the same to the intent that other men hereafter might
be infected with my follies forepassed. For though it be
a comfort *in miseriis habere consortem,* yet is it small
consolation to a fellon, to have a Coyner hanged in his
companie. And I assure you (although you will think   195
it straunge) that I have not caused them to bee im-
printed for anie vaine delight which I have (my selfe)
therein conceyved. For the most of them, being written
in my madnesse, might have yeelded then more delight
to my frantike fansie to see them published, than they   200
now do accumulate cares in my minde to set them
forth corrected: and a deformed youth had bene more
likely to set them to sale long sithence, than a reformed
man can be able now to protect them with simplicitie.
   The scope of mine intent, and the marke whereat I   205
shoote is double. I meane grounded upon two sundrie
causes: the one that being indebted unto the worlde
(at the least five thousande dayes verie vainly spent)
I may yeeld him yet some part of mine account in
these Poemes. Wherein as he may finde great diversitie   210
both in stile and sense, so may the good bee incouraged
to set mee on worke at last, though it were noone be-
fore I sought service. The other reason is, that bicause
I have (to mine owne great detriment) mispent my
golden time, I may serve as ensample to the youthfull   215
Gentlemen of England, that they runne not upon the
rocks which have brought me to shipwracke. Beware
therefore, lustie Gallants, howe you smell to these Po-
sies. And learne you to use the talent which I have
highly abused. Make me your myrrour. And if hereafter   220
you see me recover mine estate, or reedifie the decayed
walls of my youth, then beginne you sooner to builde
some foundation which may beautifie your Pallace. If
you see me sinke in distresses (notwithstanding that
you judge me quick of capacitie) then lerne you to   225

---

193. *in . . . consortem:* "to have company in miseries"
194. *Coyner:* counterfeiter
221. *reedifie:* rebuild

maynteyne your selves swimming in prosperitie, and
eschue betymes the whirlepoole of misgovernment.

Finally, I beseech you, and conjure you, that you
rather encourage me to accomplish some worthier tra-
vaile, by seeing these Posies right smelled unto, than   230
discourage me from attempting other labours, when I
shall see these first fruites rejected or misused. I have
corrected them from sundrie faultes. Which if they had
not brought suspition in the first copie, be you then out
of doubt you had never bene troubled with these sec-   235
onde presents, nor persuaded to flourishe wisely with a
two edged swoorde in your naked hands. But as I have
ment them well, so I crave of God, that they may both
pleasure and profite you for the furtherance of your
skill in any commendable enterprise. From my poore   240
house at Waltamstow in the Forest the second of Janu-
arie. 1575.

1.

The arraignment of a Lover

At Beautyes barre as I dyd stande,
When false suspect accused mee,
George (quod the Judge) holde up thy hande,
Thou art arraignde of Flatterye:
Tell therefore howe thou wylt bee tryde?   5
Whose judgement here wylt thou abyde?

My Lorde (quod I) this Lady here,
Whome I esteeme above the rest,
Doth knowe my guilte if any were:
Wherefore hir doome shall please me best,   10

---

2. *suspect:* suspicion
7. *this Lady:* i.e., Beauty
10. *doome:* judgment

Let hir bee Judge and Jurour boathe,
To trye mee guiltlesse by myne oathe.

Quod Beautie, no, it fitteth not,
A Prince hir selfe to judge the cause:
Wyll is our Justice well you wot,   15
Appointed to discusse our Lawes:
If you wyll guiltlesse seeme to goe,
God and your countrey quitte you so.

Then crafte the cryer cal'd a quest,
Of whome was falshoode formost feere,   20
A packe of pickethankes were the rest,
Which came false witnesse for to beare,
The Jurye suche, the Judge unjust,
Sentence was sayde I should be trust.

Jelous the Jayler bound mee fast,   25
To heare the verdite of the byll,
George (quod the Judge) nowe thou art cast,
Thou must goe hence to heavie hill,
And there be hangde all but the head,
God rest thy soule when thou art dead.   30

Downe fell I then upon my knee,
All flatte before Dame Beauties face,
And cryed, good Ladye pardon mee,
Which here appeale unto your grace,
You knowe if I have beene untrue,   35
It was in too much praysing you.

---

15. *wot:* know
18. *quitte:* acquit
19. *crafte:* trickery; *quest:* panel of jurors
20. *formost feere:* the leading member
21. *pickethankes:* flatterers
24. *sayde:* given; *trust:* trussed up
27. *cast:* convicted
28. *heavie hill:* alluding to Tyburn Hill, where criminals were hanged
29. *all . . . head:* the rope would be around his *neck*, not his head.
A playful allusion to the fact that the guilty speaker will never "hang his head" or "lose his head."

And though this Judge doe make suche haste,
To shead with shame my guiltlesse blood:
Yet let your pittie first bee plaste,
To save the man that meant you good,   40
So shall you shewe your selfe a Queene,
And I maye bee your servaunt scene.

(Quod Beautie) well: bicause I guesse,
What thou dost meane hencefoorth to bee,
Although thy faultes deserve no lesse,   45
Than Justice here hath judged thee,
Wylt thou be bound to stynt all strife,
And be true prisoner all thy lyfe?

Yea Madame (quod I) that I shall,
Loe fayth and trueth my suerties:
Why then (quod shee) come when I call,   50
I aske no better warrantise.
Thus am I Beauties bounden thrall,
At hir commaunde when shee doth call.
            Ever or never   55

2.

A straunge passion of a Lover

Amid my Bale I bath in blisse,
I swim in heaven, I sinke in hell:
I find amends for every misse,
And yet my moane no tongue can tell.

---

39. *plaste:* placed, directed
47. *stynt:* stop
52. *warrantise:* guarantee
55. *Ever or never:* a motto, or "posy"; Gascoigne attached one of these,
in Latin or English, to each of the poems in A *Hundreth Sundrie Flowres*
(1573) and *The Posies* (1575). Cf. Spenser's practice in *The Shepheardes
Calender.*
1. *Bale:* Torment

I live and love, what wold you more: 5
As never lover liv'd before.

I laugh sometimes with little lust,
So jest I oft and feele no joye:
Myne ease is builded all on trust:
And yit mistrust breedes myne anoye. 10
I live and lacke, I lacke and have:
I have and misse the thing I crave.

These things seeme strange, yet are they trew,
Beleeve me sweete my state is such,
One pleasure which I wold eschew, 15
Both slakes my grief and breedes my grutch.
So doth one paine which I would shoon,
Renew my joyes where grief begoon.

Then like the larke that past the night.
In heavy sleepe with cares opprest: 20
Yit when shee spies the pleasant light,
She sends sweete notes from out hir brest.
So sing I now because I thinke
How joyes approch, when sorrowes shrinke.

And as fayre *Philomene* againe, 25
Can watch and singe when other sleepe:
And taketh pleasure in hir payne,
To wray the woo that makes hir weepe.
So sing I now for to bewray
The lothsome life I lead alway. 30

The which to thee (deare wenche) I write,
That know'st my mirth, but not my moane:
I praye God graunt thee deepe delight,
To live in joyes when I am gone.

---

7. *lust:* pleasure
16. *grutch:* grudge
17. *shoon:* shun
25. *Philomene:* the nightingale
26. *other:* others
28. *wray:* reveal

I cannot live, it wyll not bee: 35
I dye to thinke to part from thee.
Ferenda Natura

3.

The Divorce of a Lover

Divorce me nowe good death, from love and lingring life,
That one hath bene my concubine, that other was my wife.
In youth I lived with love, she had my lustye dayes,
In age I thought with lingering life to stay my wandering wais,
But now abusde by both, I come for to complaine,   5
To thee good death, in whom my helpe doth wholy now
    remain,
My libell loe behold: wherein I doe protest,
The processe of my plaint is true, in which my griefe doth rest.
First love my concubine (whome I have kept so trimme,
Even she for whome I seemd of yore, in seas of joy to
    swimme: 10
To whome I dare avowe, that I have served as well,
And played my part as gallantly, as he that beares the bell)
She cast me of long since, and holdes me in disdaine,
I cannot pranke to please hir nowe, my vaunting is but vaine.
My writhled cheekes bewraye, that pride of heate is past, 15
My stagring steppes eke tell the trueth, that nature fadeth fast,
My quaking crooked joyntes, are combred with the crampe,
The boxe of oyle is wasted wel, which once dyd feede my
    lampe.
The greenesse of my yeares, doth wyther now so sore,
That lusty love leapes quite awaye, and lyketh me no more, 20
And love my lemman gone, what lyking can I take?

---

37. *Ferenda Natura:* "Nature is to be borne"
7. *libell:* the legal document with which the plaintiff begins his suit
10. *of yore:* formerly
12. *beares the bell:* wins the prize
14. *pranke:* sport, caper; *vaunting:* boasting
15. *writhled:* wrinkled; *bewraye:* betray
16. *eke:* also
21. *lemman:* mistress

In lothsome lyfe that crokcd croane, although she be my make?
Shee cloyes me with the cough, hir comfort is but cold,
She bids me give mine age for almes, wher first my youth was
    sold.
No day can passe my head, but she beginnes to brall,   25
No mery thoughts conceived so fast, but she confounds them
    al.
When I pretend to please, she overthwarts me still,
When I would faynest part with hir, she overwayes my will.
Be judge then gentle death, and take my cause in hand,
Consider every circumstaunce, marke how the case doth
    stand.   30
Percase thou wilte aledge, that cause thou canst none see,
But that I like not of that one, that other likes not me:
Yes gentle judge give eare, and thou shalt see me prove,
My concubine incontinent, a common whore is love.
And in my wyfe I find, such discord and debate,   35
As no man living can endure the tormentes of my state.
Wherefore thy sentence say, devorce me from them both,
Since only thou mayst right my wronges, good death nowe be
    not loath.
But cast thy pearcing dart, into my panting brest,
That I may leave both love and life, & thereby purchase
    rest.   40
     Haud ictus sapio

4.

The Lullabie of a Lover

Sing lullaby, as women doe,
Wherewith they bring their babes to rest,

---

22. *croane:* crone; *make:* mate
24. *give . . . almes:* i.e., become a beggar in my old age
27. *overthwarts:* thwarts, crosses
28. *overwayes:* overrules
31. *Percase:* Perhaps
41. *Haud . . . sapio:* "Even though struck down, I have not learned wisdom"

And lullaby can I sing to,
As womanly as can the best.
With lullaby they still the childe,   5
And if I be not much beguild,
Full many wanton babes have I,
Which must be stild with lullabie.

First lullaby my youthfull yeares,
It is nowe time to go to bed,   10
For croocked age and hoary heares,
Have wone the haven within my head:
With Lullaby then youth be still,
With Lullaby content thy will,
Since courage quayles, and commes behind,   15
Go sleepe, and so beguile thy minde.

Next Lullaby my gazing eyes,
Which wonted were to glaunce apace.
For every Glasse maye nowe suffise,
To shewe the furrowes in my face: 20
With Lullabye then winke awhile,
With Lullabye your lookes beguile:
Lette no fayre face, nor beautie brighte,
Entice you efte with vayne delighte.

And Lullaby my wanton will,   25
Lette reasons rule nowe reigne thy thought,
Since all to late I finde by skyll,
Howe deare I have thy fansies bought:
With Lullaby nowe tak thyne ease,
With Lullaby thy doubtes appease: 30
For trust to this, if thou be styll,
My body shall obey thy will.

Eke Lullaby my loving boye,
My little Robyn take thy rest,

---

18. *wonted were:* were accustomed; *apace:* directly
21. *winke:* shut your eyes
24. *efte:* again
27. *skyll:* sad experience
34. *little Robyn:* the reference is phallic

Since age is colde, and nothing coye, 35
Keepe close thy coyne, for so is best:
With Lullaby be thou content,
With Lullaby thy lustes relente,
Lette others pay which hath mo pence,
Thou art to pore for such expence. 40

Thus Lullabye my youth, myne eyes,
My will, my ware, and all that was,
I can no mo delayes devise,
But welcome payne, let pleasure passe:
With Lullaby now take your leave, 45
With Lullaby your dreames deceive,
And when you rise with waking eye,
Remember then this Lullabye.
   Ever or Never

5.

Gascoignes good morrow

You that have spent the silent night,
In sleepe and quiet rest,
And joye to see the cheerefull lyght
That ryseth in the East:
Now cleare your voyce, now chere your hart, 5
Come helpe me nowe to sing:
Eche willing wight come beare a part,
To prayse the heavenly King.

And you whome care in prison keepes,
Or sickenes doth suppresse, 10
Or secret sorowe breakes your sleepes,
Or dolours doe distresse:

---

39. *mo:* more
42. *ware:* "sexual equipment"
7. *wight:* creature

Yet beare a parte in dolfull wise,
Yea thinke it good accorde,
And acceptable sacrifice,   15
Eche sprite to prayse the lorde.

The dreadfull night with darkesomnesse,
Had over spread the light,
And sluggish sleepe with drowsynesse,
Had over prest our might: 20
A glasse wherin you may beholde,
Eche storme that stopes our breath,
Our bed the grave, our clothes lyke molde,
And sleepe like dreadfull death.

Yet as this deadly night did laste,   25
But for a little space,
And heavenly daye nowe night is past,
Doth shewe his pleasaunt face:
So must we hope to see Gods face,
At last in heaven on hie,   30
When we have chang'd this mortall place,
For Immortalitie.

And of such happes and heavenly joyes,
As then we hope to holde,
All earthly sightes and worldly toyes,   35
Are tokens to beholde.
The daye is like the daye of doome,
The sunne, the Sonne of man,
The skyes the heavens, the earth the tombe
Wherein we rest till than.   40

The Rainbowe bending in the skye,
Bedeckte with sundrye hewes,

---

14. *accorde:* harmony
16. *sprite:* spirit
20. *over prest:* overcome
21. *glasse:* mirror
33. *happes:* strokes of good fortune

Is like the seate of God on hye,
And seemes to tell these newes:
That as thereby he promised,   45
To drowne the world no more,
So by the bloud which Christ hath shead,
He will our helth restore.

The mistie cloudes that fall somtime,
And overcast the skyes,   50
Are like to troubles of our time,
Which do but dymme our eyes:
But as suche dewes are dryed up quite,
When *Phoebus* shewes his face,
So are such fansies put to flighte,   55
Where God doth guide by grace.

The caryon Crowe, that lothsome beast,
Which cryes agaynst the rayne,
Both for hir hewe and for the rest,
The Devill resembleth playne: 60
And as with gonnes we kill the Crowe,
For spoyling our releefe,
The Devill so must we overthrowe,
With gonshote of beleefe.

The little byrdes which sing so swete,   65
Are like the angelles voyce,
Which render God his prayses meete,
And teache us to rejoyce:
And as they more esteeme that myrth,
Than dread the nights anoy,   70
So muste we deeme our days on earth,
But hell to heavenly joye.

Unto which Joyes for to attayne
God graunt us all his grace,

---

45. *he promised:* i.e., after Noah's flood (Genesis 9:12–17)
54. *Phoebus:* the sun
57. *caryon:* eater of carrion
59. *hewe:* color

And sende us after worldly payne,   75
In heaven to have a place.
Where wee maye still enjoy that light,
Which never shall decaye:
Lorde for thy mercy lend us might,
To see that joyfull daye.   80
     Haud ictus sapio

6.

Gascoygnes good night

When thou hast spent the lingring day in pleasure and delight,
Or after toyle and wearie waye, dost seeke to rest at nighte:
Unto thy paynes or pleasures past, adde this one labour yet,
Ere sleepe close up thyne eye to fast, do not thy God forget,
But searche within thy secret thoughts, what deeds did thee
     befal: 5
And if thou find amisse in ought, to God for mercy call.
Yea though thou find nothing amisse, which thou canst cal to
     mind,
Yet ever more remember this, there is the more behind:
And thinke how well so ever it be, that thou hast spent the
     daye,
It came of God, and not of thee, so to direct thy waye.   10
Thus if thou trie thy dayly deedes, and pleasure in this payne,
Thy life shall clense thy corne from weeds, & thine shal be the
     gaine:
But if thy sinfull sluggishe eye, will venter for to winke,
Before thy wading will may trye, how far thy soule maye sinke,
Beware and wake, for else thy bed, which soft & smoth is
     made,   15
May heape more harm upon thy head, than blowes of enmies
     blade.

---

6. *ought:* anything
11. *trie:* test
13. *venter . . . winke:* dare to close

Thus if this paine procure thine ease, in bed as thou doest lye,
Perhaps it shall not God displease, to sing thus soberly:
I see that sleepe is lent me here, to ease my wearye bones,
As death at laste shall eke appeere, to ease my greevous
    grones.   20
My dayly sportes, my panch full fed, have causde my drousie
    eye,
As carelesse life in quiet led, might cause my soule to dye:
The stretching armes, the yauning breath, which I to bedward
    use,
Are patternes of the pangs of death, when life will me refuse:
And of my bed eche sundrye part in shaddowes doth
    resemble,   25
The sundry shapes of deth, whose dart shal make my flesh
    to tremble.
My bed it selfe is like the grave, my sheetes the winding sheete,
My clothes the mould which I must have, to cover me most
    meete:
The hungry fleas which friske so freshe, to wormes I can
    compare,
Which greedily shall gnaw my fleshe, & leave the bones ful
    bare: 30
The waking Cock that early crowes to weare the night awaye,
Puts in my minde the trumpe that blowes before the latter day.
And as I ryse up lustily, when sluggish sleepe is past,
So hope I to rise joyfully, to Judgement at the last.
Thus wyll I wake, thus wyll I sleepe, thus wyl I hope to
    ryse,   35
Thus wyll I neither waile nor weepe, but sing in godly wyse.
My bones shall in this bed remaine, my soule in God shall
    trust,
By whome I hope to ryse againe from death and earthly dust.
      Haud ictus sapio

---

21. *panch:* paunch, belly
28. *mould:* earth; *meete:* fittingly

7.

Alexander Nevile *delivered him this theame*, Sat cito,
si sat bene, *whereupon hee compiled these seven
Sonels in sequence, therin bewraying his owne* Nimis
cito: *and therwith his* Vix bene, *as foloweth.*

In haste poste haste, when first my wandring minde,
Behelde the glistring Courte with gazing eye,
Suche deepe delightes I seemde therin to finde,
As might beguile a graver guest than I.
The stately pompe of Princes and their peeres,   5
Did seeme to swimme in flouddes of beaten goulde,
The wanton world of yong delightfull yeeres,
Was not unlyke a heaven for to behoulde.
Wherin dyd swarme (for every saint) a Dame,
So faire of hue, so freshe of their attire,   10
As might excell dame *Cinthia* for Fame,
Or conquer *Cupid* with his owne desire.
These and suche lyke were baytes that blazed still
Before myne eye to feede my greedy will.

2. Before mine eye to feede my greedy will,   15
Gan muster eke mine olde acquainted mates,
Who helpt the dish (of vayne delighte) to fill
My empty mouth with dayntye delicates:
And folishe boldenesse toke the whippe in hande,
To lashe my life into this trustlesse trace,   20
Til all in haste I leapte a loofe from lande,
And hoyste up sayle to catche a Courtly grace:

Title: Nevile: Alexander Nevile (1544–1614), poet, translator of Seneca, secretary to Archbishop Matthew Parker. *him:* i.e., Gascoigne. *Sat . . . bene:* "If it be well, let it be quickly." *Nimis cito:* "Too quickly." *Vix bene:* "Scarcely well."
11. *Cinthia:* Diana, goddess of chastity
16. *Gan:* Began to; *eke:* also
21. *a loofe:* aloft

Eche lingring daye did seeme a world of wo,
Till in that haplesse haven my head was brought:
Waves of wanhope so tost me to and fro,   25
In deepe dispayre to drowne my dreadfull thought:
Eche houre a day eche day a yeare did seeme,
And every yeare a worlde my will did deeme.

3. And every yeare a worlde my will did deeme,
Till lo, at last, to Court nowe am I come,   30
A seemely swayne, that might the place beseeme,
A gladsome guest embraste of all and some:
Not there contente with common dignitie,
My wandring eye in haste, (yea poste poste haste)
Behelde the blazing badge of braverie,   35
For wante wherof, I thought my selfe disgraste:
Then peevishe pride puffte up my swelling harte,
To further foorth so hotte an enterprise:
And comely cost beganne to playe his parte,
In praysing patternes of mine owne devise.   40
Thus all was good that might be got in haste,
To princke me up, and make me higher plaste.

4. To prinke me up and make me higher plaste,
All came to late that taryed any time,
Pilles of provision pleased not my taste,   45
They made my heeles to heavie for to clime:
Mee thought it best that boughes of boystrous oake,
Should first be shread to make my feathers gaye.
Tyll at the last a deadly dinting stroake,
Brought downe the bulke with edgetooles of decaye: 50
Of every farme I then let flye a lease,
To feede the purse that payde for peevishnesse,
Till rente and all were falne in suche disease,
As scarce coulde serve to mayntayne cleanlynesse:

---

25. *wanhope:* despair
35. *badge of braverie:* i.e., expensive clothes
42. *princke me up:* show me off
45. *Pilles of provision:* i.e., the provisions made by his family for him, his inheritance
47. *boughes . . . oake:* i.e., he sold the trees on his lands

They bought, the bodie, fine, ferme, lease, and lande,   55
All were to little for the merchauntes hande.

5. All were to little for the merchauntes hande,
And yet my braverye bigger than his booke:
But when this hotte accompte was coldly scande,
I thought highe time about me for to looke: 60
With heavie cheare I caste my head abacke,
To see the fountaine of my furious race.
Comparde my losse, my living, and my lacke,
In equall balance with my jolye grace.
And sawe expences grating on the grounde   65
Like lumpes of lead to presse my pursse full ofte,
When light rewarde and recompence were founde,
Fleeting like feathers in the winde alofte:
These thus comparde, I left the Courte at large,
For why? the gaines doth seeldome quitte the charge.   70

6. For why? the gaines doth seldome quitte the charge,
And so saye I, by proofe too dearely bought,
My haste mad wast, my brave and brainsicke barge,
Did float to fast, to catch a thing of nought:
With leasure, measure, meane, and many mo,   75
I mought have kept a chayre of quiet state,
But hastie heads can not bee setled so,
Till croked Fortune give a crabbed mate:
As busie braynes muste beate on tickle toyes,
As rashe invention breedes a rawe devise,   80
So sodayne falles doe hinder hastie joyes,
And as swifte baytes doe fleetest fyshe entice.
So haste makes waste, and therefore nowe I saye,
No haste but good, where wisdome makes the waye.

---

55. *fine:* a legal agreement through which lands were conveyed; *ferme:* fixed annual rent
59. *accompte:* account
70. *quitte:* compensate for
72. *proofe:* experience
73. *mad:* made
76. *mought:* might
79. *tickle:* uncertain, treacherous
84. *No . . . good:* reversing the emphasis given by the original motto to the poem

7. *No haste but good,* where wisdome makes the waye,　85
For profe whereof, behold the simple snayle,
(Who sees the souldiers carcasse caste a waye,
With hotte assaulte the Castle to assayle,)
By line and leysure clymes the loftye wall,
And winnes the turrettes toppe more conningly,　90
Than doughtye Dick, who loste his life and all,
With hoysting up his head to hastilye.
The swiftest bitche brings foorth the blyndest whelpes,
The hottest Fevers coldest crampes ensue,
The nakedst neede hathe over latest helpes:　95
With *Nevyle* then I finde this proverbe true,
That *haste makes waste,* and therefore still I saye,
No haste but good, where wisdome makes the waye.
Sic tuli

8.

A *Sonet written in prayse of the browne beautie,*
compiled for the love of Mistresse E. P. as foloweth.

The thriftles thred which pampred beauty spinnes,
In thraldom binds the foolish gazing eyes:
As cruell Spiders with their crafty ginnes,
In worthlesse webbes doe snare the simple Flies.
The garments gay, the glittring golden gite,　5
The tysing talk which flowes from *Pallas* pooles:
The painted pale, the (too much) red made white,
Are smiling baytes to fishe for loving fooles.
But lo, when eld in toothlesse mouth appeares,

---

94. *ensue:* follow
95. *over latest:* which come too late
99. *Sic tuli:* "I have borne it in this manner"
Title: Mistresse E. P.: unidentified.
3. *ginnes:* devices, traps
5. *gite:* gown
6. *tysing:* enticing; *Pallas pooles:* i.e., pools of wisdom
7. *pale:* pallor

And hoary heares in steede of beauties blaze: 10
Then had I wist, doth teach repenting yeares,
The tickle track of craftie *Cupides* maze.
Twixt faire and foule therfore, twixt great and small,
A lovely nutbrowne face is best of all.
      Si fortunatus infoelix   15

9.

Councell given to master Bartholmew Withipoll *a little before his latter journey to Geane.* 1572.

Mine owne good *Bat,* before thou hoyse up saile,
To make a furrowe in the foming seas,
Content thy selfe to heare for thine availe,
Such harmelesse words, as ought thee not displease.
First in thy journey, jape not over much,   5
What? laughest thou *Batte,* bicause I write so plaine?
Beleeve me now it is a friendly touch,
To use fewe words where friendship doth remaine.
And for I finde that fault hath runne to fast,
Both in thy flesh and fancie too sometime,   10
Me thinks plaine dealing biddeth me to cast
This bone at first amid my dogrell rime.
But shall I say, to give thee grave advise
(Which in my head is (God he knowes) full geazon)?
Then marke me well, and though I be not wise,   15
Yet in my rime, thou maist perhaps find reason.

---

11. *wist:* known
15. *Si . . . infoelix:* "If fortunate, unhappy"
Title: *Bartholmew Withipoll:* Gascoigne's friend was the son of Edmund Withypoll. He was journeying to Genoa (*Geane*) to collect revenue there which had been left him in his father's will. Bartholmew died in November 1573.
1. *Mine . . . Bat:* cf. Wyatt's satire, "Myne owne John Poyntz." *hoyse:* hoist
5. *jape:* sport, wanton
14. *geazon:* lacking

First every day, beseech thy God on knee,
So to direct thy staggring steppes alway,
That he which every secrete thought doth see
May holde thee in, when thou wouldst goe astray: 20
And that he deigne to sende thee safe retoure,
And quicke dispatche of that whiche is thy due:
Lette this (my *Batte*) be bothe thy prime and houre,
Wherin also commend to *Nostre Dieu*,
Thy good Companion and my verie frend,   25
To whom I shoulde (but time woulde not permitte)
Have taken paine some ragged ryme to sende
In trustie token, that I not forget
His curtesie: but this is debte to thee,
I promysde it, and now I meane to pay: 30
What was I saying? sirra, will you see
How soone my wittes were wandering astraye?
I saye, praye thou for thee and for thy mate,
So shipmen sing, and though the note be playne,
Yet sure the musike is in heavenly state,   35
When frends sing so, and know not how to fayne.
The nexte to GOD, thy Prince have still in mynde
Thy countreys honor, and the common wealth:
And flee from them, which fled with every wynde
From native soyle, to forraine coastes by stealth: 40
Theyr traynes are trustlesse, tending still to treason,
Theyr smoothed tongues are lyned all with guyle,
Their power slender, scarsly woorthe two peason,
Their malice much, their wittes are full of wyle:
Eschue them then, and when thou seest them, say,   45
Da, da, sir *K*, I may not come at you,

---

22. *thy due:* perhaps alluding to Withypoll's inheritance
23. *prime and houre:* referring to the hour of prime (9 A.M.), at which prayers were regularly said
25. *Companion:* perhaps the *a Pencoyde* mentioned later at line 146
31. *sirra:* sir
39. *them:* the English Catholic exiles of Elizabeth's reign
41. *traynes:* seductive plots
43. *peason:* peas
46. *Da . . . K:* apparently a nonsense formula; *come at:* have anything to do with

264

You cast a snare your countrey to betraye,
And woulde you have me trust you now for true?
Remembre *Batte* the foolish blink eyed boye
Which was at *Rome,* thou knowest whome I meane,   50
Remember eke the preatie beardless toye,
Whereby thou foundst a safe returne to *Geane,*
Doe so againe: (God shielde thou shouldst have neede,)
But rather so, than to forsweare thy selfe:
A loyall hearte, (beleeve this as thy Creede)   55
Is evermore more woorth than worldly pelfe.
And for one lesson, take this more of mee,
There are three Ps almost in every place,
From whiche I counsell thee alwayes to flee,
And take good hede of them in any case,   60
The first is poyson, perillous in deede
To such as travayle with a heavie pursse:
And thou my *Batte* beware, for thou hast neede,
Thy pursse is lynde with paper, which is wursse:
Thy billes of credite wil not they, thinkst thou,   65
Be bayte to sette *Italyan* hands on woorke?
Yes by my faye, and never worse than nowe,
When every knave hath leysure for to lurke,
And knoweth thou commest for the shelles of Christe:
Beware therefore where ever that thou go,   70
It may fall out that thou shalte be entiste
To suppe sometimes with a *Magnifico,*
And have a *Fico* foysted in thy dishe,
Bycause thou shouldest disgeste thy meate the better:
Beware therefore, and rather feede on fishe,   75
Than learne to spell fyne fleshe with such a Letter.

49. *foolish . . . boye:* Prouty suggests that this may have been Bat himself
on his earlier trip to Italy. The "pretty, beardless toy" of line 51 remains
unexplained. "Toy" could mean "trifle" or "trick" as well as "pet" or
"darling."
67. *faye:* faith
69. *shelles of Christe:* the allusion has not been satisfactorily explained.
In the 1590s, "shells" was a thieves' cant term for money. Perhaps the
revenues Bat hoped to collect were derived from ecclesiastical wealth.
73. *Fico foysted:* fig concealed. Poison was often given in figs.
76. *spell . . . Letter:* eat the finer, but poisoned, meats. The letter is P.

Some may present thee with a pounde or twaine
Of Spanishe soape to washe thy lynnen white:
Beware therefore, and thynke it were small gayne,
To save thy shirte, and cast thy skinne off quite: 80
Some cunning man maye teache thee for to ryde,
And stuffe thy saddle all with Spanishe wooll,
Or in thy stirrops have a toye so tyde,
As both thy legges may swell thy buskins full:
Beware therfore, and beare a noble porte, 85
Drynke not for thyrste before an other taste:
Lette none outlandishe Taylour take disporte
To stuffe thy doublet full of such Bumbaste,
As it may cast thee in unkindely sweate,
And cause thy haire per companie to glyde, 90
Straungers are fyne in many a propre feate:
Beware therefore: the seconde *P.* is Pryde,
More perillous than was the first by farre,
For that infects but bloud and leaves the bones,
This poysons all, and mindes of men doth marre, 95
It findeth nookes to creepe in for the nones:
First from the minde it makes the heart to swell,
From thence the flesh is pampred every parte,
The skinne is taught in Dyers shoppes to dwell,
The haire is curlde or frisled up by arte: 100
Beleeve mee *Batte,* our Countreymen of late
Have caughte such knackes abroade in forayne lande,
That most men call them *Devils incarnate,*
So singular in theyr conceites they stande:

---

78. *Spanishe soape:* soap which left its poison in the clothes washed in it
82. *Spanishe wooll:* impregnated with poison, it would poison anyone who came in contact with it
83. *toye:* trifle, ornament
84. *buskins:* leggings. Swollen legs were a sign of poisoning.
86. *before . . . taste:* unless someone else has drunk first
88. *Bumbaste:* padding (poisoned) for clothes
89. *unkindely:* unnatural
90. *per . . . glyde:* to fall out in bunches—another symptom of poisoning
91. *Straungers . . . feate:* Foreigners know many a subtle trick
96. *for the nones:* on any occasion
103. *Devils incarnate:* echoing Roger Ascham's tirade against the Italianate Englishman in *The Scholemaster* (1568). Ascham cited the proverb, *Inglese Italianato è un diabolo incarnato.*
104. *conceites:* thoughts, devices

266

Nowe sir, if I shall see your maistershippe   105
Come home disguysde and cladde in queynt araye,
As with a piketoothe byting on your lippe,
Your brave *Mustachyos* turnde the *Turky* waye,
A Coptanckt hatte made on a Flemmish blocke,
A nightgowne cloake downe trayling to your toes,   110
A slender sloppe close couched to your docke,
A curtold slipper, and a shorte silke hose:
Bearing your Rapier pointe above the hilte,
And looking bigge like *Marquise of all Beefe*,
Then shall I coumpte your toyle and travayle spilte,   115
Bycause my seconde P, with you is cheefe.
But forwardes nowe, although I stayde a while,
My hindmost P, is worsse than bothe these two,
For it both bones and bodie doth defile,
With fouler blots than bothe those other doo.   120
Shorte tale to make, this P, can beare no blockes,
(God shielde me *Batte*, should beare it in his breast)
And with a dashe it spelleth piles and pockes
A perlous P, and woorsse than bothe the reste:
Now though I finde no cause for to suspect   125
My *Batte* in this, bycause he hath bene tryde,
Yet since such Spanish buttons can infect
Kings, Emperours, Princes and the world so wide,
And since those sunnes do mellowe men so fast
As most that travayle come home very ripe   130

---

107. *piketoothe:* toothpick
108. *Turky:* Turkish
109. *Coptanckt hatte:* high-crowned hat made in the shape of a sugarloaf
111. *sloppe . . . docke:* pantaloons tightly fitted to your behind
112. *curtold:* pointed, with curling toes; *hose:* pair of stockings
115. *coumpte:* reckon; *spilte:* ruined
118–34. In the 1573 version of this poem, Gascoigne's third P was Papistry, not piles and pox (syphilis). Other anti-Catholic references in 1573 were also excised for the *Posies* of 1575.
121. *beare no blockes:* brook no opposition
124. *perlous:* perilous
127. *buttons:* swellings, pimples. Syphilis was thought to have been introduced into Europe from America by the Spaniards.

Although (by sweate) they learne to live and last
When they have daunced after *Guydoes* pype:
Therfore I thought it meete to warne my frende
Of this foule *P*, and so an ende of *Ps*.
Now for thy diet marke my tale to ende, 135
And thanke me then, for that is all my fees.
See thou exceede not in three double *Us*,
The first is Wine, which may enflame thy bloud,
The second Women, such as haunte the stewes,
The thirde is Wilfulnesse, which dooth no good. 140
These three eschue, or temper them alwayes:
So shall my *Batte* prolong his youthful yeeres,
And see long *George* againe, with happie dayes,
Who if he bee as faithfull to his feeres,
As hee was wonte, will dayly pray for *Batte*, 145
And for *a Pencoyde:* and if it fall out so,
That *James a Parrye* doo but make good that,
Which he hath sayde: and if he bee (no, no)
The best companion that long *George* can finde,
Then at the *Spawe* I promise for to bee 150
In *Auguste* nexte, if God turne not my minde,
Where as I would bee glad thy selfe to see:
Till then farewell, and thus I ende my song,
Take it in gree, for else thou doest mee wrong.
Haud ictus sapio

---

131. *by sweate:* the Elizabethan treatment for the disease was the "sweating-tub"
132. *after Guydoes pype:* i.e., to an Italian tune. "Guido" may simply be a generic reference or it may allude to Guido d'Arezzo (d. 1050), inventor of the Guidonian scale.
139. *stewes:* whorehouses
143. *long George:* Gascoigne himself
144. *feeres:* companions
146. *a Pencoyde:* Prouty identifies him as Sir William Morgan of Pencoyde, an Elizabethan soldier of fortune, perhaps Bat's companion on his voyage
147. *James a Parrye:* a Welshman who had been involved with Sir John Scudamore in a wardship case. The exact point of Gascoigne's reference here is obscure, but he may have promised Gascoigne money.
150. *the Spawe:* Spa, near Liège in Belgium
154. *in gree:* in good part

10.

Gascoignes woodmanship written to the L. Grey of Wilton upon this occasion, the sayd L. Grey delighting (amongst many other good qualities) in chusing of his winter deare, & killing the same with his bowe, did furnishe the Aucthor with a crossebowe *cum pertinenciis* and vouchsaved to use his company in the said exercise, calling him one of his woodmen. Now the Aucthor shooting very often, could never hitte any deare, yea and oftentimes he let the heard passe by as though he had not seene them. Whereat when this noble Lord tooke some pastime, and had often put him in remembrance of his good skill in choosing, and readinesse in killing of a winter deare, he thought good thus to excuse it in verse.

My woorthy Lord, I pray you wonder not,
To see your woodman shoote so ofte awrie,
Nor that he stands amased like a sot,
And lets the harmlesse deare (unhurt) go by.
Or if he strike a Doe which is but carren,   5
Laugh not good Lord, but favoure such a fault,
Take will in worth, he would faine hit the barren,
But though his harte be good, his happe is naught:
And therefore now I crave your Lordships leave,
To tell you plaine what is the cause of this: 10
First if it please your honour to perceyve,
What makes your woodman shoote so ofte amisse,
Beleeve me L. the case is nothing strange,
He shootes awrie almost at every marke,
His eyes have bene so used for to raunge,   15
That now God knowes they be both dimme and darke.

Title: *L. Grey:* Arthur, Lord Grey of Wilton, who succeeded to the title in 1562. He had estates at Whaddon in Buckinghamshire and Wrest in Bedfordshire. The poem was written in late 1572 or early 1573. *cum pertinenciis:* with its appurtenances
5. *carren:* with young and hence unfit to eat
7. *will in worth:* his intention in good part; *the barren:* does without fawns
8. *happe:* luck

For proofe, he beares the note of follie now,
Who shotte sometimes to hit Philosophie,
And aske you why? forsooth I make avow,
Bicause his wanton wittes went all awrie.   20
Next that, he shot to be a man of lawe,
And spent sometime with learned *Litleton*,
Yet in the end, he proved but a dawe,
For lawe was darke and he had quickly done.
Then could he with *Fitzharbert* such a braine,   25
As *Tully* had, to write the lawe by arte,
So that with pleasure or with litle paine,
He might perhaps have caught a trewants parte.
But all to late, he most mislikte the thing,
Which most might helpe to guide his arrow streight: 30
He winked wrong, and so let slippe the string,
Which cast him wide, for all his queint conceit.
From thence he shotte to catch a courtly grace,
And thought even there to wield the world at will,
But out alas he much mistooke the place,   35
And shot awrie at every rover still.
The blasing baits which drawe the gazing eye,
Unfethered there his first affection,
No wonder then although he shot awrie,
Wanting the feathers of discretion.   40
Yet more than them, the marks of dignitie,
He much mistooke and shot the wronger way,
Thinking the purse of prodigalitie,
Had bene best meane to purchase such a pray.

---

18. *Philosophie:* i.e., as a university student
22. *Litleton:* Sir Thomas Littleton, whose fifteenth-century text, *Littleton's Tenures*, was used at the Inns of Court
23. *dawe:* jackdaw, dunce
25. *Fitzharbert:* Sir Anthony Fitzherbert, whose *La Grande Abridgement* of 1514 was an attempt to systematize English law. Gascoigne would have liked to have been able to compile such an abridgement so that he could play truant (line 28) whenever he wished.
26. *Tully:* Cicero
31. *winked:* aimed
32. *cast him:* made his shot go; *queint conceit:* foolish fancy (of his own ability)
35. *out:* to his sorrow
36. *rover:* random mark

He thought the flattring face which fleareth still,   45
Had bene full fraught with all fidelitie,
And that such wordes as courtiers use at will,
Could not have varied from the veritie.
But when his bonet buttened with gold,
His comelie cape begarded all with gay,   50
His bumbast hose, with linings manifold,
His knit silke stocks and all his queint aray,
Had pickt his purse of all the Peter pence,
Which might have paide for his promotion,
Then (all to late) he found that light expence,   55
Had quite quencht out the courts devotion.
So that since then the tast of miserie,
Hath bene alwayes full bitter in his bit,
And why? forsooth bicause he shot awrie,
Mistaking still the markes which others hit.   60
But now behold what marke the man doth find,
He shootes to be a souldier in his age,
Mistrusting all the vertues of the minde,
He trusts the power of his personage.
As though long limmes led by a lusty hart,   65
Might yet suffice to make him rich againe;
But Flushyng fraies have taught him such a parte,
That now he thinks the warres yeeld no such gaine.
And sure I feare, unlesse your lordship deigne,
To traine him yet into some better trade,   70
It will be long before he hit the veine,
Whereby he may a richer man be made.

---

45. *fleareth:* smiles fawningly
49. *buttened with gold:* with a gold button on it
50. *begarded . . . gay:* gaily trimmed
51. *bumbast hose:* upper stockings padded with cotton
52. *stocks:* lower, or nether, stockings
53. *Peter pence:* i.e., money for bribes. Peter's pence was an annual tax paid to Rome before the Reformation.
55. *light:* careless
67. *Flushyng fraies:* Gascoigne took part in skirmishes at Flushing in the summer of 1572

He cannot climbe as other catchers can,
To leade a charge before himselfe be led;
He cannot spoile the simple sakeles man, 75
Which is content to feede him with his bread.
He cannot pinch the painefull souldiers pay,
And sheare him out his share in ragged sheetes,
He cannot stoupe to take a greedy pray
Upon his fellowes groveling in the streetes. 80
He cannot pull the spoyle from such as pill,
And seeme full angrie at such foule offence,
Although the gayne content his greedie will,
Under the cloake of contrarie pretence:
And now adayes, the man that shootes not so, 85
May shoote amisse, even as your Woodman dothe:
But then you marvell why I lette them go,
And never shoote, but saye farewell forsooth:
Alas my Lord, while I doe muze hereon,
And call to minde my youthfull yeares myspente, 90
They give mee suche a boane to gnawe upon,
That all my senses are in silence pente.
My minde is rapte in contemplation,
Wherein my dazeled eyes onely beholde,
The blacke houre of my constellation, 95
Which framed mee so lucklesse on the molde:
Yet therewithall I can not but confesse,
That vayne presumption makes my heart to swell,
For thus I thinke, not all the worlde (I guesse)
Shootes bet than I, nay some shootes not so well. 100
In *Aristotle* somewhat did I learne,
To guyde my manners all by comelynesse,
And *Tullie* taught me somewhat to discerne
Betweene sweete speeche and barbarous rudenesse.

---

73. *catchers:* those who "catch on," grasping, ambitious men
75. *spoile:* rob; *sakeles:* innocent
78. *sheare . . . sheetes:* give him ragged sheets for his pay
80. *groveling:* drunken
81. *pill:* plunder
95. *blacke . . . constellation:* the unfavorable position of the planets when
I was born
96. *molde:* earth

272

Olde *Parkyns, Rastall,* and *Dan Bractens* bookes,   105
Did lende mee somewhat of the lawlesse Lawe;
The craftie Courtiers with their guylefull lookes,
Must needes put some experience in my mawe:
Yet can not these with many maystries mo,
Make me shoote streyght at any gaynfull pricke,   110
Where some that never handled such a bow,
Can hit the white, or touch it neare the quicke,
Who can nor speake, nor write in pleasant wise,
Nor leade their life by *Aristotles* rule,
Nor argue well on questions that arise,   115
Nor pleade a case more than my Lord Mairs mule;
Yet can they hit the marks that I do misse,
And winne the meane which may the man mainteyne.
Now when my minde doth mumble upon this,
No wonder then although I pine for payne: 120
And whiles mine eyes beholde this mirrour thus,
The hearde goeth by, and farewell gentle does:
So that your Lordship quickely may discusse
What blindes mine eyes so ofte (as I suppose).
But since my Muse can to my Lorde reherse   125
What makes me misse, and why I doe not shoote,
Let me imagine in this woorthlesse verse,
If right before mee, at my standings foote
There stoode a Doe, and I should strike hir deade,
And then shee prove a carrian carkas too,   130

---

105. *Parkyns:* John Parkins, who published a legal text, *Perutilio Tractatus,*
in 1530; *Rastall:* John Rastell (d. 1536) or William his son (d. 1564),
both of whom published legal books. John was the brother-in-law of Sir
Thomas More. *Dan Bractens:* Henry Bracton, famous thirteenth-century
jurist
108. *mawe:* gullet
109. *maystries mo:* other special skills
110. *pricke:* peg at the center of the target
112. *white:* circle surrounding the center of the target; *quicke:* heart
114. *Aristotle's rule:* probably a reference to Aristotle's ethical formulation,
according to which virtue consists of a mean between two extremes
116. *Mairs:* Mayor's
118. *meane:* means
125. *reherse:* relate, narrate
128. *standings:* hunting position

What figure might I finde within my head,
To scuse the rage whiche rulde mee so to doo?
Some myght interprete by playne paraphrase,
That lacke of skill or fortune ledde the chaunce,
But I must otherwise expounde the case.   135
I say *Jehova* did this Doe advaunce,
And made hir bolde to stande before mee so,
Till I had thrust mine arrowe to hir harte,
That by the sodaine of hir overthrowe,
I myght endevour to amende my parte,   140
And turne myne eyes that they no more beholde,
Such guylefull markes as seeme more than they be:
And though they glister outwardely like golde,
Are inwardly but brasse, as men may see:
And when I see the milke hang in hir teate,   145
Me thinkes it sayth, olde babe now learne to sucke,
Who in thy youth couldst never learne the feate
To hitte the whytes whiche live with all good lucke.
Thus have I tolde my Lorde, (God graunt in season)
A tedious tale in rime, but little reason.   150

   Haud ictus sapio

11.

 Farewell with a mischeife, written by a lover being dis-
daynefullye abjected by a dame of highe calling, Who had
chosen (in his place) a playe fellow of baser condition: & ther-
fore he determined to step a side, and before his departure
giveth hir this farwell in verse.

Thy byrth, thy beautie, nor thy brave attyre,
(Disdaynfull Dame, which doest me double wrong)
Thy hygh estate, which sets thy harte on fire,
Or newe found choyse, which cannot serve thee long
Shall make me dread, with pen for to reherse,   5
Thy skittish deedes, in this my parting verse.

---

131. *figure:* metaphor, image
139. *sodaine:* suddenness
Title: abjected: rejected

For why thou knowest, and I my selfe can tell,
By many vowes, how thou to me wert bound:
And how for joye, thy hart did seeme to swell,
And in delight how thy desires were drownd.　　　　10
When of thy will the walles I did assayle,
Wherin fond fancie fought for mine avayle.

And though my mind have small delight to vaunt,
Yet must I vowe my hart to thee was true:
My hand was always able for to daunt,　　　　15
Thy slaundrous fooes and kepe theyr tongues in mew.
My head (though dull) was yet of such devise,
As might have kept thy name always in price.

And for the rest my body was not brave,
But able yet, of substaunce to allaye,　　　　20
The raging lust, wherein thy limbes did rave,
And quench the coales which kindled thee to playe.
Such one I was, and such always wyl be,
For worthy Dames, but then I meane not thee.

For thou hast caught a proper paragon,　　　　25
A theefe, a cowarde, and a Peacocke foole:
An Ase, a milkesop, and a minion,
Which hath no oyle, thy furyous flames to coole;
Such on he is, a pheare for thee most fit,
A wandring gest, to please thy wavering wit.　　　　30

A theefe I counte him for he robbes us both,
Thee of thy name, and me of my delight:
A coward is he noted where he goeth,
Since every child is match to him in might.
And for his pride no more, but marke his plumes,　　　　35
The which to princke he dayes and nights consumes.

---

7. *For why:* Because
13. *vaunt:* boast
16. *in mew:* cooped up
18. *in price:* highly esteemed
29. *on:* a one; *pheare:* companion
34. *match . . . might:* as strong as he is
36. *princke:* primp ·

The rest thy selfe in secret sorte can judge,
He rides not me, thou knowest his sadell best:
And though these tricks of thine mought make me grudg,
And kindle wrath in my revenging brest, 40
Yet of my selfe, and not to please thy mind,
I stand content my rage in rule to binde.

And farre from thee now must I take my flight,
Where tongues maye tell, (and I not see) thy fall:
Where I maye drinke these druggs of thy dispite, 45
To purge my Melancholike mind with all.
In secrete so, my stomacke will I sterve,
Wishing thee better than thou doest deserve.
            Spraeta tamen vivunt

12.

The Steele Glas

The Nightingale, whose happy noble hart,
No dole can daunt, nor fearful force affright,
Whose chereful voice doth comfort saddest wights,
When she hir self hath little cause to sing,
Whom lovers love, bicause she plaines their greves, 5
She wraies their woes and yet relieves their payne,
Whom worthy mindes, always esteemed much,
And gravest yeares, have not disdainde hir notes:
(Only that king proud *Tereus* by his name
With murdring knife, did carve hir pleasant tong, 10
To cover so his owne foule filthy fault).

---

39. *mought:* might
49. *Spraeta . . . vivunt:* "Things which are scorned still live"
Title: first published in 1576. For Raleigh's dedicatory poem, see Raleigh, no. 1.
2. *dole:* suffering
5. *plaines their greves:* laments over their griefs
6. *wraies:* reveals
9. *Tereus:* Gascoigne alludes to the story of Philomela and her sister Procne, which he then proceeds (lines 56ff.) to allegorize

This worthy bird hath taught my weary Muze,
To sing a song in spight of their despight,
Which worke my woe, withouten cause or crime,
And make my backe a ladder for their feete,   15
By slaundrous steppes and stayres of tickle talke,
To clyme the throne, wherin my selfe should sitte.
O *Phylomene*, then helpe me now to chaunt:
And if dead beastes, or living byrdes have ghosts,
Which can conceive the cause of carefull mone,   20
When wrong triumphes and right is overtrodde,
Then helpe me now, O byrd of gentle bloud,
In barrayne verse to tell a frutefull tale,
A tale (I meane) which may content the mindes
Of learned men and grave Philosophers.   25

And you my Lord, (whose happe hath heretofore
Bene lovingly to reade my reckles rimes,
And yet have deignde with favor to forget
The faults of youth, which past my hasty pen:
And therwithall have graciously vouchsafte,   30
To yeld the rest, much more than they deservde)
Vouchsafe (lo now) to reade and to peruse,
This rimles verse, which flowes from troubled mind.
Synce that the line of that false caytife king
(Which ravished fayre *Phylomene* for lust,   35
And then cut out, hir trustie tong for hate)
Lives yet (my Lord), which words I weepe to write.
They live, they live, (alas the worse my lucke)
Whose greedy lust, unbridled from their brest,
Hath raunged long about the world so wyde   40
To finde a pray for their wide open mouthes,
And me they found, (O wofull tale to tell)
Whose harmelesse hart perceivde not their deceipt.

16. *tickle:* slippery, untrustworthy
23. *barrayne:* barren, sterile
26. *my Lord:* Lord Grey of Wilton. See no. 10, note to title. *happe:* luck, lot
34. *caytife king:* the cowardly Tereus
43. *harmelesse:* innocent

But that my Lord may playnely understand
The mysteries of all that I do meane, 45
I am not he whom slaunderous tongues have tolde
(False tongues in dede & craftie subtile braines)
To be the man which ment a common spoyle
Of loving dames, whose eares wold heare my words
Or trust the tales devised by my pen. 50
I n'am a man, as some do thinke I am,
(Laugh not good Lord) I am in dede a dame,
Or at the least, a right *Hermaphrodite*:
And who desires at large to knowe my name,
My birth, my line, and every circumstance, 55
Lo reade it here, *Playne dealyng* was my Syre,
And he begat me by *Simplycitie*;
A paire of twinnes at one selfe burden borne,
My sistr' and I into this world were sent.
My Systers name was pleasant *Poesys*, 60
And I my selfe had *Satyra* to name,
Whose happe was such, that in the prime of youth,
A lusty ladde, a stately man to see,
Brought up in place where pleasures did abound,
(I dare not say in court for both myne eares) 65
Beganne to woo my sister, not for wealth,
But for hir face was lovely to beholde,
And therewithall hir speeche was pleasant stil.
This Nobles name was called *vayne Delight*,
And in his trayne he had a comely crewe 70
Of guylefull wights: *False semblant* was the first,
The second man was *Flearing flattery*

---

45. *mysteries . . . meane:* secret meanings contained in my verse
46. *tolde:* said
48. *which . . . spoyle:* who intended a general ravaging
51. *n'am:* am not
54. *who:* whoever
58. *one selfe burden:* one and the same birth
60–61. *Poesys . . . Satyra:* Poetry (Procne in the classical myth) and Satire (Philomela)
71. *wights:* followers; *semblant:* appearance
72. *Flearing:* smiling in a fawning way

278

(Brethren by like, or very neare of kin),
Then followed them *Detraction* and *Deceite.*
Sym Swash did beare a buckler for the first,   75
False witnesse was the seconde stemly page;
And thus wel armd and in good equipage,
This Galant came unto my fathers courte
And woed my sister, for she elder was
And fayrer eke, but out of doubt (at least)   80
Hir pleasant speech surpassed mine so much,
That *vayne Delight* to hir adrest his sute.
Short tale to make, she gave a free consent,
And forth she goeth to be his wedded make,
Entyst percase with glosse of gorgeous shewe,   85
(Or else perhappes, persuaded by his peeres),
That constant love had herbord in his brest;
Such errors growe where suche false Prophets preach.
How so it were, my Syster likte him wel,
And forth she goeth, in Court with him to dwel,   90
Where when she had some yeeres ysojorned,
And saw the world and marked eche mans minde,
A *deepe Desire* hir loving hart enflamde,
To see me sit by hir in seemely wise,
That companye might comfort hir sometimes,   95
And sound advice might ease hir wearie thoughtes:
And forth with speede, (even at hir first request)
Doth *vaine Delight* his hasty course direct;
To seeke me out his sayles are fully bent,
And winde was good to bring me to the bowre   100
Whereas she lay that mourned dayes and nights
To see hir selfe so matchte and so deceivde;

---

73. *Brethren by like:* Probably brothers
75. *buckler:* small, round shield
76. *stemly:* the 1575 edition originally read *seemly,* which was corrected to *stemly* on the errata page. If the correction is not itself a printer's error, then *stemly* may mean "descended from the same stem" (False Witness as the natural attendant of Deceit).
80. *eke:* too
84. *make:* mate
85. *Entyst percase:* Enticed perhaps; *glosse:* glossy appearance
87. *herbord:* harbored
91. *ysojorned:* lived

And when the wretch, (I cannot terme him bet)
Had me on seas ful farre from friendly help,
A sparke of lust did kindle in his brest,   105
And bad him harke to songs of *Satyra.*
I selly soule (which thought no body harme)
Gan cleere my throte, and strave to sing my best,
Which pleasde him so and so enflamde his hart,
That he forgot my sister *Poesys*   110
And ravisht me, to please his wanton minde.
Not so content, when this foule fact was done,
(Yfraught with feare, least that I should disclose
His incest and his doting darke desire)
He causde straight wayes the formost of his crew   115
With his compeare to trie me with their tongues:
And when their guiles could not prevaile to winne
My simple mynde from tracke of trustie truth,
Nor yet deceyt could bleare mine eyes through fraude,
Came Slander then, accusing me, and sayde   120
That I entist *Delyght* to love & luste.
Thus was I caught, poore wretch that thought none il.
And furthermore to cloke their own offence,
They clapt me fast in cage of *Myserie,*
And there I dwelt full many a doleful day,   125
Until this theefe, this traytor vaine *Delight,*
Cut out my tong with *Raysor* of *Restraynte,*
Least I should wraye this bloudy deede of his.

And thus (my Lord) I live a weary life,
Not as I seemd, a man sometimes of might,   130
But womanlike, whose teares must venge hir harms.
And yet even as the mighty gods did daine

---

103. *terme him bet:* find a better name for him
107. *selly:* simple
108. *strave:* strove
112. *fact:* deed
113. *Yfraught:* Filled; *least:* lest
115. *formost:* foremost
116. *compeare:* comrade. The two "persuaders" are probably the *False semblant* and *Flearing flattery* mentioned above at lines 71–72.
128. *wraye:* betray
132. *daine:* deign

For *Philomele*, that thoughe hir tong were cutte,
Yet should she sing a pleasant note sometimes:
So have they deignd, by their devine decrees,   135
That with the stumps of my reproved tong,
I may sometimes *Reprovers* deedes reprove,
And sing a verse to make them see themselves.

Then thus I sing this selly song by night,
Like *Phylomene*, since that the shining Sunne   140
Is now eclypst, which wont to lend me light.

And thus I sing, in corner closely cowcht
Like *Philomene*, since that the stately cowrts,
Are now no place for such poore byrds as I.

And thus I sing, with pricke against my brest,   145
Like *Philomene*, since that the privy worme,
Which makes me se my reckles youth mispent,
May well suffise to keepe me waking still.

And thus I sing, when pleasant spring begins,
Like *Philomene*, since every janglyng byrd,   150
Which squeaketh loude, shall never triumph so,
As though my muze were mute and durst not sing.

And thus I sing, with harmelesse true intent,
Like *Philomene*, when as percase (meane while)
The Cuckowe suckes mine eggs by foule deceit,   155
And lickes the sweet, which might have fed me first.

---

133. *Philomele*: Gascoigne uses either this form or "Philomene" (cf. line 140) indifferently. Both were current.
141. *wont*: used
145. *pricke*: thorn
146. *privy worme*: secret snake (in his heart)
152. *muze*: muse
155. *Cuckowe*: the cuckoo was notorious for stealing other birds' eggs and laying its own in their nests
156. *the sweet*: i.e., the meat within the eggs

And thus I meane in mournfull wise to sing,
A rare conceit, (God graunt it like my Lorde)
A trustie tune, from auncient clyffes conveyed,
A playne song note, which cannot warble well.　　160

For whyles I mark this weak and wretched world,
Wherin I see howe every kind of man
Can flatter still and yet deceives himselfe,
I seeme to muse, from whence such errour springs,
Such grosse conceits, such mistes of darke mistake,　　165
Such *Surcuydry*, such weening over well,
And yet in dede such dealings too too badde;
And as I stretch my weary wittes, to weighe
The cause therof and whence it should proceede,
My battred braynes, (which now be shrewdly brusde,　　170
With cannon shot, of much misgovernment)
Can spye no cause, but onely one conceite,
Which makes me thinke the world goeth stil awry.

I see and sigh, (bycause it makes me sadde)
That pevishe pryde, doth al the world possesse,　　175
And every wight, will have a looking glasse
To see himselfe, yet so he seeth him not:
Yea shal I say? a glasse of common glasse,
Which glistreth bright and shewes a seemely shew
Is not enough; the days are past and gon　　180
That Berral glasse, with foyles of lovely brown,
Might serve to shew a seemely favord face.
That age is deade and vanisht long ago,
Which thought that steele both trusty was & true,
And needed not a foyle of contraries,　　185

---

158. *conceit:* imaginative fiction
159. *clyffes:* musical clefs
166. *Surcuydry:* pride; *weening over well:* (people) who think too much of themselves
170. *shrewdly:* severely, badly
178. *glasse . . . glasse:* i.e., an ordinary mirror
181. *Berral:* beryl; *foyles:* metal sheets used as backing for a mirror
185. *foyle of contraries:* which would give back a deceptive, unreal reflection

But shewde al things, even as they were in deede.
In steade whereof our curious yeares can finde
The christal glas, which glimseth brave & bright,
And shewes the thing much better than it is,
Beguylde with foyles, of sundry subtil sights,   190
So that they seeme and covet not to be.

This is the cause (beleve me now my Lorde)
That Realmes do rewe from high prosperity,
That kings decline from princely government,
That Lords do lacke their auncestors good wil,   195
That knights consume their patrimonie still,
That gentlemen do make the merchant rise,
That plowmen begge and craftesmen cannot thrive,
That clergie quayles and hath smal reverence,
That laymen live by moving mischiefe stil,   200
That courtiers thrive at latter Lammas day,
That officers can scarce enrich their heyres,
That Souldiours sterve or prech at Tiborne crosse,
That lawyers buye and purchase deadly hate,
That merchants clyme and fal againe as fast,   205
That roysters brag above their betters rome,
That sicophants are counted jolly guests,
That *Lais* leades a Ladies life alofte,
And *Lucrece* lurkes with sobre bashful grace.

This is the cause (or else my Muze mistakes)   210
That things are thought which never yet were wrought,
And castels buylt above in lofty skies,
Which never yet had good foundation.

---

187. *curious:* artificial, novelty-seeking
193. *rewe:* fall, decline
197. *That . . . rise:* i.e., by buying too much from them and thus going
into debt
200. *moving mischiefe:* committing evil deeds
201. *latter . . . day:* i.e., a day that will never come. Lammas Day was
August 1, a harvest festival.
203. *prech . . . crosse:* i.e., are hanged as thieves on Tyburn Hill
206. *roysters:* roisterers, rowdies; *rome:* social position
208. *Lais:* the famous Greek courtesan
209. *Lucrece:* the chaste Roman matron, raped by Tarquin

And that the same may seme no feined dreame,
But words of worth and worthy to be wayed,   215
I have presumde my Lord for to present
With this poore glasse, which is of trustie Steele,
And came to me by wil and testament
Of one that was a Glassemaker in deede.

Lucylius, this worthy man was namde,   220
Who at his death bequeathed the christal glasse,
To such as love to seme but not to be,
And unto those that love to see themselves,
How foule or fayre soever that they are,
He gan bequeath a glasse of trustie Steele,   225
Wherin they may be bolde alwayes to looke,
Bycause it shewes all things in their degree.
And since myselfe (now pride of youth is past)
Do love to be and let al seeming passe,
Since I desire to see my selfe in deed,   230
Not what I would, but what I am or should,
Therfore I like this trustie glasse of Steele.

Wherin I see a frolike favor frounst
With foule abuse, of lawlesse lust in youth:
Wherin I see a *Sampsons* grim regarde   235
Disgraced yet with *Alexanders* bearde:
Wherein I see a corps of comely shape
(And such as might beseeme the courte full wel)
Is cast at heele by courting al to soone:
Wherein I see a quicke capacitye,   240

---

215. *wayed:* weighed
220. *Lucylius:* the father of Roman satire (second century B.C.)
227. *in their degree:* according to their true value
233. *frolike . . . frounst:* a happy-go-lucky face wrinkled
234. *of:* accused of. A marginal gloss in 1575 refers lines 233–34 to "The author himselfe."
235. *regarde:* appearance
236. *bearde:* Alexander the Great reputedly had a very small beard
237. *corps:* body
239. *cast at heele:* reduced to groveling

284

Berayde with blots of light Inconstancie:
An age suspect bycause of youthes misdeedes.
A poets brayne possest with layes of love:
A *Caesars* minde and yet a *Codrus* might,
A Souldiours hart, supprest with feareful doomes: 245
A Philosopher, foolishly fordone.
And to be playne, I see my selfe so playne,
And yet so much unlike that most I seemde,
As were it not that Reason ruleth me,
I should in rage this face of mine deface   250
And cast this corps downe headlong in dispaire,
Bycause it is so farre unlike it selfe.

And therwithal, to comfort me againe,
I see a world of worthy government,
A common welth with policy so rulde,   255
As neither lawes are sold nor justice bought,
Nor riches sought unlesse it be by right.
No crueltie nor tyrannie can raigne,
No right revenge doth rayse rebellion,
No spoyles are tane although the sword prevaile,   260
No ryot spends the coyne of common welth,
No rulers hoard the countries treasure up,
No man growes riche by subtilty nor sleight:
All people dreade the magistrates decree,
And al men feare the scourge of mighty Jove.   265
Lo this (my lord) may wel deserve the name
Of such a lande, as milke and hony flowes.
And this I see within my glasse of Steel,

---

241. *Berayde:* Betrayed
242. *An age suspect:* A man suspected in his maturity
244. *Codrus:* the last king of Athens (ca. 1068 B.C.), who, powerless against the Spartans, sacrificed himself in order to save his people
245. *doomes:* judgments
246. *fordone:* come to ruin
259. *right:* just
260. *tane:* taken
261. *ryot:* wastefulness
267. *as:* in which

Set forth even so, by *Solon* (worthy wight)
Who taught king *Croesus* what it is to seme 270
And what to be, by proofe of happie end.
The like *Lycurgus, Lacedemon* king,
Did set to shew by viewe of this my glasse,
And left the same a mirour to behold
To every prince of his posterity. 275

But now (aye me) the glasing christal glasse
Doth make us thinke that realmes and townes are rych
Where favor sways the sentence of the law,
Where al is fishe that cometh to the net,
Where mighty power doth over rule the right, 280
Where injuries do foster secret grudge,
Where bloudy sword maks every booty prize,
Where banquetting is compted comly cost,
Where officers grow rich by princes pens,
Where purchase commes by covyn and deceit, 285
And no man dreads but he that cannot shift,
Nor none serve God, but only tongtide men.
Againe I see, within my glasse of Steele,
But foure estates, to serve eche country Soyle,
The King, the Knight, the Pesant, & the Priest. 290
The King should care for al the subjectes still,
The Knight should fight for to defende the same,
The Peasant he, should labor for their ease,
And Priests shuld pray for them & for themselves.

---

269. *Solon:* lawgiver of ancient Greece (638–559 B.C.)
270. *Croesus:* last king of Lydia (d. 546 B.C.). According to Herodotus
(I, 29ff., 86–87), Solon, in exile, was asked by Croesus who were the
happiest men. Solon named Bion and other humble Greek philosophers.
Solon's own death was reported to have been serene, which may explain
Gascoigne's *by proofe of happie end* in line 271.
272. *Lycurgus:* the legendary lawgiver of Sparta (*Lacedemon*); the reforms
ascribed to him are now dated about 600 B.C.
276. *glasing:* obscuring, distorting
282. *maks:* makes
283. *compted . . . cost:* viewed as a fitting expense
284. *pens:* perhaps the pens used by princes to sign warrants, but more
likely "pence" (money) which corrupt officials steal from their princes
285. *purchase:* gain, acquisition; *covyn:* sly trickery

But out alas, such mists do bleare our eyes,   295
And christal glosse, doth glister so therwith,
That Kings conceive their care is wonderous great
When as they beat their busie restles braynes,
To maintaine pompe and high triumphant sights,
To fede their fil of daintie delicates,   300
To glad their harts with sight of pleasant sports,
To fil their eares with sound of instruments,
To breake with bit the hot coragious horse,
To deck their haules with sumpteous cloth of gold,
To cloth themselves with silkes of straunge devise,   305
To search the rocks for pearles & pretious stones,
To delve the ground for mines of glistering gold:
And never care to maynteine peace and rest,
To yeld reliefe where needy lacke appears,
To stop one eare until the poore man speake,   310
To seme to sleepe when Justice still doth wake,
To gard their lands from sodaine sword and fier,
To feare the cries of giltles suckling babes,
Where ghosts may cal for vengeance on their bloud,
And stirre the wrath of mightie thundring Jove.   315

I speake not this by any english king,
Nor by our Queene, whose high forsight provids
That dyre debate is fledde to foraine Realmes,
Whiles we injoy the golden fleece of peace.
But there to turne my tale, from whence it came,   320
In olden dayes, good kings and worthy dukes
(Who sawe themselves in glasse of trusty Steele)
Contented were with pompes of little pryce,
And set their thoughtes on regal governement.

And order was, when Rome did florish most,   325
That no man might triumph in stately wise,
But such as had with blowes of bloudy blade

304. *haules:* halls
316. *by:* with reference to
318. *debate:* strife

Five thousand foes in foughten field foredone.
Now he that likes to loke in Christal glasse,
May see proud pomps in high triumphant wise,   330
Where never blowe was delt with enemie.

When *Sergius* devised first the meane
To pen up fishe within the swelling floud,
And so content his mouth with daintie fare,
Then followed fast excesse on Princes bordes,   335
And every dish was chargde with new conceits,
To please the taste of uncontented mindes.
But had he seene the streine of straunge devise,
Which *Epicures* do now adayes invent,
To yeld good smacke unto their daintie tongues: 340
Could he conceive how princes paunch is fillde
With secret cause of sickenesse (oft) unseene,
Whiles lust desires much more than nature craves,
Then would he say that al the Romane cost
Was common trash compard to sundrie Sauce   345
Which princes use to pamper Appetite.

O Christal Glasse, thou settest things to shew,
Which are (God knoweth) of little worth in dede.
Al eyes behold, with eagre deepe desire,
The Faulcon flye, the grehounde runne his course,   350
The bayted Bul and Beare at stately stake,
These Enterluds, these newe Italian sportes,
And every gawde that glads the minde of man:
But fewe regard their needy neighbours lacke,
And fewe beholde by contemplation   355

---

328. *in . . . fordone*: slain on the battlefield. Roman triumphs were granted
to victorious generals by the Senate according to certain set rules.
332. *Sergius*: Caius Sergius Orata, a notorious Roman voluptuary; *meane*:
method
336. *chargde*: loaded; *conceits*: delicacies
338. *streine*: strain, flow
340. *smacke*: taste
351. *bayted . . . stake*: bull and bear baiting were popular London sports
352. *Enterluds*: dramatic performances exhibited as part of an elaborate
entertainment
353. *gawde*: trick, prank

The joyes of heaven, ne yet the paines of hel.
Fewe loke to lawe, but al men gaze on lust.

A swete consent of Musicks sacred sound,
Doth rayse our mindes, (as rapt) al up on high,
But sweeter soundes, of concorde, peace, and love,   360
Are out of tune and jarre in every stoppe.

To tosse and turne the sturdie trampling stede,
To bridle him and make him meete to serve,
Deserves (no doubt) great commendation.
But such as have their stables ful yfraught   365
With pampred Jades, ought therwithal to wey
What great excesse upon them may be spent,
How many pore, (which nede nor brake nor bit)
Might therwithal in godly wise be fedde,
And kings ought not so many horse to have.   370

The sumpteous house declares the princes state,
But vaine excesse bewrayes a princes faults.

Our bumbast hose, our treble double ruffes,
Our sutes of Silke, our comely garded capes,
Our knit silke stockes, and spanish lether shoes,   375
(Yea velvet serves, ofttimes to trample in)
Our plumes, our spangs, and al our queint aray,
Are pricking spurres, provoking filthy pride,
And snares (unseen) which leade a man to hel.

How live the Mores, which spurne at glistring perle,   380
And scorne the costs which we do holde so deare?
How? how but wel? and weare the precious pearle
Of peerlesse truth, amongst them published,

---

358. *consent:* harmony
365. *yfraught:* filled
374. *garded:* trimmed
377. *spangs:* spangles
380. *Mores:* Moors. Cf. *Othello,* V, ii, 347–48. *spurne at:* hold in contempt
383. *published:* well known

(Which we enjoy and never wey the worth).
They would not then the same (like us) despise, 385
Which (though they lacke) they live in better wise
Than we, which holde the worthles pearle so deare.
But glittring gold, which many yeares lay hidde,
Til gredy mindes gan search the very guts
Of earth and clay to finde out sundrie moulds 390
(As redde and white, which are by melting made
Bright gold and silver, mettals of mischiefe)
Hath now enflamde the noblest Princes harts
With foulest fire of filthy Avarice;
And seldome seene that kings can be content 395
To kepe their bounds, which their forefathers left:
What causeth this, but greedy golde to get?
Even gold, which is the very cause of warres,
The neast of strife, and nourice of debate,
The barre of heaven, and open way to hel. 400
But is this strange? when Lords when Knights & Squires
(Which ought defende the state of common welth)
Are not afrayd to covet like a King?
O blinde desire: oh high aspiring harts.
The country Squire doth covet to be Knight, 405
The Knight a Lord, the Lord an Erle or a Duke,
The Duke a King, the King would Monarke be,
And none content with that which is his own.
Yet none of these can see in Christal glasse
(Which glistereth bright, & bleares their gasing eyes) 410
How every life beares with him his disease.
But in my glasse, which is of trustie steele,
I can perceive how kingdomes breede but care,
How Lordship lives with lots of lesse delight
(Though cappe and knee do seeme a reverence, 415
And courtlike life is thought an other heaven)
Than common people finde in every coast.

---

384. *wey:* weigh, consider carefully
390. *moulds:* kinds of ore
399. *nourice:* nurse, nourisher
411. *him his:* it its
414. *with lots:* in conditions
415. *cappe and knee:* doffing the cap and bending the knee (to a superior)

The Gentleman, which might in countrie keepe
A plenteous boorde and feed the fatherlesse
With pig and goose, with mutton, beefe and veale   420
(Yea now and then, a capon and a chicke)
Wil breake up house and dwel in market townes,
A loytring life, and like an *Epicure*.

But who (meane while) defends the common welth?
Who rules the flocke, when sheperds so are fled?   425
Who stayes the staff, which shuld uphold the state?
Forsoth good Sir, the Lawyer leapeth in,
Nay rather leapes both over hedge and ditch,
And rules the rost, but fewe men rule by right.

O Knights, O Squires, O Gentle blouds yborne,   430
You were not borne al onely for your selves:
Your countrie claymes some part of al your paines.
There should you live and therin should you toyle,
To hold up right, and banish cruel wrong,
To helpe the pore, to bridle backe the riche,   435
To punish vice, and vertue to advaunce,
To see God servde, and *Belzebub* supprest.
You should not trust lieftenaunts in your rome,
And let them sway the scepter of your charge,
Whiles you (meane while) know scarcely what is don,   440
Nor yet can yeld accompt if you were callde.

The stately lord, which woonted was to kepe
A court at home, is now come up to courte,
And leaves the country for a common prey
To pilling, polling, brybing, and deceit: 445
(Al which his presence might have pacified,
Or else have made offenders smel the smoke).

---

437. *Belzebub:* Beelzebub, the devil
438. *rome:* office
441. *yeld accompt:* give a satisfactory account
442. *woonted was:* used
445. *pilling, polling:* ruining by depredation and extortion

And now the youth which might have served him
In comely wise, with countrey clothes yclad,
And yet therby bin able to preferre 450
Unto the prince and there to seke advance:
Is faine to sell his landes for courtly cloutes,
Or else sits still and liveth like a loute,
(Yet of these two, the last fault is the lesse):
And so those imps which might in time have sprong 455
Alofte (good lord) and servde to shielde the state,
Are either nipt with such untimely frosts,
Or else growe crookt because they be not proynd.

These be the Knights which shold defend the land,
And these be they which leave the land at large. 460
Yet here percase, it wilbe thought I rove
And runne astray, besides the kings high way,
Since by the Knights, of whom my text doth tell
(And such as shew most perfect in my glasse)
Is ment nomore, but worthy Souldiours 465
Whose skil in armes and long experience
Should still uphold the pillers of the worlde.
Yes out of doubt, this noble name of Knight
May comprehend, both Duke, Erle, lorde, Knight, Squire,
Yea gentlemen, and every gentle borne. 470

But if you wil constraine me for to speake,
What souldiours are, or what they ought to be
(And I my selfe of that profession)
I see a crew, which glister in my glasse,
The bravest bande that ever yet was sene: 475
Behold behold, where *Pompey* commes before,
Where *Manlius* and *Marius* insue,

450. *preferre:* be preferred
452. *cloutes:* "pieces of cloth"
455. *imps:* tender shoots
458. *proyned:* pruned
476. *Pompey:* Roman triumvir (106–48 B.C.)
477. *Manlius:* probably Marcus Manlius Capitolinus (d. 384 B.C.); *Marius:* Gaius Marius (d. 86 B.C.), Roman general

292

Æmilius and *Curius* I see,
Palamedes and *Fabius maximus*,
And eke their mate, *Epaminondas* loe,   480
Protesilaus and *Phocyon* are not farre,
Pericles stands in rancke amongst the rest,
Aristomenes may not be forgot,
Unlesse the list of good men be disgrast.

Behold (my lord) these souldiours can I spie   485
Within my glasse, within my true Steele glasse.

I see not one therin, which seekes to heape
A world of pence, by pinching of dead payes,
And so beguiles the prince in time of nede,
When muster day, and foughten fielde are odde.   490
Since *Pompey* did enrich the common heaps,
And *Paulus* he (*Æmilius* surnamed)
Returnde to *Rome* no richer than he went,
Although he had so many lands subdued,
And brought such treasure to the common chests   495
That fourescore yeres the state was (after) free
From grevous taske and imposition.
Yea since againe, good *Marcus Curius*,

---

478. *Æmilius:* Lucius Aemilius Paullus, killed at the battle of Cannae
(216 B.C.), or his son Macedonicus (229–160 B.C.); *Curius:* Manius
Curius Dentatus (d. 272 B.C.), Roman general, famed for his incorrupti-
bility
479. *Palamedes:* Greek hero who died at the siege of Troy; *Fabius maximus:*
Quintus Fabius Maximus Cunctator (d. 203 B.C.), Roman general in the
Second Punic War
480. *Epaminondas:* Theban general (d. 362 B.C.)
481. *Protesilaus:* Greek leader at Troy; *Phocyon:* Athenian general (d.
317 B.C.)
482. *Pericles:* Athenian statesman (d. 429 B.C.)
483. *Aristomenes:* national hero of Messenia in the seventh century B.C.
488. *pinching . . . payes:* stealing the pay of dead men
490. *When . . . odde:* i.e., when there is a big discrepancy between the
number of soldiers listed as mustered and those who actually fight in a
given battle. Cf. Falstaff's recruiting practices in *Henry IV, Part II.* Lines
491–500 are printed in italic in the 1576 edition, as are lines 513–20, 528–
36, 544–54, and 562–65.
498. *Marcus:* Probably Gascoigne's error for "Manius." See above, line
478 n.

Thought sacriledge himselfe for to advaunce,
And see his souldiours pore or live in lacke.   500

I see not one within this glasse of mine,
Whose fethers flaunt and flicker in the winde,
As though he were all onely to be markt,
When simple snakes, which go not halfe so gay,
Can leave him yet a furlong in the field: 505
And when the pride of all his peacockes plumes,
Is daunted downe with dastard dreadfulnesse.
And yet in towne he jetted every streete
As though the god of warres (even *Mars* himself)
Might wel (by him) be lively counterfayte,   510
Though much more like the coward *Constantine*.
I see none such (my Lorde), I see none such,
Since *Phocion*, which was in deed a *Mars*
And one which did much more than he wold vaunt,
Contented was to be but homely clad.   515
And *Marius* (whose constant hart could bide
The very vaines of his forwearied legges
To be both cut and carved from his corps)
Could never yet contented be to spend
One idle groate, in clothing nor in cates.   520

I see not one, (my Lord) I see not one
Which stands somuch, upon his paynted sheath
(Bycause he hath perchaunce at *Bolleyn* bene
And loytered since then in idlenesse)
That he accompts no Soldiour but himselfe,   525
Nor one that can despise the learned brayne,

---

503. *all onely:* himself alone
507. *dreadfulnesse:* fearfulness
508. *jetted:* promenaded through
510. *lively counterfayte:* imitated to the life
511. *Constantine:* Gascoigne probably alludes, not to Constantine the Great, but to the usurping emperor Constantine, who was killed at Ravenna in 411
517. *forwearied:* utterly exhausted
520. *groate:* a silver coin worth fourpence; *cates:* provisions
523. *Bolleyn:* Boulogne, captured by Henry VIII in 1544

Which joyneth reading with experience.
Since *Palamedes* and *Ulisses* both,
Were much esteemed for their pollicies
Although they were not thought long trained men,　　530
Epamynondas eke was much esteemde
Whose Eloquence was such in all respects,
As gave no place unto his manly hart.
And *Fabius* surnamed *Maximus*,
Could joyne such learning with experience,　　535
As made his name more famous than the rest.

These bloudy beasts apeare not in my glasse
Which cannot rule their sword in furious rage,
Nor have respecte to age nor yet to kinde:
But downe goeth al where they get upper hand.　　540
Whose greedy harts so hungrie are to spoyle,
That few regard the very wrath of God,
Which greeved is at cries of giltlesse bloud.
Pericles was a famous man of warre,
And victor eke in nine great foughten fields,　　545
Wherof he was the general in charge.
Yet at his death he rather did rejoyce
In clemencie than bloudy victorie.
Be still (quoth he) you grave *Athenians*,
(Who whispered and tolde his valiant facts)　　550
You have forgot my greatest glorie got.
For yet (by me, nor mine occasion)
Was never sene a mourning garment worne.
O noble words, wel worthy golden writ.
Beleve me (Lord) a souldiour cannot have　　555
Too great regarde wheron his knife should cut.

Ne yet the men, which wonder at their wounds,
And shewe their scarres to every commer by,
Dare once be seene within my glasse of Steele;

---

539. *kinde*: kindred
550. *facts*: deeds
552–53. *by . . . worne*: i.e., I never caused nor gave occasion that a mourning garment was worn

For so the faults of *Thraso* and his trayne   560
(Whom *Terence* told, to be but bragging brutes)
Might sone appeare to every skilful eye.
Bolde *Manlius* could close and wel convey
Ful thirtie wounds (and three) upon his head,
Yet never made nor bones nor bragges therof.   565

What should I speake of drunken Soldiours?
Or lechers lewde, which fight for filthy lust?
Of whom that one can sit and bybbe his fil,
Consume his coyne, (which might good corage yeld,
To such as march and move at his commaunde)   570
And makes himselfe a worthy mocking stocke
Which might deserve (by sobre life) great laude.
That other dotes and driveth forth his dayes
In vaine delight and foule concupiscence,
When works of weight might occupie his hedde.   575
Yea therwithal he puts his owne fonde heade
Under the belt of such as should him serve,
And so becoms example of much evil,
Which should have servde as lanterne of good life:
And is controlde, wheras he should commaund.   580
Augustus Caesar, he which might have made
Both feasts and banquets bravely as the best,
Was yet content (in campe) with homely cates,
And seldome dranke his wine unwatered.
Aristomenes dayned to defende   585
His dames of prize, whom he in warres had won,
And rather chose to die in their defence,
Then filthy men should foyle their chastitie.
This was a wight wel worthy fame and prayse.

O Captayns come, and Souldiours come apace,   590
Behold my glasse, and you shall see therin

---

560. *Thraso:* the braggart soldier in Terence's *Eunuchus*
563. *convey:* bear
568. *Of whom that:* At whose expense; *bybbe:* imbibe
572. *laude:* praise
586. *dames of prize:* lady prisoners
588. *Then:* Than; *foyle:* violate

Proud *Crassus* bagges consumde by covetise,
Great *Alexander* drounde in drunkennesse,
Caesar and *Pompey* spilt with privy grudge,
Brennus beguild with lightnesse of beliefe,   595
Cleomenes by ryot not regarded,
Vespasian disdayned for deceit,
Demetrius light set by for his lust,
Whereby at last he dyed in prison pent.

Hereto percase, some one man will alledge   600
That Princes pence are pursed up so close,
And faires do fall so seldome in a yeare,
That when they come provision must be made
To fende the frost in hardest winter nights.

Indeed I finde, within this glasse of mine,   605
Justinian, that proude ungrateful prince,
Which made to begge bold *Belisarius*
His trustie man, which had so stoutly fought
In his defence, with evry enimy.
And *Scypio* condemnes the Romaine rule,   610
Which suffred him (that had so truely served)
To leade pore life at his (*Lynternum*) ferme,

---

592. *Crassus:* Marcus Licinius Crassus (d. 53 B.C.), who made a huge fortune through speculation; *bagges:* money bags; *covetise:* avarice
594. *spilt . . . grudge:* destroyed by secret quarrels
595. *Brennus:* Galatian leader who invaded Greece and attacked Delphi in 279 B.C.
596. *Cleomenes:* probably Cleomenes of Naucratis, whom Alexander the Great made regent of Egypt in 332–31 B.C. He was later executed by Ptolemy I for exploiting (*ryot*) the wealth of Egypt. *by:* because of
597. *Vespasian:* Roman emperor (d. A.D. 79). He does not seem to have been especially noted for deceitfulness.
598. *Demetrius:* among the various Demetriuses of classical history, Demetrius I of Macedonia (336–283 B.C.) seems the best candidate. After his surrender to Seleucus he was encouraged (and did) drink himself to death. *light set by:* held in slight regard
604. *fende:* fend off
606. *Justinian:* Roman emperor of the East (A.D. 527–65). His great general, Belisarius (d. 565) lived in disfavor after Narses replaced him in 548.
610. *Scypio:* Scipio Africanus (237–183 B.C.), Roman general. His *ferme* (country estate) was at Liternum, now the village of Patria, in Campania.

Which did deserve such worthy recompence.
Yea herewithal most Souldiours of our time
Beleeve for truth, that proude *Justinian*   615
Did never die, without good store of heyres,
And *Romanes* race cannot be rooted out,
Such yssewe springs of such unplesant budds.

But shal I say? this lesson learne of me,
When drums are dumb and sound not dub a dub,   620
Then be thou eke as mewet as a mayde
(I preach this sermon but to souldiours)
And learne to live within thy bravries bounds.
Let not the Mercer pul thee by the sleeve
For sutes of silke, when cloth may serve thy turne;   625
Let not thy scores come robbe thy needy purse,
Make not the catchpol rich by thine arrest.

Are thou a Gentle? live with gentle friendes,
Which wil be glad thy companie to have,
If manhoode may with manners well agree.   630

Art thou a serving man? then serve againe,
And stint to steale as common souldiours do.

Art thou a craftsman? take thee to thine arte,
And cast off slouth which loytreth in the Campes.

Art thou a plowman pressed for a shift?   635
Then learne to clout thine old cast cobled shoes,
And rather bide at home with barley bread,
Than learne to spoyle, as thou hast seene some do.

---

621. *eke:* too; *mewet:* mute
626. *scores:* debts
627. *catchpol:* sheriff's officer who arrests for debt
628. *Gentle:* gentleman
632. *stint:* cease
635. *shift:* way to earn a living
636. *clout:* patch, repair; *cast:* cast off
638. *spoyle:* rob

Of truth (my friendes and my companions eke)
Who lust by warres to gather lawful welth,   640
And so to get a right renoumed name,
Must cast aside al common trades of warre,
And learne to live as though he knew it not.

Well, thus my Knight hath held me al to long,
Bycause he bare such compasse in my glasse.   645
High time were then to turne my wery pen,
Unto the Peasant comming next in place,
And here to write the summe of my conceit.
I do not meane alonely husbandmen,
Which till the ground, which dig, delve, mow, and sowe,   650
Which swinke and sweate, whiles we do sleepe and snort
And serch the guts of earth for greedy gain;
But he that labors any kind of way
To gather gaines and to enrich himselfe,
By King, by Knight, by holy helping Priests,   655
And al the rest, that live in common welth,
(So that his gaines, by greedy guyles be got)
Him can I compt a Peasant in his place.
Al officers, all advocates at lawe,
Al men of arte, which get goodes greedily,   660
Must be content to take a Peasants rome.

A strange devise, and sure my Lord wil laugh
To see it so, desgested in degrees.
But he which can in office drudge and droy,
And crave of al (although even now a dayes   665
Most officers commaund that shuld be cravde);

641. *renoumed:* renowned
645. *bare such compasse:* took up so much space
648. *conceit:* ideas
649. *alonely:* only
658. *compt:* reckon
663. *desgested in degrees:* set forth in digest form according to the ranks of society
664. *droy:* toil
665. *crave:* desire
666. *that:* what

He that can share from every pention payde
A Peeter peny weying halfe a pounde,
He that can plucke sir *Bennet* by the sleeve,
And finde a fee in his pluralitie,   670
He that can winke at any foule abuse,
As long as gaines come trouling in therwith,
Shal such come see themselves in this my glasse?
Or shal they gaze, as godly good men do?
Yea let them come: but shal I tell you one thing?   675
How ere their gownes be gathred in the backe
With organe pipes of old king *Henries* clampe,
How ere their cappes be folded with a flappe,
How ere their beardes be clipped by the chinne,
How ere they ride or mounted are on mules,   680
I compt them worse than harmeles homely hindes,
Which toyle in dede to serve our common use.

Strange tale to tel: all officers be blynde,
And yet their one eye, sharpe as *Linceus* sight,
That one eye winks, as though it were but blynd,   685
That other pries and peekes in every place.
Come naked neede? and chance to do amisse?
He shal be sure to drinke upon the whippe.
But privie gaine (that bribing busie wretch)
Can finde the meanes to creepe and cowch so low,   690
As officers can never see him slyde,
Nor heare the trampling of his stealing steppes.
He comes (I thinke) upon the blinde side stil.

---

667. *pention:* pension
668. *Peeter peny:* unjust "cut." See no. 10, line 53 n.
669. *sir Bennet:* said generically for a typical clergyman
670. *finde . . . pluralitie:* extract a fee from him because he holds (illegally) more than one living
672. *trouling:* rolling
676. *How ere:* Howsoever
677. *organe pipes:* large, rounded flutings; *Henries clampe:* i.e., like the fashion which prevailed in Henry VIII's days
681. *hindes:* rustics, farm laborers
684. *Linceus:* Lynceus of Messenia, one of the Argonauts, who was famed for the sharpness of his sight
688. *drinke . . . whippe:* get or merit a flogging

These things (my Lord) my glasse now sets to shew,
Whereas long since all officers were seene   695
To be men made out of another moulde.
Epamynond, of whome I spake before
(Which was long time an officer in *Thebes*)
And toylde in peace aswel as fought in warre,
Would never take or bribe or rich reward.   700
And thus he spake, to such as sought his helpe:
If it be good (quoth he) that you desire,
Then wil I do it for the vertues sake:
If it be badde no bribe can me infecte.
If so it be for this my common weale,   705
Then am I borne and bound by duetie both
To see it done, withouten furder words.
But if it be unprofitable thing,
And might empaire, offende, or yeld anoy
Unto the state, which I pretende to stay,   710
Then al the gold (quoth he) that growes on earth
Shal never tempt my free consent thereto.

How many now wil treade *Zeleucus* steps?
Or who can byde *Cambyses* cruel dome?
Cruel? nay just (yea softe, and peace, good sir)   715
For Justice sleepes and Troth is jested out.

O that al kings would (*Alexander* like)
Hold evermore, one finger streight stretcht out,
To thrust in eyes of all their master theeves.

---

697. *before:* cf. above, line 480
700. first *or:* either
707. *furder:* further
710. *pretende to stay:* profess to support
713. *Zeleucus:* Seleucus I (d. 280 B.C.), general of Alexander the Great and founder of the Seleucid dynasty. A most humane and just ruler.
714. *Cambyses:* King of Persia (d. 521 B.C.), son of Cyrus the Great. He changed from a just ruler to a tyrannical madman in the latter part of his reign. *dome:* judgment. Herodotus (*History,* Book III) tells many stories about Cambyses, but to which of his *Cruel? nay just* acts Gascoigne refers is uncertain.

But *Brutus* died without posteritie, 720
And *Marcus Crassus* had none issue male,
Cicero slipt unsene out of this world,
With many mo which pleaded romaine pleas
And were content to use their eloquence
In maintenance of matters that were good. 725
Demosthenes in *Athens* usde his arte,
(Not for to heape himselfe great hourds of gold)
But stil to stay the towne from deepe deceite
Of *Philips* wyles, which had besieged it.
Where shal we reade, that any of these foure 730
Did ever pleade as carelesse of the trial?
Or who can say they builded sumpteously?
Or wroong the weake out of his own by wyles?
They were (I trowe) of noble houses borne,
And yet content to use their best devoire, 735
In furdering eche honest harmelesse cause.
They did not rowte (like rude unringed swine,)
To roote nobilitie from heritage.
They stoode content with gaine of glorious fame,
(Bycause they had respect to equitie) 740
To leade a life like true Philosophers.
Of all the bristle bearded Advocates

---

720. *Brutus:* Marcus Junius Brutus (d. 42 B.C.), who committed suicide
after the battle of Philippi
721. *Marcus Crassus:* with Caesar and Pompey he formed the first triumvi-
rate in 60 B.C.; killed after being defeated by the Parthians in 53 B.C. He
did, however, have a son, Publius Licinus, who died with his father.
722. *slipt unsene:* little is known about the last months of Cicero's life.
He died in 43 B.C., a sacrifice made by Octavian to quiet Antony's animos-
ity.
723. *many . . . pleas:* i.e., many other great Roman lawyers who defended
just causes
726. *Demosthenes:* Athenian orator and statesman (d. 322 B.C.) who at-
tacked Philip of Macedon in a series of great speeches (*the Philippics*)
728. *stay:* keep
731. *carelesse . . . trial:* i.e., as if they were unconcerned over the outcome
of the trial
733. *wroong . . . wyles:* cunningly extorted the weak man's possessions
from him
735. *devoire:* effort
737. *rowte:* dig in the ground with their noses; *unringed:* untamed, with no
rings in their snouts

302

That ever lovde their fees above the cause,
I cannot see (scarce one) that is so bolde
To shewe his face and fayned Phisnomie   745
In this my glasse: but if he do (my Lorde)
He shewes himselfe to be by very kinde
A man which meanes at every time and tide,
To do smal right but sure to take no wrong.

And master Merchant, he whose travaile ought   750
Commodiously to doe his countrie good,
And by his toyle the same for to enriche,
Can finde the meane to make *Monopolyes*
Of every ware that is accompted strange.
And feeds the vaine of courtiers vaine desires   755
Until the court have courtiers cast at heele,
Quia non habent vestes Nuptiales.

O painted fooles, whose harebrainde heads must have
More clothes attones than might become a king:
For whom the rocks in forain Realmes must spin,   760
For whom they carde, for whom they weave their webbes
For whom no wool appeareth fine enough,
(I speake not this by english courtiers
Since english wool was ever thought most worth)
For whom al seas are tossed to and fro,   765
From whom these purples come from *Persia,*
The crimosine and lively red from *Inde:*
For whom soft silks do sayle from *Sericane,*
And all queint costs do come from fardest coasts:
Whiles in meane while, that worthy Emperour,   770

745. *fayned Phisnomie:* false countenance
754. *ware . . . strange:* commodity which is thought to be unusual
756. *cast at heele:* rejected with contempt
757. *Quia . . . Nuptiales:* because they have no marriage garments. An ironic allusion to Matthew 22:11–14.
759. *attones:* at any given moment
760. *rocks:* distaffs on spinning wheels
763. *by:* concerning
767. *Inde:* India
768. *Sericane:* China, or eastern Asia taken generically
770. *Emperour:* Augustus Caesar

Which rulde the world and had all welth at wil,
Could be content to tire his wearie wife,
His daughters and his niepces everychone,
To spin and worke the clothes that he should weare,
And never carde for silks or sumpteous cost,   775
For cloth of gold or tinsel figurie,
For Baudkin, broydrie, cutworks, nor conceits.
He set the shippes of merchantmen on worke,
With bringing home oyle, graine, and savrie salt
And such like wares, as served common use.   780

Yea for my life, those merchants were not woont
To lend their wares at reasonable rate,
(To gaine no more but *Cento por cento*)
To teach yong men the trade to sel browne paper,
Yea Morrice bells, and byllets too sometimes,   785
To make their coyne a net to catch yong frye.
To binde such babes in father Derbies bands,
To stay their steps by statute Staples staffe,
To rule yong roysters with *Recognisance*,
To read *Arithmeticke* once every day,   790
In Woodstreat, Bredstreat, and in Pultery
(Where such schoolmaisters keepe their counting house)
To fede on bones when flesh and fell is gon,

773. *niepces everychone:* all his nieces
775. *carde:* cared
776. *tinsel figurie:* cloth figured with tinsel
777. *Baudkin . . . conceits:* rich shot silk, embroidered cloth, cloth with patterns cut out of it, artfully devised material
779. *savrie:* savory
782. *reasonable:* the word is used ironically by Gascoigne
783. *Cento por cento:* such and such a percentage
784. *browne paper:* coarse paper used for wrapping
785. *Morrice bells:* used in morris dances; *byllets:* love letters
786. *frye:* i.e., men
787. *father . . . bands:* a rigid form of bond by which a debtor was bound and put in the power of a moneylender
788. *stay:* support; *statute . . . staffe:* i.e., by bonds of record which made the lands of the debtor subject to seizure if he did not pay up in time
789. *roysters:* riotous fellows; *Recognisance:* a bond or pledge
791. *Woodstreat . . . Pultery:* streets of London where moneylenders had their shops
793. *fell:* skin

To keepe their byrds ful close in caytives cage,
(Who being brought to libertie at large   795
Might sing perchaunce, abroade, when sunne doth shine
Of their mishaps & how their fethers fel)
Untill the canker may their corpse consume.

These knackes (my lord) I cannot cal to minde,
Bycause they shewe not in my glasse of steele.   800
But holla: here, I see a wondrous sight,
I see a swarme of Saints within my glasse:
Beholde, behold, I see a swarme in deede
Of holy Saints, which walke in comely wise,
Not deckt in robes, nor garnished with gold,   805
But some unshod, yea some ful thinly clothde,
And yet they seme so heavenly for to see,
As if their eyes were al of Diamonds,
Their face of Rubies, Saphires, and Jacincts,
Their comly beards and heare of silver wiers.   810
And to be short, they seeme Angelycall.
What should they be, (my Lord) what should they be?

O gratious God, I see now what they be.
These be my priests, which pray for evry state,
These be my priests, devorced from the world,   815
And wedded yet, to heaven and holynesse,
Which are not proude, nor covet to be riche.
Which go not gay, nor fede on daintie foode,
Which envie not, nor knowe what malice meanes,
Which loth all lust, disdayning drunkenesse,   820
Which cannot faine, which hate hypocrisie.
Which never sawe Sir *Simonies* deceits.
Which preach of peace, which carpe contentions,
Which loyter not but labour al the yeare,
Which thunder threts of gods most grevous wrath,   825
And yet do teach that mercie is in store.

---

799. *knackes:* tricks
809. *Jacincts:* jacinths, zircons
823. *carpe:* speak against

Lo these (my Lord) be my good praying priests,
Descended from, *Melchysedec* by line,
Cosens to Paule, to Peter, James, and John,
These be my priests, the seasning of the earth,   830
Which wil not leese their Savrinesse, I trowe.

Not one of these (for twentie hundreth groats)
Wil teach the text that byddes him take a wife,
And yet be combred with a concubine.

Not one of these wil reade the holy write   835
Which doth forbid all greedy usurie,
And yet receive a shilling for a pounde.

Not one of these wil preach of patience,
And yet be found as angry as a waspe.

Not one of these can be content to sit   840
In Taverns, Innes, or Alehouses all day,
But spends his time devoutly at his booke.

Not one of these will rayle at rulers wrongs,
And yet be blotted with extortion.

Not one of these, wil paint out worldly pride,   845
And he himselfe as gallaunt as he dare.

Not one of these rebuketh avarice,
And yet procureth proude pluralities.

Not one of these reproveth vanitie
(Whiles he him selfe, with hauke upon his fist   850
And houndes at heele) doth quite forget his text.

---

828. *Melchysedec*: Melchizedek, the priest and king of Salem (Genesis 14:18)
832. *groats*: silver coins worth fourpence
835. *write*: scripture
848. *procureth . . . pluralities* i.e., obtains a license to hold more than one living at a time

Not one of these corrects contentions
For trifling things: and yet will sue for tythes.

Not one of these (not one of these my Lord)
Will be ashamde to do even as he teacheth.   855

My priests have learnt to pray unto the Lord,
And yet they trust not in their lyplabour.

My priests can fast and use al abstinence
From vice and sinne, and yet refuse no meats.

My priests can give in charitable wise,   860
And love also to do good almes dedes,
Although they trust not in their owne deserts.

My priestes can place all penaunce in the hart,
Without regard of outward ceremonies.

My priestes can keepe their temples undefyled,   865
And yet defie all Superstition.

Lo now my Lorde, what thinke you by my priests?
Although they were the last that shewed themselves,
I saide at first their office was to pray,
And since the time is such even now a dayes   870
As hath great nede of prayers truely prayde,
Come forth my priests, and I wil bydde your beades,
I wil presume (although I be no priest)
To bide you pray as Paule and Peter prayde.

Then pray my priests, yea pray to god himselfe,   875
That he vouchsafe (even for his Christes sake)
To give his word free passage here on earth,
And that his church (which now is Militant)

---

867. *by*: of
872. *bydde . . . beades*: say your prayers for you

May soone be sene triumphant over all,
And that he deigne to ende this wicked world,   880
Which walloweth stil in Sinks of filthy sinne.

Eke pray my priests, for Princes and for Kings,
Emperours, Monarks, Duks, and all estates,
Which sway the sworde of royal government
(Of whom our Queene, which lives without compare,   885
Must be the chiefe in bydding of my beades,
Else I deserve to lese both beades and bones)
That God give light unto their noble mindes
To maintaine truth, and therwith stil to wey
That here they reigne not onely for themselves,   890
And that they be but slaves to common welth,
Since al their toyles and all their broken sleeps
Shal scant suffize, to hold it stil upright.

Tell some (in *Spaine*) how close they kepe their closets,
How selde the winde doth blow upon their cheeks,   895
While as (mene while) their sunburnt sutours sterve
And pine before their processe be preferrde.
Then pray (my priests) that god will give his grace
To such a prince, his fault in time to mende.

Tel some (in *France*) how much they love to dance,   900
While sutours daunce attendaunce at the dore.
Yet pray (my priests) for prayers princes mende.

Tel some (in *Portugale*) how colde they be,
In setting forth of right religion:
Which more esteme the present pleasures here,   905
Then stablishing of God his holy worde.
And pray (my Priests) least god such princes spit
And vomit them out of his angrie mouth.

---

887. *lese:* lose
889. *wey:* weigh, consider
894. *close . . . closets:* secret they are in their private chambers
897. *processe be preferrde:* suit be given a hearing

Tel some (*Italian*) princes, how they winke
At stinking stewes, and say they are (forsooth)   910
A remedy to quench foule filthy luste:
When as in dede they be the sinkes of sinne.
And pray (my priests) that God wil not impute
Such wilful facts unto such princes charge,
When he himselfe commaundeth every man   915
To do none ill, that good may growe therby.

And pray likewise, for all that rulers be
By kings commaundes as their lieftenants here,
Al magistrates, al councellours, and all
That sit in office or Authoritie.   920
Pray, pray, (my priests) that neither love nor mede
Do sway their minds from furdering of right,
That they be not too saintish nor too sowre,
But beare the bridle evenly betwene both,
That stil they stoppe one eare to heare him speake   925
Which is accused, absent as he is:
That evermore, they mark what moode doth move
The mouth which makes the information,
That faults forpaste (so that they be not huge,
Nor do exceed the bonds of loyaltie)   930
Do never quench their charitable minde,
When as they see repentance hold the reines
Of heady youth, which wont to runne astray.
That malice make no mansion in their minds,
Nor envy frete to see how vertue clymes.   935
The greater Birth, the greater glory sure,
If deeds mainteine their auncestors degree.

Eke pray (my Priests) for them and for yourselves,
For Bishops, Prelats, Archdeanes, deanes, and Priests

---

910. *stewes:* brothels
914. *facts:* deeds
918. *lieftenants:* lieutenants
921. *mede:* reward
922. *furdering:* advancing, furthering
928. *makes:* gives

And al that preach, or otherwise professe   940
Gods holy word, and take the cure of soules.
Pray pray that you and every one of you
May walke upright in your vocation.
And that you shine like lamps of perfect life,
To lende a light and lanterne to our feete.   945

Say therwithal that some (I see them, I,
Wheras they fling in *Flaunders* all afarre,
For why my glasse wil shew them as they be)
Do neither care for God nor yet for devill,
So libertie may launch about at large.   950

And some again (I see them wel enough
And note their names, in *Liegelande* where they lurke)
Under pretence of holy humble harts
Would plucke adowne al princely *Dyademe*.
Pray, pray (my priests) for these, they touch you neere. 955

Shrinke not to say that some do (Romainelike)
Esteme their pall and habyte overmuche.
And therfore pray (my priests) lest pride prevaile.

Pray that the soules of sundrie damned gosts
Do not come in and bring good evidence   960
Before the God, which judgeth al mens thoughts,
Of some whose welth made them neglect their charge
Til secret sinnes (untoucht) infecte their flocks
And bredde a scab, which brought the shep to bane.

Some other ranne before the greedy woolfe,   965
And left the folde unfended from the fox,

---

941. *cure of*: responsibility for the health of
947. *fling . . . all afarre*: i.e., throw aside all restraints
952. *Liegelande*: i.e., in Belgium, near Liège. Gascoigne refers to the English recusants in exile abroad.
957. *pall and habyte*: i.e., ecclesiastical vestments and robes
964. *scab*: scabies, mange; *bane*: destruction
966. *unfended*: unprotected

Which durst nor barke nor bawle for both theyr eares.
Then pray (my priests) that such no more do so.

Pray for the nources, of our noble Realme,
I meane the worthy Universities,   970
(And *Cantabridge* shal have the dignitie,
Wherof I was unworthy member once)
That they bring up their babes in decent wise:
That *Philosophy* smel no secret smoke
Which *Magike* makes in wicked mysteries: 975
That *Logike* leape not over every stile,
Before he come a furlong neare the hedge,
With curious *Quids* to maintain argument.
That *Sophistrie* do not deceive it selfe,
That *Cosmography* keepe his compasse wel,   980
And such as be *Historiographers*
Trust not to much in every tatlyng tong,
Nor blynded be by partialitie.
That *Phisicke* thrive not over fast by murder:
That *Numbring* men in al their evens and odds   985
Do not forget that only *Unitie*
Unmeasurable, infinite, and one.
That *Geometrie* measure not so long,
Til all their measures out of measure be:
That *Musike* with his heavenly harmonie   990
Do not allure a heavenly minde from heaven,
Nor set mens thoughts in worldly melodie,
Til heavenly *Hierarchies* be quite forgot:
That *Rhetorick* learne not to overreache:
That *Poetrie* presume not for to preache,   995
And bite mens faults with *Satyres* corosives,
Yet pamper up hir owne with pultesses:

967. *for . . . eares:* i.e., because they were afraid of being harmed themselves
969. *nources:* nurses
978. *curious Quids:* adventitious "Whys?"
980. *keepe his compasse:* stay within its bounds
984. *Phisicke:* the medical faculty
986. *only Unitie:* i.e., God
996. *Satyres corosives:* harsh satires
997. *pultesses:* soft, medicinal compresses

Or that she dote not uppon *Erato*,
Which should invoke the good *Caliope*:
That *Astrologie* looke not over high,   1000
And light (meane while) in every pudled pit:
That *Grammer* grudge not at our english tong,
Bycause it stands by *Monosyllaba*,
And cannot be declind as others are.
Pray thus (my priests) for universities.   1005
And if I have forgotten any Arte,
Which hath bene taught or exercised there,
Pray you to god, the good be not abusde
With glorious shewe of overloding skill.

Now these be past (my priests) yet shal you pray 1010
For common people, eche in his degree,
That God vouchsafe to graunt them al his grace.
Where should I now beginne to bidde my beades?
Or who shal first be put in common place?
My wittes be wearie and my eyes are dymme,   1015
I cannot see who best deserves the roome,
Stand forth good *Peerce*, thou plowman by thy name,
Yet so the Sayler saith I do him wrong:
That one contends his paines are without peare,
That other saith that none be like to his,   1020
In dede they labour both exceedingly.
But since I see no shipman that can live
Without the plough, and yet I many see
(Which live by lande) that never sawe the seas:
Therfore I say, stand forth *Peerce* plowman first, 1025
Thou winst the roome by verie worthinesse.

Behold him (priests) & though he stink of sweat
Disdaine him not: for shal I tel you what?

---

998. *Erato:* the muse of amorous poetry
999. *Caliope:* the muse of heroic poetry
1003. *stands by Monosyllaba:* relies on monosyllables
1009. *overloding:* overbearing
1017. *Peerce:* so-called after Langland's *Piers Plowman*
1019. *peare:* equal

312

Such clime to heaven before the shaven crownes.
But how? forsooth, with true humilytie.   1030
Not that they hoord their grain when it is cheape,
Nor that they kill the calfe to have the milke,
Nor that they set debate betwene their lords,
By earing up the balks that part their bounds:
Nor for because they can both crowche & creep   1035
(The guilefulst men that ever God yet made)
When as they meane most mischiefe and deceite,
Nor that they can crie out on landelordes lowde,
And say they racke their rents an ace to high,
When they themselves do sel their landlords lambe   1040
For greater price then ewe was wont be worth.
I see you *Peerce*, my glasse was lately scowrde.
But for they feed with frutes of their gret paines
Both King and Knight and priests in cloyster pent:
Therefore I say that sooner some of them   1045
Shal scale the walles which leade us up to heaven,
Than cornfed beasts whose bellie is their God,
Although they preach of more perfection.

And yet (my priests) pray you to God for *Peerce*,
As *Peerce* can pinch it out for him and you.   1050
And if you have a *Paternoster* spare
Then shal you pray for Saylers (God them send
More mind of him when as they come to lande,
For towarde shipwracke many men can pray)
That they once learne to speake without a lye,   1055
And meane good faith without blaspheming othes:
That they forget to steale from every fraight,

1029. *shaven crownes:* i.e., the clergy
1033. *set debate:* stir up strife
1034. *earing . . . balks:* plowing up the ridges which were supposed to serve as boundary lines between furrowed fields
1041. *then . . . wont:* than an ewe used to
1042. *scowrde:* scoured, polished
1050. *As:* Since; *pinch it out:* i.e., gain merit through his suffering
1051. *Paternoster spare:* a spare "Our Father"
1054. *towarde:* when confronted with
1057. *fraight:* cargo

And for to forge false cockets, free to passe:
That manners make them give their betters place
And use good words, though deeds be nothing gay.   1060

But here me thinks, my priests begin to frowne,
And say that thus they shal be overchargde,
To pray for al which seme to do amisse:
And one I heare, more saucie than the rest,
Which asketh me when shal our prayers end?   1065

I tel thee (priest) when shoomakers make shoes,
That are wel sowed, with never a stitch amisse,
And use no crafte in uttring of the same:
When Taylours steale no stuffe from gentlemen,
When Tanners are with Corriers wel agreede,   1070
And both so dresse their hydes that we go dry:
When Cutlers leave to sel olde rustie blades,
And hide no crackes with soder nor deceit:
When tinkers make no more holes than they founde,
When thatchers thinke their wages worth their worke,   1075
When colliers put no dust into their sacks,
When maltemen make us drinke no firmentie,
When Davie Diker diggs and dallies not,
When smithes shoo horses as they would be shod,
When millers toll not with a golden thumbe,   1080
When bakers make not barme beare price of wheat,
When brewers put no bagage in their beere,
When butchers blowe not over al their fleshe,
When horsecorsers beguile no friends with Jades,
When weavers weight is found in huswives web.   1085
(But why dwel I so long among these lowts?)

1058. *cockets . . . passe:* customs documents, so that goods may come in
without duty
1068. *uttring:* offering for sale
1070. *Corriers:* curriers
1077. *firmentie:* frumenty, hulled wheat boiled in milk
1080. *toll . . . thumbe:* i.e., act dishonestly by giving false measure
1081. *barme:* yeast, leaven
1082. *bagage:* refuse, dirt
1084. *horsecorsers:* jobbing dealers in horses

When mercers make more bones to swere and lye,
When vintners mix no water with their wine,
When printers passe none errours in their bookes,
When hatters use to bye none olde cast robes,   1090
When goldsmithes get no gains by sodred crownes,
When upholsters sel fethers without dust,
When pewterers infect no Tin with leade,
When drapers draw no gaines by giving day,
When perchmentiers put in no ferret Silke,   1095
When Surgeons heale al wounds without delay.
(Tush these are toys, but yet my glas sheweth al).

When purveyours provide not for themselves,
When Takers take no brybes nor use no brags,
When customers, conceale no covine usde,   1100
When Searchers see al corners in a shippe,
(And spie no pens by any sight they see)
When shrives do serve all processe as they ought,
When baylifes strain none other thing but strays,
When auditours their counters cannot change,   1105
When proude surveyours take no parting pens,
When Silver sticks not on the Tellers fingers,
And when receivers pay as they receive,
When al these folke have quite forgotten fraude.

(Againe (my priests) a little by your leave)   1110
When Sicophants can finde no place in courte,
But are espied for *Ecchoes* as they are,
When roysters ruffle not above their rule,

1087. *make . . . lye:* have more scruples about swearing and lying
1090. *cast:* cast-off (the old rags would be used to make hats)
1094. *giving day:* offering credit
1095. *perchmentiers:* parchment makers; *ferret Silke:* floss silk (which would weaken the parchment)
1100. *covine:* trickery
1102. *pens:* money (being brought in illegally)
1103. *shrives:* sheriffs; *processe:* summons
1104. *strain:* distrain, seize
1105. *counters:* systems of reckoning
1106. *pens:* pence

Nor colour crafte by swearing precious coles:
When Fencers fees are like to apes rewards, 1115
A peece of breade and therwithal a bobbe:
When *Lays* lives not like a ladies peare,
Nor useth art in dying of hir heare.
When al these things are ordred as they ought,
And see themselves within my glasse of steele, 1120
Even then (my priests) may you make holyday,
And pray no more but ordinarie prayers.

And yet therin, I pray you (my good priests)
Pray stil for me and for my Glasse of steele,
That it (nor I) do any minde offend 1125
Bycause we shew all colours in their kinde.
And pray for me, that (since my hap is such
To see men so) I may perceive myselfe.
O worthy words to ende my worthlesse verse,
Pray for me Priests, I pray you pray for me. 1130

FINIS

Tam Marti, quam Mercurio

EPILOGUS

Alas (my lord) my hast was al to hote,
I shut my glasse before you gasde your fill,
And at a glimse my seely selfe have spied 1135
A stranger trowpe than any yet were sene:
Beholde (my lord) what monsters muster here,
With Angels face and harmefull helish harts,

1114. *colour crafte:* disguise their cunning; *precious coles:* "precious coals,"
an obsolete exclamation
1116. *bobbe:* perhaps a small coin worth 1½ pence. But "bob" may here
mean "a blow with the fist."
1117. *Lays:* see above, line 208 n.; *peare:* equal
1121. *holyday:* holiday
1132. *Tam . . . Mercurio:* Gascoigne's personal motto ("As Mars, so
Mercury") combines his double ideal of the soldier and the scholar
1135. *seely:* simple
1136. *trowpe:* troop

With smyling lookes and depe deceitful thoughts,
With tender skinnes and stony cruel mindes, 1140
With stealing steppes, yet forward feete to fraude.
Behold, behold, they never stande content,
With God, with kinde, with any helpe of Arte,
But curle their locks with bodkins & with braids,
But dye their heare with sundry subtill sleights, 1145
But paint and slicke til fayrest face be foule,
But bumbast, bolster, frisle, and perfume:
They marre with muske the balme which nature made,
And dig for death in dellicatest dishes.
The yonger sorte come pyping on apace, 1150
In whistles made of fine enticing wood,
Til they have caught the birds for whom they bryded.
The elder sorte go stately stalking on,
And on their backs they beare both land and fee,
Castles and Towres, revenewes and receits, 1155
Lordships and manours, fines, yea fermes and al.
What should these be? (speake you my lovely lord)
They be not men: for why? they have no beards.
They be no boyes, which weare such side long gowns.
They be no Gods, for al their gallant glosse. 1160
They be no divels, (I trow) which seme so saintish.
What be they? women? masking in mens weedes?
With dutchkin dublets and with Jerkins jaggde?
With Spanish spangs and ruffes fet out of France,
With high copt hattes and fethers flaunt a flaunt? 1165
They be so sure even *Wo* to *Men* in dede.
Nay then (my lord) let shut the glasse apace,
High time it were for my pore Muse to winke,

1143. *kinde:* nature
1152. *bryded:* played the part of a bride. Gascoigne is attacking effeminacy at court.
1156. *fines:* legal agreements for the conveying of land; *fermes:* fixed yearly rents
1160. *glosse:* outward appearance
1163. *dutchkin:* like those worn in Germany; *Jerkins jaggde:* close-fitting slashed jackets
1164. *spangs:* spangles; *fet:* fetched
1165. *copt:* peaked
1167. *apace:* immediately

Since al the hands, al paper, pen, and inke,
Which ever yet this wretched world possest, 1170
Cannot describe this Sex in colours dewe:
No no (my lord) we gased have inough,
(And I too much, God pardon me therfore)
Better loke of than loke an ace to farre:
And better mumme than meddle overmuch. 1175
But if my Glasse do like my lovely lord,
We wil espie, some sunny Sommers day,
To loke againe and see some semely sights.
Meane while, my Muse right humbly doth besech
That my good lorde accept this ventrous verse, 1180
Until my braines may better stuffe devise.

FINIS:

Tan Marti, quam Mercurio

1.

Certayne notes of Instruction concerning the making of verse or ryme in English, written at the request of Master Edouardo Donati.

Signor Edouardo, since promise is debt, and you (by
the lawe of friendship) do burden me with a promise
that I shoulde lende you instructions towards the mak-
ing of English verse or ryme, I will assaye to discharge
the same, though not so perfectly as I would, yet as 5
readily as I may: and therwithall I pray you consider
that *Quot homines, tot Sententiae,* especially in Po-
etrie, wherein (neverthelesse) I dare not challenge any
degree, and yet will I at your request adventure to set

1174. *of:* off
1180. *ventrous:* adventurous, daring
Title: First published in 1575. Gascoigne's friend, Edward Donati, has not
been identified with certainty.
7. *Quot . . . Sententiae:* "So many men, so many opinions"

down my simple skill in such simple manner as I have   10
used, referring the same hereafter to the correction of
the *Laureate*. And you shall have it in these few poynts
followyng.

The first and most necessarie poynt that ever I
founde meete to be considered in making of a delecta-   15
ble poeme is this, to grounde it upon some fine inven-
tion. For it is not inough to roll in pleasant woordes,
nor yet to thunder in *Rym, Ram, Ruff* by letter (quoth
my master *Chaucer*) nor yet to abounde in apt voca-
bles, or epythetes, unlesse the Invention have in it also   20
aliquid salis. By this *aliquid salis*, I meane some good
and fine devise, shewing the quicke capacitie of a writer:
and where I say some *good and fine invention*, I meane
that I would have it both fine and good. For many inven-
tions are so superfine, that they are *Vix good*. And againe   25
many Inventions are *good*, and yet not *finely* handled.
And for a general forwarning: what Theame soever you
do take in hande, if you do handle it but *tanquam in
oratione perpetua*, and never studie for some depth of
devise in the Invention, & some figures also in the   30
handlyng thereof: it will appeare to the skilfull Reader
but a tale of a tubbe. To deliver unto you generall
examples it were almoste unpossible, sithence the
occasions of Inventions are (as it were) infinite: never-
thelesse take in worth mine opinion, and perceyve   35
my furder meanyng in these few poynts. If I should
undertake to wryte in prayse of a gentlewoman, I
would neither praise hir christal eye, not hir cherrie
lippe, &c. For these things are *trita et obvia*. But I

12. *the Laureate*: those who have won the poet's crown
18. *Rum, Ram, Ruff*: the phrase comes from Chaucer's Parson, who uses it in his prologue to describe alliterative verse
21. *aliquid salis*: literally, "some salt"
25. *Vix*: scarcely
28-29. *tanquam . . . perpetua*: "as if it were an endless discourse"
32. *tale . . . tubbe*: a worthless tale
33. *sithence*: since
35. *in worth*: for what it is worth
39. *trita et obvia*: "trite and obvious"

would either finde some supernaturall cause wherby   40
my penne might walke in the superlative degree, or
els I would undertake to aunswere for any imperfection
that shee hath, and thereupon rayse the prayse of hir
commendacion. Likewise if I should disclose my pre-
tence in love, I would eyther make a straunge discourse   45
of some intollerable passion, or finde occasion to pleade
by the example of some historie, or discover my dis-
quiet in shadowes *per Allegoriam,* or use the covertest
meane that I could to avoyde the uncomely customes
of common writers. Thus much I adventure to deliver   50
unto you (my freend) upon the rule of Invention,
which of all other rules is most to be marked, and
hardest to be prescribed in certayne and infallible rules;
neverthelesse to conclude therein, I would have you
stand most upon the excellencie of your Invention, &   55
sticke not to studie deepely for some fine devise. For
that beyng founde, pleasant woordes will follow well
inough and fast inough.

2 Your Invention being once devised, take heede
that neither pleasure of rime, nor varietie of devise,   60
do carie you from it: for as to use obscure & darke
phrases in a pleasant Sonet, is nothing delectable, so
to entermingle merie jests in a serious matter is an
Indecorum.

3 I will next advise you that you hold the just meas-   65
ure wherwith you begin your verse; I will not denie but
this may seeme a preposterous ordre: but bycause I
covet rather to satisfie you particularly, than to under-
take a generall tradition, I wil not somuch stand upon
the manner as the matter of my precepts. I say then,   70
remember to holde the same measure wherwith you
begin, whether it be in a verse of six syllables, eight,
ten, twelve, &c. and though this precept might seeme
ridiculous unto you, since every yong scholler can con-

---

48. *per Allegoriam:* "through allegory"; *covertest:* most secret
56. *sticke:* hesitate
69. *tradition:* treatment

ceive that he ought to continue in the same measure   75
wherwith he beginneth, yet do I see and read many
mens Poems now adayes, whiche beginning with the
measure of xii. in the first line, & xiiii. in the second
(which is the common kinde of verse), they wil yet (by
that time they have passed over a few verses) fal into   80
xiiii. & fourtene, *et sic de similibus*, the which is
either forgetfulnes or carelesnes.

4 And in your verses remember to place every worde
in his natural *Emphasis* or sound, that is to say in such
wise, and with such length or shortnesse, elevation or   85
depression of sillables, as it is commonly pronounced
or used: to expresse the same we have three maner of
accents, *gravis, levis, et circumflexa,* the whiche I
would english thus, the long accent, the short accent,
& that whiche is indifferent: the grave accent is marked   90
by this caracte,∕ the light accent is noted thus,∖ &
the circumflexe or indifferent is thus signified ∼: the
grave accent is drawn out or elevate, and maketh that
sillable long whereupon it is placed: the light accent
is depressed or snatched up, and maketh that sillable   95
short upon the which it lighteth: the circumflexe
accent is indifferent, sometimes short, sometimes long,
sometimes depressed & sometimes elevate. For example
of th' emphasis or natural sound of words, this word
Treasure, hath the grave accent upon the first sillable,   100
whereas if it shoulde be written in this sorte, *Treasúre,*
nowe were the second sillable long, & that were con-
trarie to the common use wherwith it is pronounced.
For furder explanation hereof, note you that commonly
now a dayes in english rimes (for I dare not cal them   105
English verses) we use none other order but a foote of
two sillables, wherof the first is depressed or made
short, & the second is elevate or made long: and that
sound or scanning continueth throughout the verse.

---

79. *common kinde:* i.e., poulter's measure. See below, lines 320–24.
81. *et . . . similibus:* "and so on in like manner"
106–7. *foote . . . sillables:* i.e., the iambic foot

We have used in times past other kindes of Meeters: 110
as for example this following:

No wight in this world, that wealth can attayne,

Unlesse he beleve, that all is but vayne.

Also our father *Chaucer* hath used the same libertie
in feete and measures that the Latinists do use: and 115
who so ever do peruse and well consider his workes,
he shall finde that although his lines are not alwayes
of one selfe same number of Syllables, yet beyng redde
by one that hath understanding, the longest verse and
that which hath most Syllables in it, will fall (to the 120
eare) correspondent unto that whiche hath fewest sil-
lables in it: and like wise that whiche hath in it fewest
syllables, shalbe founde yet to consist of woordes that
have suche naturall sounde, as may seeme equall in
length to a verse which hath many moe sillables 125
of lighter accentes. And surely I can lament that wee are
fallen into suche a playne and simple manner of wryt-
ing, that there is none other foote used but one: wherby
our Poemes may justly be called Rithmes, and cannot
by any right challenge the name of a Verse. But since it 130
is so, let us take the forde as we finde it, and lette me set
downe unto you suche rules or precepts that even in
this playne foote of two syllables you wreste no woorde
from his natural and usuall sounde; I do not meane
hereby that you may use none other wordes but of twoo 135
sillables, for therein you may use discretion according
to occasion of matter: but my meaning is that all the
wordes in your verse be so placed as the first sillable
may sound short or be depressed, the second long or
elevate, the third shorte, the fourth long, the fifth 140

---

115. *Latinists:* Latin poets. Chaucer's metrics were misunderstood until
late in the eighteenth century.

shorte, &c. For example of my meaning in this point
marke these two verses:

I understand your meanyng by your eye.
Your meaning I understand by your eye.

In these two verses there seemeth no difference at all,   145
since the one hath the very selfe same woordes that the
other hath, and yet the latter verse is neyther true nor
pleasant, & the first verse may passe the musters. The
fault of the latter verse is that this worde *understand* is
therein so placed as the grave accent falleth upon *der*,   150
and therby maketh *der*, in this worde understand to be
elevated: which is contrarie to the naturall or usual pro-
nunciation: for we say *understand*, and not *under-
stand*.

  5 Here by the way I think it not amisse to forewarne   155
you that you thrust as few wordes of many sillables into
your verse as may be: and hereunto I might alledge
many reasons: first the most auncient English wordes
are of one sillable, so that the more monasyllables that
you use, the truer Englishman you shall seeme, and the   160
lesse you shall smell of the Inkehorne. Also wordes of
many syllables do cloye a verse and make it unpleasant,
whereas woordes of one syllable will more easily fall
to be shorte or long as occasion requireth, or wilbe
adapted to become circumflexe or of an indifferent   165
sounde.

  6 I would exhorte you also to beware of rime without
reason: my meaning is hereby that your rime leade you
not from your firste Invention, for many wryters when
they have layed the platforme of their invention, are   170
yet drawen sometimes (by ryme) to forget it or at least
to alter it, as when they cannot readily finde out a

worde whiche maye rime to the first (and yet continue
their determinate Invention) they do then eyther
botche it up with a worde that will ryme (howe small 175
reason soever it carie with it) or els they alter their first
worde and so percase decline or trouble their former
Invention: But do you alwayes hold your first deter-
mined Invention, and do rather searche the bottome of
your braynes for apte wordes, than chaunge good rea- 180
son for rumbling rime.

7 To help you a little with ryme (which is also a
plaine yong schollers lesson) worke thus: when you
have set downe your first verse, take the last worde
thereof and coumpt over all the wordes of the selfe 185
same sounde by order of the Alphabete: As for ex-
ample, the laste woord of your firste line is *care*, to
ryme therwith you have *bare, clare, dare, fare, gare,*
hare, and *share, mare, snare, rare, stare,* & *ware,* &c. Of
all these take that which best may serve your purpose, 190
carying reason with rime: and if none of them will
serve so, then alter the laste worde of your former
verse, but yet do not willingly alter the meanyng of
your Invention.

8 You may use the same Figures or Tropes in verse 195
which are used in prose, and in my judgement they
serve more aptly, and have greater grace in verse than
they have in prose: but yet therein remembre this old
adage, *Ne quid nimis,* as many wryters which do not
know the use of any other figure than that which is ex- 200
pressed in repeticion of sundrie wordes beginning all
with one letter, the whiche (beyng modestly used)
lendeth good grace to a verse: but they do so hunte a
letter to death, that they make it *Crambé,* and *Crambe*
bis positum mors est: therfore *Ne quid nimis.* 205

9 Also asmuche as may be, eschew straunge words,

---

174. *determinate:* predetermined
177. *percase decline:* perhaps deviate from
199. *Ne quid nimis:* "Nothing too much"
204–5. *Crambé . . . est:* "Cabbage served twice is death"; the proverb
echoes Juvenal, *Satires,* VII, 154

or *obsoleta et inusitata,* unlesse the Theame do give just occasion: marie in some places a straunge worde doth drawe attentive reading, but yet I woulde have you therein to use discretion.   210

10 And asmuch as you may, frame your stile to *per-spicuity* and to be sensible: for the haughty obscure verse doth not much delight, and the verse that is to easie is like a tale of a rosted horse: but let your Poeme be such as may both delight and draw attentive readyng,   215 and therewithal may deliver such matter as be worth the marking.

11 You shall do very well to use your verse after thenglishe phrase, and not after the maner of other languages: The Latinists do commonly set the adjective   220 after the Substantive: As for example *Femina pulchra, ædes altæ, etc.* but if we should say in English a woman fayre, a house high, &c. it would have but small grace: for we say a good man, and not a man good, &c. And yet I will not altogether forbidde it you, for in some   225 places, it may be borne, but not so hardly as some use it which wryte thus:

Now let us go to Temple ours,
I will go visit mother myne &c.

Surely I smile at the simplicite of such devisers which   230 might aswell have sayde it in playne English phrase, and yet have better pleased all eares, than they satisfie their owne fancies by suche *superfinesse.* Therefore even as I have advised you to place all wordes in their naturall or most common and usuall pronunciation, so would I   235 wishe you to frame all sentences in their mother phrase and proper *Idioma,* and yet sometimes (as I have sayd before) the contrarie may be borne, but that is rather where rime enforceth, or *per licentiam Poeticam,* than it is otherwise lawfull or commendable.   240

12 This poeticall licence is a shrewde fellow, and covereth many faults in a verse; it maketh wordes longer, shorter, of mo sillables, of fewer, newer, older,

---

207. *obsoleta et inusitata:* "obsolete and unused" words

truer, falser, and to conclude it turkeneth all things at
pleasure, for example, *ydone* for *done, adowne* for 245
downe, orecome for *overcome, tane* for *taken, power
for powre, heaven for heavn, thewes* for good partes
or good qualities, and a numbre of other whiche were
but tedious and needelesse to rehearse, since your owne
judgement and readyng will soone make you espie such 250
advauntages.

13 There are also certayne pauses or restes in a verse
whiche may be called *Ceasures,* whereof I would be
lothe to stande long, since it is at discretion of the
wryter, and they have bene first devised (as should 255
seeme) by the Musicians: but yet thus much I will ad-
venture to wryte, that in mine opinion in a verse of
eight sillables, the pause will stand best in the middest,
in a verse of tenne it will best be placed at the ende of
the first foure sillables: in a verse of twelve, in the 260
midst, in verses of twelve in the firste and fouretene in
the seconde, wee place the pause commonly in the
midst of the first, and at the ende of the first eight sil-
lables in the second. In Rithme royall, it is at the wryt-
ers discretion, and forceth not where the pause be untill 265
the ende of the line.

14 And here bycause I have named Rithme royall,
I will tell you also mine opinion aswell of that as of the
names which other rymes have commonly borne here-
tofore. Rythme royall is a verse of tenne sillables, and 270
seven such verses make a staffe, whereof the first and
thirde lines do aunswer (acrosse) in like terminations
and rime, the second, fourth, and fifth, do likewise
answere eche other in terminations, and the two last do
combine and shut up the Sentence: this hath bene 275
called Rithme royall, & surely it is a royall kinde of
verse serving best for grave discourses. There is also an-
other kind called Ballade, and thereof are sundrie sortes:

244. *turkeneth:* alters
253. *Ceasures:* caesurae
265. *forceth:* matters
271. *staffe:* stanza

for a man may write ballade in a staffe of sixe lines,
every line conteyning eighte or sixe sillables, whereof   280
the firste and third, second and fourth do rime acrosse,
and the fifth and sixth do rime togither in conclusion.
You may write also your ballad of tenne sillables
rimyng as before is declared, but these two were wont
to be most commonly used in ballade, which propre   285
name was (I thinke) derived of this worde in Italian
Ballare, whiche signifieth to daunce. And in deed those
kinds of rimes serve beste for daunces or light matters.
Then have you also a rondlette, the which doth al-
wayes end with one self same foote or repeticion, and   290
was thereof (in my judgement) called a rondelet. This
may consist of such measure as best liketh the wryter.
Then have you Sonnets; some think that all Poemes
(being short) may be called Sonets, as in deede it is a
diminutive worde derived of *Sonare,* but yet I can beste   295
allowe to call those Sonets whiche are of fouretene
lynes, every line conteyning tenne syllables. The firste
twelve do ryme in staves of foure lines by crosse meetre,
and the last twoo ryming togither do conclude the
whole. There are Dyzaynes, & Syxaines which are of ten   300
lines, and of sixe lines, commonly used by the French,
which some English writers do also terme by the name
of Sonettes. Then is there an old kinde of Rithme
called Verlayes, derived (as I have redde) of this worde
Verd whiche betokeneth Greene, and *Laye* which be-   305
tokeneth a Song, as if you would say greene Songes:
but I muste tell you by the way, that I never redde
any verse which I saw by aucthoritie called *Verlay,* but
one, and that was a long discourse in verses of tenne
sillables, whereof the foure first did ryme acrosse, and   310
the fifth did aunswere to the firste and thirde, breaking
off there, and so going on to another termination. Of

295–96. *I can beste allowe:* this passage probably did much to establish the
more limited meaning of "sonnet" in sixteenth-century English. Gascoigne
defines the so-called Shakespearean sonnet (ababcdcdefefgg) and not the
Italian (abbaabbacdecde).
304. *Verlayes:* Gascoigne's etymology is incorrect

this I could shewe example of imitation in mine own
verses written to the right honorable the Lord *Grey of
Wilton* upon my journey into *Holland*, &c. There are 315
also certaine Poemes devised of tenne syllables, whereof
the first aunswereth in termination with the fourth,
and the second and thirde answere eche other: these
are more used by other nations than by us, neyther can
I tell readily what name to give them. And the com- 320
monest sort of verse which we use now adayes (*viz.* the
long verse of twelve and fourtene sillables) I know not
certainly howe to name it, unless I should say that it
doth consist of Poulters measure, which giveth xii. for
one dozen and xiiii. for another. But let this suffise (if 325
it be not to much) for the sundrie sortes of verses
which we use now adayes.

15 In all these sortes of verses when soever you un-
dertake to write, avoyde prolixitie and tediousnesse, &
ever as neare as you can, do finish the sentence and 330
meaning at the end of every staffe where you wright
staves, & at the end of every two lines where you write
by cooples or poulters measure: for I see many writers
which draw their sentences in length, & make an ende
at latter Lammas: for commonly before they end, the 335
Reader hath forgotten where he begon. But do you (if
you wil follow my advise) eschue prolixitie and knit up
your sentences as compendiously as you may, since
brevitie (so that it be not drowned in obscuritie) is
most commendable. 340

16 I had forgotten a notable kinde of ryme, called
ryding rime, and that is suche as our Mayster and Fa-
ther *Chaucer* used in his Canterburie tales, and in di-
vers other delectable and light enterprises: but though
it come to my remembrance somewhat out of order, it 345

313–14. *mine own verses:* "Gascoignes voyage into Holland" (1572)
324. *Poulters measure:* i.e., a measure like that which an inconsistent
(and possibly dishonest) poultry merchant might give. Cf. "baker's dozen."
333. *by cooples:* in couplets
335. *latter Lammas:* i.e., never. Cf. above, no. 12, line 201 n.
342. *ryding rime:* Gascoigne gives no formal definition of this type

shall not yet come altogether out of time, for I will
nowe tell you a conceipt whiche I had before forgotten
to wryte: you may see (by the way) that I holde a pre-
posterous order in my traditions, but as I sayde before
I wryte moved by good wil, and not to shewe my skill.   350
Then to returne too my matter, as this riding rime
serveth must aptly to wryte a merie tale, so Rythme
royall is fittest for a grave discourse. Ballades are beste
of matters of love, and rondlettes moste apt for the
beating or handlyng of an adage or common proverbe: 355
Sonets serve as well in matters of love as of discourse:
Dizaymes and Sixames for shorte Fantazies: Verlayes
for an effectuall proposition, although by the name you
might otherwise judge of Verlayes, and the long verse
of twelve and fouretene sillables, although it be now   360
adayes used in all Theames, yet in my judgement it
would serve best for Psalmes and Himpnes.

I woulde stande longer in these traditions, were it
not that I doubt mine owne ignoraunce, but as I
sayde before, I know that I write to my freende, and   365
affying my selfe thereupon, I make an ende.

347. *a conceipt*: an idea
362. *Himpnes*: hymns
366. *affying*: trusting

SIR WALTER RALEIGH
1552–1618

1.

Walter Rawely of the middle
Temple, in commendation of the Steele Glasse

Swete were the sauce would please ech kind of tast,
The life likewise were pure that never swerved,
For spyteful tongs, in cankred stomackes plaste,
Deeme worst of things, which best (percase) deserved:
But what for that? This medcine may suffyse,   5
To scorne the rest, and seeke to please the wise.

Though sundry mindes in sundry sorte do deeme,
Yet worthiest wights yelde prayse for every payne,
But envious braynes do nought (or light) esteme
Such stately steppes as they cannot attaine.   10
For who so reapes renowne above the rest
With heapes of hate, shall surely be opprest.

Wherefore to write my censure of this booke,
This Glasse of Steele, unpartially doth shewe,
Abuses all, to such as in it looke,   15
From prince to poore, from high estate to lowe;

Title: middle Temple; Raleigh, though not a law student, resided at the
Middle Temple in 1575. This prefatory poem to the *Steele Glasse* (1576;
see Gascoigne, no. 12) was his first published poem.
3. *cankred:* diseased; *plaste:* placed
4. *percase:* perhaps
8. *wights yelde:* men grant
13. *censure:* judgment

As for the verse, who list like trade to trye,
I feare me much, shal hardly reach so high.

2.

The Excuse

Calling to minde mine eie long went about
T" entice my hart to seeke to leave my brest,
All in a rage I thought to pull it out,
By whose device I liv'd in such unrest,
What could it say to purchase so my grace?   5
Forsooth that it had seene my Mistres face.

Another time I likewise call to minde,
My hart was he that all my woe had wrought.
For he my brest the fort of Love resignde,
When of such warrs my fancie never thought,   10
What could it say, when I would him have slaine?
But he was yours, and had forgone me cleane.

At length when I perceiv'd both eie and hart,
Excusde themselves, as guiltles of mine ill,
I found my selfe was cause of all my smart,   15
And tolde my selfe, my selfe now slay I will:
But when I found my selfe to you was true,
I lov'd my selfe, bicause my selfe lov'd you.

3.

The Advice

Many desire, but few or none deserve
To win the Fort of thy most constant will;

---

17. *the verse:* Gascoigne's poem was the first sustained attempt at blank
verse in original English composition
1. *mine:* that mine

Therefore take heed, let fancy never swerve
But unto him that will defend thee still.
For this be sure, the fort of fame once won, 5
Farewell the rest, thy happy dayes are done.

Many desire, but few or none deserve
To pluck the flowers and let the leaves to fall;
Therefore take heed, let fancy never swerve,
But unto him that will take leaves and all. 10
For this be sure, the flower once pluckt away,
Farewell the rest, thy happy days decay.

Many desire, but few or none deserve
To cut the corn, not subject to the sickle.
Therefore take heed, let fancy never swerve, 15
But constant stand, for Mowers mindes are fickle.
For this be sure, the crop being once obtain'd
Farewell the rest, the soil will be disdain'd.

4.

The Nimphs reply to the Sheepheard

If all the world and love were young,
And truth in every Sheepheards tongue,
These pretty pleasures might me move,
To live with thee, and be thy love.

Time drives the flocks from field to fold, 5
When Rivers rage, and Rocks grow cold,
And Philomell becommeth dombe,
The rest complaines of cares to come.

The flowers doe fade, and wanton fieldes,
To wayward winter reckoning yeeldes, 10

Title: Raleigh's is perhaps the most famous reply to Marlowe's lyric, q.v.
7. *Philomell:* the nightingale
9. *wanton:* poorly cultivated

A honny tongue, a hart of gall,
Is fancies spring, but sorrowes fall.

Thy gownes, thy shooes, thy beds of Roses,
Thy cap, thy kirtle, and thy poesies,
Soone breake, soone wither, soone forgotten: 15
In follie ripe, in reason rotten.

Thy belt of straw and Ivie buddes,
Thy Corall claspes and Amber studdes,
All these in mee no meanes can move,
To come to thee, and be thy love.   20

But could youth last, and love still breede,
Had joyes no date, nor age no neede,
Then these delights my minde might move,
To live with thee, and be thy love.

5.

Sir Walter Ralegh to the Queen

Our Passions are most like to Floods and streames,
The shallow Murmure, but the Deep are Dumb.
So when Affections yeeld Discourse, it seems
The bottom is but shallow whence they come.
They that are Rich in Words must needs discover   5
That they are Poore in that which makes a Lover.

Wrong not, deare Empresse of my Heart,
   The Meritt of true Passion,
With thinking that Hee feels no Smart,
   That sues for no Compassion: 10
Since, if my Plaints serve not to prove
   The Conquest of your Beauty,
It comes not from Defect of Love,
   But from Excesse of duety.

---

21. *still:* always
22. *date:* end

For knowing that I sue to serve　　　　　　15
　A Saint of such Perfection,
As all desire, but none deserve,
　A place in her Affection:
I rather chuse to want Reliefe
　Then venture the Revealing;　　　　　　20
When Glory recommends the Griefe,
　Despaire distrusts the Healing.

Thus those desires that aime too high,
　For any mortall Lover,
When Reason cannot make them dye,　　　25
　Discretion will them Cover.
Yet when discretion dothe bereave
　The Plaints that they should utter,
Then your discretion may perceive,
　That Silence is a Suitor.　　　　　　　　30

Silence in Love bewraies more Woe,
　Then Words, though ne'r so Witty,
A Beggar that is dumb, yee know,
　Deserveth double Pitty.
Then misconceive not (dearest Heart)　　35
　My true though secret Passion;
Hee smarteth most that hides his smart,
　And sues for no Compassion.

6.

A Poem of Sir Walter Rawleighs

Nature that washt her hands in milke
　And had forgott to dry them,
In stead of earth tooke snow and silke
　At Loves request to trye them;
If she a mistresse could compose　　　　　5
To please Loves fancy out of those.

---

19. *want:* lack
31. *bewraies:* reveals

Her eyes he would should be of light,
  A Violett breath, and Lipps of Jelly,
Her haire not blacke, nor over bright,
  And of the softest downe her Belly,   10
As for her inside hee'ld have it
Only of wantonnesse and witt.

At Loves entreaty such a one
  Nature made, but with her beauty
She hath framed a heart of stonė;   15
  So as Love by ill destinie
Must dye for her whom nature gave him
Because her darling would not save him.

But Time which nature doth despise,
  And rudely gives her love the lye,   20
Makes hope a foole and sorrow wise,
  His hands doth neither wash, nor dry,
But being made of steele and rust,
Turnes snow and silke and milke to dust.

The Light, the Belly, lipps and breath,   25
  He dimms, discolours, and destroyes,
With those he feedes but fills not death,
  Which sometimes were the foode of Joyes;
Yea Time doth dull each lively witt,
And dryes all wantonnes with it.   30

Oh cruell Time which takes in trust
  Our youth, our Joyes and all we have,
And payes us but with age and dust,
  Who in the darke and silent grave
When we have wandred all our wayes   35
Shutts up the story of our dayes.

---

22. *doth:* the MS. reads *doe*
26. *discolours:* MS. *discovers*

7.

As you came from the holy land
    Of Walsinghame,
Mett you not with my true love
    By the way as you came?

How shall I know your trew love   5
    That have mett many one,
As I went to the holy lande
    That have come, that have gone?

She is neyther whyte nor browne
    Butt as the heavens fayre,   10
There is none hathe a forme so divine
    In the earth or the ayre.

Such an one did I meet, good Sir,
    Suche an Angelyke face,
Who lyke a queene, lyke a nymph, did appere   15
    By her gate, by her grace.

She hath lefte me here all alone,
    All allone as unknowne,
Who somtymes did me lead with her selfe,
    And me lovde as her owne.   20

Whats the cause that she leaves you alone
    And a new waye doth take;
Who loved you once as her owne
    And her joye did you make?

I have lovde her all my youth,   25
    Butt now ould, as you see,
Love lykes not the fallyng frute
    From the wythered tree.

---

2. *Walsinghame:* a famous medieval shrine, destroyed in 1538. Raleigh's
poem is probably based on an old ballad.
16. *gate:* gait, graceful walk

Know that love is a careless chylld
    And forgets promyse paste,   30
He is blynd, he is deaff when he lyste
    And in faythe never faste.

His desyre is a dureless contente
    And a trustless joye,
He is wonn with a world of despayre   35
    And is lost with a toye.

Of women kynde suche indeed is the love,
    Or the word Love abused,
Under which many chyldysh desyres
    And conceytes are excusde.   40

Butt true Love is a durable fyre
    In the mynde ever burnynge;
Never sycke, never ould, never dead,
    From itt selfe never turnynge.

8.

The Lie

Goe soule, the bodies guest,
    Upon a thankelesse arrant,
Feare not to touch the best,
    The truth shall be thy warrant:
Goe, since I needs must die,   5
    And give the world the lie.

---

33. *dureless:* unlasting, evanescent
40. *conceytes:* ideas
Title: this poem has been attributed to Donne, to Joshua Sylvester, and to others, as well as to Raleigh; but most scholars remain convinced of the latter's authorship. A number of contemporary "answers" to it are extant. The best date for the poem is 1593–96.
2. *arrant:* errand

Say to the Court it glowes,
  And shines like rotten wood,
Say to the Church it showes
  Whats good, and doth no good.   10
If Church and Court reply,
  Then give them both the lie.

Tell Potentates they live
  Acting by others action,
Not loved unlesse they give,   15
  Not strong but by affection.
If Potentates reply,
  Give Potentates the lie.

Tell men of high condition,
  That mannage the estate,   20
Their purpose is ambition,
  Their practise onely hate:
And if they once reply,
  Then give them all the lie.

Tell them that brave it most,   25
  They beg for more by spending,
Who in their greatest cost
  Seek nothing but commending.
And if they make replie,
  Then give them all the lie.   30

Tell zeale it wants devotion,
  Tell love it is but lust,
Tell time it meets but motion,
  Tell flesh it is but dust.
And wish them not replie   35
  For thou must give the lie.

---

14. *by:* Davison's text reads *but*
28. *Seek:* Davison reads *like*
33. *meets:* metes, measures

338

Tell age it daily wasteth,
  Tell honour how it alters.
Tell beauty how she blasteth
  Tell favour how it falters   40
And as they doe reply
  Give every one the lie.

Tell wit how much it wrangles
  In tickle points of nycenesse,
Tell wisedome she entangles   45
  Her selfe in over wisenesse.
And when they doe reply
  Straight give them both the lie.

Tell Phisicke of her boldnes,
  Tell skill it is prevention: 50
Tell charity of coldnes,
  Tell law it is contention,
And as they doe reply
  So give them still the lie.

Tell fortune of her blindnesse,   55
  Tell nature of decay,
Tell friendship of unkindnesse,
  Tell justice of delay.
And if they will reply,
  Then give them all the lie.   60

Tell Arts they have no soundnesse,
  But vary by esteeming,
Tell schooles they want profoundnes
  And stand too much on seeming.
If Arts and schooles reply,   65
  Give arts and schooles the lie.

_____

39. *blasteth*: withers
44. *tickle*: slippery; *nycenesse*: scrupulosity, fastidiousness
49. *Phisicke*: the art of medicine
62. *by esteeming*: according to the way in which they are esteemed

Tell faith its fled the Citie,
  Tell how the country erreth,
Tell manhood shakes off pittie,
  Tell vertue least preferreth,   70
And if they doe reply,
  Spare not to give the lie.

So when thou hast as I
  Commanded thee, done blabbing,
Although to give the lie,   75
  Deserves no lesse then stabbing,
Stab at thee he that will,
  No stab thy soule can kill.

9.

The passionate mans Pilgrimage

Give me my Scallop shell of quiet,
My staffe of Faith to walke upon,
My Scrip of Joy, Immortall diet,
My bottle of salvation:
My Gowne of Glory, hopes true gage,   5
And thus Ile take my pilgrimage.
Blood must be my bodies balmer,
No other balme will there be given
Whilst my soule like a white Palmer
Travels to the land of heaven,   10
Over the silver mountaines,
Where spring the Nectar fountaines:

---

69. *shakes:* i.e., it shakes
70. *least preferreth:* it prefers the least
Title: Generally supposed to have been written immediately after Raleigh's
trial in 1603. He was condemned to death on November 17 and reprieved
on December 6.
1. *Scallop shell:* used traditionally as a pilgrim's badge
3. *Scrip:* bag, knapsack
5. *gage:* pledge

And there Ile kisse
The Bowle of blisse,
And drink my eternall fill   15
On every milken hill.
My soule will be a drie before,
But after, it will nere thirst more.

And by the happie blisfull way
More peacefull Pilgrims I shall see,   20
That have shooke off their gownes of clay,
And goe appareld fresh like mee.
Ile bring them first
To slake their thirst,
And then to tast those Nectar suckets   25
At the cleare wells
Where sweetnes dwells,
Drawne up by Saints in Christall buckets.

And when our bottles and all we,
Are fild with immortalitie: 30
Then the holy paths weele travell
Strewde with Rubies thicke as gravell,
Seelings of Diamonds, Saphire floores,
High walles of Corall and Pearle Bowres.

From thence to heavens Bribeles hall   35
Where no corrupted voyces brall,
No Conscience molten into gold,
Nor forg'd accusers bought and sold,
No cause deferd, nor vaine spent Jorney,
For there Christ is the Kings Atturney: 40
Who pleades for all without degrees,
And he hath Angells, but no fees.

---

17. *a drie:* dried out
25. *suckets:* sweetmeats
31. *weele:* we shall
33. *Seelings:* Ceilings
42. *Angells:* punning on the name of a contemporary coin

When the grand twelve million Jury,
Of our sinnes and sinfull fury,
Gainst our soules blacke verdicts give,   45
Christ pleades his death, and then we live;
Be thou my speaker, taintles pleader,
Unblotted Lawyer, true proceeder,
Thou movest salvation even for almes:
Not with a bribed Lawyers palmes.   50

And this is my eternall plea,
To him that made Heaven, Earth and Sea,
Seeing my flesh must die so soone,
And want a head to dine next noone,   55
Just at the stroke when my vaines start and spred
Set on my soule an everlasting head.
Then am I readie like a palmer fit,
To tread those blest paths which before I writ.

10.

On the Life of Man

What is our life? a play of passion,
Our mirth the musicke of division,
Our mothers wombes the tyring houses be,
When we are drest for this short Comedy,
Heaven the Judicious sharpe spector is,   5
That sits and markes still who doth act amisse,
Our graves that hide us from the searching Sun,
Are like drawne curtaynes when the play is done,
Thus march we playing to our latest rest,
Onely we dye in earnest, that's no Jest.   10

---

2. *division:* variation
3. *tyring houses:* dressing rooms
5. *spector:* spectator, but "specter" too

11.

*These verses following were made by
Sir Walter Rawleigh the night before
he dyed and left att the Gate howse*

Even such is tyme which takes in trust
Our yowth, our Joyes, and all we have,
And payes us butt with age and dust;
Who in the darke and silent grave
When we have wandred all our wayes   5
Shutts up the storye of our dayes.
And from which earth and grave and dust
The Lord shall rayse me up I trust.

Title: Ralcigh was executed on October 29, 1618.

EDMUND SPENSER
1552–99

Amoretti

I

Happy ye leaves when as those lilly hands,
Which hold my life in their dead doing might,
Shall handle you and hold in loves soft bands,
Lyke captives trembling at the victors sight.
And happy lines, on which with starry light,   5
Those lamping eyes will deigne sometimes to look
And reade the sorrowes of my dying spright,
Written with teares in harts close bleeding book.
And happy rymes bath'd in the sacred brooke,
Of *Helicon* whence she derived is,   10
When ye behold that Angels blessed looke,
My soules long lacked foode, my heavens blis.
Leaves, lines, and rymes, seeke her to please alone,
Whom if ye please, I care for other none.

II

Unquiet thought, whom at the first I bred,
Of th' inward bale of my love pined hart:

---

2. *dead doing:* having the power to cause death
6. *lamping:* flashing, beaming
7. *spright:* spirit
8. *close:* hidden
10. *Helicon . . . is:* Helicon is the Boeotian mountain sacred to the Muses; *she* refers to the brook (Aganippe) that rose ("derived is") in the mountain
2. *bale:* sorrow

And sithens have with sighes and sorrowes fed,
Till greater then my wombe thou woxen art.
Breake forth at length out of the inner part,   5
In which thou lurkest lyke to vipers brood:
And seeke some succour both to ease my smart
And also to sustayne thy selfe with food.
But if in presence of that fayrest proud
Thou chance to come, fall lowly at her feet: 10
And with meeke humblesse and afflicted mood,
Pardon for thee, and grace for me intreat.
Which if she graunt, then live, and my love cherish,
If not, die soone, and I with thee will perish.

III

The soverayne beauty which I doo admyre,
Witnesse the world how worthy to be prayzed:
The light wherof hath kindled heavenly fyre,
In my fraile spirit by her from basenesse raysed.
That being now with her huge brightnesse dazed,   5
Base thing I can no more endure to view:
But looking still on her I stand amazed,
At wondrous sight of so celestiall hew.
So when my toung would speak her praises dew,
It stopped is with thoughts astonishment: 10
And when my pen would write her titles true,
It ravisht is with fancies wonderment:
Yet in my hart I then both speake and write,
The wonder that my wit cannot endite.

IV

New yeare forth looking out of Janus gate,
Doth seeme to promise hope of new delight:
And bidding th'old Adieu, his passed date
Bids all old thoughts to die in dumpish spright.

----

3. *sithens:* since
4. *wombe:* abdomen; *woxen art:* have grown. The idea of giving birth hovers over this line.
11. *humblesse:* humility
4. *dumpish spright:* depressed spirits

And calling forth out of sad Winters night,   5
Fresh love, that long hath slept in cheerlesse bower:
Wils him awake, and soone about him dight
His wanton wings and darts of deadly power.
For lusty spring now in his timely howre,
Is ready to come forth him to receive: 10
And warnes the Earth with divers colord flowre,
To decke hir selfe, and her faire mantle weave.
Then you faire flowre, in whom fresh youth doth raine,
Prepare your selfe new love to entertaine.

V

Rudely thou wrongest my deare harts desire,
In finding fault with her too portly pride:
The thing which I doo most in her admire,
Is of the world unworthy most envide.
For in those lofty lookes is close implide,   5
Scorn of base things, & sdeigne of foule dishonor:
Thretning rash eies which gaze on her so wide,
That loosely they ne dare to looke upon her.
Such pride is praise, such portlinesse is honor,
That boldned innocence beares in hir eies: 10
And her faire countenance like a goodly banner,
Spreds in defiaunce of all enemies.
Was never in this world ought worthy tride,
Without some spark of such self-pleasing pride.

VI

Be nought dismayd that her unmoved mind,
Doth still persist in her rebellious pride:

---

7. *dight:* put on
2. *portly:* stately
4. *envide:* envied
6. *sdeigne:* scorn
7. *so wide:* in so many places
8. *That . . . her:* not to dare to look upon her in any loose way
10. *boldned:* emboldened
13. *ought:* anything

Such love not lyke to lusts of baser kynd,
The harder wonne, the firmer will abide.
The durefull Oake, whose sap is not yet dride,   5
Is long ere it conceive the kindling fyre:
But when it once doth burne, it doth divide
Great heat, and makes his flames to heaven aspire.
So hard it is to kindle new desire,
In gentle brest that shall endure for ever: 10
Deepe is the wound, that dints the parts entire
With chast affects, that naught but death can sever.
Then thinke not long in taking litle paine,
To knit the knot, that ever shall remaine.

VII

Fayre eyes, the myrrour of my mazed hart,
What wondrous vertue is contaynd in you
The which both lyfe and death forth from you dart
Into the object of your mighty view?
For when ye mildly looke with lovely hew,   5
Then is my soule with life and love inspired:
But when ye lowre, or looke on me askew
Then doe I die, as one with lightning fyred.
But since that lyfe is more then death desyred,
Looke ever lovely, as becomes you best,   10
That your bright beams of my weak eies admyred,
May kindle living fire within my brest.
Such life should be the honor of your light,
Such death the sad ensample of your might.

---

5. *durefull:* long-lasting
7. *divide:* give forth in various directions
8. *his:* its
11. *dints:* strikes
12. *affects:* emotions, feelings
14. *knit the knot:* i.e., the marriage knot
1. *mazed:* bewildered
14. *ensample:* example

VIII

More then most faire, full of the living fire,
Kindled above unto the maker neere:
No eies but joyes, in which al powers conspire,
That to the world naught else be counted deare.
Thrugh your bright beames doth not the blinded guest,   5
Shoot out his darts to base affections wound:
But Angels come to lead fraile mindes to rest
In chast desires on heavenly beauty bound.
You frame my thoughts and fashion me within,
You stop my toung, and teach my hart to speake   10
You calme the storme that passion did begin,
Strong thrugh your cause, but by your vertue weak.
Dark is the world, where your light shined never;
Well is he borne, that may behold you ever.

IX

Long-while I sought to what I might compare
Those powrefull eies, which lighten my dark spright,
Yet find I nought on earth to which I dare
Resemble th'ymage of their goodly light.
Not to the Sun: for they doo shine by night;   5
Nor to the Moone: for they are changed never;
Nor to the Starres: for they have purer sight;
Nor to the fire: for they consume not ever;
Nor to the lightning: for they still persever;
Nor to the Diamond: for they are more tender;   10
Nor unto Christall: for nought may them sever;
Nor unto glasse: such basenesse mought offend her;
Then to the Maker selfe they likest be,
Whose light doth lighten all that here we see.

No. VIII This is the only sonnet in the *Amoretti* that employs the Shake-
spearean rhyme scheme.
4. *Resemble:* Compare
12. *mought:* may
13. *selfe:* Himself

X

Unrighteous Lord of love what law is this,
That me thou makest thus tormented be:
The whiles she lordeth in licentious blisse
Of her freewill, scorning both thee and me.
See how the Tyrannesse doth joy to see   5
The huge massacres which her eyes do make:
And humbled harts brings captives unto thee,
That thou of them mayst mightie vengeance take.
But her proud hart doe thou a little shake
And that high look, with which she doth comptroll   10
All this worlds pride bow to a baser make,
And al her faults in thy black booke enroll.
That I may laugh at her in equall sort,
As she doth laugh at me and makes my pain her sport.

XI

Dayly when I do seeke and sew for peace,
And hostages doe offer for my truth:
She cruell warriour doth her selfe addresse
To battell, and the weary war renew'th.
Ne wilbe moov'd with reason or with rewth,   5
To graunt small respit to my restlesse toile:
But greedily her fell intent poursewth,
Of my poore life to make unpitteid spoile.
Yet my poore life, all sorrowes to assoyle,
I would her yield, her wrath to pacify: 10
But then she seekes with torment and turmoyle,
To force me live and will not let me dy.

---

3. *licentious:* unlimited
5. *Tyrannesse:* female tyrant
8. *of:* on
11. *make:* mate
1. *sew:* sue
5. *rewth:* compassion
7. *fell:* cruel; *poursewth:* pursueth
8. *unpitteid spoile:* pitiless plunder
9. *assoyle:* remove

All paine hath end and every war hath peace,
But mine no price nor prayer may surcease.

XII

One day I sought with her hart-thrilling eies,
To make a truce and termes to entertaine:
All fearelesse then of so false enimies,
Which sought me to entrap in treasons traine.
So as I then disarmed did remaine,   5
A wicked ambush which lay hidden long
In the close covert of her guilefull eyen,
Thence breaking forth did thick about me throng.
Too feeble I t'abide the brunt so strong,
Was forst to yeeld my selfe into their hands: 10
Who me captiving streight with rigorous wrong,
Have ever since me kept in cruell bands.
So Ladie, now to you I doo complaine,
Against your eies that justice I may gaine.

XIII

In that proud port, which her so goodly graceth,
Whiles her faire face she reares up to the skie:
And to the ground her eie lids low embaseth,
Most goodly temperature ye may descry,
Myld humblesse mixt with awfull majesty,   5
For looking on the earth whence she was borne:
Her minde remembreth her mortalitie,
What so is fayrest shall to earth returne.
But that same lofty countenance seemes to scorne
Base thing, and thinke how she to heaven may clime: 10

---

14. *surcease:* bring to an end
1. *hart-thrilling:* heart-piercing
4. *traine:* snare
7. *covert:* hiding place
11. *streight:* straitly, strictly
12. *bands:* bonds
1. *port:* bearing
3. *embaseth:* casts down
5. *humblesse:* humility

Treading downe earth as lothsome and forlorne,
That hinders heavenly thoughts with drossy slime.
Yet lowly still vouchsafe to looke on me,
Such lowlinesse shall make you lofty be.

XIV

Retourne agayne my forces late dismayd,
Unto the siege by you abandon'd quite,
Great shame it is to leave like one afrayd,
So fayre a peece for one repulse so light.
Gaynst such strong castles needeth greater might,　　　　5
Then those small forts which ye were wont belay,
Such haughty mynds enur'd to hardy fight,
Disdayne to yield unto the first assay.
Bring therefore all the forces that ye may,
And lay incessant battery to her heart,　　　　10
Playnts, prayers, vowes, ruth, sorrow, and dismay,
Those engins can the proudest love convert.
And if those fayle, fall downe and dy before her,
So dying live, and living do adore her.

XV

Ye tradefull Merchants that with weary toyle,
Do seeke most pretious things to make your gain:
And both the Indias of their treasures spoile,
What needeth you to seeke so farre in vaine?
For loe my love doth in her selfe containe　　　　5
All this worlds riches that may farre be found,
If Saphyres, loe her eies be Saphyres plaine,
If Rubies, loe hir lips be Rubies sound:
If Pearles, hir teeth be pearles both pure and round;
If Yvorie, her forhead yvory weene;　　　　10

---

1. *dismayd:* put to rout
6. *belay:* lay siege to
7. *enur'd:* accustomed
10. *weene:* think

If Gold, her locks are finest gold on ground;
If silver, her faire hands are silver sheenc.
But that which fairest is, but few behold,
Her mind adornd with vertues manifold.

XVI

One day as I unwarily did gaze
On those fayre eyes my loves immortall light:
The whiles my stonisht hart stood in amaze,
Through sweet illusion of her lookes delight.
I mote perceive how in her glauncing sight,   5
Legions of loves with little wings did fly:
Darting their deadly arrowes fyry bright,
At every rash beholder passing by.
One of those archers closely I did spy,
Ayming his arrow at my hart: 10
When suddenly with twincle of her eye,
The Damzell broke his misintended dart.
Had she not so doon, sure I had bene slayne,
Yet as it was, I hardly scap't with paine.

XVII

The glorious pourtraict of that Angels face,
Made to amaze weake mens confused skil:
And this worlds worthlesse glory to embase,
What pen, what pencill can expresse her fill?
For though he colours could devize at will,   5

---

11. *on ground:* to be found anywhere
12. *silver sheene:* shining silver
3. *stonisht:* astonished
5. *mote:* could
12. *misintended:* maliciously aimed
14. *hardly scap't:* barely escaped
1. *pourtraict:* portrait
3. *embase:* lower
4. *fill:* fullness

And eke his learned hand at pleasure guide:
Least trembling it his workmanship should spill,
Yet many wondrous things there are beside.
The sweet eye-glaunces, that like arrowes glide,
The charming smiles, that rob sence from the hart: 10
The lovely pleasance and the lofty pride,
Cannot expressed be by any art.
A greater craftesmans hand thereto doth neede,
That can expresse the life of things indeed.

XVIII

The rolling wheele that runneth often round,
The hardest steele in tract of time doth teare:
And drizling drops that often doe redound,
The firmest flint doth in continuance weare.
Yet cannot I with many a dropping teare,   5
And long intreaty soften her hard hart:
That she will once vouchsafe my plaint to heare,
Or looke with pitty on my payneful smart.
But when I pleade, she bids me play my part,
And when I weep, she sayes teares are but water: 10
And when I sigh, she sayes I know the art,
And when I waile she turnes hir selfe to laughter.
So doe I weepe, and wayle, and pleade in vaine,
Whiles she as steele and flint doth still remayne.

XIX

The merry Cuckow, messenger of Spring,
His trompet shrill hath thrise already sounded:

---

7. *Least:* Lest; *spill:* ruin
11. *pleasance:* pleasantness
13. *doth neede:* is necessary
2. *tract:* course
3. *redound:* overflow
4. *in continuance:* by continuing
14. *still:* always

That warnes al lovers wayt upon their king,
Who now is comming forth with girland crouned.
With noyse whereof the quyre of Byrds resounded   5
Their anthemes sweet devized of loves prayse,
That all the woods theyr ecchoes back rebounded,
As if they knew the meaning of their layes.
But mongst them all, which did Loves honor rayse
No word was heard of her that most it ought,   10
But she his precept proudly disobayes,
And doth his ydle message set at nought.
Therefore O love, unlesse she turne to thee
Ere Cuckrow end, let her a rebell be.

                              xx

In vaine I seeke and sew to her for grace,
And doe myne humbled hart before her poure:
The whiles her foot she in my necke doth place,
And tread my life downe in the lowly floure.
And yet the Lyon that is Lord of power,   5
And reigneth over every beast in field:
In his most pride disdeigneth to devoure
The silly lambe that to his might doth yield.
But she more cruell and more salvage wylde,
Then either Lyon or the Lyonesse: 10
Shames not to be with guiltlesse bloud defylde,
But taketh glory in her cruelnesse.
Fayrer then fayrest, let none ever say,
That ye were blooded in a yeelded pray.

---

5. *quyre:* choir
7. Cf. the refrain in the *Epithalamion,* "The woods shall to me answer, and
my eccho ring."
8. *layes:* songs
10. *most it ought:* owed most to Love
12. *ydle:* trivial; *set at nought:* view as worthless
7. *most:* greatest; *disdeigneth:* disdains
8. *silly:* simple, innocent
9. *salvage:* savage
14. *blooded . . . pray:* first tasted blood on a prey that had already sur-
rendered

354

XXI

Was it the worke of nature or of Art?
Which tempred so the feature of her face:
That pride and meeknesse mixt by equall part,
Doe both appeare t'adorne her beauties grace.
For with mild pleasance, which doth pride displace,   5
She to her loves doth lookers eyes allure:
And with sterne countenance back again doth chace
Their looser lookes that stir up lustes impure.
With such strange termes her eyes she doth inure,
That with one looke she doth my life dismay: 10
And with another doth it streight recure,
Her smile me drawes, her frowne me drives away.
Thus doth she traine and teach me with her lookes,
Such art of eyes I never read in bookes.

XXII

This holy season fit to fast and pray,
Men to devotion ought to be inclynd:
Therefore, I lykewise on so holy day,
For my sweet Saynt some service fit will find.
Her temple fayre is built within my mind,   5
In which her glorious ymage placed is,
On which my thoughts doo day and night attend
Lyke sacred priests that never thinke amisse.
There I to her as th'author of my blisse,
Will builde an altar to appease her yre: 10
And on the same my hart will sacrifise,
Burning in flames of pure and chast desyre:
The which vouchsafe O goddesse to accept,
Amongst thy deerest relicks to be kept.

9. *termes:* conditions; *inure:* exercise
11. *streight recure:* immediately recover

XXIII

Penelope for her *Ulisses* sake,
Deviz'd a Web her wooers to deceave:
In which the worke that she all day did make
The same at night she did againe unreave,
Such subtile craft my Damzell doth conceave,   5
Th'importune suit of my desire to shonne:
For all that I in many dayes doo weave,
In one short houre I find by her undonne.
So when I thinke to end that I begonne,
I must begin and never bring to end: 10
For with one looke she spils that long I sponne,
And with one word my whole years work doth rend.
Such labour like the Spyders web I fynd,
Whose fruitlesse worke is broken with least wynd.

XXIV

When I behold that beauties wonderment,
And rare perfection of each goodly part:
Of natures skill the onely complement,
I honor and admire the makers art.
But when I feele the bitter balefull smart,   5
Which her fayre eyes unwares doe worke in mee:
That death out of theyr shiny beames doe dart,
I thinke that I a new *Pandora* see.
Whom all the Gods in councell did agree,
Into this sinfull world from heaven to send: 10

---

4. *unreave:* unravel
6. *importune:* importunate, urgent; *shonne:* shun
1. *wonderment:* wonderful quality
6. *unwares:* without her being aware of it
8. *Pandora:* the wife of Epimetheus in Greek myth, created by Hephaestus to punish men for Prometheus' theft of fire. The box she opened contained all evil things. Spenser's use of her here balances the figures of Penelope and Daphne employed in sonnets XXIII and XXVIII.

That she to wicked men a scourge should bee,
For all their faults with which they did offend.
But since ye are my scourge I will intreat,
That for my faults ye will me gently beat.

XXV

How long shall this lyke dying lyfe endure,
And know no end of her owne mysery:
But wast and weare away in termes unsure,
Twixt feare and hope depending doubtfully.
Yet better were attonce to let me die,   5
And shew the last ensample of your pride:
Then to torment me thus with cruelty,
To prove your powre, which I too wel have tride.
But yet if in your hardned brest ye hide,
A close intent at last to shew me grace: 10
Then all the woes and wrecks which I abide,
As meanes of blisse I gladly wil embrace.
And wish that more and greater they might be,
That greater meede at last may turne to mee.

XXVI

Sweet is the Rose, but growes upon a brere;
Sweet is the Junipere, but sharpe his bough;
Sweet is the Eglantine, but pricketh nere;
Sweet is the firbloome, but his braunches rough.
Sweet is the Cypresse, but his rynd is tough,   5
Sweet is the nut, but bitter is his pill;
Sweet is the broome-flowre, but yet sowre enough;

---

3. *termes unsure:* uncertain conditions
4. *depending:* suspended
10. *close:* secret
14. *meede:* reward
1. *brere:* briar
3. *nere:* i.e., if one comes too near to it
4. *firbloome:* fir tree
5. *rynd:* bark
6. *pill:* shell

And sweet is Moly, but his root is ill.
So every sweet with soure is tempred still,
That maketh it be coveted the more: 10
For easie things that may be got at will,
Most sorts of men doe set but little store.
Why then should I accoumpt of little paine,
That endlesse pleasure shall unto me gaine.

XXVII

Faire proud now tell me why should faire be proud,
Sith all worlds glorie is but drosse uncleane:
And in the shade of death it selfe shall shroud,
How ever now thereof ye little weene.
That goodly Idoll now so gay beseene,   5
Shall doffe her fleshes borowd fayre attyre:
And be forgot as it had never beene,
That many now much worship and admire.
Ne any then shall after it inquire,
Ne any mention shall thereof remaine: 10
But what this verse, that never shall expyre,
Shall to you purchas with her thankles paine.
Faire be no lenger proud of that shall perish,
But that which shal you make immortall, cherish.

XXVIII

The laurell leafe, which you this day doe weare,
Gives me great hope of your relenting mynd:

---

8. *Moly:* a fabulous white flower with a black root; used by Ulysses as a charm against Circe's magic
13. *accoumpt of:* mind a
1. *faire:* someone who is beautiful
4. *weene:* expect
5. *gay beseene:* gaily arrayed
12. *her:* i.e., the verse's
13. *lenger:* longer

For since it is the badg which I doe beare,
Ye bearing it doe seeme to me inclind:
The powre thereof, which ofte in me I find,   5
Let it lykewise your gentle brest inspire
With sweet infusion, and put you in mind
Of that proud mayd, whom now those leaves attyre:
Proud *Daphne* scorning Phaebus lovely fyre,
On the Thessalian shore from him did flie: 10
For which the gods in theyr revengefull yre
Did her transforme into a laurell tree.
Then fly no more fayre love from Phebus chace,
But in your brest his leafe and love embrace.

XXIX

See how the stubborne damzell doth deprave
My simple meaning with disdaynfull scorne:
And by the bay which I unto her gave,
Accoumpts my selfe her captive quite forlorne.
The bay (quoth she) is of the victours borne,   5
Yielded them by the vanquisht as theyr meeds,
And they therewith doe poetes heads adorne,
To sing the glory of their famous deedes.
But sith she will the conquest challeng needs,
Let her accept me as her faithfull thrall,   10
That her great triumph which my skill exceeds,
I may in trump of fame blaze over all.
Then would I decke her head with glorious bayes,
And fill the world with her victorious prayse.

---

3. *badg . . . beare:* the laurel wreath is the poet's crown. Apollo (Phoebus),
from whom Daphne fled, is also the god of poets.
1. *deprave:* disparage
3. *by the bay:* garlands made of bay leaves were worn, as Spenser explains,
by both conquerors and poets
4. *Accoumpts my selfe:* Accounts me
9. *sith:* since
12. *trump:* trumpet; *blaze:* proclaim

XXX

My love is lyke to yse, and I to fyre;
How comes it then that this her cold so great
Is not dissolv'd through my so hot desyre,
But harder growes the more I her intreat?
Or how comes it that my exceeding heat   5
Is not delayd by her hart frosen cold:
But that I burne much more in boyling sweat,
And feele my flames augmented manifold?
What more miraculous thing may be told
That fire which all thing melts, should harden yse: 10
And yse which is congeald with sencelesse cold,
Should kindle fyre by wonderfull devyse.
Such is the powre of love in gentle mind,
That it can alter all the course of kynd.

XXXI

Ah why hath nature to so hard a hart
Given so goodly giftes of beauties grace?
Whose pryde depraves each other better part,
And all those pretious ornaments deface.
Sith to all other beastes of bloody race,   5
A dreadfull countenaunce she given hath:
That with theyr terrour al the rest may chace,
And warne to shun the daunger of theyr wrath.
But my proud one doth worke the greater scath,
Through sweet allurement of her lovely hew: 10
That she the better may in bloody bath,
Of such poore thralls her cruell hands embrew.
But did she know how ill these two accord,
Such cruelty she would have soone abhord.

1. *yse:* ice
2. *cold:* coldness
11. *sencelesse:* inanimate
14. *kynd:* nature
9. *scath:* harm
12. *embrew:* saturate

XXXII

The paynefull smith with force of fervent heat,
The hardest yron soone doth mollify:
That with his heavy sledge he can it beat,
And fashion to what he it list apply.
Yet cannot all these flames in which I fry,   5
Her hart more harde then yron soft awhit:
Ne all the playnts and prayers with which I
Doe beat on th'andvyle of her stubberne wit:
But still the more she fervent sees my fit:
The more she frieseth in her wilfull pryde: 10
And harder growes the harder she is smit,
With all the playnts which to her be applyde.
What then remaines but I to ashes burne,
And she to stones at length all frosen turne?

XXXIII

Great wrong I doe, I can it not deny,
To that most sacred Empresse my dear dred,
Not finishing her Queene of faery,
That mote enlarge her living prayses dead:
But lodwick, this of grace to me aread: 5
Doe ye not thinck th'accomplishment of it,
Sufficient worke for one mans simple head,

---

2. *mollify:* soften
3. *That:* So that
4. *fashion . . . apply:* shape it into whatever form he may wish
6. *soft awhit:* soften one bit
10. *frieseth:* freezes
2. *Empresse:* Queen Elizabeth, to whom the first three books of *The Fairie Queene* had been dedicated in 1590. Spenser's plan for the poem, as outlined in his introductory letter to Raleigh, called for twelve books. Books IV–VI were published in 1596 and two additional cantos on Mutability first appeared in 1609. *dred:* object of awe
4. *mote:* may; *dead:* i.e., after her death
5. *lodwick:* Spenser's friend Lodowick Bryskett (d. 1611), poet, translator, and Irish civil servant. This sonnet is addressed to him. *this . . . aread:* be gracious enough to advise me about this

All were it as the rcst but rudely writ.
How then should I without another wit:
Thinck ever to endure so taedious toyle,   10
Sins that this one is tost with troublous fit,
Of a proud love, that doth my spirite spoyle.
Ceasse then, till she vouchsafe to grawnt me rest,
Or lend you me another living brest.

XXXIV

Lyke as a ship that through the Ocean wyde,
By conduct of some star doth make her way,
Whenas a storme hath dimd her trusty guyde,
Out of her course doth wander far astray.
So I whose star, that wont with her bright ray,   5
Me to direct, with cloudes is overcast,
Doe wander now in darknesse and dismay,
Through hidden perils round about me plast.
Yet hope I well, that when this storme is past
My *Helice* the lodestar of my lyfe   10
Will shine again, and looke on me at last,
With lovely light to cleare my cloudy grief.
Till then I wander carefull comfortlesse,
In secret sorow and sad pensivenesse.

XXXV

My hungry eyes through greedy covetize,
Still to behold the object of their paine:
With no contentment can themselves suffize,
But having pine and having not complaine.

---

8. *as the rest:* i.e., the first three books; *rudely:* unskillfully
9. *wit:* brain
11. *Sins:* Since; *tost:* tossed, disturbed
2. *By conduct of:* Led by
8. *plast:* placed
10. *Helice:* probably the constellation Ursa Major; *lodestar:* pole star
No. XXXV This sonnet later reappears as number LXXXIII, where the
only change is "seeing" for "having" in l. 6.
1. *covetize:* covetousness
2. *Still:* Always

For lacking it they cannot lyfe sustayne,   5
And having it they gaze on it the more:
In their amazement lyke *Narcissus* vaine
Whose eyes him starv'd: so plenty makes me poore.
Yet are mine eyes so filled with the store
Of that faire sight, that nothing else they brooke,   10
But lothe the things which they did like before,
And can no more endure on them to looke.
All this worlds glory seemeth vayne to me,
And all their showes but shadowes saving she.

XXXVI

Tell me when shall these wearie woes have end,
Or shall their ruthlesse torment never cease:
But al my dayes in pining languor spend,
Without hope of aswagement or release.
Is there no meanes for me to purchace peace,   5
Or make agreement with her thrilling eyes:
But that their cruelty doth still increace,
And dayly more augment my miseryes.
But when ye have shewed all extremityes,
Then thinke how litle glory ye have gayned: 10
By slaying him, whose lyfe though ye despyse,
Mote have your life in honour long maintayned.
But by his death which some perhaps will mone,
Ye shall condemned be of many a one.

XXXVII

What guyle is this, that those her golden tresses,
She doth attyre under a net of gold:

---

7. *amazement:* infatuation
8. *him starv'd:* caused him to die (because he drowned in trying to embrace his own reflection on the water)
14. *saving she:* except for her
4. *aswagement:* relief
6. *thrilling:* piercing
12. *Mote:* Could

And with sly skill so cunningly them dresses,
That which is gold or heare, may scarsc bc told?
Is it that mens frayle eyes, which gaze too bold,   5
She may entangle in that golden snare:
And being caught may craftily enfold,
Theyr weaker harts, which are not wel aware?
Take heed therefore, myne eyes, how ye doe stare
Henceforth too rashly on that guilefull net,   10
In which if ever ye entrapped are,
Out of her bands ye by no meanes shall get.
Fondnesse it were for any being free,
To covet fetters, though they golden bee.

XXXVIII

Arion, when through tempests cruel wracke,
He forth was thrown into the greedy seas:
Through the sweet musick which his harp did make
Allu'rd a Dolphin him from death to ease.
But my rude musick, which was wont to please   5
Some dainty eares, cannot with any skill,
The dreadfull tempest of her wrath appease,
Nor move the Dolphin from her stubborne will.
But in her pride she dooth persever still,
All carelesse how my life for her decayse: 10
Yet with one word she can it save or spill,
To spill were pitty, but to save were prayse.
Chose rather to be praysed for dooing good,
Then to be blam'd for spilling guiltlesse blood.

XXXIX

Sweet smile, the daughter of the Queene of love,
Expressing all thy mothers powrefull art:
With which she wonts to temper angry Jove,

---

13. *Fondnesse:* Foolishness
1. *Arion:* a famous seventh-century Greek lyre player. Cf. Spenser's use of
Orpheus in XLIV.
11. *spill:* ruin
3. *wonts:* is accustomed

When all the gods he threats with thundring dart.
Sweet is thy vertue as thy selfe sweet art,   5
For when on me thou shinedst late in sadnesse:
A melting pleasance ran through every part,
And me revived with hart robbing gladnes.
Whylest rapt with joy resembling heavenly madnes,
My soule was ravisht quite as in a traunce: 10
And feeling thence no more her sorowes sadnesse,
Fed on the fulnesse of that chearefull glaunce.
More sweet than Nectar or Ambrosiall meat,
Seemd every bit, which thenceforth I did eat.

XL

Mark when she smiles with amiable cheare,
And tell me whereto can ye lyken it:
When on each eyelid sweetly doe appeare
An hundred Graces as in shade to sit.
Lykest it seemeth in my simple wit   5
Unto the fayre sunshine in somers day:
That when a dreadfull storme away is flit,
Thrugh the broad world doth spred his goodly ray
At sight whereof each bird that sits on spray,
And every beast that to his den was fled: 10
Comes forth afresh out of their late dismay,
And to the light lift up theyr drouping hed.
So my storme beaten hart likewise is cheared,
With that sunshine when cloudy looks are cleared.

XLI

Is it her nature or is it her will,
To be so cruell to an humbled foe:
If nature, then she may it mend with skill,
If will, then she at will may will forgoe.
But if her nature and her wil be so,   5
That she will plague the man that loves her most:

---

9. *Whylest:* Until
9. *spray:* twig

And take delight t'encrease a wretches woe,
Then all her natures goodly guifts are lost.
And that same glorious beauties ydle boast,
Is but a bayt such wretches to beguile: 10
As being long in her loves tempest tost,
She meanes at last to make her piteous spoyle.
O fayrest fayre let never it be named,
That so fayre beauty was so fowly shamed.

XLII

The love which me so cruelly tormenteth,
So pleasing is in my extreamest paine:
That all the more my sorrow it augmenteth,
The more I love and doe embrace my bane.
Ne doe I wish (for wishing were but vaine)   5
To be acquit fro my continuall smart:
But joy her thrall for ever to remayne,
And yield for pledge my poore captyved hart:
The which that it from her may never start,
Let her, yf please her, bynd with adamant chayne: 10
And from all wandring loves which mote pervart
His safe assurance strongly it restrayne.
Onely let her abstaine from cruelty,
And doe me not before my time to dy.

XLIII

Shall I then silent be or shall I speake?
And if I speake, her wrath renew I shall:
And if I silent be, my hart will breake,
Or choked be with overflowing gall.
What tyranny is this both my hart to thrall,   5
And eke my toung with proud restraint to tie?
That nether I may speake nor thinke at all,
But like a stupid stock in silence die.

---

12. *piteous spoyle:* mournful prey
11. *mote pervart:* might pervert

Yet I my hart with silence secretly
Will teach to speak, and my just cause to plead: 10
And eke mine eies with meeke humility,
Love learned letters to her eyes to read.
Which her deep wit, that true harts thought can spel,
Wil soone conceive, and learne to construe well.

XLIV

When those renoumed noble Peres of Greece,
Thrugh stubborn pride amongst themselves did jar
Forgetfull of the famous golden fleece,
Then Orpheus with his harp theyr strife did bar.
But this continuall cruell civill warre,   5
The which my selfe against my selfe doe make:
Whilest my weak powres of passions warreid arre,
No skill can stint nor reason can aslake.
But when in hand my tunelesse harp I take,
Then doe I more augment my foes despight: 10
And griefe renew, and passions doe awake,
To battaile fresh against my selfe to fight.
Mongst whome the more I seeke to settle peace,
The more I fynd their malice to increace.

XLV

Leave lady in your glasse of christall clene,
Your goodly selfe for evermore to vew:
And in my selfe, my inward selfe I meane,
Most lively lyke behold your semblant trew.
Within my hart, though hardly it can shew,   5

---

12. *Love . . . letters:* letters which he has been taught by love
13. *spel:* decipher
1. *renoumed:* renowned; *Peres:* peers, the Argonauts, with whom Orpheus sailed in their quest for the Golden Fleece
2. *jar:* quarrel
7. *warreid:* harried by war
8. *aslake:* appease
10. *despight:* disdain
4. *lively lyke:* lifelike; *semblant:* reflection

Thing so divine to vew of earthly eye:
The fayre Idea of your celestiall hew,
And every part remaines immortally:
And were it not that through your cruelty,
With sorrow dimmed and deformd it were: 10
The goodly ymage of your visnomy,
Clearer then christall would therein appere.
But if your selfe in me ye playne will see,
Remove the cause by which your fayre beames darkned be.

XLVI

When my abodes prefixed time is spent,
My cruell fayre streight bids me wend my way:
But then from heaven most hideous stormes are sent
As willing me against her will to stay.
Whom then shall I or heaven or her obay,   5
The heavens know best what is the best for me:
But as she will, whose will my life doth sway,
My lower heaven, so it perforce must bee.
But ye high hevens, that all this sorowe see,
Sith all your tempests cannot hold me backe: 10
Aswage your stormes, or else both you and she,
With both together me too sorely wrack.
Enough it is for one man to sustaine,
The stormes, which she alone on me doth raine.

XLVII

Trust not the treason of those smyling lookes,
Untill ye have theyr guylefull traynes well tryde:
For they are lyke but unto golden hookes,
That from the foolish fish theyr bayts doe hyde:
So she with flattring smyles weake harts doth guyde   5
Unto her love and tempte to theyr decay,

---

11. *visnomy:* countenance
1. *prefixed:* fixed beforehand
5. i.e., shall I obey heaven or her?
2. *traynes:* snares

Whome being caught she kills with cruell pryde,
And feeds at pleasure on the wretched pray:
Yet even whylst her bloody hands them slay,
Her eyes looke lovely and upon them smyle: 10
That they take pleasure in her cruell play,
And dying doe them selves of payne beguyle.
O mighty charm which makes men love theyr bane,
And thinck they dy with pleasure, live with payne.

XLVIII

Innocent paper, whom too cruell hand,
Did make the matter to avenge her yre:
And ere she could thy cause wel understand,
Did sacrifize unto the greedy fyre.
Well worthy thou to have found better hyre,   5
Then so bad end for hereticks ordayned:
Yet heresy nor treason didst conspire,
But plead thy maisters cause unjustly payned.
Whom she all carelesse of his griefe constrayned
To utter forth th'anguish of his hart: 10
And would not heare, when he to her complayned,
The piteous passion of his dying smart.
Yet live for ever, though against her will,
And speake her good, though she requite it ill.

XLIX

Fayre cruell, why are ye so fierce and cruell?
Is it because your eyes have powre to kill?
Then know, that mercy is the mighties jewell,
And greater glory thinke to save, then spill.
But if it be your pleasure and proud will,   5

---

5. *hyre:* reward
6. *for . . . ordayned:* convicted heretics were burned at the stake
7-8. i.e., you plotted neither heresy nor treason, but rather pleaded the
cause of your unjustly pained master
3. *mighties:* Almighty's
4. *spill:* destroy

To shew the powre of your imperious eyes:
Then not on him that never thought you ill,
But bend your force against your enemyes.
Let them feele th'utmost of your crueltyes,
And kill with looks, as Cockatrices doo: 10
But him that at your footstoole humbled lies,
With mercifull regard, give mercy too.
Such mercy shal you make admyred to be,
So shall you live by giving life to me.

L

Long languishing in double malady,
Of my harts wound and of my bodies griefe:
There came to me a leach that would apply
Fit medicines for my bodies best reliefe.
Vayne man (quod I) that hast but little priefe: 5
In deep discovery of the mynds disease,
Is not the hart of all the body chiefe?
And rules the members as it selfe doth please.
Then with some cordialls seeke first to appease,
The inward languour of my wounded hart, 10
And then my body shall have shortly ease:
But such sweet cordialls passe Physitions art.
Then my lyfes Leach doe you your skill reveale,
And with one salve both hart and body heale.

LI

Doe I not see that fayrest ymages
Of hardest Marble are of purpose made?
For that they should endure through many ages,
Ne let theyr famous moniments to fade.
Why then doe I, untrainde in lovers trade, 5

10. *Cockatrices:* the cockatrice was a fabulous serpent, said to be able to
kill by a mere glance
3. *leach:* doctor
5. *priefe:* experience
4. *moniments:* persons whom they commemorate

Her hardnes blame which I should more comend?
Sith never ought was excellent assayde,
Which was not hard t'atchive and bring to end.
Ne ought so hard, but he that would attend,
Mote soften it and to his will allure: 10
So doe I hope her stubborne hart to bend,
And that it then more stedfast will endure.
Onely my paines wil be the more to get her,
But having her, my joy wil be the greater.

LII

So oft as homeward I from her depart,
I goe lyke one that having lost the field:
Is prisoner led away with heavy hart,
Despoyld of warlike armes and knowen shield.
So doe I now my selfe a prisoner yeeld,   5
To sorrow and to solitary paine:
From presence of my dearest deare exylde,
Longwhile alone in languor to remaine.
There let no thought of joy or pleasure vaine,
Dare to approch, that may my solace breed: 10
But sudden dumps and drery sad disdayne,
Of all worlds gladnesse more my torment feed.
So I her absens will my penaunce make,
That of her presens I my meed may take.

LIII

The Panther knowing that his spotted hyde,
Doth please all beasts but that his looks them fray:
Within a bush his dreadfull head doth hide,
To let them gaze whylest he on them may pray.
Right so my cruell fayre with me doth play,   5
For with the goodly semblant of her hew:

---

8. *t'atchive:* to achieve
11. *dumps:* depressions
14. *meed:* reward
2. *fray:* frighten
6. *semblant:* image

She doth allure me to mine owne decay,
And then no mercy will unto me shew.
Great shame it is, thing so divine in view,
Made for to be the worlds most ornament: 10
To make the bayte her gazers to embrew,
Good shames to be to ill an instrument.
But mercy doth with beautie best agree,
As in theyr maker ye them best may see.

LIV

Of this worlds Theatre in which we stay,
My love lyke the Spectator ydly sits
Beholding me that all the pageants play,
Disguysing diversly my troubled wits.
Sometimes I joy when glad occasion fits, 5
And mask in myrth lyke to a Comedy:
Soone after when my joy to sorrow flits,
I waile and make my woes a Tragedy.
Yet she beholding me with constant eye,
Delights not in my merth nor rues my smart: 10
But when I laugh she mocks, and when I cry
She laughes, and hardens evermore her hart.
What then can move her? if nor merth nor mone,
She is no woman, but a sencelesse stone.

LV

So oft as I her beauty doe behold,
And therewith doe her cruelty compare:
I marvaile of what substance was the mould
The which her made attonce so cruell faire.
Not earth; for her high thoghts more heavenly are, 5
Not water; for her love doth burne like fyre:

---

10. *most:* greatest
11. *embrew:* stain (with blood)
12. *shames:* is ashamed
No. LV 5–8. the four elements, earth, air, fire, and water, of the traditional cosmology

Not ayre; for she is not so light or rare,
Not fyre; for she doth friese with faint desire.
Then needs another Element inquire
Whereof she mote be made; that is the skye.　　　　10
For to the heaven her haughty lookes aspire:
And eke her mind is pure immortall hye.
Then sith to heaven ye lykened are the best;
Be lyke in mercy as in all the rest:

LVI

Fayre ye be sure, but cruell and unkind,
As is a Tygre that with greedinesse
Hunts after bloud, when he by chauce doth find
A feeble beast, doth felly him oppresse.
Fayre be ye but proud and pittilesse,　　　　　　5
As is a storme, that all things doth prostrate:
Finding a tree alone all comfortlesse,
Beats on it strongly it to ruinate.
Fayre be ye sure, but hard and obstinate,
As is a rocke amidst the raging floods:　　　　　10
Gaynst which a ship of succour desolate,
Doth suffer wreck both of her selfe and goods.
That ship, that tree, and that same beast am I,
Whom ye doe wreck, doe ruine, and destroy.

LVII

Sweet warriour when shall I have peace with you?
High time it is, this warre now ended were:
Which I no lenger can endure to sue,
Ne your incessant battry more to beare:

---

9. i.e., another element must be sought out
10. *mote:* could
12. *pure . . . hye:* purely immortal in the highest way
1. *sure:* certainly
4. *felly:* cruelly
8. *ruinate:* bring to ruin
11. *of . . . desolate:* without hope of rescue
3. *sue:* follow

So weake my powres, so sore my wounds appeare,   5
That wonder is how I should live a jot,
Seeing my hart through launched every where
With thousand arrowes, which your eies have shot:
Yet shoot ye sharpely still, and spare me not,
But glory thinke to make these cruel stoures.   10
Ye cruell one, what glory can be got,
In slaying him that would live gladly yours?
Make peace therefore, and graunt me timely grace.
That al my wounds wil heale in little space.

LVIII

By her that is most assured of her selfe.

Weake is th'assurance that weake flesh reposeth,
In her owne powre, and scorneth others ayde:
That soonest fals when as she most supposeth
Her selfe assurd, and is of nought affrayd.
All flesh is frayle, and all her strength unstayd,   5
Like a vaine bubble blowen up with ayre:
Devouring tyme and changeful chance have prayd
Her glories pride that none may it repayre.
Ne none so rich or wise, so strong or fayre,
But fayleth trusting on his owne assurance: 10
And he that standeth on the hyghest stayre
Fals lowest: for on earth nought hath enduraunce.
Why then doe ye proud fayre, misdeeme so farre,
That to your selfe ye most assured arre.

LIX

Thrise happie she, that is so well assured
Unto her selfe and setled so in hart:

---

7. *launched:* pierced
10. *stoures:* attacks
Heading. By: Concerning.
5. *unstayd:* unsupported
7. *prayd:* preyed on
8. *that:* in such a way that
13. *misdeeme:* misjudge

That nether will for better be allured,
Ne feard with worse to any chaunce to start,
But like a steddy ship doth strongly part   5
The raging waves and keepes her course aright:
Ne ought for tempest doth from it depart,
Ne ought for fayrer weathers false delight.
Such selfe assurance need not feare the spight,
Of grudging foes, ne favour seek of friends: 10
But in the stay of her owne stedfast might,
Nether to one her selfe nor other bends.
Most happy she that most assured doth rest,
But he most happy who such one loves best.

                              LX

They that in course of heavenly spheares are skild,
To every planet point his sundry yeare:
In which her circles voyage is fulfild,
As Mars in three score yeares doth run his spheare.
So since the winged God his planet cleare,   5
Began in me to move, one yeare is spent:
The which doth longer unto me appeare,
Then al those fourty which my life outwent.
Then by that count, which lovers books invent,
The spheare of Cupid fourty yeares containes: 10
Which I have wasted in long languishment,
That seemd the longer for my greater paines.
But let my loves fayre Planet short her wayes
This year ensuing, or else short my dayes.

---

4. *Ne . . . start:* i.e., not afraid that any accident will change her for the
worse
2. *point:* appoint. The planetary year reckoned the time it took for a
planet to return to its original position in its revolution around the sun.
Ptolemy estimated the period of Mars at seventy-nine years.
5. *winged God:* Cupid
8. *outwent:* had passed through previously. If Spenser is to be taken
literally, this calculation gives the date 1593 for the composition of the
sonnet.
13. *short:* shorten

LXI

The glorious image of the makers beautie,
My soverayne saynt, the Idoll of my thought,
Dare not henceforth above the bounds of dewtie,
T'accuse of pride, or rashly blame for ought.
For being as she is divinely wrought,   5
And of the brood of Angels hevenly borne:
And with the crew of blessed Saynts upbrought,
Each of which did her with theyr guifts adorne:
The bud of joy, the blossome of the morne,
The beame of light, whom mortal eyes admyre: 10
What reason is it then but she should scorne
Base things, that to her love too bold aspire?
Such heavenly formes ought rather worshipt be,
Then dare be lov'd by men of meane degree.

LXII

The weary yeare his race now having run,
The new begins his compast course anew:
With shew of morning mylde he hath begun,
Betokening peace and plenty to ensew.
So let us, which this chaunge of weather vew,   5
Chaunge eeke our mynds and former lives amend,
The old yeares sinnes forepast let us eschew,
And fly the faults with which we did offend.
Then shall the new yeares joy forth freshly send,
Into the glooming world his gladsome ray: 10
And all these stormes which now his beauty blend,
Shall turne to caulmes and tymely cleare away.

4. *ought:* anything
7. *crew:* band; *upbrought:* brought up, raised
14. *meane:* low
2. *compast:* circular
7. *forepast:* gone by
10. *glooming:* gloomy
11. *blend:* dim

So likewise love cheare you your heavy spright,
And chaunge old yeares annoy to new delight.

LXIII

After long stormes and tempests sad assay,
Which hardly I endured heretofore:
In dread of death and daungerous dismay,
With which my silly barke was tossed sore:
I doe at length descry the happy shore,   5
In which I hope ere long for to arryve,
Fayre soyle it seemes from far and fraught with store
Of all that deare and daynty is alyve.
Most happy he that can at last atchyve,
The joyous safety of so sweet a rest: 10
Whose least delight sufficeth to deprive,
Remembrance of all paines which him opprest.
All paines are nothing in respect of this,
All sorrowes short that gaine eternall blisse.

LXIV

Coming to kisse her lyps, (such grace I found)
Me seemd I smelt a gardin of sweet flowres:
That dainty odours from them threw around
For damzels fit to decke their lovers bowres.
Her lips did smell lyke unto Gillyflowers,   5
Her ruddy cheekes lyke unto Roses red:
Her snowy browes lyke budded Bellamoures,
Her lovely eyes lyke Pincks but newly spred,
Her goodly bosome lyke a Strawberry bed,
Her neck lyke a bounch of Cullambynes: 10
Her brest lyke lillyes, ere theyr leaves be shed,
Her nipples lyke yong blossomd Jessemynes,
Such fragrant flowres doe give most odorous smell,
But her sweet odour did them all excell.

---

1. *sad assay:* grievous affliction
7. *Bellamoures:* these flowers have not been identified. The name means,
literally, "fair loves."

LXV

The doubt which ye misdeeme, fayre love, is vaine,
That fondly feare to loose your liberty,
When loosing one, two liberties ye gayne,
And make him bond that bondage earst dyd fly.
Sweet be the bands, the which true love doth tye,   5
Without constraynt or dread of any ill:
The gentle birde feeles no captivity
Within her cage, but singes and feeds her fill.
There pride dare not approch, nor discord spill
The league twixt them, that loyal love hath bound: 10
But simple truth and mutuall good will,
Seekes with sweet peace to salve each others wound:
There fayth doth fearlesse dwell in brasen towre,
And spotlesse pleasure builds her sacred bowre.

LXVI

To all those happy blessings which ye have,
With plenteous hand by heaven upon you thrown:
This one disparagement they to you gave,
That ye your love lent to so meane a one.
Yee whose high worths surpassing paragon,   5
Could not on earth have found one fit for mate,
Ne but in heaven matchable to none,
Why did ye stoup unto so lowly state.
But ye thereby much greater glory gate,
Then had ye sorted with a princes pere: 10
For now your light doth more it selfe dilate,
And in my darknesse greater doth appeare.

---

1. *misdeeme:* mistakenly conceive
2. *fondly:* foolishly; *loose:* lose
12. *salve:* heal
4. *meane:* low
9. *gate:* got, obtained
10. *sorted:* consorted; *pere:* equal

Yet since your light hath once enlumind me,
With my reflex yours shall encreased be.

LXVII

Lyke as a huntsman after weary chace,
Seeing the game from him escapt away:
Sits downe to rest him in some shady place,
With panting hounds beguiled of their pray.
So after long pursuit and vaine assay,   5
When I all weary had the chace forsooke,
The gentle deare returnd the selfe-same way,
Thinking to quench her thirst at the next brooke.
There she beholding me with mylder looke,
Sought not to fly, but fearelesse still did bide: 10
Till I in hand her yet halfe trembling tooke,
And with her owne goodwill hir fyrmely tyde.
Strange thing me seemd to see a beast so wyld,
So goodly wonne with her owne will beguyld.

LXVIII

Most glorious Lord of lyfe that on this day,
Didst make thy triumph over death and sin:
And having harrowd hell, didst bring away
Captivity thence captive us to win.
This joyous day, deare Lord, with joy begin,   5
And grant that we for whom thou diddest dye
Being with thy deare blood clene washt from sin,
May live for ever in felicity.
And that thy love we weighing worthily,
May likewise love thee for the same againe: 10

---

13. *enlumind:* illuminated
14. *reflex:* light reflected from me
4. *beguiled:* cheated
5. *assay:* attempt
1. *this day:* Easter Day
3. *harrowd hell:* "plundered" hell, by opening up its gates after his death
and releasing the patriarchs and prophets who had been confined there

And for thy sake that all lyke deare didst buy,
With love may one another entertayne.
So let us love, deare love, lyke as we ought,
Love is the lesson which the Lord us taught.

LXIX

The famous warriors of the anticke world,
Used Trophees to erect in stately wize:
In which they would the records have enrold,
Of theyr great deeds and valarous emprize.
What trophee then shall I most fit devize,   5
In which I may record the memory
Of my loves conquest, peerelesse beauties prise,
Adorn'd with honour, love, and chastity.
Even this verse vowd to eternity,
Shall be thereof immortall moniment: 10
And tell her prayse to all posterity,
That may admire such worlds rare wonderment.
The happy purchase of my glorious spoile,
Gotten at last with labour and long toyle.

LXX

Fresh spring the herald of loves mighty king,
In whose cote armour richly are displayd,
All sorts of flowers the which on earth do spring
In goodly colours gloriously arrayd.
Goe to my love, where she is carelesse layd,   5
Yet in her winters bowre not well awake:
Tell her the joyous time wil not be staid

---

11. *lyke deare:* at an equally expensive rate; *buy:* ransom
1. *anticke:* ancient
2. *wize:* manner
4. *valarous emprize:* valiant undertakings
7. *prise:* excellence
13. *purchase:* achievement; *spoile:* conquest, plunder; cf. "the spoils of war"
2. *cote armour:* vest embroidered with heraldic designs
5. *carelesse:* without care, quietly
7. *staid:* controlled. To take time "by the forelock" (l. 8) is to take advantage of the immediate opportunity.

Unlesse she doe him by the forelock take.
Bid her therefore her selfe soone ready make,
To wayt on love amongst his lovely crew: 10
Where every one that misseth then her make,
Shall be by him amearst with penance dew.
Make haste therefore sweet love, whilest it is prime,
For none can call againe the passed time.

LXXI

I joy to see how in your drawen work,
Your selfe unto the Bee ye doe compare;
And me unto the Spyder that doth lurke,
In close awayt to catch her unaware.
Right so your selfe were caught in cunning snare   5
Of a deare foe, and thralled to his love:
In whose streight bands ye now captived are
So firmely, that ye never may remove.
But as your worke is woven all about,
With woodbynd flowers and fragrant Eglantine: 10
So sweet your prison you in time shall prove,
With many deare delights bedecked fyne.
And all thensforth eternall peace shall see,
Betweene the Spyder and the gentle Bee.

LXXII

Oft when my spirit doth spred her bolder winges,
In mind to mount up to the purest sky:
It down is weighd with thoght of earthly things
And clogd with burden of mortality,

---

10. *crew:* band of attendants
11. *misseth . . . make:* has no mate
12. *amearst:* punished
13. *prime:* early morning
1. *drawen work:* ornamental work done by drawing out threads in a cloth
4. *awayt:* ambush
7. *streight:* close
9. *about:* possibly an error in the first edition for "above," which would preserve the rhyme scheme

Where when that soverayne beauty it doth spy,   5
Resembling heavens glory in her light:
Drawne with sweet pleasures bayt, it back doth fly,
And unto heaven forgets her former flight.
There my fraile fancy fed with full delight,
Doth bath in blisse and mantleth most at ease: 10
Ne thinks of other heaven, but how it might
Her harts desire with most contentment please.
Hart need not with none other happinesse,
But here on earth to have such hevens blisse.

LXXIII

Being my selfe captyved here in care,
My hart, whom none with servile bands can tye:
But the fayre tresses of your golden hayre,
Breaking his prison forth to you doth fly.
Lyke as a byrd that in ones hand doth spy   5
Desired food, to it doth make his flight:
Even so my hart, that wont on your fayre eye
To feed his fill, flyes backe unto your sight.
Doe you him take, and in your bosome bright,
Gently encage, that he may be your thrall: 10
Perhaps he there may learne with rare delight,
To sing your name and prayses over all.
That it hereafter may you not repent,
Him lodging in your bosome to have lent.

LXXIV

Most happy letters fram'd by skilfull trade,
With which that happy name was first desynd:
The which three times thrise happy hath me made,
With guifts of body, fortune and of mind.
The first my being to me gave by kind,   5
From mothers womb deriv'd by dew descent,

---

10. *mantleth:* rests on its perch
7. *wont:* was accustomed
1. *fram'd . . . trade:* drawn . . . practice
2. *desynd:* designed

The second is my sovereigne Queene most kind,
That honour and large richesse to me lent.
The third my love, my lives last ornament,
By whom my spirit out of dust was raysed: 10
To speake her prayse and glory excellent,
Of all alive most worthy to be praysed.
Ye three Elizabeths for ever live,
That three such graces did unto me give.

LXXV

One day I wrote her name upon the strand,
But came the waves and washed it away:
Agayne I wrote it with a second hand,
But came the tyde, and made my paynes his pray.
Vayne man, sayd she, that doest in vaine assay,   5
A mortall thing so to immortalize.
For I my selve shall lyke to this decay,
And eek my name bee wyped out lykewize.
Not so, (quod I) let baser things devize,
To dy in dust, but you shall live by fame: 10
My verse your vertues rare shall eternize,
And in the hevens wryte your glorious name:
Where whenas death shall all the world subdew,
Our love shall live, and later life renew.

LXXVI

Fayre bosome fraught with vertues richest tresure,
The neast of love, the lodging of delight:
The bowre of blisse, the paradice of pleasure,
The sacred harbour of that hevenly spright.
How was I ravisht with your lovely sight,   5
And my frayle thoughts too rashly led astray?
Whiles diving deepe through amorous insight,
On the sweet spoyle of beautie they did pray.

---

9. *quod*: quoth; *devize*: contrive, resolve
11. *eternize*: make eternal

And twixt her paps like early fruit in May,
Whose harvest seemd to hasten now apace: 10
They loosely did theyr wanton winges display,
And there to rest themselves did boldly place.
Sweet thoughts I envy your so happy rest,
Which oft I wisht, yet never was so blest.

LXXVII

Was it a dreame, or did I see it playne,
A goodly table of pure yvory:
All spred with juncats, fit to entertayne,
The greatest Prince with pompous roialty.
Mongst which there in a silver dish did ly, 5
Twoo golden apples of unvalewd price:
Far passing those which Hercules came by,
Or those which Atalanta did entice.
Exceeding sweet, yet voyd of sinfull vice,
That many sought yet none could ever taste, 10
Sweet fruit of pleasure brought from paradice
By love himselfe and in his garden plaste.
Her brest that table was so richly spredd,
My thoughts the guests, which would thereon have fedd.

LXXVIII

Lackyng my love I go from place to place,
Lyke a young fawne that late hath lost the hynd:
And seeke each where, where last I sawe her face,
Whose ymage yet I carry fresh in mynd.
I seeke the fields with her late footing synd, 5
I seeke her bowre with her late presence deckt,

---

3. *juncats:* sweet dishes, usually made from cream
6. *unvalewd:* invaluable
7. *passing:* surpassing; *Hercules:* one of his twelve labors involved the stealing of the golden apples of the Hesperides
8. *Atalanta:* who lost her race with her suitor Hippomenes when she stopped to pick up the golden apples he threw in her way
12. *plaste:* placed
2. *the hynd:* its mother
5. *footing synd:* footsteps marked

Yet nor in field nor bowre I her can fynd:
Yet field and bowre are full of her aspect.
But when myne eyes I thereunto direct,
They ydly back returne to me agayne,   10
And when I hope to see theyr trew object,
I fynd my selfe but fed with fancies vayne.
Ceasse then myne eyes, to seeke her selfe to see,
And let my thoughts behold her selfe in mee.

LXXIX

Men call you fayre, and you doe credit it,
For that your selfe ye dayly such doe see:
But the trew fayre, that is the gentle wit,
And vertuous mind, is much more praysd of me.
For all the rest, how ever fayre it be,   5
Shall turne to nought and loose that glorious hew:
But onely that is permanent and free
From frayle corruption, that doth flesh ensew.
That is true beautie: that doth argue you
To be divine and borne of heavenly seed: 10
Deriv'd from that fayre Spirit, from whom al true
And perfect beauty did at first proceed.
He onely fayre, and what he fayre hath made,
All other fayre lyke flowres untymely fade.

LXXX

After so long a race as I have run
Through Faery land, which those six books compile,
Give leave to rest me being halfe fordonne,
And gather to my selfe new breath awhile.
Then as a steed refreshed after toyle,   5
Out of my prison I will breake anew:

---

8. *aspect:* image, presence
8. *that . . . ensew:* which afflicts the flesh
2. *six books:* Books I–VI of *The Faerie Queene,* one half of Spenser's twelve-book plan, were published in 1596. Cf. above, no. XXXIII.
3. *fordonne:* finished

And stoutly will that second worke assoyle,
With strong endevour and attention dew.
Till then give leave to me in pleasant mew,
To sport my muse and sing my loves sweet praise: 10
The contemplation of whose heavenly hew,
My spirit to an higher pitch will rayse.
But let her prayses yet be low and meane,
Fit for the handmayd of the Faery Queene.

LXXXI

Fayre is my love, when her fayre golden heares,
With the loose wynd ye waving chance to marke:
Fayre when the rose in her red cheekes appeares,
Or in her eyes the fyre of love does sparke.
Fayre when her brest lyke a rich laden barke, 5
With pretious merchandize she forth doth lay:
Fayre when that cloud of pryde, which oft doth dark
Her goodly light with smiles she drives away.
But fayrest she, when so she doth display,
The gate with pearles and rubyes richly dight: 10
Throgh which her words so wise do make their way
To beare the message of her gentle spright.
The rest be works of natures wonderment,
But this the worke of harts astonishment.

LXXXII

Joy of my life, full oft for loving you
I blesse my lot, that was so lucky placed:
But then the more your owne mishap I rew,
That are so much by so meane love embased.
For had the equall hevens so much you graced 5
In this as in the rest, ye mote invent
Som hevenly wit, whose verse could have enchased

---

7. *assoyle:* deliver
9. *mew:* retreat
4. *embased:* disgraced
5. *equall:* just
6. *mote:* could
7. *enchased:* engraved

386

Your glorious name in golden moniment.
But since ye deignd so goodly to relent
To me your thrall, in whom is little worth,   10
That little that I am, shall all be spent,
In setting your immortall prayses forth.
Whose lofty argument uplifting me,
Shall lift you up unto an high degree.

LXXXIII

My hungry eyes, through greedy covetize,
Still to behold the object of theyr payne:
With no contentment can themselves suffize,
But having pine, and having not complayne.
For lacking it, they cannot lyfe sustayne,   5
And seeing it, they gaze on it the more:
In theyr amazement lyke Narcissus vayne
Whose eyes him starv'd: so plenty makes me pore.
Yet are myne eyes so filled with the store
Of that fayre sight, that nothing else they brooke: 10
But loath the things which they did like before,
And can no more endure on them to looke.
All this worlds glory seemeth vayne to me,
And all theyr shewes but shadowes saving she.

LXXXIV

Let not one sparke of filthy lustfull fyre
Breake out, that may her sacred peace molest:
Ne one light glance of sensuall desyre
Attempt to work her gentle mindes unrest.
But pure affections bred in spotlesse brest,   5
And modest thoughts breathd from wel tempred sprites
Goe visit her in her chast bowre of rest,
Accompanyde with angelick delightes.
There fill your selfe with those most joyous sights,

No. LXXXIII This sonnet repeats no. XXXV.
6. *seeing:* no. XXXV reads *having*

The which my selfe could never yet attayne: 10
But speake no word to her of these sad plights,
Which her too constant stiffenesse doth constrayn.
Onely behold her rare perfection,
And blesse your fortunes fayre election.

LXXXV

The world that cannot deeme of worthy things,
When I doe praise her, say I doe but flatter:
So does the Cuckow, when the Mavis sings,
Begin his witlesse note apace to clatter.
But they that skill not of so heavenly matter,   5
All that they know not, envy or admyre:
Rather then envy let them wonder at her,
But not to deeme of her desert aspyre.
Deepe in the closet of my parts entyre,
Her worth is written with a golden quill: 10
That me with heavenly fury doth inspire,
And my glad mouth with her sweet prayses fill.
Which when as fame in her shrill trump shal thunder
Let the world chose to envy or to wonder.

LXXXVI

Venemous toung tipt with vile adders sting,
Of that selfe kynd with which the Furies fell
Theyr snaky heads doe combe, from which a spring
Of poysoned words and spitefull speeches well.
Let all the plagues and horrid paines of hell,   5
Upon thee fall for thine accursed hyre:

---

12. *stiffenesse:* stubbornness
14. *election:* choice
3. *Mavis:* thrush
5. *skill not:* have no knowledge of
8. *deeme . . . aspyre:* think of aspiring to a level upon which they might deserve something of her
2. *selfe:* very, same
4. *well:* rise up
6. *hyre:* reward

That with false forged lyes, which thou didst tel,
In my true love did stirre up coles of yre,
The sparkes whereof let kindle thine own fyre,
And catching hold on thine owne wicked hed   10
Consume thee quite, that didst with guile conspire
In my sweet peace such breaches to have bred.
Shame be thy meed, and mischiefe thy reward,
Dew to thy selfe that it for me prepard.

LXXXVII

Since I did leave the presence of my love,
Many long weary dayes I have outworne:
And many nights, that slowly seemd to move
Theyr sad protract from evening untill morne.
For when as day the heaven doth adorne,   5
I wish that night the noyous day would end:
And when as night hath us of light forlorne,
I wish that day would shortly reascend.
Thus I the time with expectation spend,
And faine my griefe with chaunges to beguile,   10
That further seemes his terme still to extend,
And maketh every minute seeme a myle.
So sorrow still doth seeme too long to last,
But joyous houres doo fly away too fast.

LXXXVIII

Since I have lackt the comfort of that light,
The which was wont to lead my thoughts astray:
I wander as in darkenesse of the night,
Affrayd of every dangers least dismay.
Ne ought I see, though in the clearest day,   5

---

4. *protract:* protraction
6. *noyous:* vexatious
7. *us . . . forlorne:* taken away light from us
11. *terme:* limit
5. *ought:* aught, anything

When others gaze upon theyr shadowes vayne:
But th'onely image of that heavenly ray,
Whereof some glance doth in mine eie remayne.
Of which beholding th'Idaea playne,
Through contemplation of my purest part: 10
With light thereof I doe my selfe sustayne,
And thereon feed my love-affamisht hart.
But with such brightnesse whylest I fill my mind,
I starve my body and mine eyes doe blynd.

LXXXIX

Lyke as the Culver on the bared bough,
Sits mourning for the absence of her mate:
And in her songs sends many a wishfull vow,
For his returne that seemes to linger late.
So I alone now left disconsolate,   5
Mourne to my selfe the absence of my love:
And wandring here and there all desolate,
Seek with my playnts to match that mournful dove:
Ne joy of ought that under heaven doth hove,
Can comfort me, but her owne joyous sight: 10
Whose sweet aspect both God and man can move,
In her unspotted pleasauns to delight.
Dark is my day, whyles her fayre light I mis,
And dead my life that wants such lively blis.

I

In youth before I waxed old,
The blynd boy Venus baby,
For want of cunning made me bold,
In bitter hyve to grope for honny.

---

9. *th'Idaea:* the Platonic "idea" or pure form
12. *love-affamisht:* starved by love
1. *Culver:* dove
9. *hove:* hover, remain
12. *pleasauns:* pleasantness
14. *wants such lively:* lacks such vital
The four Anacreontic poems that follow the sonnets of the *Amoretti* are unnumbered in the original edition.

But when he saw me stung and cry,   5
He tooke his wings and away did fly.

II

As Diane hunted on a day,
She chaunst to come where Cupid lay,
    His quiver by his head:
One of his shafts she stole away,
And one of hers did close convay,   5
    Into the others stead:
With that love wounded my loves hart,
But Diane beasts with Cupids dart.

III

I saw in secret to my Dame,
How little Cupid humbly came:
    And sayd to her All hayle my mother.
But when he saw me laugh, for shame
His face with bashfull blood did flame,   5
    Not knowing Venus from the other,
Then never blush Cupid (quoth I)
For many have err'd in this beauty.

IV

Upon a day as love lay sweetly slumbring,
    All in his mothers lap:
A gentle Bee with his loud trumpet murm'ring,
    About him flew by hap.
Whereof when he was wakened with the noyse,   5
    And saw the beast so small:
Whats this (quoth he) that gives so great a voyce,
    That wakens men withall.
        In angry wize he flyes about,
        And threatens all with corage stout.   10

---

5. *close convay:* secretly transfer
6. *stead:* place
4. *hap:* chance
9. *wize:* manner

To whom his mother closely smiling sayd,
    Twixt earnest and twixt game:
See thou thy selfe likewise art lyttle made,
    If thou regard the same.
And yet thou suffrest neyther gods in sky,   15
    Nor men in earth to rest:
But when thou art disposed cruelly,
    Theyr sleepe thou doost molest.
        Then eyther change thy cruelty,
        Or give lyke leave unto the fly.   20

Nathlesse the cruell boy not so content,
    Would needs the fly pursue:
And in his hand with heedlesse hardiment,
    Him caught for to subdue.
But when on it he hasty hand did lay,   25
    The Bee him stung therefore:
Now out alasse (he cryde) and welaway,
    I wounded am full sore:
        The fly that I so much did scorne,
        Hath hurt me with his little horne.   30

Unto his mother straight he weeping came,
    And of his griefe complayned:
Who could not chose but laugh at his fond game,
    Though sad to see him pained.
Think now (quod she) my sonne how great the smart   35
    Of those whom thou dost wound:
Full many thou hast pricked to the hart,
    That pitty never found:
        Therefore henceforth some pitty take,
        When thou doest spoyle of lovers make.   40

She tooke him streight full pitiously lamenting,
    And wrapt him in her smock:
She wrapt him softly, all the while repenting,
    That he the fly did mock.

---

20. *fly:* insect
23. *headlesse hardiment:* reckless boldness

She drest his wound and it embaulmed wel 45
    With salve of soveraigne might:
And then she bath'd him in a dainty well
    The well of deare delight.
      Who would not oft be stung as this,
      To be so bath'd in Venus blis. 50

The wanton boy was shortly wel recured,
    Of that his malady:
But he soone after fresh againe enured,
    His former cruelty.
And since that time he wounded hath my selfe 55
    With his sharpe dart of love:
And now forgets the cruell carelesse elfe,
    His mothers heast to prove.
      So now I languish, till he please,
      My pining anguish to appease. 60

Epithalamion

1.

Ye learned sisters which have oftentimes
Beene to me ayding, others to adorne:
Whom ye thought worthy of your gracefull rymes,
That even the greatest did not greatly scorne
To heare theyr names sung in your simple layes, 5
But joyed in theyr prayse.
And when ye list your owne mishaps to mourne,
Which death, or love, or fortunes wreck did rayse,
Your string could soone to sadder tenor turne,

---

51. *recured:* recovered
53. *enured:* put into practice
58. *His . . . prove:* To comply with his mother's request
Epithalamion The stanzas are unnumbered in the original edition (1595).
1. *learned sisters:* the Muses
7. *ye list:* it pleased you
8. *wreck:* violence

And teach the woods and waters to lament   10
Your dolefull dreriment.
Now lay those sorrowfull complaints aside,
And having all your heads with girland crownd,
Helpe me mine owne loves prayses to resound,
Ne let the same of any be envide: 15
So Orpheus did for his owne bride,
So I unto my selfe alone will sing,
The woods shall to me answer and my Eccho ring.

2.

Early before the worlds light giving lampe,
His golden beame upon the hils doth spred,   20
Having disperst the nights unchearefull dampe,
Doe ye awake and with fresh lusty hed,
Go to the bowre of my beloved love,
My truest turtle dove
Bid her awake; for Hymen is awake,   25
And long since ready forth his maske to move,
With his bright Tead that flames with many a flake,
And many a bachelor to waite on him,
In theyr fresh garments trim.
Bid her awake therefore and soone her dight,   30
For lo the wished day is come at last,
That shall for al the paynes and sorrowes past,
Pay to her usury of long delight,
And whylest she doth her dight,
Doe ye to her joy and solace sing,   35
That all the woods may answer and your eccho ring.

---

11. *dreriment:* sadness
16. *Orpheus:* after the death of Eurydice upon a riverbank, Orpheus sang
his lament for her along the lonely shore. Later, through the magic of his
singing, he brought her back from the underworld.
25. *Hymen:* the god of marriage
26. *maske:* masque
27. *Tead:* torch; *flake:* flash (of fire)
30. *dight:* dress

3.

Bring with you all the Nymphes that you can heare
Both of the rivers and the forrests greene:
And of the sea that neighbours to her neare,
Al with gay girlands goodly wel beseene.   40
And let them also with them bring in hand,
Another gay girland
For my fayre love of lillyes and of roses,
Bound truelove wize with a blew silke riband.
And let them make great store of bridale poses,   45
And let them eeke bring store of other flowers
To deck the bridale bowers.
And let the ground whereas her foot shall tread,
For feare the stones her tender foot should wrong
Be strewed with fragrant flowers all along,   50
And diapred lyke the discolored mead.
Which done, doe at her chamber dore awayt,
For she will waken strayt,
The whiles doe ye this song unto her sing,
The woods shall to you answer and your Eccho ring.   55

4.

Ye Nymphes of Mulla which with carefull heed,
The silver scaly trouts doe tend full well,
And greedy pikes which use therein to feed,
(Those trouts and pikes all others doo excell)

---

37. *Bring . . . heare:* i.e., Bring here with you all etc.
39. *neighbours . . . neare:* Spenser's bride, Elizabeth Boyle, was from
Kilcoran, Ireland, on the bay of Youghal
40. *beseene:* appearing
44. *riband:* ribbon
45. *poses:* posies, bouquets
46. *eeke:* also
51. *diapred:* variegated; *discolored:* of different colors
53. *strayt:* in a moment
56. *Mulla:* the Awbeg, an Irish river

And ye likewise which keepe the rushy lake,   60
Where none doo fishes take,
Bynd up the locks the which hang scatterd light,
And in his waters which your mirror make,
Behold your faces as the christall bright,
That when you come whereas my love doth lie,   65
No blemish she may spie.
And eke ye lightfoot mayds which keepe the deere,
That on the hoary mountayne use to towre,
And the wylde wolves which seeke them to devoure,
With your steele darts doo chace from comming neer   70
Be also present heere,
To helpe to decke her and to help to sing,
That all the woods may answer and your eccho ring.

5.

Wake now my love, awake; for it is time,
The Rosy Morne long since left Tithones bed,   75
All ready to her silver coche to clyme,
And Phoebus gins to shew his glorious hed.
Hark how the cheerefull birds do chaunt theyr laies
And carroll of loves praise.
The merry Larke hir mattins sings aloft,   80
The thrush replyes, the Mavis descant playes,
The Ouzell shrills, the Ruddock warbles soft,
So goodly all agree with sweet consent,
To this dayes merriment.
Ah my deere love why doe ye sleepe thus long,   85
When meeter were that ye should now awake,
T'awayt the comming of your joyous make,

---

67. *deere:* the 1595 edition reads "dore"
68. *towre:* soar
75. *Tithones:* Tithonus', the consort of Eos, the dawn
77. *gins:* begins
80. *mattins:* morning prayers
81. *Mavis:* another kind of thrush; *descant:* melodious accompaniment to a musical theme
82. *Ouzell:* blackbird; *Ruddock:* redbreast
83–84. *agree . . . To:* accord with in sweet harmony
86. *meeter were:* it would be more fitting
87. *make:* mate

And hearken to the birds lovelearned song,
The deawy leaves among.
For they of joy and pleasance to you sing,   90
That all the woods them answer and theyr eccho ring.

6.

My love is now awake out of her dreame,
And her fayre eyes like stars that dimmed were
With darksome cloud, now shew theyr goodly beams
More bright then Hesperus his head doth rere.   95
Come now ye damzels, daughters of delight,
Helpe quickly her to dight,
But first come ye fayre houres which were begot
In loves sweet paradice, of Day and Night,
Which doe the seasons of the yeare allot,   100
And al that ever in this world is fayre
Doe make and still repayre.
And ye three handmayds of the Cyprian Queene,
The which doe still adorne her beauties pride,
Helpe to addorne my beautifullest bride.   105
And as ye her array, still throw betweene
Some graces to be seene,
And as ye use to Venus, to her sing,
The whiles the woods shal answer and your eccho ring.

7.

Now is my love all ready forth to come,   110
Let all the virgins therefore well awayt,
And ye fresh boyes that tend upon her groome
Prepare your selves; for he is comming strayt.
Set all your things in seemely good aray
Fit for so joyfull day,   115
The joyfulst day that ever sunne did see.
Faire Sun, shew forth thy favourable ray,

---

95. *Hesperus:* the evening star; *rere:* raise
103. *three . . . Queene:* the three graces who wait upon Venus
104. *still:* always

And let thy lifull heat not fervent be
For feare of burning her sunshyny face,
Her beauty to disgrace.   120
O fayrest Phoebus, father of the Muse,
If ever I did honour thee aright,
Or sing the thing, that mote thy mind delight,
Doe not thy servants simple boone refuse,
But let this day let this one day be myne,   125
Let all the rest be thine.
Then I thy soverayne prayses loud wil sing,
That all the woods shal answer and theyr eccho ring.

8.

Harke how the Minstrels gin to shrill aloud
Their merry Musick that resounds from far,   130
The pipe, the tabor, and the trembling Croud,
That well agree withouten breach or jar.
But most of all the Damzels doe delite,
When they their tymbrels smyte,
And thereunto doe daunce and carrol sweet,   135
That all the sences they doe ravish quite,
The whyles the boyes run up and downe the street,
Crying aloud with strong confused noyce,
As if it were one voyce.
Hymen io Hymen, Hymen they do shout,   140
That even to the heavens theyr shouting shrill
Doth reach, and all the firmament doth fill,
To which the people standing all about,
As in approvance doe thereto applaud
And loud advaunce her laud,   145

---

118. *lifull:* full of life
123. *mote:* could
124. *boone:* favor requested
131. *pipe:* flutelike instrument; *tabor:* drum; *Croud:* early form of the fiddle
134. *tymbrels:* tambourines
138. *noyce:* sound
142. *firmament:* sky
144. *approvance:* approval
145. *laud:* praise

And evermore they Hymen Hymen sing,
That al the woods them answer and theyr eccho ring.

9.

Loe where she comes along with portly pace,
Lyke Phoebe from her chamber of the East,
Arysing forth to run her mighty race,   150
Clad all in white, that seemes a virgin best.
So well it her beseemes that ye would weene
Some angell she had beene.
Her long loose yellow locks lyke golden wyre,
Sprinckled with perle, and perling flowres a tweene,   155
Doe lyke a golden mantle her attyre,
And being crowned with a girland greene,
Seeme lyke some mayden Queene.
Her modest eyes abashed to behold
So many gazers, as on her do stare,   160
Upon the lowly ground affixed are.
Ne dare lift up her countenance too bold,
But blush to heare her prayses sung so loud,
So farre from being proud.
Nathlesse doe ye still loud her prayses sing,   165
That all the woods may answer and your eccho ring.

10.

Tell me ye merchants daughters did ye see
So fayre a creature in your towne before,
So sweet, so lovely, and so mild as she,
Adornd with beautyes grace and vertues store,   170
Her goodly eyes lyke Saphyres shining bright,
Her forehead yvory white,

---

148. *portly:* dignified
149. *Phoebe:* Diana, the goddess of the moon
152. *weene:* think
155. *perling:* rippling
165. *Nathlesse:* Nevertheless
170. *store:* richness, abundance

Her cheekes lyke apples which the sun hath rudded,
Her lips lyke cherryes charming men to byte,
Her brest like to a bowle of creame uncrudded,   175
Her paps lyke lyllies budded,
Her snowie necke lyke to a marble towre,
And all her body like a pallace fayre,
Ascending uppe with many a stately stayre,
To honors seat and chastities sweet bowre.   180
Why stand ye still ye virgins in amaze,
Upon her so to gaze,
Whiles ye forget your former lay to sing,
To which the woods did answer and your eccho ring.

11.

But if ye saw that which no eyes can see,   185
The inward beauty of her lively spright,
Garnisht with heavenly guifts of high degree,
Much more then would ye wonder at that sight,
And stand astonisht lyke to those which red
Medusaes mazeful hed.   190
There dwels sweet love and constant chastity,
Unspotted fayth and comely womanhood,
Regard of honour and mild modesty,
There vertue raynes as Queene in royal throne,
And giveth lawes alone.   195
The which the base affections doe obay,
And yeeld theyr services unto her will,
Ne thought of thing uncomely ever may
Thereto approch to tempt her mind to ill.
Had ye once seene these her celestial threasures,   200
And unrevealed pleasures,

173. *rudded:* reddened
175. *uncrudded:* uncurdled
186. *lively spright:* vital spirit
189. *red:* looked at
190. *Medusaes:* Medusa was a mythical monster with snaky locks; anyone who gazed at her was turned to stone; *mazeful:* confounding
198. *uncomely:* improper

Then would ye wonder and her prayses sing,
That al the woods should answer and your echo ring.

12.

Open the temple gates unto my love,
Open them wide that she may enter in,   205
And all the postes adorne as doth behove,
And all the pillours deck with girlands trim,
For to recyve this Saynt with honour dew,
That commeth in to you.
With trembling steps and humble reverence,   210
She commeth in, before th'almighties vew,
Of her ye virgins learne obedience,
When so ye come into those holy places,
To humble your proud faces:
Bring her up to th'high altar that she may,   215
The sacred ceremonies there partake,
The which do endlesse matrimony make,
And let the roring Organs loudly play;
The praises of the Lord in lively notes,
The whiles with hollow throates   220
The Choristers the joyous Antheme sing,
That al the woods may answere and their eccho ring.

13.

Behold whiles she before the altar stands
Hearing the holy priest that to her speakes
And blesseth her with his two happy hands,
How the red roses flush up in her cheekes,   225
And the pure snow with goodly vermill stayne,
Like crimsin dyde in grayne,
That even th'Angels which continually,
About the sacred Altare doe remaine,   230

---

208. *recyve:* receive
226. *vermill:* vermilion
227. *crimsin . . . grayne:* crimson fast dyed

Forget their service and about her fly,
Ofte peeping in her face that seemes more fayre,
The more they on it stare.
But her sad eyes still fastened on the ground,
Are governed with goodly modesty, 235
That suffers not one looke to glaunce awry,
Which may let in a little thought unsownd.
Why blush ye love to give to me your hand,
The pledge of all our band?
Sing ye sweet Angels, Alleluya sing, 240
That all the woods may answere and your eccho ring.

14.

Now al is done; bring home the bride againe,
Bring home the triumph of our victory,
Bring home with you the glory of her gaine,
With joyance bring her and with jollity. 245
Never had man more joyfull day then this,
Whom heaven would heape with blis.
Make feast therefore now all this live long day,
This day for ever to me holy is,
Poure out the wine without restraint or stay, 250
Poure not by cups, but by the belly full,
Poure out to all that wull,
And sprinkle all the postes and wals with wine,
That they may sweat, and drunken be withall.
Crowne ye God Bacchus with a coronall, 255
And Hymen also crowne with wreathes of vine,
And let the Graces daunce unto the rest;
For they can doo it best:
The whiles the maydens doe theyr carroll sing,
To which the woods shal answer and theyr eccho ring. 260

239. *band:* bond, tie
245. *joyance:* joyfulness
252. *wull:* will
255. *coronall:* wreath of flowers

402

15.

Ring ye the bels, ye yong men of the towne,
And leave your wonted labors for this day:
This day is holy; doe ye write it downe,
That ye for ever it remember may.
This day the sunne is in his chiefest hight,   265
With Barnaby the bright,
From whence declining daily by degrees,
He somewhat loseth of his heat and light,
When once the Crab behind his back he sees.
But for this time it ill ordained was,   270
To chose the longest day in all the yeare,
And shortest night, when longest fitter weare:
Yet never day so long, but late would passe.
Ring ye the bels, to make it weare away,
And bonefiers make all day,   275
And daunce about them, and about them sing:
That all the woods may answer, and your eccho ring.

16.

Ah when will this long weary day have end,
And lende me leave to come unto my love?
How slowly do the houres theyr numbers spend?   280
How slowly does sad Time his feathers move?
Hast thee O fayrest Planet to thy home
Within the Westerne fome:
Thy tyred steedes long since have need of rest.
Long though it be, at last I see it gloome,   285
And the bright evening star with golden creast
Appeare out of the East.

---

266. *Barnaby the bright:* the feast of St. Barnabas (June 11), the longest
day of the year in the old calendar
269. *the Crab:* Cancer, the astrological sign
281. *his feathers:* cf. "the wings of time"
284. *steedes:* the horses which drew the chariot of the sun
285. *gloome:* begin to grow dark

Fayre childe of beauty, glorious lampe of love
That all the host of heaven in rankes doost lead,
And guydest lovers through the nightes dread,   290
How chearefully thou lookest from above,
And seemst to laugh atweene thy twinkling light
As joying in the sight
Of these glad many which for joy doe sing,
That all the woods them answer and their echo ring.   295

17.

Now ceasse ye damsels your delights forepast;
Enough is it, that all the lay was youres:
Now day is doen, and night is nighing fast:
Now bring the Bryde into the brydall boures.
Now night is come, now soone her disaray,   300
And in her bed her lay;
Lay her in lillies and in violets,
And silken courteins over her display,
And odourd sheetes, and Arras coverlets.
Behold how goodly my faire love does ly   305
In proud humility;
Like unto Maia, when as Jove her tooke,
In Tempe, lying on the flowry gras,
Twixt sleepe and wake, after she weary was,
With bathing in the Acidalian brooke.   310
Now it is night, ye damsels may be gon,
And leave my love alone,
And leave likewise your former lay to sing:
The woods no more shal answere, nor your echo ring.

---

290. *nightes:* pronounced here as a disyllable
292. *atweene:* between
296. *forepast:* gone by
298. *nighing:* drawing near
299. *boures:* bowers
304. *odourd:* scented; *Arras:* a town in Artois, famous for its woven cloth and tapestries
307. *Maia:* the eldest of the Pleiades, who became the mother of Hermes after Jupiter seduced her

18.

Now welcome night, thou night so long expected, 315
That long daies labour doest at last defray,
And all my cares, which cruell love collected,
Hast sumd in one, and cancelled for aye:
Spread thy broad wing over my love and me,
That no man may us see, 320
And in thy sable mantle us enwrap,
From feare of perrill and foule horror free.
Let no false treason seeke us to entrap,
Nor any dread disquiet once annoy
The safety of our joy: 325
But let the night be calme and quietsome,
Without tempestuous storms or sad afray:
Lyke as when Jove with fayre Alcmena lay,
When he begot the great Tirynthian groome:
Or lyke as when he with thy selfe did lie, 330
And begot Majesty.
And let the mayds and yongmen cease to sing:
Ne let the woods them answer, nor theyr eccho ring.

19.

Let no lamenting cryes, nor dolefull teares,
Be heard all night within nor yet without:
Ne let false whispers breeding hidden feares, 335
Breake gentle sleepe with misconceived dout.
Let no deluding dreames, nor dreadful sights
Make sudden sad affrights;
Ne let housefyres, nor lightnings helpelesse harmes, 340
Ne let the Pouke, nor other evill sprights,
Ne let mischivous witches with theyr charmes,

---

318. *for aye:* forever
329. *great . . . groome:* Hercules, the son of Alcmena and Jupiter
337. *misconceived:* falsely imagined
340. *helpelesse:* irremediable
341. *the Pouke:* Puck, Robin Goodfellow

Ne let hob Goblins, names whose sence we see not,
Fray us with things that be not.
Let not the shriech Oule, nor the Storke be heard: 345
Nor the night Raven that still deadly yels,
Nor damned ghosts cald up with mighty spels,
Nor griesly vultures make us once affeard:
Ne let th'unpleasant Quyre of Frogs still croking
Make us to wish theyr choking. 350
Let none of these theyr drery accents sing;
Ne let the woods them answer, nor theyr eccho ring.

20.

But let stil Silence trew night watches keepe,
That sacred peace may in assurance rayne,
And tymely sleep, when it is tyme to sleepe, 355
May poure his limbs forth on your pleasant playne,
The whiles an hundred little winged loves,
Like divers fethered doves,
Shall fly and flutter round about your bed,
And in the secret darke, that none reproves, 360
Their prety stealthes shal worke, and snares shal spread
To filch away sweet snatches of delight,
Conceald through covert night.
Ye sonnes of Venus, play your sports at will,
For greedy pleasure, carelesse of your toyes, 365
Thinks more upon her paradise of joyes,
Then what ye do, albe it good or ill.
All night therefore attend your merry play,
For it will soone be day:
Now none doth hinder you, that say or sing, 370
Ne will the woods now answer, nor your Eccho ring.

---

344. *Fray:* Frighten
345. *shriech Oule:* screech owl; *Storke:* conceived of here as a bird of ill omen
346. *yels:* cries
349. *Quyre:* choir; *still:* always
363. *covert:* covered, hidden
367. *albe it:* whether it is

21.

Who is the same, which at my window peepes?
Or whose is that faire face, that shines so bright,
Is it not Cinthia, she that never sleepes,
But walkes about high heaven al the night? 375
O fayrest goddesse, do thou not envy
My love with me to spy:
For thou likewise didst love, though now unthought,
And for a fleece of woll, which privily,
The Latmian shephard once unto thee brought, 380
His pleasures with thee wrought.
Therefore to us be favorable now;
And sith of wemens labours thou hast charge,
And generation goodly dost enlarge,
Encline thy will t'effect our wishfull vow, 385
And the chast wombe informe with timely seed,
That may our comfort breed:
Till which we cease our hopefull hap to sing,
Ne let the woods us answere, nor our Eccho ring.

22.

And thou great Juno, which with awful might 390
The lawes of wedlock still dost patronize,
And the religion of the faith first plight
With sacred rites hast taught to solemnize:
And eeke for comfort often called art
Of women in their smart, 395
Eternally bind thou this lovely band,
And all thy blessings unto us impart.
And thou glad Genius, in whose gentle hand,

374. *Cinthia:* the moon
376. *envy:* begrudge
379. *privily:* secretly
380. *Latmian shephard:* Endymion, with whom the moon fell in love
383. *sith:* since
386. *informe:* implant
388. *hap:* lot
395. *smart:* pain (of childbirth)
398. *Genius:* guardian spirit who watches over procreation

The bridale bowre and geniall bed remaine,
Without blemish or staine, 400
And the sweet pleasures of theyr loves delight
With secret ayde doest succour and supply,
Till they bring forth the fruitfull progeny,
Send us the timely fruit of this same night.
And thou fayre Hebe, and thou Hymen free, 405
Grant that it may so be.
Til which we cease your further prayse to sing,
Ne any woods shal answer, nor your Eccho ring.

23.

And ye high heavens, the temple of the gods,
In which a thousand torches flaming bright 410
Doe burne, that to us wretched earthly clods:
In dreadful darknesse lend desired light;
And all ye powers which in the same remayne,
More than we men can fayne,
Poure out your blessing on us plentiously, 415
And happy influence upon us raine,
That we may raise a large posterity,
Which from the earth, which they may long possesse,
With lasting happinesse,
Up to your haughty pallaces may mount, 420
And for the guerdon of theyr glorious merit
May heavenly tabernacles there inherit,
Of blessed Saints for to increase the count.
So let us rest, sweet love, in hope of this,
And cease till then our tymely joyes to sing, 425
The woods no more us answer, nor our eccho ring.

---

405. *Hebe:* Juno's daughter, who became the bride of Hercules
420. *haughty:* lofty
421. *guerdon:* reward

24.

Song made in lieu of many ornaments,
With which my love should duly have bene dect,
Which cutting off through hasty accidents,
Ye would not stay your dew time to expect,
But promist both to recompens,
Be unto her a goodly ornament,
And for short time an endlesse moniment.

430

Prothalamion
Or
A Spousall Verse made by
Edm. Spenser.
IN HONOUR OF THE DOU-
ble mariage of the two Honorable & vertuous
Ladies, the Ladie Elizabeth *and the Ladie* Katherine
Somerset, Daughters to the Right Honourable the
Earle of *Worcester* and espoused to the two worthie
Gentlemen M. *Henry Gilford,* and
M. *William Peter* Esquyers.

Prothalamion

1.

Calme was the day, and through the trembling ayre,
Sweete breathing *Zephyrus* did softly play

---

428. *dect:* decked, arrayed
Title: First published in 1596. "Prothalamion" means literally "before the
marriage." Spenser celebrates the visit of the two brides to Essex House a
little before their marriage.
2. *Zephyrus:* the west wind

A gentle spirit, that lightly did delay
Hot *Titans* beames, which then did glyster fayre:
When I whom sullein care,   5
Through discontent of my long fruitlesse stay
In Princes Court, and expectation vayne
Of idle hopes, which still doe fly away,
Like empty shaddowes, did aflict my brayne,
Walkt forth to ease my payne   10
Along the shoare of silver streaming *Themmes*,
Whose rutty Bancke, the which his River hemmes,
Was paynted all with variable flowers,
And all the meades adornd with daintie gemmes,
Fit to decke maydens bowres,   15
And crowne their Paramours,
Against the Brydale day, which is not long:
    Sweete *Themmes* runne softly, till I end my Song.

2.

There, in a Meadow, by the Rivers side,
A Flocke of *Nymphes* I chaunced to espy,   20
All lovely Daughters of the Flood thereby,
With goodly greenish locks all loose untyde,
As each had bene a Bryde,
And each one had a little wicker basket,
Made of fine twigs entrayled curiously,   25
In which they gathered flowers to fill their flasket:
And with fine Fingers, cropt full feateously
The tender stalkes on hye.
Of every sort, which in that Meadow grew,
They gathered some; the Violet pallid blew,   30

---

4. *Titans:* the sun's; *glyster:* glitter
12. *rutty:* full of roots
13. *variable:* of various colors
17. *Against:* In preparation for; *long:* distant
21. *Flood:* river
22. *untyde:* the custom was for brides to wear their hair loose at weddings
25. *entrayled curiously:* artfully woven
26. *flasket:* shallow basket
27. *cropt full feateously:* picked very deftly

The little Dazie, that at evening closes,
The virgin Lillie, and the Primrose trew,
With store of vermeil Roses,
To decke their Bridegromes posies,
Against the Brydale day, which was not long: 35
    Sweete *Themmes* runne softly, till I end my Song.

3.

With that, I saw two Swannes of goodly hewe,
Come softly swimming downe along the Lee;
Two fairer Birds I yet did never see:
The snow which doth the top of *Pindus* strew,   40
Did never whiter shew,
Nor *Jove* himselfe when he a Swan would be
For love of *Leda*, whiter did appeare:
Yet *Leda* was they say as white as he,
Yet not so white as these, nor nothing neare;   45
So purely white they were,
That even the gentle streame, the which them bare,
Seem'd foule to them, and bad his billowes spare
To wet their silken feathers, least they might
Soyle their fayre plumes with water not so fayre,   50
And marre their beauties bright,
That shone as heavens light,
Against their Brydale day, which was not long:
    Sweete *Themmes* runne softly, till I end my Song.

4.

Eftsoones the *Nymphes*, which now had Flowers their fill,   55
Ran all in haste, to see that silver brood,
As they came floating on the Christal Flood.
Whom when they sawe, they stood amazed still,
Their wondring eyes to fill,

---

33. *vermeil:* vermilion
40. *Pindus:* Mount Pindus in Thessaly, the seat of the Muses
43. *Leda:* seduced by Jupiter, who appeared to her in the form of a swan

Them seem'd they never saw a sight so fayre,   60
Of Fowles so lovely, that they sure did deeme
Them heavenly borne, or to be that same payre
Which through the Skie draw *Venus* silver Teeme,
For sure they did not seeme
To be begot of any earthly Seede,   65
But rather Angels or of Angels breede:
Yet were they bred of *Somers-heat* they say,
In sweetest Season, when each Flower and weede
The earth did fresh aray,
So fresh they seem'd as day,   70
Even as their Brydale day, which was not long:
    Sweete *Themmes* runne softly, till I end my Song.

5.

Then forth they all out of their baskets drew,
Great store of Flowers, the honour of the field,
That to the sense did fragrant odours yeild,   75
All which upon those goodly Birds they threw,
And all the Waves did strew,
That like old *Peneus* Waters they did seeme,
When downe along by pleasant *Tempes* shore
Scattred with Flowres, through *Thessaly* they streeme,   80
That they appeare through Lillies plenteous store,
Like a Brydes Chamber flore:
Two of those *Nymphes,* meane while, two Garlands bound,
Of freshest Flowres which in that Mead they found,
The which presenting all in trim Array,   85
Their snowie Foreheads therewithall they crownd,
Whil'st one did sing this Lay,
Prepar'd against that Day,
Against their Brydale day, which was not long:
    Sweete *Themmes* runne softly, till I end my Song.   90

---

61. *Fowles:* birds
67. *Somers-heat:* a pun on "Somerset," the sisters' family name
78. *Peneus:* a river in Thessaly that flows through the vale of Tempe

6.

Ye gentle Birdes, the worlds faire ornament,
And heavens glorie, whom this happie hower
Doth leade unto your lovers blisfull bower,
Joy may you have and gentle hearts content
Of your loves couplement: 95
And let faire *Venus*, that is Queene of love,
With her heart-quelling Sonne upon you smile,
Whose smile they say, hath vertue to remove
All Loves dislike, and friendships faultie guile
For ever to assoile.   100
Let endlesse Peace your steadfast hearts accord,
And blessed Plentie wait upon your bord,
And let your bed with pleasures chast abound,
That fruitfull issue may to you afford,
Which may your foes confound,   105
And make your joyes redound,
Upon your Brydale day, which is not long:
  Sweete *Themmes* run softlie, till I end my Song.

7.

So ended she; and all the rest around
To her redoubled that her undersong,   110
Which said, their bridale daye should not be long.
And gentle Eccho from the neighbour ground,
Their accents did resound.
So forth, those joyous Birdes did passe along,
Adowne the Lee, that to them murmurde low,   115
As he would speake, but that he lackt a tong
Yeat did by signes his glad affection show,
Making his streame run slow.

---

95. *couplement:* union
97. *heart-quelling:* heart-subduing
99. *Loves dislike:* dislike of love
100. *assoile:* clear away
110. *redoubled:* re-echoed
115. *Lee:* surface of the river

And all the foule which in his flood did dwell
Gan flock about these twaine, that did excell   120
The rest, so far, as *Cynthia* doth shend
The lesser starres. So they enranged well,
Did on those two attend,
And their best service lend,
Against their wedding day, which was not long: 125
    Sweete *Themmes* run softly, till I end my song.

8.

At length they all to mery *London* came,
To mery London, my most kyndly Nurse,
That to me gave this Lifes first native sourse:
Though from another place I take my name,   130
An house of auncient fame.
There when they came, whereas those bricky towres,
The which on *Themmes* brode aged backe doe ryde,
Where now the studious Lawyers have their bowers
There whylome wont the Templer Knights to byde,   135
Till they decayd through pride:
Next whereunto there standes a stately place,
Where oft I gayned giftes and goodly grace
Of that great Lord, which therein wont to dwell,
Whose want too well now feeles my freendles case: 140
But Ah here fits not well
Olde woes but joyes to tell
Against the bridale daye, which is not long:
    Sweete *Themmes* runne softly, till I end my Song.

---

121. *shend:* put to shame
128. *my . . . Nurse:* Spenser was born and bred in London, but claimed
kinship with the Spensers of Althorpe, a distinguished family
132. *bricky towres:* the Temple, one of the Inns of Court; formerly owned
by the order of Knights Templar, which was dissolved at the Reformation
137. *a stately place:* Leicester House, where Spenser's early patron, the
Earl of Leicester (l. 139), had lived. In 1596 it was the residence of the
Earl of Essex (l. 145).

9.

Yet therein now doth lodge a noble Peer,   145
Great *Englands* glory and the Worlds wide wonder,
Whose dreadfull name, late through all *Spaine* did thunder,
And *Hercules* two pillors standing neere,
Did make to quake and feare:
Faire branch of Honor, flower of Chevalrie,   150
That fillest *England* with thy triumphes fame,
Joy have thou of thy noble victorie,
And endlesse happinesse of thine owne name
That promiseth the same:
That through thy prowesse and victorious armes,   155
Thy country may be freed from forraine harmes:
And great *Elisaes* glorious name may ring
Through al the world, fil'd with thy wide Alarmes,
Which some brave muse may sing
To ages following,   160
Upon the Brydale day, which is not long:
     Sweete *Themmes* runne softly, till I end my Song.

10.

From those high Towers, this noble Lord issuing,
Like Radiant *Hesper* when his golden hayre
In th'*Ocean* billowes he hath Bathed fayre,   165
Descended to the Rivers open vewing,
With a great traine ensuing.
Above the rest were goodly to bee seene
Two gentle Knights of lovely face and feature
Beseeming well the bower of anie Queene,   170
With gifts of wit and ornaments of nature,
Fit for so goodly stature:

---

147. *all Spaine:* alluding to Essex's 1596 raid on Cádiz, where a Spanish
fleet was burned in the harbor
148. *pillors:* the pillars of Hercules, rocks on either side of the strait of
Gibraltar
158. *Alarmes:* sudden assaults

That like the twins of *Jove* they seem'd in sight,
Which decke the Bauldricke of the Heavens bright.
They two forth pacing to the Rivers side,   175
Received those two faire Brides, their Loves delight,
Which at th'appointed tyde,
Each one did make his Bryde,
Against their Brydale day, which is not long:
    Sweete *Themmes* runne softly, till I end my Song.   180

---

173. *twins of Jove:* Castor and Pollux, who became the constellation
Gemini
174. *Bauldricke:* literally, a sword belt. The reference is to the zodiac, in
which the stars appear like jewels on a belt.
177. *tyde:* time

SIR PHILIP SIDNEY

1554–86

Astrophil and Stella

1.

Loving in truth, and faine in verse my love to show,
That she (deare she) might take some pleasure of my paine:
Pleasure might cause her reade, reading might make her know,
Knowledge might pitie winne, and pitie grace obtaine,
I sought fit words to paint the blackest face of woe,   5
Studying inventions fine, her wits to entertaine:
Oft turning others leaves, to see if thence would flow
Some fresh and fruitfull showers upon my sunne-burn'd braine.
But words came halting forth, wanting Inventions stay,
Invention Natures child, fled step-dame Studies blowes,   10
And others feete still seem'd but strangers in my way.
Thus great with child to speake, and helplesse in my throwes,
Biting my trewand pen, beating my selfe for spite,
Foole, said my Muse to me, looke in thy heart and write.

2.

Not at the first sight, nor with a dribbed shot
Love gave the wound, which while I breathe will bleed:

This sonnet is in hexameters, not pentameters. Throughout the sequence,
Sidney's metrical variations will well repay study.
9. *stay:* support
11. *still:* always
12. *throwes:* throes
13. *trewand:* truant
1. *dribbed:* dribbled. The archery image appropriately describes Cupid's arrows. Cf. No. 5, l. 5.

But knowne worth did in mine of time proceed,
Till by degrees it had full conquest got.
I saw and liked, I liked but loved not,   5
I loved, but straight did not what *Love* decreed:
At length to *Loves* decrees, I forc'd, agreed,
Yet with repining at so partiall lot.
Now even that footstep of lost libertie
Is gone, and now like slave-borne *Muscovite*,   10
I call it praise to suffer Tyrannie;
And now employ the remnant of my wit,
To make me selfe beleeve, that all is well,
While with a feeling skill I paint my hell.

3.

Let daintie wits crie on the Sisters nine,
That bravely maskt, their fancies may be told:
Or *Pindares* Apes, flaunt they in phrases fine,
Enam'ling with pied flowers their thoughts of gold:
Or else let them in statelier glorie shine,   5
Ennobling new found Tropes with problemes old:
Or with strange similies enrich each line,
Of herbes or beastes, which *Inde* or *Afrike* hold.
For me in sooth, no Muse but one I know:
Phrases and Problemes from my reach do grow,   10
And strange things cost too deare for my poore sprites.
How then? even thus: in *Stellas* face I reed,
What Love and Beautie be, then all my deed
But Copying is, what in her Nature writes.

---

6. *straight:* at once
10. *Muscovite:* resident of Moscow—a serf
13. *me:* my
1. *crie on:* make demands on; *Sisters nine:* the nine Muses
2. *maskt:* dressed
3. *Pindares Apes:* imitators of the Greek poet (522?–443? B.C.)
4. *pied:* of various colors
6. *Tropes:* figures of speech
8. *Inde or Afrike:* India or Africa
9. *sooth:* truth
10. *grow:* escape
11. *sprites:* spirits
13. *deed:* task

4.

Vertue alas, now let me take some rest,
Thou setst a bate betweene my will and wit,
If vaine love have my simple soule opprest,
Leave what thou likest not, deale not thou with it.
Thy scepter use in some old *Catoes* brest;   5
Churches or schooles are for thy seate more fit:
I do confesse, pardon a fault confest:
My mouth too tender is for thy hard bit.
But if that needs thou wilt usurping be,
The litle reason that is left in me,   10
And still th'effect of thy perswasions prove:
I sweare, my heart such one shall shew to thee,
That shrines in flesh so true a Deitie,
That Vertue, thou thy selfe shalt be in love.

5.

It is most true, that eyes are form'd to serve
The inward light: and that the heavenly part
Ought to be king, from whose rules who do swerve,
Rebels to Nature strive for their owne smart.
It is most true, what we call *Cupids* dart,   5
An image is, which for our selves we carve;
And, fooles, adore in temple of our hart,
Till that good God make Church and Churchman starve.
True, that true Beautie Vertue is indeed,
Whereof this Beautie can be but a shade,   10
Which elements with mortall mixture breed:
True, that on earth we are but pilgrims made,
And should in soule up to our countrey move:
True, and yet true that I must *Stella* love.

2. *bate:* debate
5. *Catoes:* the renowned Roman Stoic (95–46 B.C.)
12. *one:* a one

6.

Some Lovers speake when they their Muses entertaine,
Of hopes begot by feare, of wot not what desires:
Of force of heav'nly beames, infusing hellish paine:
Of living deaths, deare wounds, faire stormes and freesing fires:
Some one his song in *Jove*, and *Joves* strange tales attires,   5
Bordred with buls and swans, powdred with golden raine:
Another humbler wit to shepheard's pipe retires,
Yet hiding royall bloud full oft in rurall vaine.
To some a sweetest plaint, a sweetest stile affords,
While teares powre out his inke, and sighs breathe out his
    words: 10
His paper, pale dispaire, and paine his pen doth move.
I can speake what I feele, and feele as much as they,
But thinke that all the Map of my state I display,
When trembling voice brings forth that I do *Stella* love.

7.

When Nature made her chiefe worke, *Stellas* eyes,
In colour blacke, why wrapt she beames so bright?
Would she in beamie blacke, like painter wise,
Frame daintiest lustre, mixt of shades and light?
Or did she else that sober hue devise,   5
In object best to knit and strength our sight,
Least if no vaile these brave gleames did disguise,
They sun-like should more dazle then delight?

2–4. *Of . . . fires:* the conventional paradoxes of the Petrarchan tradition
2. *wot not:* they know not
6. *Bordred:* embroidered. Jupiter became a bull to mate with Europa, a swan when he took Leda, and a shower of gold when he came to Danae.
8. *rurall vaine:* a country manner
10. *powre:* pour
3. *beamie:* radiant
5. *else:* otherwise
6. *strength:* strengthen
7. *vaile:* veil

Or would she her miraculous power show,
That whereas blacke seemes Beauties contrary,   10
She even in blacke doth make all beauties flow?
Both so and thus, she minding *Love* should be
Placed ever there, gave him this mourning weed,
To honor all their deaths, who for her bleed.

8.

Love borne in *Greece*, of late fled from his native place,
Forc'd by a tedious proofe, that Turkish hardned hart,
Is no fit marke to pierce with his fine pointed dart:
And pleasd with our soft peace, staid here his flying race.
But finding these North clymes do coldly him embrace,   5
Not usde to frozen clips, he strave to find some part,
Where with most ease and warmth he might employ his art:
At length he perch'd himself in *Stellas* joyfull face,
Whose faire skin, beamy eyes like morning sun on snow,
Deceiv'd the quaking boy, who thought from so pure light,   10
Effects of lively heat, must needs in nature grow.
But she most faire, most cold, made him thence take his flight
To my close heart, where while some firebrands he did lay,
He burnt unwares his wings, and cannot fly away.

9.

Queene *Vertues* court, which some call *Stellas* face,
Prepar'd by Natures choisest furniture,
Hath his front built of Alablaster pure;
Gold is the covering of that stately place.
The doore by which sometimes comes forth her Grace,   5

---

2. *tedious proofe:* painful experience
5. *these North clymes:* the northern climate
6. *clips:* embraces; *strave:* strove
10. *quaking:* shivering
11. *lively:* lifelike
13. *close:* secret
2. *choisest:* some of the early texts read *chiefest*

Red Porphir is, which locke of pearle makes surt:
Whose porches rich (which name of cheekes endure)
Marble mixt red and white do enterlace.
The windowes now through which this heav'nly guest
Looks over the world, and can find nothing such,　　　　10
Which dare claime from those lights the name of best.
Of touch they are that without touch doth touch,
Which *Cupids* selfe from Beauties mind did draw:
Of touch they are, and poore I am their straw.

10.

Reason, in faith thou art well serv'd, that still
Wouldst brabling be with sence and love in me:
I rather wisht thee clime the Muses hill,
Or reach the fruite of Natures choisest tree,
Or seeke heavns course, or heavns inside to see:　　　　5
Why shouldst thou toyle our thornie soile to till?
Leave sense, and those which senses objects be:
Deale thou with powers of thoughts, leave love to will.
But thou wouldst needs fight both with love and sence,
With sword of wit, giving wounds of dispraise,　　　　10
Till downe-right blowes did foyle thy cunning fence:
For soone as they strake thee with *Stellas* rayes,
Reason thou kneel'dst, and offeredst straight to prove
By reason good, good reason her to love.

---

6. *Porphir:* porphyry
7. *rich:* the first of many puns in the sequence upon the name of Lord
Rich. Cf. nos. 13 and 24. *which . . . endure:* which allow themselves to be
called "cheeks"
10. *over:* to be pronounced as a monosyllable (o'er)
12. *Of touch:* i.e., basanite; cf. "true as touchstones"
13. *mind:* an alternative reading in the early editions is *myne*
14. *straw:* which is attracted by the magnetic force of Stella's eyes. The
touchstone was believed to be magnetic.
2. *brabling:* arguing
11. *cunning fence:* artful defense
12. *strake:* struck

11.

In truth, o Love, with what a boyish kind
Thou doest proceed in thy most serious wayes:
That when the heav'n to thee his best displayes,
Yet of that best thou leav'st the best behind.
For like a child that some faire booke doth find,   5
With guilded leaves or colourd Velume playes,
Or at the most on some fine picture stayes,
But never heeds the fruit of writers mind:
So when thou saw'st in Natures cabinet
Stella, thou straight lookst babies in her eyes,   10
In her cheekes pit thou didst they pitfould set:
And in her breast bopeepe or couching lyes,
Playing and shining in each outward part:
But, foole, seekst not to get into her hart.

12.

Cupid, because thou shin'st in *Stellas* eyes,
That from her lockes, thy daunces, none scapes free,
That those lips sweld, so full of thee they bee,
That her sweete breath makes oft thy flames to rise,
That in her breast thy pap well sugred lies,   5
That her Grace gracious makes thy wrongs, that she
What words so ere she speak perswades for thee,
That her cleare voyce lifts thy fame to the skies.

---

1. *kind:* manner
6. *guilded . . . Velume:* as Putzel notes, "only the richest manuscripts and illuminated books were embellished with gold leaf and printed or written on vellum"
7. *stayes:* remains looking
10. *lookst . . . eyes:* a common Elizabethan conceit: each lover can see his own reflection in the eyes of his beloved. The overtones suggest procreation.
11. *pitfould:* trap
12. *bopeepe . . . lyes:* you played hide-and-go-seek (or lay hidden)
2 *That:* Because (so too in ll. 3–8); *daunces:* Ringler emends to *day-nets,* i.e., the lures (mirrors) with which larks were dazzled. The image of Stella's hair as Cupid's "dances" is equally possible. *scapes:* escapes

Thou countest *Stella* thine, like those whose powers
Having got up a breach by fighting well,   10
Crie, Victorie, this faire day all is ours.
O no, her heart is such a Cittadell,
So fortified with wit, stor'd with disdaine,
That to win it, is all the skill and paine.

13.

Phoebus was Judge between *Jove, Mars,* and *Love,*
Of those three gods, whose armes the fairest were:
Joves golden shield did Eagle sables beare,
Whose talents held young *Ganimed* above:
But in Vert field *Mars* bare a golden speare,   5
Which through a bleeding heart his point did shove:
Each had his creast, *Mars* caried *Venus* glove,
Jove on his helme the thunderbolt did reare.
Cupid then smiles, for on his crest there lies
Stellas faire haire, her face he makes his shield,   10
Where roses gueuls are borne in silver field.
Phoebus drew wide the curtaines of the skies,
To blaze these last, and sware devoutly then,
The first, thus matcht, were scantly Gentlemen.

---

10. *got . . . breach:* made a break in the wall of a fortified city
14. *That . . . paine:* everything depends on the skill (and suffering) with which one approaches such a city (Stella), who is not to be taken easily
1. *Phoebus:* the sun god. Sidney offers a variation on the theme of the quarrel among Venus, Minerva, and Diana. At the same time, he devises a heraldic emblem that portrays the arms of the Devereux family (l. 11), from which Stella (Penelope Devereux, now Lady Rich) came. Cf. Richard B. Young, "English Petrarke: A Study of Sidney's *Astrophel and Stella,*" in *Three Renaissance Studies* (New Haven, Yale University Press, 1958). In Sidney's contest, Jupiter blazons his homosexual affair with Ganymede and Mars his love for Venus (Vulcan's wife); Cupid, in contrast to these lascivious amours, presents Stella's chastity as his chief love.
4. *talents:* talons
5. *Vert field:* a green background
8. *reare:* raise
11. *roses gueuls:* red discs, the Devereux arms
13. *sware:* swore
14. *The first:* i.e., Jupiter and Mars; *scantly:* scarcely

14.

Alas have I not paine enough my friend,
Upon whose breast a fiercer Gripe doth tire,
Then did on him who first stale downe the fire,
While *Love* on me doth all his quiver spend,
But with your Rubarb words yow must contend,   5
To grieve me worse, in saying that Desire
Doth plunge my wel-form'd soule even in the mire
Of sinfull thoughts, which do in ruine end?
If that be sinne which doth the maners frame,
Well staid with truth in word and faith of deed,   10
Readie of wit and fearing nought but shame:
If that be sinne which in fixt hearts doth breed
A loathing of all loose unchastitie,
Then Love is sinne, and let me sinfull be.

15.

You that do search for everie purling spring,
Which from the ribs of old *Parnassus* flowes,
And everie floure not sweet perhaps, which growes
Neare thereabouts into your Poesie wring.
You that do Dictionaries methode bring   5
Into your rimes, running in ratling rowes:
You that poore *Petrarchs* long deceased woes,
With new-borne sighes and denisend wit do sing.

---

2. *Gripe doth tire:* hold does tear
3. *him:* Prometheus; *stale:* stole
5. *Rubarb:* cynical
7. *even:* right
9. *maners:* morals
10. *staid:* supported
2. *Parnassus:* the seat of the Muses. Sidney proceeds to attack those who
draw their inspiration solely from classical sources.
4. *wring:* wrest
5. *Dictionaries method:* i.e., alliteration
7. *Petrarchs . . . woes:* Petrarch (1300–74) established the sonnet tradi-
tion with his *Sonnets to Laura*
8. *denisend:* naturalized

You take wrong waies those far-fet helpes be such,
As do bewray a want of inward tuch: 10
And sure at length stolne goods do come to light
But if (both for your love and skill) your name
You seeke to nurse at fullest breasts of Fame,
Stella behold, and then begin to endite.

16.

In nature apt to like when I did see
Beauties, which were of manie Carrets fine,
My boiling sprites did thither soone incline,
And, Love, I thought that I was full of thee:
But finding not those restlesse flames in me,   5
Which others said did make their soules to pine:
I thought those babes of some pinnes hurt did whine,
By my soule judging what Loves paine might be.
But while I thus with this yong Lyon plaid;
Mine eyes (shall I say curst or blest) beheld   10
Stella; now she is nam'd, need more be said?
In her sight I a lesson new have speld,
I now have learn'd Love right, and learn'd even so,
As who by being poisond doth poison know.

17.

His mother deare *Cupid* offended late,
Because that *Mars* growne slacker in her love,
With pricking shot he did not throughly move,
To keepe the pace of their first loving state.

---

9. *far-fet:* farfetched
10. *bewray . . . tuch:* betray a lack of inward touch
2. *Carrets:* carats
7. *pinnes:* pin's
9. *plaid:* played
12. *speld:* spelled, puzzled out
1. *mother:* Venus
3. *pricking shot:* with direct aim on the target (*prick*); *throughly:* thoroughly

The boy refusde for feare of *Marses* hate,   5
Who threatned stripes, if he his wrath did prove:
But she in chafe him from her lap did shove,
Brake bow, brake shafts, while *Cupid* weeping sate:
Till that his grandame *Nature* pittying it,
Of *Stellas* browes made him two better bowes,   10
And in her eyes of arrowes infinit.
O how for joy he leapes, o how he crowes,
And straight therewith like wags new got to play,
Fals to shrewd turnes, and I was in his way.

18.

With what sharpe checkes I in my selfe am shent,
When into Reasons audite I do go:
And by just counts my selfe a banckrout know
Of all those goods, which heav'n to me have lent:
Unable quite to pay even Natures rent,   5
Which unto it by birthright I do ow:
And which is worse, no good excuse can show,
But that my wealth I have most idly spent.
My youth doth waste, my knowledge brings forth toyes,
My wit doth strive those passions to defend,   10
Which for reward spoile it with vaine annoyes.
I see my course to loose my selfe doth bend:
I see and yet no greater sorow take,
Then that I loose no more for *Stellas* sake.

19.

On *Cupids* bow how are my heart-strings bent,
That see my wracke, and yet embrace the same?

---

6. *stripes:* beatings; *prove:* experience
7. *chafe:* a heat
13. *wags:* rascals; *new . . . play:* just beginning to play
14. *shrewd turnes:* mischievous tricks
1. *checkes:* rebuffs; *shent:* ashamed
3. *banckrout:* bankrupt
12. *loose:* lose. So too in l. 14.

When most I glorie, then I feele most shame:
I willing run, yet while I run, repent.
My best wits still their owne disgrace invent: 5
My verie inke turnes straight to *Stellas* name;
And yet my words, as them my pen doth frame,
Avise themselves that they are vainely spent.
For though she passe all things, yet what is all
That unto me, who fare like him that both   10
Lookes to the skies, and in a ditch doth fall?
O let me prop my mind yet in his growth,
And not in Nature, for best fruits unfit:
Scholler, said *Love*, bend hitherward your wit.

20.

Flie, fly, my friends, I have my death wound; fly,
See there that boy, that murthring boy I say,
Who like a theefe, hid in darke bush doth ly,
Till bloudie bullet get him wrongfull pray.
So Tyran he no fitter place could spie,   5
Nor so faire levell in so secret stay,
As that sweete blacke which vailes the heav'nly eye:
There himselfe with his shot he close doth lay.
Poore passenger, passe now thereby I did,
And staid pleasd with the prospect of the place,   10
While that blacke hue from me the bad guest hid:
But straight I saw motions of lightning grace,
And then descried the glistring of his dart:
But ere I could flie thence, it pierc'd my heart.

---

9. *passe:* surpass
10. *him:* the Greek astronomer Thales is said to have fallen into a ditch while looking at the stars
12. *yet in his:* still in its
2. *murthring:* murdering
5. *Tyran:* tyrant
6. *levell:* aim
9. *passenger:* passer-by
13. *glistring:* glittering

21.

Your words my friend (right healthfull caustiks) blame
My young mind marde, whom *Love* doth windlas so,
That mine owne writings like bad servants show
My wits, quicke in vaine thoughts, in vertue lame:
That *Plato* I read for nought, but if he tame   5
Such coltish yeeres, that to my birth I owe
Nobler desires, least else that friendly foe,
Great expectation, weare a traine of shame.
For since mad March great promise made of me,
If now the May of my yeares much decline,   10
What can be hoped my harvest time will be?
Sure you say well, your wisdomes golden mine,
Dig deepe with learnings spade, now tell me this,
Hath this world ought so faire as *Stella* is?

22.

In highest way of heav'n the Sunne did ride,
Progressing then from faire twinnes gold'n place:
Having no scarfe of clowds before his face,
But shining forth of heate in his chiefe pride;
When some faire Ladies by hard promise tied,   5
On horsebacke met him in his furious race,
Yet each prepar'd with fannes wel-shading grace,
From that foes wounds their tender skinnes to hide.
Stella alone with face unarmed marcht,
Either to do like him which open shone,   10
Or carelesse of the wealth because her owne:
Yet were the hid and meaner beauties parcht,

---

1. *caustiks:* abrasives
2. *windlas:* wind about
8. *traine of shame:* disgraceful retinue
14. *ought:* aught
1. *way:* road, path
2. *twinnes:* Gemini, in the zodiac

Her daintiest bare went free; the cause was this,
The Sunne which others burn'd, did her but kisse.

23.

The curious wits seeing dull pensivenesse
Bewray it selfe in my long setled eyes,
Whence those same fumes of melancholy rise,
With idle paines, and missing ayme, do guesse.
Some that know how my spring I did addresse,   5
Deeme that my Muse some fruit of knowledge plies:
Others, because the Prince my service tries,
Thinke that I thinke state errours to redresse.
But harder Judges judge ambitions rage,
Scourge of it selfe, still climing slipprie place,   10
Holds my young braine captiv'd in golden cage.
O fooles, or over-wise, alas the race
Of all my thoughts hath neither stop nor start,
But only *Stellas* eyes and *Stellas* hart.

24.

Rich fooles there be, whose base and filthy hart
Lies hatching still the goods wherein they flow:
And damning their owne selves to *Tantals* smart,
Wealth breeding want, more blist, more wretched grow.
Yet to those fooles heav'n such wit doth impart,   5
As what their hands do hold, their heads do know,
And knowing *Love*, and loving lay apart,
As sacred things, far from all daungers show.

---

13. *daintiest bare:* i.e., her unprotected face
5. *my spring . . . addresse:* I gave myself to scholarship while still a youth
7. *the Prince:* i.e., Queen Elizabeth. Sidney did not, in fact, receive any state employment before 1586.
12. *race:* course
1. *Rich:* this sonnet puns on the name of Penelope Devereux's husband, Robert Lord Rich, whom she married on November 1, 1581
3. *Tantals:* Tantalus'
4. *blist:* blessed

But that rich foole who by blind Fortunes lot,
The richest gemme of Love and life enjoyes,   10
And can with foule abuse such beauties blot;
Let him deprived of sweet but unfelt joyes,
(Exil'd for ay from those high treasures, which
He knowes not) grow in only follie rich.

25.

The wisest scholler of the wight most wise,
By *Phoebus* doome, with sugred sentence sayes,
That Vertue if it once met with our eyes,
Strange flames of *Love* it in our soules would raise.
But for that man with paine this truth descries,   5
Whiles he each thing in senses ballance wayes,
And so nor will, nor can behold those skies,
Which inward sunne to *Heroicke* minde displaies.
Vertue of late with vertuous care to ster
Love of her selfe, tooke *Stellas* shape, that she   10
To mortall eyes might sweetly shine in her.
It is most true, for since I her did see,
Vertues great beautie in that face I prove,
And find th'effect, for I do burne in love.

26.

Though dustie wits dare scorne Astrologie,
And fooles can thinke those Lampes of purest light,
Whose numbers, weighs, greatnesse, eternitie,
Promising wonders, wonder do invite:

---

13. *ay*: ever
14. *only follie*: folly alone
1. *wight*: man, i.e., Socrates, Plato's teacher
2. *doome*: judgement
3–8. *That . . . displaies*: As Ringler notes, Sidney is following Cicero's version (*De Officiis*, i. 15) of this Platonic commonplace
5. *for*: because
9. *ster*: stir
13. *prove*: experience
1. *dustie*: earthy
3. *weighs*: ways, the paths of the stars

To have for no cause birthright in the skie,   5
But for to spangle the blacke weeds of night:
Or for some brawle, which in that chamber hie,
They should still daunce to please a gazers sight.
For me, I do Nature unidle know,
And know great causes, great effects procure: 10
And know those Bodies high raigne on the low.
And if these rules did faile, proofe makes me sure,
Who oft fore-judge my after-following race,
By only those two starres in *Stellas* face.

27.

Because I oft in darke abstracted guise,
Seeme most alone in greatest companie:
With dearth of words, or answers quite awrie,
To them that would make speech of speech arise.
They deeme, and of their doome the rumour flies,   5
That poison foule of bubling pride doth lie:
So in my swelling breast that only I
Fawne on me selfe, and others to despise:
Yet pride I thinke doth not my soule possesse,
Which lookes too oft in his unflattring glasse: 10
But one worse fault *Ambition*, I confesse,
That makes me oft my best friends overpasse,
Unseene, unheard, while thought to highest place
Bends all his powers, even unto *Stellas* grace.

28.

You that with allegories curious frame,
Of others children changelings use to make,

---

6. *weeds:* clothing
7. *brawle:* a circular dance; *hie:* high
11. *on:* over
12. *proofe:* experience
5. *doome:* judgment
1. *curious frame:* meticulous structure

With me those paines for Gods sake do not take:
I list not dig so deepe for brasen fame.
When I say, *Stella*, I do meane the same   5
Princesse of Beautie, for whose only sake,
The raines of *Love* I love, though never slake,
And joy therein, though Nations count it shame.
I beg no subject to use eloquence,
Nor in hid wayes do guide Philosophie: 10
Looke at my hands for no such quintessence;
But know that I in pure simplicitie,
Breathe out the flames which burne within my heart,
Love onely reading unto me this art.

29.

Like some weake Lords, neighbord by mighty kings,
To keepe themselves and their chiefe cities free,
Dc easly yeeld, that all their coasts may be
Ready to store their campes of needfull things:
So *Stellas* heart finding what power *Love* brings,   5
To keepe it selfe in life and liberty,
Doth willing graunt, that in the frontiers he
Use all to helpe his other conquerings:
And thus her heart escapes, but thus her eyes
Serve him with shot, her lips his heralds arre: 10
Her breasts his tents, legs his triumphall carre:
Her flesh his food, her skin his armour brave,
And I, but for because my prospect lies
Upon that coast, am giv'n up for a slave.

30.

Whether the Turkish new-moone minded be
To fill his hornes this yeare on Christian coast:

---

4. *list not:* do not care to; *brasen:* made of brass
6. *only sake:* sake alone
7. *raines:* reins, curbs
13. *but for because:* because; *prospect:* situation
1. *Turkish:* the topical allusions in this sonnet (to political affairs) all point
to 1582. The "new-moone" here is the Turkish crescent.

434

How *Poles* right king meanes without leave of hoast,
To warme with ill-made fire cold *Moscovy.*
If French can yet three parts in one agree, 5
What now the Dutch in their full diets boast,
How *Holland* hearts, now so good townes be lost,
Trust in the shade of pleasing *Orange* tree.
How *Ulster* likes of that same golden bit,
Wherewith my father once made it halfe tame, 10
If in the Scotch Court be no weltring yet.
These questions busie wits to me do frame;
I cumbred with good maners, answer do,
But know not how, for still I thinke of you.

31.

With how sad steps o Moone, thou climb'st the skies,
How silently, and with how wanne a face,
What may it be, that even in heav'nly place
That busie archer his sharpe arrowes tries?
Sure if that long with *Love* acquainted eyes 5
Can judge of *Love*, thou feel'st a Lovers case;
I reade it in thy lookes, thy languisht grace
To me that feele the like, thy state descries.

3. *right king:* Stephen Batory, crowned in 1576, despite the claims of the Emperor, Maximilian II, to the throne. He invaded Russia (*Moscovy*) in 1580 and the campaign continued for two years. *without . . . hoast:* without the permission of the Moscovites
4. *ill-made fire:* red-hot cannonballs, used by Batory in his siege operations
5. *French:* the three French factions in 1582 were the Catholics, the Politiques (moderates), and the Protestant Huguenots
6. *Dutch:* Germans. The pun on "diets" later in the line is clear.
8. *Orange:* William, Prince of Orange, who ruled Holland from 1576 to 1584
9–10. *Ulster . . . tame:* Sidney's father (Sir Henry) had been governor of Ireland for three terms in the 1570s
11. *Scotch:* alluding to the turbulent politics of Scotland in the 1570s and 1580s
12. *frame:* put
13. *do:* make
2. *wanne:* wan, pale
4. *busie archer:* Cupid
6. *case:* situation
8. *descries:* reveals

Then ev'n of fellowship, o Moone, tell me
Is constant *Love* deem'd there but want of wit? 10
Are Beauties there as proud as here they be?
Do they above love to be lov'd, and yet
Those Lovers scorne whom that *Love* doth possesse?
Do they call *Vertue* there ungratefulnesse?

32.

Morpheus the lively sonne of deadly sleepe,
Witnesse of life to them that living die:
A Prophet oft, and oft an historie,
A Poet eke, as humours fly or creepe,
Since thou in me so sure a power doest keepe, 5
That never I with close up sense do lie,
But by thy worke (my *Stella*) I descrie,
Teaching blind eyes both how to smile and weepe.
Vouchsafe of all acquaintance this to tell,
Whence hast thou Ivorie, Rubies, pearle and gold, 10
To shew her skin, lips, teeth and head so well?
Foole, answers he, no *Indes* such treasures hold,
But from thy heart, while my sire charmeth thee,
Sweet *Stellas* image I do steale to mee.

33.

I might, unhappie word, o me, I might,
And then would not, or could not see my blisse:
Till now wrapt in a most infernall night,
I find how heav'nly day, wretch, I did misse.
Hart rent thy selfe, thou doest thy selfe but right, 5
No lovely *Paris* made thy *Hellen* his:

---

1. *Morpheus:* the god of sleep; *lively:* lifelike; *deadly:* deathlike
4. *eke:* also
6. *close up:* closed up
12. *Indes:* Indias (East and West)
4. *wretch,:* the 1598 folio has no punctuation before or after this word
5. *rent:* tear
6. *Paris:* who started the Trojan War by abducting Helen

No force, no fraud, robd thee of thy delight,
Nor Fortune of thy fortune author is:
But to my selfe my selfe did give the blow,
While too much wit (forsooth) so troubled me,   10
That I respects for both our sakes must show:
And yet could not by rising Morne foresee
How faire a day was neare, o punisht eyes,
That I had bene more foolish or more wise.

34.

Come let me write, and to what end? to ease
A burthned hart, how can words ease, which are
The glasses of thy dayly vexing care?
Oft cruell fights well pictured forth do please.
Art not asham'd to publish thy disease?   5
Nay, that may breed my fame, it is so rare:
But will not wise men thinke thy words fond ware?
Then be they close, and so none shall displease.
What idler thing, then speake and not be hard?
What harder thing then smart, and not to speake?   10
Peace, foolish wit, with wit my wit is mard.
Thus write I while I doubt to write, and wreake
My harmes on Inks poore losse, perhaps some find
Stellas great powrs, that so confuse my mind.

35.

What may words say, or what may words not say,
Where truth it selfe must speake like flatterie?

---

11. *I respects . . . show:* because of our reputations, I must pay attention to
what other people say about us
2. *burthned:* burdened
3. *glasses:* reflectors, mirrors
5. *publish thy disease:* reveal your illness
7. *fond ware:* foolish merchandise
8. *close:* secret
9. *hard:* heard
12. *doubt:* fear; *wreake:* avenge

Within what bounds can one his liking stay,
Where Nature doth with infinite agree?
What *Nestors* counsell can my flames alay,   5
Since Reason selfe doth blow the cole in me?
And ah what hope, that hope should once see day,
Where *Cupid* is sworne page to Chastity?
Honour is honour'd, that thou doest possesse
Him as thy slave, and now long needy Fame   10
Doth even grow rich, naming my *Stellas* name.
Wit learnes in thee perfection to expresse,
Not thou by praise, but praise in thee is raisde:
It is a praise to praise, when thou art praisde.

36.

Stella, whence doth this new assault arise,
A conquerd yelden, ransackt heart to winne?
Whereto long since through my long battred eyes,
Whole armies of thy beauties entred in.
And there long since, *Love* thy Lieutenant lies,   5
My forces razde, thy banners raisd within:
Of conquest, do not these effects suffice,
But wilt now warre upon thine owne begin?
With so sweete voice, and by sweete Nature so
In sweetest strength, so sweetly skild withall,   10
In all sweete stratagems, sweete Arte can show,
That not my soule, which at thy foot did fall,
Long since forc'd by thy beames, but stone nor tree
By Sences priviledge, can scape from thee.

---

3. *stay:* retain, hold
5. *Nestors:* the wise man who guided the fortunes of the Greeks during the
siege of Troy
11. *even:* monosyllabic; *rich:* another pun upon Lord Rich's name
2. *yelden:* yielded (Ringler's emendation); the 1598 folio reads *golden*
6. *banners raisd:* as a sign of triumph, once his forces had been defeated
(*razde*)
13–14. *but . . . thee:* not even stones and trees, normally unaffected by an
appeal to the senses, can escape from Stella

438

37.

My mouth doth water, and my breast doth swell,
My tongue doth itch, my thoughts in labour be:
Listen then Lordings with good eare to me,
For of my life I must a riddle tell.
Toward *Auroras* Court a Nymph doth dwell,   5
Rich in all beauties which mans eye can see:
Beauties so farre from reach of words, that we
Abase her praise, saying she doth excell:
Rich in the treasure of deserv'd renowne,
Rich in the riches of a royall hart,   10
Rich in those gifts which give th'eternall crowne;
Who though most rich in these and everie part,
Which make the patents of true worldly blisse,
Hath no misfortune, but that Rich she is.

38.

This night while sleepe begins with heavy wings
To hatch mine eyes, and that unbitted thought
Doth fall to stray, and my chiefe powres are brought
To leave the scepter of all subject things.
The first that straight my fancies error brings   5
Unto my mind, is *Stellas* image, wrought
By *Loves* owne selfe, but with so curious drought,
That she, me thinks, not onely shines but sings.
I start, looke, hearke, but what in closde up sence
Was held, in opend sense it flies away,   10

---

2. *in labour:* as before childbirth
5. *Auroras:* goddess of the dawn
6. *Rich:* the pun on the name of Stella's husband runs through the sonnet;
1598's punctuation in l. 14 is especially effective
13. *make the patents:* guarantee the grants
2. *hatch:* close; *unbitted:* taken off the bit, unrestrained
5. *error:* wandering
7. *curious drought:* artful draftsmanship
8. *That . . . sings:* Stella is starlike (her name) but her music also produces a heavenly harmony
10. *opend:* revealed

Leaving me nought but wailing eloquence:
I seeing better sights in sights decay,
Cald it anew, and wooed sleepe againe:
But him her host that unkind guest had slaine.

39.

Come sleepe, o sleepe, the certaine knot of peace,
The baiting place of wit, the balme of woe,
The poore mans wealth, the prisoners release,
Th'indifferent Judge betweene the high and low;
With shield of proofe shield me from out the prease   5
Of those fierce darts, dispaire at me doth throw:
O make in me those civill warres to cease;
I will good tribute pay if thou do so.
Take thou of me smooth pillowes, sweetest bed,
A chamber deafe to noise, and blind to light: 10
A rosie garland, and a wearie hed:
And if these things, as being thine by right,
Move not thy heavy grace, thou shalt in me
Livelier then else-where *Stellas* image see.

40.

As good to write as for to lie and grone,
O *Stella* deare, how much thy power hath wrought,
That hast my mind, none of the basest, brought
My still kept course, while other sleepe to mone.
Alas, if from the height of Vertues throne,   5
Thou canst vouchsafe the influence of a thought
Upon a wretch, that long thy grace hath sought;
Weigh then how I by thee am overthrowne:
And then, thinke thus, although thy beautie be

---

13. *wooed*: disyllabic
2. *baiting*: resting
4. *indifferent*: impartial
5. *of proofe*: tried by experience; *prease*: throng
14. *Livelier*: More lifelike
1. *grone*: groan
4. *still*: always; *other*: others; *mone*: moan

Made manifest by such a victorie,   10
Yet noblest Conquerours do wreckes avoid.
Since then thou hast so farre subdued me,
That in my heart I offer still to thee,
O do not let thy Temple be destroyd.

41.

Having this day my horse, my hand, my launce
Guided so well, that I obtain'd the prize,
Both by the judgement of the English eyes,
And of some sent from that sweet enemie *Fraunce*.
Horsemen my skill in horsmanship advaunce: 5
Towne-folkes my strength, a daintier judge applies
His praise to sleight, which from good use doth rise:
Some luckie wits impute it but to chaunce:
Others, because of both sides I do take
My bloud from them, who did excell in this,   10
Thinke Nature me a man of armes did make.
How farre they shot awrie? the true cause is,
Stella lookt on, and from her hav'nly face
Sent forth the beames, which made so faire my race.

42.

O eyes, which do the Spheares of beautie move,
Whose beames be joyes, whose joyes all vertues be,
Who while they make *Love* conquer, conquer *Love*,
The schooles where *Venus* hath learn'd Chastitie.
O eyes, where humble lookes most glorious prove,   5
Only lov'd Tyrants, just in cruelty,
Do not, o do not from poore me remove,
Keepe still my Zenith, ever shine on me.

11. *wreckes:* complete destruction
13. *offer:* make a sacrifice
5. *advaunce:* praise
7. *sleight:* skill; *use:* practice
10. *My . . . this:* Sidney's father, grandfather, and maternal uncles had
often participated in tournaments
13. *hav'nly:* heavenly
14. *race:* course, run (in the tournaments)

For though I never see them, but straight wayes
My life forgets to nourish languisht sprites;   10
Yet still on me, o eyes, dart downe your rayes:
And if from Majestie of sacred lights,
Oppressing mortall sense, my death proceed,
Wrackes Triumphs be, which *Love* (high set) doth breed.

43.

Faire eyes, sweet lips, deare heart, that foolish I
Could hope by *Cupids* helpe on you to pray;
Since to himselfe he doth your gifts apply,
As his maine force, choise sport, and easefull stay.
For when he will see who dare him gainesay,   5
Then with those eyes he lookes, lo by and by
Each soule doth at *Loves* feet his weapons lay,
Glad if for her he give them leave to die.
When he will play, then in her lips he is,
Where blushing red, that *Loves* selfe them doth love,   10
With either lip he doth the other kisse:
But when he will for quiets sake remove
From all the world, her heart is then his rome,
Where well he knowes, no man to him can come.

44.

My words I know do well set forth my mind,
My mind bemones his sense of inward smart;
Such smart may pitie claime of any hart,
Her heart, sweete heart, is of no Tygres kind:
And yet she heares, and yet no pitie I find;   5

---

9. *straight wayes:* immediately
10. *sprites:* spirits
14. *Wrackes . . . be:* Let my pains become triumphs; *high set:* aimed at the most ideal goal
2. *pray:* prey
6. *by and by:* at once
13. *rome:* room
2. *his:* its

But more I crie, lesse grace she doth impart,
Alas, what cause is there so overthwart,
That Noblenesse it selfe makes thus unkind?
I much do guesse, yet find no truth save this,
That when the breath of my complaints doth tuch   10
Those daintie dores unto the Court of blisse,
The heav'nly nature of that place is such,
That once come there, the sobs of mine annoyes
Are metamorphosd straight to tunes of joyes.

45.

Stella oft sees the verie face of wo
Painted in my beclowded stormie face:
But cannot skill to pitie my disgrace,
Not though thereof the cause her selfe she know:
Yet hearing late a fable, which did show   5
Of Lovers never knowne, a grievous case,
Pitie thereof gate in her breast such place,
That from that sea deriv'd teares spring did flow.
Alas, if Fancy drawne by imag'd things,
Though false, yet with free scope more grace doth breed   10
Then servants wracke, where new doubts honor brings;
Then thinke my deare, that you in me do reed
Of Lovers ruine some sad Tragedie:
I am not I, pitie the tale of me.

46.

I curst thee oft, I pitie now thy case,
Blind-hitting boy, since she that thee and me

---

6. *more:* the more
7. *overthwart:* perverse
8. *unkind:* unnatural
3. *cannot skill:* isn't able
5. *fable:* story
7. *gate:* got
11. *Then:* Than
2. *boy:* Cupid

Rules with a becke, so tyrannizeth thee,
That thou must want or food, or dwelling place.
For she protests to banish thee her face,   5
Her face? O *Love*, a Rogue thou then shouldst be!
If *Love* learne not alone to love and see,
Without desire to feed of further grace.
Alas poore wag, that now a scholler art
To such a schoole-mistresse, whose lessons new   10
Thou needs must misse, and so thou needs must smart.
Yet Deare, let me his pardon get of you,
So long (though he from booke myche to desire)
Till without fewell you can make hot fire.

47.

What have I thus betrayed my libertie?
Can those blacke beames such burning markes engrave
In my free side? or am I borne a slave,
Whose necke becomes such yoke of tyranny?
Or want I sense to feele my miserie?   5
Or sprite, disdaine of such disdaine to have?
Who for long faith, tho dayly helpe I crave,
May get no almes but scorne of beggerie.
Vertue awake, Beautie but beautie is,
I may, I must, I can, I will, I do   10
Leave following that, which it is gaine to misse.
Let her do: soft, but here she comes, go to,
Unkind, I love you not: O me, that eye
Doth make my heart give to my tongue the lie.

---

3. *becke:* nod
9. *wag:* vagabond
12. *get:* obtain
13. *from . . . desire:* becomes a truant from the school of virtue and succumbs to desire
14. *fewell:* fuel
2. *burning markes:* brands
6. *sprite:* spirit
11. *Leave:* Desist from; *misse:* lack
12. *do:* do what she will. Some editors emend to *go; go to:* begone
13. *unkind:* unnatural

48.

Soules joy, bend not those morning starres from me,
Where Vertue is made strong by Beauties might,
Where *Love* is chastnesse, Paine doth learne delight,
And Humblenesse growes one with Majestie.
What ever may ensue, o let me be   5
Copartner of the riches of that sight:
Let not mine eyes be hel-driv'n from that light:
O looke, o shine, o let me die and see.
For though I oft my selfe of them bemone,
That through my heart their beamie darts be gone: 10
Whose curelesse wounds even now most freshly bleed:
Yet since my death-wound is already got,
Deare Killer, spare not thy sweet cruell shot:
A kind of grace it is to slay with speed.

49.

I on my horse, and *Love* on me doth trie
Our horsmanships, while by strange worke I prove
A horsman to my horse, a horse to *Love;*
And now mans wrongs in me, poore beast, descrie.
The raine wherewith my Rider doth me tie,   5
Are humbled thoughts, which bit of Reverence move,
Curb'd in with feare, but with guilt bosse above
Of Hope, which makes it seeme faire to the eye.
The Wand is Will, thou Fancie Saddle art,
Girt fast by memorie, and while I spurre   10
My horse, he spurres with sharpe desire my hart:
He sits me fast, how ever I do sturre:
And now hath made me to his hand so right,
That in the Manage myselfe takes delight.

---

3. *chastnesse:* chastity
7. *hel-driv'n:* driven to hell
11. *curelesse:* irremediable
5. *raine:* rein
7. *guilt bosse:* golden knob
12. *sturre:* stir

50.

Stella, the fulnesse of my thoughts of thee
Cannot be staid within my panting breast,
But they do swell and struggle forth of me,
Till that in words thy figure be exprest.
And yet as soone as they so formed be,   5
According to my Lord *Loves* owne behest:
With sad eyes I their weake proportion see,
To portrait that which in this world is best.
So that I cannot chuse but write my mind,
And cannot chuse but put out what I write,   10
While these poore babes their death in birth do find:
And now my pen these lines had dashed quite,
But that they stopt his furie from the same,
Because their forefront bare sweet *Stellas* name.

51.

Pardon mine eares, both I and they do pray,
So may your tongue still fluently proceed,
To them that do such entertainment need,
So may you still have somewhat new to say.
On silly me do not the burthen lay   5
Of all the grave conceits your braine doth breed;
But find some *Hercules* to beare, in steed
Of *Atlas* tyr'd, your wisedomes heav'nly sway.
For me, while you discourse of courtly tides,
Of cunning fishers in most troubled streames,   10

---

2. *staid:* contained
3. *of:* from
6. *behest:* command
8. *portrait:* portray
13. *But that:* Except that; *his:* its (the pen's)
14. *forefront:* forehead; the first word in the first line of the sonnet is "Stella"
5. *silly:* innocent; *burthen:* burden
6. *grave conceits:* somber images
7. *Hercules:* who held up the world to relieve Atlas; *steed:* stead
9. *courtly tides:* affairs of court

Of straying wayes, when valiant errour guides:
Meane while my heart confers with *Stellas* beames,
And is even irkt that so sweet Comedie,
By such unsuted speech should hindred be.

52.

A strife is growne betweene *Vertue* and *Love*,
While each pretends that *Stella* must be his:
Her eyes, her lips, her all, saith *Love* do this,
Since they do weare his badge, most firmely prove.
But *Vertue* thus that title doth disprove,   5
That *Stella* (o deare name) that *Stella* is
That vertuous soule, sure heire of heav'nly blisse:
Not this faire outside, which our hearts doth move.
And therefore, though her beautie and her grace
Be *Loves* indeed, in *Stellas* selfe he may   10
By no pretence claime any maner place.
Well *Love*, since this demurre our sute doth stay,
Let *Vertue* have that *Stellas* selfe; yet thus,
That *Vertue* but that body graunt to us.

53.

In Martiall sports I had my cunning tride,
And yet to breake more staves did me addresse:
While with the peoples shouts I must confesse,
Youth, lucke, and praise, even fild my veines with pride.
When *Cupid* having me his slave describe,   5
In *Marses* liverie, prauncing in the presse:

---

12. *beames:* radiant beauty
13. *even:* monosyllabic
14. *unsuted:* unsuitable
11. *any maner place:* any kind of position
12. *demurre:* demurrer; *sute:* suit
1. *cunning:* skill
2. *staves:* lances—as in a tournament
4. *fild:* filled
5. *having . . . describe:* having seen me as his slave
6. *presse:* throng

What now sir foole, said he, I would no lesse,
Looke here, I say, I look'd and *Stella* spide:
Who hard by made a window send forth light,
My heart then quak'd, then dazled were mine eyes,   10
One hand forgat to rule, th'other to fight.
Nor trumpets sound I heard, nor friendly cries;
My Foe came on, and beat the aire for me,
Till that her blush taught me my shame to see.

54.

Because I breathe not love to everie one,
Nor do not use set colours for to weare,
Nor nourish speciall lockes of vowed haire,
Nor give each speech a full point of a grone.
The courtly Nymphs, acquainted with the mone   5
Of them, who in their lips *Loves* standerd beare;
What he? say they of me, now I dare sweare,
He cannot love: no, no, let him alone.
And thinke so still, so *Stella* know my mind,
Professe in deed I do not *Cupids* art;   10
But you faire maides, at length this true shall find,
That his right badge is but worne in the hart:
Dumbe Swannes, not chatring Pies, do Lovers prove,
They love indeed, who quake to say they love.

55.

Muses, I oft invoked your holy ayde,
With choisest flowers my speech to engarland so;
That it despisde in true but naked shew,
Might winne some grace in your sweet grace arraid.

8. *spide:* spied
9. *hard:* near
11. *forgat:* forgot
13. *beat . . . me:* rode into the field and found no one to confront him—
because the speaker was gazing at Stella
2. *set colours:* i.e., colors that would directly indicate my devotion to
Stella
9. *thinke:* let them think
13. *Pies:* magpies

And oft whole troupes of saddest words I staid,   5
Striving abroad a foraging to go;
Untill by your inspiring I might know,
How their blacke banner might be best displaid.
But now I meane no more your helpe to trie,
Nor other sugring of my speech to prove,   10
But on her name incessantly to crie:
For let me but name her whom I do love,
So sweete sounds straight mine eare and heart do hit,
That I well find no eloquence like it.

56.

Fy, schoole of Patience, Fy your lesson is
Far far too long to learne it without booke:
What, a whole weeke without one peece of looke,
And thinke I should not your large precepts misse?
When I might reade those letters faire of blisse,   5
Which in her face teach vertue, I could brooke
Somewhat thy lead'n counsels, which I tooke,
As of a friend that meant not much amisse:
But now that I alas do want her sight,
What, dost thou thinke that I can ever take   10
In thy cold stuffe a flegmatike delight?
No Patience, if thou wilt my good, then make
Her come, and heare with patience my desire,
And then with patience bid me beare my fire.

57.

Wo, having made with many fights his owne
Each sence of mine, each gift, each power of mind,
Growne now his slaves, he forst them out to find
The thorowest words, fit for woes selfe to grone,

---

10. *sugring:* sweetening
2. *without booke:* from memory
9. *want:* lack
11. *flegmatike:* phlegmatic, cold
12. *wilt:* desire
4. *thorowest:* most thoroughgoing

Hoping that when they might find *Stella* alone,   5
Before she could prepare to be unkind,
Her soule arm'd but with such a dainty rind,
Should soone be pierc'd with sharpnesse of the mone.
She heard my plaints, and did not only heare,
But them (so sweete is she) most sweetly sing,   10
With that faire breast making woes darknesse cleare:
A prety case! I hoped her to bring
To feele my griefes, and she with face and voice,
So sweets my paines, that my paines me rejoyce.

58.

Doubt there hath bene when with his golden chaine,
The Oratour so farre mens harts doth bind,
That no pace else their guided steps can find,
But as he them more short or slacke doth raine.
Whether with words this soveraignty he gaine,   5
Cloth'd with fine tropes, with strongest reasons lin'd,
Or else pronouncing grace, wherewith his mind
Prints his owne lively forme in rudest braine:
Now judge by this, in piercing phrases late,
The anatomy of all my woes I wrate,   10
Stellas sweete breath the same to me did reed.
O voice, o face, maugre my speeches might,
Which wooed wo, most ravishing delight,
Even those sad words, even in sad me did breed.

59.

Deare, why make you more of a dog then me?
If he do love, I burne, I burne in love:

---

7. *rind:* skin
12. *case!:* Ringler's emendation for *case* in 1598
1–2. *chaine . . . Oratour:* Ringler identifies Hercules as the orator who led crowds of people about by a golden chain issuing from his mouth
4. *raine:* rein
10. *wrate:* wrote
12. *maugre:* despite

If he waite well, I never thence would move:
If he be faire, yet but a dog can be.
Litle he is, so litle worth is he;   5
He barks, my songs thine owne voyce oft doth prove:
Bid'n perhaps he fetcheth thee a glove,
But I unbid, fetch even my soule to thee.
Yet while I languish, him that bosome clips,
That lap doth lap, nay lets in spite of spite,   10
This sowre-breath'd mate tast of those sugred lips.
Alas, if you graunt only such delight
To witlesse things, then *Love*, I hope (since wit
Becomes a clog) will soone ease me of it.

60.

When my good Angell guides me to the place,
Where all my good I do in *Stella* see,
That heav'n of joyes throwes onely downe on me
Thundred disdaines and lightnings of disgrace:
But when the ruggedst step of Fortunes race   5
Makes me fall from her sight, then sweetly she
With words, wherein the Muses treasures be,
Shewes love and pitie to my absent case.
Now I wit-beaten long by hardest Fate,
So dull am, that I cannot looke into   10
The ground of this fierce *Love* and lovely hate:
Then some good body tell me how I do,
Whose presence, absence, absence presence is;
Blist in my curse, and cursed in my blisse.

---

4. *but . . . be:* he is still only a dog
6. *prove:* try out (by singing)
9. *clips:* clasps
14. Supply *you* before *will.*
5. *race:* course
8. *case:* state
14. *Blist:* Blessed

61.

Oft with true sighes, oft with uncalled teares,
Now with slow words, now with dumbe eloquence
I *Stellas* eyes assaid, invade her eares;
But this at last is her sweet breath'd defence:
That who indeed infelt affection beares,   5
So captives to his Saint both soule and sence,
That wholly hers, all selfnesse he forbeares,
Then his desires he learnes his lives course thence.
Now since her chast mind hates this love in me,
With chastned mind, I straight must shew that she   10
Shall quickly me from what she hates remove.
O Doctor *Cupid*, thou for me reply,
Driv'n else to graunt by Angels sophistrie,
That I love not, without I leave to love.

62.

Late tyr'd with wo, even ready for to pine
With rage of *Love*, I cald my Love unkind;
She in whose eyes *Love* though unfelt doth shine,
Sweet said that I true love in her should find,
I joyed, but straight thus watred was my wine,   5
That love she did, but loved a Love not blind,
Which would not let me, whom she loved, decline
From nobler course, fit for my birth and mind:
And therefore by her Loves authority,
Wild me these tempests of vaine love to flie,   10
And anchor fast my selfe on *Vertues* shore.
Alas, if this the only mettall be
Of *Love*, new-coind to helpe my beggery,
Deare, love me not, that ye may love me more.

---

5. *infelt*: felt in the heart
8. *lives*: life's
14. *without I leave*: unless I cease
10. *Wild*: Willed

63.

O grammer rules, o now your vertues show;
So children still reade you with awfull eyes,
As my young Dove may in your precepts wise
Her graunt to me, by her owne vertue know.
For late with heart most high, with eyes most low,   5
I crav'd the thing which ever she denies:
She lightning *Love*, displaying *Venus* skies,
Least once should not be heard, twise said, No, No.
Sing then my Muse, now *Io Pean* sing,
Heav'ns envy not at my high triumphing: 10
But Grammers force with sweet successe confirme:
For Grammer sayes (o this deare *Stella* nay,)
For Grammer sayes (to Grammer who sayes nay)
That in one speech two Negatives affirme.

First song

Doubt you to whom my Muse these notes entendeth,
Which now my breast orecharg'd to Musicke lendeth:
To you, to you, all song of praise is due,
Only in you my song begins and endeth.

Who hath the eyes which marrie state with pleasure,   5
Who keepes the key of Natures chiefest treasure:
To you, to you, all song of praise is due,
Only for you the heav'n forgate all measure.

Who hath the lips, where wit in fairenesse raigneth,
Who womankind at once both deckes and stayneth:
To you, to you, all song of praise is due,   10
Onely by you *Cupid* his crowne maintaineth.

---

7. *lightning*: flashing forth
9. *Io Pean*: Io *paean*, a shout of victory
12. *nay*: deny (if you can). Other early editions read *weighe*.
5. *state*: dignity
9. *fairenesse*: beauty

Who hath the feet, whose step of sweetnesse planteth,
Who else for whom *Fame* worthy trumpets wanteth:
To you, to you, all song of praise is due, 15
Onely to you her Scepter *Venus* granteth.

Who hath the breast, whose milke doth passions nourish,
Whose grace is such, that when it chides doth cherish:
To you, to you all song of praise is due,
Onelie through you the tree of life doth flourish. 20

Who hath the hand which without stroke subdueth,
Who long dead beautie with increase reneweth:
To you, to you, all song of praise is due,
Onely at you all envie hopelesse rueth.

Who hath the haire which loosest, fastest tieth, 25
Who makes a man live then glad when he dieth:
To you, to you, all song of praise is due:
Only of you the flatterer never lieth.

Who hath the voyce, which soule from sences sunders,
Whose force but yours the bolts of beautie thunders: 30
To you, to you, all song of praise is due:
Only with you not miracles are wonders.

Doubt you to whom my Muse these notes intendeth,
Which now my breast orecharg'd to Musicke lendeth:
To you, to you, all song of praise is due: 35
Only in you my song begins and endeth.

64.

No more, my deare, no more these counsels trie,
O give my passions leave to run their race:
Let Fortune lay on me her worst disgrace,
Let folke orecharg'd with braine against me crie.
Let clouds bedimme my face, breake in mine eye, 5

---

32. *not . . . wonders:* (such) wonders are not miracles (but natural)

454

Let me no steps but of lost labour trace:
Let all the earth with scorne recount my case,
But do not will me from my *Love* to flie.
I do not envie *Aristotles* wit,
Nor do aspire to *Cæsars* bleeding fame;   10
Nor ought do care, though some above me sit:
Nor hope, nor wish another course to frame,
But that which once may win thy cruell hart
Thou art my Wit, and thou my Vertue art.

65.

Love by sure proofe I may call thee unkind,
That giv'st no better eare to my just cries:
Thou whom to me such my good turnes should bind,
As I may well recount, but none can prize:
For when nak'd boy thou couldst no harbour find   5
In this old world, growne now so too too wise:
I lodg'd thee in my heart, and being blind
By Nature borne, I gave to thee mine eyes.
Mine eyes, my light, my heart, my life, alas,
If so great services may scorned be: 10
Yet let this thought thy Tygrish courage passe:
That I perhaps am somewhat kinne to thee;
Since in thine armes, if learnd fame truth hath spread,
Thou bear'st the arrow, I the arrow head.

66.

And do I see some cause a hope to feede,
Or doth the tedious burd'n of long wo
In weakened minds, quicke apprehending breed,
Of everie image, which may comfort show?
I cannot brag of word, much lesse of deed,   5
Fortunes wheeles still with me in one sort slow,

---

12. *wish:* 1598 reads *with*
14. *arrow head:* the Sidney crest contained an arrowhead
6. *slow:* go slow; Ringler emends *Fortunes* to *Fortune,* in which case *wheeles* becomes a verb

My wealth no more, and no whit lesse my need,
Desire still on the stilts of feare doth go.
And yet amid all feares a hope there is,
Stolne to my heart since last faire night, nay day,　　　10
Stellas eyes sent to me the beames of blisse,
Looking on me, while I lookt other way:
But when mine eyes backe to their heav'n did move,
They fled with blush, which guiltie seem'd of love.

67.

Hope, art thou true, or doest thou flatter me?
Doth *Stella* now begin with piteous eye,
The ruines of her conquest to espie:
Will she take time, before all wracked be?
Her eyes-speech is translated thus by thee:　　　5
But failst thou not in phrase so heav'nly hie?
Looke on againe, the faire text better trie:
What blushing notes doest thou in margine see?
What sighes stolne out, or kild before full borne?
Hast thou found such and such like arguments?　　　10
Or art thou else to comfort me forsworne?
Well, how so thou interpret the contents,
I am resolv'd thy errour to maintaine,
Rather then by more truth to get more paine.

68.

Stella, the onely Planet of my light,
Light of my life, and life of my desire,
Chiefe good, whereto my hope doth only aspire,
World of my wealth, and heav'n of my delight.
Why doest thou spend the treasures of thy sprite,　　　5
With voice more fit to wed *Amphions* lyre,
Seeking to quench in me the noble fire,
Fed by thy worth, and blinded by thy sight?

---

4. *take time*: make use of the occasion; *wracked*: destroyed
6. *Amphions*: who built Thebes with the power of his music

And all in vaine, for while thy breath most sweet,
With choisest words, thy words with reasons rare,   10
Thy reasons firmly set on *Vertues feet,*
Labour to kill in me this killing care:
O thinke I then, what paradise of joy
It is, so faire a Vertue to enjoy.

69.

O joy, too high for my low stile to show:
O blisse, fit for a nobler state then me:
Envie, put out thine eyes, least thou do see
What Oceans of delight in me do flow.
My friend, that oft saw through all maskes my wo,   5
Come, come, and let me powre my selfe on thee;
Gone is the winter of my miserie,
My spring appeares, o see what here doth grow.
For *Stella* hath with words where faith doth shine,
Of her high heart giv'n me the monarchie: 10
I, I, o I may say, that she is mine.
And though she give but thus conditionly
This realme of blisse, while vertuous course I take,
No kings be crown'd but they some covenants make.

70.

My Muse may well grudge at my heav'nly joy,
If still I force her in sad rimes to creepe:
She oft hath drunke my teares, now hopes to enjoy
Nectar of Mirth, since I *Joves* cup do keepe.
Sonets be not bound prentise to annoy: 5
Trebles sing high, as well as bases deepe:
Griefe but *Loves* winter liverie is, the Boy
Hath cheekes to smile, as well as eyes to weepe.
Come then my Muse, shew thou height of delight
In well raisde notes, my pen the best it may   10

6. *powre . . . on:* pour out my heart to
14. *covenants:* agreements
4. *I . . . keepe:* like Ganymede, the cupbearer of the gods
5. *bound prentise:* like an apprentice in a trade

Shall paint out joy, though but in blacke and white.
Cease eager Muse, peace pen, for my sake stay,
I give you here my hand for truth of this,
Wise silence is best musicke unto blisse.

71.

Who will in fairest booke of Nature know,
How Vertue may best lodg'd in beautie be,
Let him but learne of *Love* to reade in thee
Stella, those faire lines, which true goodnesse show.
There shall he find all vices overthrow,   5
Not by rude force, but sweetest soveraigntie
Of reason, from whose light those night-birds flie;
That inward sunne in thine eyes shineth so.
And not content to be Perfections heire
Thy selfe, doest strive all minds that way to move: 10
Who marke in thee what is in thee most faire.
So while thy beautie drawes the heart to love,
As fast thy Vertue bends that love to good:
But ah, Desire still cries, give me some food.

72.

Desire, though thou my old companion art,
And oft so clings to my pure *Love*, that I
One from the other scarcely can descrie,
While each doth blow the fier of my hart;
Now from thy fellowship I needs must part,   5
Venus is taught with *Dians* wings to flie:
I must no more in thy sweet passions lie;
Vertues gold now must head my *Cupids* dart.
Service and Honor, wonder with delight,
Feare to offend, will worthie to appeare,   10
Care shining in mine eyes, faith in my sprite.
These things are left me by my only Deare;
But thou Desire, because thou wouldst have all,
Now banisht art, but yet alas how shall?

---

6. *Dians*: goddess of chastity

Second song

Have I caught my heav'nly jewell,
Teaching sleepe most faire to be?
Now will I teach her that she,
When she wakes, is too too cruell.

Since sweet sleep her eyes hath charmed,   5
The two only darts of *Love:*
Now will I with that boy prove
Some play, while he is disarmed.

Her tongue waking still refuseth,
Giving frankly niggard No: 10
Now will I attempt to know,
What No her tongue sleeping useth.

See the hand which waking gardeth,
Sleeping, grants a free resort:
Now will I invade the fort;   15
Cowards *Love* with losse rewardeth.

But o foole, thinke of the danger,
Of her just and high disdaine:
Now will I alas refraine,
Love feares nothing else but anger.   20

Yet those lips so sweetly swelling,
Do invite a stealing kisse:
Now will I but venture this,
Who will read must first learne spelling.

Oh sweet kisse, but ah she is waking,   25
Lowring beautie chastens me:
Now will I away hence flee:
Foole, more foole, for no more taking.

73.

Love still a boy, and oft a wanton is,
School'd onely by his mothers tender eye:
What wonder then if he his lesson misse,
When for so soft a rod deare play he trie?
And yet my Starre, because a sugred kisse   5
In sport I suckt, while she asleepe did lie,
Doth lowre, nay, chide; nay, threat for only this:
Sweet, it was saucie *Love*, not humble I.
But no scuse serves, she makes her wrath appeare
In Beauties throne, see now who dares come neare   10
Those scarlet judges, threatning bloudy paine?
O heav'nly foole, thy most kisse-worthie face,
Anger invests with such a lovely grace,
That Angers selfe I needs must kisse againe.

74.

I never dranke of *Aganippe* well,
Nor ever did in shade of *Tempe* sit:
And Muses scorne with vulgar braines to dwell,
Poore Layman I, for sacred rites unfit.
Some do I heare of Poets furie tell,   5
But (God wot) wot not what they meane by it:
And this I sweare by blackest brooke of hell,
I am no pick-purse of anothers wit.
How falles it then, that with so smooth an ease
My thoughts I speake, and what I speake doth flow 10
In verse, and that my veï e best wits oth please?
Guesse we the cause, What is it thu fie no:
Or so? much lesse: how then? sure thus it is:
My lips are sweet, inspired with *Stellas* kisse.

---

11. *scarlet judges:* i.e., Stella's lips
14. *Angers:* 1598 reads *Anger*
1. *Aganippe well:* a spring sacred to the Muses
2. *Tempe:* a valley in Thessaly, between Mount Olympus and Mount Ossa
6. *God wot:* God knows
8. *pick-purse:* pickpocket

75.

Of all the kings that ever here did raigne,
Edward named fourth, as first in praise I name,
Not for his faire outside, nor well lined braine;
Although lesse gifts impe feathers oft on Fame
Nor that he could young-wise, wise-valiant frame   5
His Sires revenge, joyn'd with a kingdomes gaine:
And gain'd by *Mars*, could yet mad *Mars* so tame,
That Ballance weigh'd what sword did late obtaine.
Nor that he made the Flouredeluce so fraid,
Though strongly hedg'd of bloudy Lyons pawes,   10
That wittie *Lewis* to him a tribute paid.
Nor this, nor that, nor any such small cause,
But only for this worthy knight durst prove
To loose his Crowne, rather then faile his Love.

76.

She comes, and streight therewith her shining twins do move,
Their rayes to me, who in her tedious absence lay
Benighted in cold wo, but now appeares my day,
The onely light of joy, the onely warmth of *Love*.
She comes with light and warmth, which like *Aurora* prove   5
Of gentle force, so that mine eyes dare gladly play
With such a rosie morne, whose beames most freshly gay
Scortch not, but onely do darke chilling sprites remove.
But lo, while I do speake, it groweth noone with me,
Her flamie glistring lights increase with time and place;   10
My heart cries ah, it burnes, mine eyes now dazled be:
No wind, no shade can coole, what helpe then in my case,

---

2. *Edward:* Edward IV, 1442–83, usurped the throne from Henry VI in
1461, revenging the death of his father, the Duke of York
4. *impe:* graft (a falconry term)
9. *Flouredeluce:* i.e., France, which Edward invaded in 1474. Louis XI
gave him a pension of 50,000 crowns per year at the treaty of Picquigny in
1475.
14. *loose:* lose. Edward's marriage to the widow Elizabeth Gray infuriated
the Duke of Warwick, who led a rebellion against him in 1471.
5. *Aurora:* goddess of the dawn

But with short breath, long lookes, staid feet and walking hed,
Pray that my sunne go downe with meeker beames to bed.

77.

Those lookes, whose beames be joy, whose motion is delight,
That face, whose lecture shewes what perfect beautie is:
That presence, which doth give darke hearts a living light:
That grace, which **V**enus weepes that she her selfe doth misse:
That hand, which without touch holds more then *Atlas*
    might;   5
Those lips, which make deaths pay a meane price for a kisse:
That skin, whose passe-praise hue scorns this poore terme of
    white:
Those words, which do sublime the quintessence of blisse:
That voyce, which makes the soule plant himselfe in the eares:
That conversation sweet, where such high comforts be,   10
As consterd in true speech, the name of heav'n it beares,
Makes me in my best thoughts and quietst judgement see,
That in no more but these I might be fully blest:
Yet ah, my Mayd'n Muse doth blush to tell the best.

78.

O how the pleasant aires of true love be
Infected by those vapours, which arise
From out that noysome gulfe, which gaping lies
Betweene the jawes of hellish Jealousie.
A monster, others harme, selfe-miserie,   5
Beauties plague, Vertues scourge, succour of lies:
Who his owne joy to his owne hurt applies,
And onely cherish doth with injurie.

---

13. *staid:* unable to move; *walking:* agitated
2. *whose lecture:* the reading (gazing on) of which
5. *Atlas might:* the strength of Atlas, who held the world on his shoulders
6. *deaths . . . price:* death a cheap price to pay
7. *passe-praise hue:* color surpassing praise
11. *constered:* rendered
3. *noysome:* noxious
8. *And . . . injurie:* And can cherish only by injuring

Who since he hath, by Natures speciall grace,
So piercing pawes, as spoyle when they embrace,   10
So nimble feet as stirre still, though on thornes:
So manie eyes ay seeking their owne woe,
So ample eares as never good newes know:
Is it not evill that such a Devill wants hornes?

79.

Sweet kisse, thy sweets I faine would sweetly endite,
Which even of sweetnesse sweetest sweetner art:
Pleasingst consort, where each sence holds a part,
Which coupling Doves guides *Venus* chariot right.
Best charge, and bravest retrait in *Cupids* fight,   5
A double key, which opens to the heart,
Most rich, when most his riches it impart:
Neast of young joyes, schoolmaster of delight,
Teaching the meane, at once to take and give
The friendly fray, where blowes both wound and heale,   10
The prettie death, while each in other live.
Poore hopes first wealth, ostage of promist weale,
Breakefast of *Love*, but lo, lo, where she is,
Cease we to praise, now pray we for a kisse.

80.

Sweet swelling lip, well maist thou swell in pride,
Since best wits thinke it wit thee to admire;
Natures praise, Vertues stall, *Cupids* cold fire,
Whence words, not words, but heav'nly graces slide.

---

10. *spoyle:* injure seriously
12. *ay:* ever
14. *wants hornes:* lacks a cuckold's horns
1. *endite:* write about
3. *Pleasingst consort:* Most pleasing harmony
4. *coupling Doves:* joining together the doves that draw Venus' chariot
5. *retrait:* retreat
9. *meane:* way
12. *ostage:* hostage; *weale:* happiness
3. *stall:* seat

The new *Pernassus*, where the Muses bide,   5
Sweetner of musicke, wisedomes beautifier:
Breather of life, and fastner of desire,
Where Beauties blush in Honours graine is dide.
Thus much my heart compeld my mouth to say,
But now spite of my heart my mouth will stay,   10
Loathing all lies, doubting this Flatterie is:
And no spurre can his resty race renew,
Without how farre this praise is short of you,
Sweet lip, you teach my mouth with one sweet kisse.

81.

O kisse, which doest those ruddie gemmes impart,
Or gemmes, or frutes of new-found *Paradise*,
Breathing all blisse and sweetning to the heart,
Teaching dumbe lips a nobler exercise.
O kisse, which soules, even soules together ties   5
By linkes of *Love*, and only Natures art:
How faine would I paint thee to all mens eyes,
Or of thy gifts at least shade out some part.
But she forbids, with blushing words, she sayes,
She builds her fame on higher seated praise: 10
But my heart burnes, I cannot silent be.
Then since (deare life) you faine would have me peace,
And I, mad with delight, want wit to cease,
Stop you my mouth with still still kissing me.

82.

Nymph of the gard'n, where all beauties be:
Beauties which do in excellencie passe

---

7. *fastner:* a fixative
8. *Honours . . . dide:* the royal purple of honor is dyed
10. *spite:* in spite; *stay:* be silent
11. *doubting:* fearing
12. *resty:* restive
13. *Without:* Unless
2. *Or:* Either
6. *only Natures:* Nature's alone
12. *peace:* be still

His who till death lookt in a watrie glasse,
Or hers whom naked the *Trojan* boy did see.
Sweet gard'n Nymph, which keepes the Cherrie tree,   5
Whose fruit doth farre th'*Esperian* tast surpasse:
Most sweet-faire, most faire-sweet, do not alas,
From comming neare those Cherries banish me:
For though full of desire, emptie of wit,
Admitted late by your best-graced grace,   10
I caught at one of them a hungrie bit;
Pardon that fault, once more graunt me the place,
And I do sweare even by the same delight,
I will but kisse, I never more will bite.

83.

Good brother *Philip*, I have borne you long,
I was content you should in favour creepe,
While craftily you seem'd your cut to keepe,
As though that faire soft hand did you great wrong.
I bare (with Envie) yet I bare your song,   5
When in her necke you did *Love* ditties peepe;
Nay, more foole I, oft suffered you to sleepe
In Lillies neast, where *Loves* selfe lies along.
What, doth high place ambitious thoughts augment?
Is sawcinesse reward of curtesie?   10
Cannot such grace your silly selfe content,
But you must needs with those lips billing be?
And through those lips drinke Nectar from that toong;
Leave that sir *Phip*, least off your necke be wroong.

---

3. *His:* Narcissus'; *glasse:* mirror
4. *hers:* Venus', who revealed herself naked to Paris
6. *th'Esperian:* the gardens of the Hesperides, famed for their golden apples
11. *I . . . bit:* cf. above, the Second song
1. *Philip:* as in Skelton's *Phyllyp Sparowe*, q.v.
3. *your . . . keepe:* to act with propriety
8. *Lillies neast:* i.e., Stella's bosom
14. *wroong:* wrung

Third song

If *Orpheus* voyce had force to breathe such musickes love
Through pores of sencelesse trees, as it could make them move:
If stones good measure daunc'd, the *Theban* walles to build,
To cadence of the tunes, which *Amphyons* lyre did yeeld,
More cause a like effect at leastwise bringeth: 5
O stones, o trees, learne hearing, *Stella* singeth.

If Love might sweet'n so a boy of shepheard brood,
To make a Lyzard dull to taste Loves daintie food:
If Eagle fierce could so in *Grecian* Mayd delight,
As his light was her eyes, her death his endlesse night: 10
Earth gave that Love, heav'n I trow Love refineth:
O beasts, o birds looke, Love, lo, *Stella* shineth.

The birds, beasts, stones and trees feele this, and feeling *Love*:
And if the trees, nor stones stirre not the same to prove,
Nor beasts, nor birds do come unto this blessed gaze, 15
Know, that small Love is quicke, and great Love doth amaze:
They are amaz'd, but you with reason armed,
O eyes, o eares of men, how are you charmed!

84.

High way since you my chiefe *Pernassus* be,
And that my Muse to some eares not unsweet,

---

1. *Orpheus:* whose music moved stones and trees. For Amphyon (l. 4),
see sonnet 68 above.
7. *shepheard brood:* bred up as a shepherd. The reference is to the Arcadian boy Thoas, who was saved from robbers by a dragon (*Lyzard*, l. 8)
he had nurtured.
9. *Eagle:* this story, like the preceding one, comes from Pliny's *Natural
History.* The maid of Sestos cared for an eagle, which, when she died, flew
into her funeral pyre.
11. *trow:* trust
16. *small . . . quicke:* Cupid's love is lively; *great Love* probably refers to
Venus (Putzel)
1. *Pernassus:* the mountain of the Muses; Sidney applies it to the "highway" because the latter now inspires his verse

Tempers her words to trampling horses feet,
More oft then to a chamber melodie.
Now blessed you, beare onward blessed me   5
To her, where I my heart safelest shall meet,
My Muse and I must you of dutie greet
With thankes and wishes, wishing thankfully.
Be you still faire, honoured by publike heed,
By no encrochment wrongd, nor time forgot: 10
Nor blam'd for bloud, nor sham'd for sinfull deed.
And that you know, I envy you no lot
Of highest wish, I wish you so much blisse,
Hundreds of yeares you *Stellas* feet may kisse.

85.

I see the house, my heart thy selfe containe,
Beware full sailes drowne not thy tottring barge:
Least joy by Nature apt sprites to enlarge,
Thee to thy wracke beyond thy limits straine.
Nor do like Lords, whose weake confused braine,   5
Not pointing to fit folkes each undercharge,
While everie office themselves will discharge,
With doing all, leave nothing done but paine.
But give apt servants their due place, let eyes
See Beauties totall summe summ'd in her face: 10
Let eares heare speech, which wit to wonder ties.
Let breath sucke up those sweetes, let armes embrace
The globe of weale, lips *Loves* indentures make:
Thou but of all the kingly Tribute take.

Fourth song

Onely joy, now here you are,
Fit to heare and ease my care:

---

3. *Tempers:* Tunes
6. *safelest:* most safely (because away from court, where rumors fly)
1. *house:* at the end of the journey described in no. 84
6. *pointing . . . undercharge:* appointing menial tasks to suitable servants
13. *globe of weale:* wealth of happiness (which she offers); *indentures:* Ringler notes the pun on "contracts" and "indentations"

Let my whispering voyce obtaine,
Sweete reward for sharpest paine:
Take me to thee, and thee to me.   5
No, no, no, no, my Deare, let be.

Night hath closd all in her cloke,
Twinckling starres Love-thoughts provoke:
Danger hence good care doth keepe,
Jealousie it selfe doth sleepe: 10
Take me to thee, and thee to me.
No, no, no, no, my Deare, let be.

Better place no wit can find,
Cupids yoke to loose or bind:
These sweet flowers on fine bed too,   15
Us in their best language woo:
Take me to thee, and thee to me.
No, no, no, no, my Deare, let be.

This small light the Moone bestowes,
Serves thy beames but to disclose,   20
So to raise my hap more hie;
Feare not else, none can us spie:
Take me to thee, and thee to me.
No, no, no, no, my Deare, let be.

That you heard was but a Mouse,   25
Dumbe sleepe holdeth all the house:
Yet a sleepe, me thinkes they say,
Yong folkes, take time while you may:
Take me to thee, and thee to me.
No, no, no, no, my Deare, let be.   30

---

6. *No . . . be*: The last line of each stanza in this song is spoken by Stella.
Sidney's fourth and eighth songs inspired many later imitations; cf., e.g.,
Donne's *The Extasie* and Herbert of Cherbury's *An Ode upon a Question
moved.*
21. *hap*: fortune
28. *take . . . may*: echoing Horace's *carpe diem* theme

Niggard Time threats, if we misse
This large offer of our blisse:
Long stay ere he graunt the same:
Sweet then, while each thing doth frame:
Take me to thee, and thee to me.   35
No, no, no, no, my Deare let be.

Your faire mother is a bed,
Candles out, and curtaines spread:
She thinkes you do letters write:
Write, but let me first endite: 40
Take me to thee, and thee to me.
No, no, no, no, my Deare, let be.

Sweet alas, why strive you thus?
Concord better fitteth us:
Leave to *Mars* the force of hands,   45
Your power in your beautie stands:
Take thee to me, and me to thee.
No, no, no, no, my Deare, let be.

Wo to me, and do you sweare
Me to hate, but I forbeare,   50
Cursed be my destines all,
That brought me so high to fall:
Soone with my death I will please thee.
No, no, no, no, my Deare, let be.

86.

Alas, whence came this change of lookes? if I
Have chang'd desert, let mine owne conscience be
A still felt plague, to selfe condemning me:
Let wo gripe on my heart, shame loade mine eye.

---

44. *fitteth:* 1598 misprints *fitteh*
49. *and do you:* if you do
51. *destines:* fates
2. *Have . . . desert:* Am less deserving than I was
3. *A still:* An always
4. *gripe on:* seize

But if all faith, like spotlesse Ermine ly   5
Safe in my soule, which only doth to thee
(As his sole object of felicitie)
With wings of *Love* in aire of wonder flie.
O ease your hand, treate not so hard your slave:
In justice paines come not till faults do call,   10
Or if I needs (sweet Judge) must torments have,
Use something else to chast'n me withall,
Then those blest eyes, where all my hopes do dwell,
No doome should make once heav'n become his hell.

Fift song

While favour fed my hope, delight with hope was brought,
Thought waited on delight, and speech did follow thought:
Then grew my tongue and pen records unto thy glory:
I thought all words were lost, that were not spent of thee:
I thought each place was darke but where thy lights would
    be,   5
And all eares worse then deafe, that heard not out thy storie.

I said, thou wert most faire, and so indeed thou art:
I said, thou art most sweet, sweet poison to my heart:
I said, my soule was thine (o that I then had lyed)
I said, thine eyes were starres, thy breasts the milk'n way,   10
Thy fingers *Cupids* shafts, thy voyce the Angels lay:
And all I said so well, as no man it denied.

But now that hope is lost, unkindnesse kils delight,
Yet thought and speech do live, though metamorphosd quite:
For rage now rules the raines, which guided were by
    Pleasure.   15
I thinke now of thy faults, who late thought of thy praise,
That speech falles now to blame, which did thy honour raise,
The same key op'n can, which can locke up a treasure.

---

14. *doome:* judgment; *once:* one's
4. *of:* on
11. *lay:* song
15. *raines:* reins, which may mean here "loins" or "kidneys," viewed as the
seat of the affections

470

Thou then whom partiall heavens conspir'd in one to frame,
The proofe of Beautie's worth, th'enheritrix of fame,   20
The mansion seat of blisse, and just excuse of Lovers;
See now those feathers pluckt, wherewith thou flew most high:
See what clouds of reproch shall darke thy honours skie,
Whose owne fault casts him downe, hardly high seat recovers.

And o my Muse, though oft you luld her in your lap,   25
And then a heav'nly child gave her Ambrosian pap:
And to that braine of hers your hidnest gifts infused,
Since she disdaining me, doth you in me disdaine:
Suffer not her to laugh, while both we suffer paine:
Princes in subjects wrongd, must deeme themselves abused.   30

Your Client poore my selfe, shall *Stella* handle so?
Revenge, revenge, my Muse. Defiance trumpet blow:
Threat'n what may be done, yet do more then you threat'n.
Ah, my sute granted is, I feele my breast doth swell:
Now child, a lesson new you shall begin to spell: 35
Sweet babes must babies have, but shrewd gyrles must be beat'n.

Thinke now no more to heare of warme fine odourd snow,
Nor blushing Lillies, nor pearles ruby-hidden row,
Nor of that golden sea, whose waves in curles are brok'n:
But of thy soule, so fraught with such ungratefulnesse,   40
As where thou soone mightst helpe, most faith dost most
      oppresse,
Ungrateful who is cald, the worst of evils is spok'n:

Yet worse then worst, I say thou art a theefe, a theefe?
Now God forbid. A theef, and of worst theeves the cheefe:
Theeves steal for need, and steale but goods, which paine
      recovers,   45
But thou rich in all joyes, doest rob my joyes from me,
Which cannot be restor'd by time nor industrie:
Of foes the spoile is evill, far worse of constant lovers.

---

19. *partiall:* biased
27. *hidnest:* most hidden
32. *Defiance:* Defiance's
36. *babies:* dolls; *shrewd:* shrewish

Yet gentle English theeves do rob, but will not slay;
Thou English murdring theefe, wilt have harts for thy pray: 50
The name of murdrer now on thy faire forehead sitteth:
And even while I do speake, my death wounds bleeding be:
Which (I protest) proceed from only Cruell thee,
Who may and will not save, murder in truth committeth.

But murder private fault seemes but a toy to thee,   55
I lay then to thy charge unjustest Tyrannie,
If Rule by force without all claime a Tyran showeth,
For thou doest lord my heart, who am not borne thy slave,
And which is worse, makes me most guiltlesse torments have,
A rightfull Prince by unright deeds a Tyran groweth.   60

Lo you grow proud with this, for tyrans make folke bow:
O foule rebellion then I do appeach thee now;
Rebell by Natures law, Rebell by law of reason,
Thou sweetest subject wert borne in the realme of Love,
And yet against thy Prince thy force dost dayly prove: 65
No vertue merits praise, once toucht with blot of Treason.

But valiant Rebels oft in fooles mouthes purchase fame:
I now then staine thy white with vagabunding shame,
Both Rebell to the Sunne, and Vagrant from the mother;
For wearing *Venus* badge, in every part of thee,   70
Unto *Dianaes* traine thou runaway didst flie:
Who faileth one, is false, though trusty to another.

What is not this enough? nay farre worse commeth here;
A witch I say thou art, though thou so faire appeare;
For I protest, my sight never thy face enjoyeth,   75
But I in me am chang'd, I am alive and dead:
My feete are turn'd to rootes, my hart becommeth lead,
No witchcraft is so evill, as which mans mind destroyeth.

---

58. *lord:* lord over
62. *appeach:* impeach, accuse
68. *vagabunding:* acting like a vagabond
69. *Sunne:* son
71. *flie:* flee

Yet witches may repent, thou art far worse then they,
Alas, that I am forst such evill of thee to say,   80
I say thou art a Devill though clothd in Angels shining:
For thy face tempts my soule to leave the heav'n for thee,
And thy words of refuse, do powre even hell on mee:
Who tempt, and tempted plague, are Devils in true defining.

You then ungratefull thiefe, you murdring Tyran you,   85
You Rebell run away, to Lord and Lady untrue,
You witch, you Divill (alas) you still of me beloved,
You see what I can say; mend yet your froward mind,
And such skill in my Muse you reconcil'd shall find,
That all these cruell words your praises shall be proved.   90

Sixt song

O you that heare this voice,
O you that see this face,
Say whether of the choice
Deserves the former place:
Feare not to judge this bate,   5
For it is void of hate.

This side doth beauty take,
For that doth Musike speake,
Fit oratours to make
The strongest judgements weake: 10
The barre to plead their right,
Is only true delight.

Thus doth the voice and face,
These gentle Lawyers wage,
Like loving brothers case,   15
For fathers heritage:

---

83. *refuse:* refusal; *powre:* pour
3. *whether:* which
4. *former:* foremost
5. *bate:* debate
14. *wage:* hire

That each while each contends,
It selfe to other lends.

For beautie beautifies,
With heavenly hew and grace,   20
The heavenly harmonies;
And in this faultlesse face,
The perfect beauties be
A perfect harmony.

Musicke more loftly swels   25
In speeches nobly placed:
Beauty as farre excels,
In action aptly graced:
A friend each party drawes,
To countenance his cause: 30

Love more affected seemes
To beauties lovely light,
And wonder more esteemes
Of Musicke wondrous might:
But both to both so bent,   35
As both in both are spent.

Musike doth witnesse call
The eare, his truth to trie:
Beauty brings to the hall,
The judgement of the eye,   40
Both in their objects such,
As no exceptions tutch.

The common sence, which might
Be Arbiter of this,
To be forsooth upright,   45
To both sides partiall is:
He layes on this chiefe praise,
Chiefe praise on that he laies.

---

40. *The:* 1598 reads *Eye-*
47. *this:* 1598 reads *this side*

Then reason Princesse hy,
Whose throne is in the mind,   50
Which Musicke can in sky
And hidden beauties find,
Say whether thou wilt crowne,
With limitlesse renowne.

Seventh song

Whose senses in so evill consort, their stepdame Nature laies,
That ravishing delight in them most sweete tunes do not raise;
Or if they do delight therein, yet are so closde with wit,
As with sententious lips to set a title vaine on it:
O let them heare these sacred tunes, and learne in wonders
    schooles,   5
To be in things past bounds of wit fooles, if they be not fooles.

Who have so leaden eyes, as not to see sweet beauties show,
Or seeing, have so wodden wits, as not that worth to know;
Or knowing, have so muddy minds, as not to be in love;
Or loving, have so frothy thoughts, as easly thence to
    move: 10
O let them see these heavenly beames, and in faire letters reede
A lesson fit, both sight and skill, love and firme love to breede.

Heare then, but then with wonder heare; see but adoring see,
No mortall gifts, no earthly fruites, now here descended be:
See, do you see this face? a face? nay image of the skies,   15
Of which the two life-giving lights are figured in her eyes:
Heare you this soule-invading voice, and count it but a voice?
The very essence of their tunes, when Angels do rejoyce.

Eight song

In a grove most rich of shade,
Where birds wanton musicke made,

---

8. *wodden:* wooden, dull
2. *wanton:* sportive

May then yong his pide weedes showing,
New perfumed with flowers fresh growing,

Astrophel with *Stella* sweete,   5
Did for mutuall comfort meete,
Both within themselves oppressed,
But each in the other blessed.

Him great harmes had taught much care,
Her faire necke a foule yoke bare,   10
But her sight his cares did banish,
In his sight her yoke did vanish.

Wept they had, alas the while,
But now teares themselves did smile,
While their eyes by love directed,   15
Enterchangeably reflected.

Sigh they did, but now betwixt
Sighs of woes were glad sighs mixt,
With armes crost, yet testifying
Restlesse rest, and living dying.   20

Their eares hungry of each word,
Which the deere tongue would afford,
But their tongues restraind from walking,
Till their harts had ended talking.

But when their tongues could not speake,   25
Love it selfe did silence breake;
Love did set his lips asunder,
Thus to speake in love and wonder:

Stella soveraigne of my joy,
Faire triumpher of annoy,   30

---

3. *pide weedes*: many-colored garments
10. *foule yoke*: i.e., her marriage to Lord Rich
30. *of*: over

Stella starre of heavenly fier,
Stella loadstar of desier.

Stella, in whose shining eyes,
Are the lights of *Cupids* skies,
Whose beames where they once are darted,   35
Love therewith is streight imparted.

Stella, whose voice when it speakes,
Senses all asunder breakes;
Stella, whose voice when it singeth,
Angels to acquaintance bringeth.   40

Stella, in whose body is
Writ each character of blisse,
Whose face all, all beauty passeth,
Save thy mind which yet surpasseth.

Graunt, o graunt, but speech alas,   45
Failes me fearing on to passe,
Graunt, o me, what am I saying?
But no fault there is in praying.

Graunt, o deere, on knees I pray,
(Knees on ground he then did stay)   50
That not I but since I love you,
Time and place for me may move you.

Never season was more fit,
Never roome more apt for it;
Smiling ayre allowes my reason,   55
These birds sing; now use the season.

This small wind which so sweete is,
See how it the leaves doth kisse,
Ech tree in his best attiring,
Sense of love to love inspiring.   60

---

32. *loadstar:* magnet
55. *allowes my reason:* supports my case

Love makes earth the water drinke,
Love to earth makes water sinke;
And if dumbe things be so witty,
Shall a heavenly grace want pitty?

There his hands in their speech, faine   65
Would have made tongues language plaine;
But her hands his hands repelling,
Gave repulse all grace excelling.

Then she spake; her speech was such,
As not eares but hart did tuch: 70
While such wise she love denied,
As yet love she signified.

Astrophel sayd she, my love
Cease in these effects to prove:
Now be still, yet still beleeve me,   75
Thy griefe more then death would grieve me.

If that any thought in me,
Can tast comfort but of thee,
Let me fed with hellish anguish,
Joylesse, hopelesse, endlesse languish.   80

If those eyes you praised, be
Half so deere as you to me,
Let me home returne, starke blinded
Of those eyes, and blinder minded.

If to secret of my hart,   85
I do any wish impart,
Where thou art not formost placed,
Be both wish and I defaced.

---

71. *such wise:* in such ways
73–74. *my . . . prove:* don't try to test my love through these displays of
passion

If more may be sayd, I say,
All my blisse in thee I lay;   90
If thou love, my love content thee,
For all love, all faith is meant thee,

Trust me while I thee deny,
In my selfe the smart I try,
Tyran honour doth thus use thee,   95
Stellas selfe might not refuse thee.

Therefore, Deere, this no more move,
Least though I leave not thy love,
Which too deep in me is framed,
I should blush when thou art named.   100

Therewithall away she went,
Leaving him so passion rent,
With what she had done and spoken,
That therewith my song is broken.

Ninth song

Go my flocke, go get you hence,
Seeke a better place of feeding,
Where you may have some defence
Fro the stormes in my breast breeding,
And showers from mine eyes proceeding.   5

Leave a wretch, in whom all wo
Can abide to keepe no measure,
Merry flocke, such one forgo,
Unto whom mirth is displeasure,
Only rich in mischiefes treasure.   10

---

94. *smart I try:* pain I feel
95. *Tyran:* Tyrant
102. *so:* 1598 reads *to*
4. *Fro:* From

Yet alas before you go,
Heare your wofull maisters story,
Which to stones I els would show:
Sorrow onely then hath glory,
When tis excellently sory.   15

Stella fiercest shepherdesse,
Fiercest but yet fairest ever;
Stella whom o heavens do blesse,
Tho against me shee persever,
Tho I blisse enherit never.   20

Stella hath refused me,
Stella who more love hath proved,
In this caitife hart to be,
Then can in good eawes be moved
Toward *Lamkins* best beloved.   25

Stella hath refused me,
Astrophel that so wel served,
In this pleasant spring must see
While in pride flowers be preserved,
Himselfe onely winter-sterved.   30

Why alas doth she then sweare,
That she loveth me so dearely,
Seing me so long to beare
Coles of love that burne so clearely;
And yet leave me helplesse meerely?   35

Is that love? forsooth I trow,
If I saw my good dog grieved,
And a helpe for him did know,
My love should not be beleeved,
But he were by me releeved.   40

---

23. *caitife:* wretched
30. *winter-sterved:* starved by winter
40. *But:* Unless

No, she hates me, wellaway,
Faining love, somewhat to please me:
For she knowes, if she display
All her hate, death soone would seaze me,
And of hideous torments ease me.   45

Then adieu, deere flocke adieu:
But alas, if in your straying
Heavenly *Stella* meete with you,
Tell her in your piteous blaying,
Her poore slaves unjust decaying.   50

87.

When I was forst from *Stella* ever deere,
Stella food of my thoughts, hart of my hart,
Stella whose eyes make all my tempests cleere,
By iron lawes of duty to depart:
Alas I found, that she with me did smart,   5
I saw that teares did in her eyes appeare;
I saw that sighes her sweetest lips did part,
And her sad words my saddest sence did heare.
For me, I wept to see pearles scattered so,
I sighd her sighes, and wailed for her wo,   10
Yet swam in joy, such love in her was seene.
Thus while th' effect most bitter was to me,
And nothing then the cause more sweet could be,
I had bene vext, if vext I had not beene.

88.

Out traytour absence, darest thou counsell me,
From my deare Captainnesse to run away?

---

41. *wellaway:* woe is me
49. *blaying:* baaing
1. *forst:* forced
4. *iron . . . duty:* cf. *Tyran honour* in the Eight song (l. 95)
13. *then:* than

Because in brave array heere marcheth she,
That to win me, oft shewes a present pay?
Is faith so weake? or is such force in thee? 5
When Sun is hid, can starres such beames display?
Cannot heavns food once felt, keepe stomakes free
From base desire on earthly cates to pray.
Tush absence while thy mistes eclipse that light,
My Orphan sence flies to the inward sight, 10
Where memory sets foorth the beams of love.
That where before hart loved and eyes did see,
In hart both sight and love now coupled be;
United powers make each the stronger prove.

89.

Now that of absence the most irksome night,
With darkest shade doth overcome my day;
Since *Stellas* eyes wont to give me my day,
Leaving my Hemisphere, leave me in night,
Each day seemes long, and longs for long-staid night, 5
The night as tedious, wooes th'approch of day;
Tired with the dusty toiles of busie day,
Languisht with horrors of the silent night;
Suffering the evils both of the day and night,
While no night is more darke then is my day, 10
Nor no day hath lesse quiet then my night:
With such bad mixture of my night and day,
That living thus in blackest winter night,
I feele the flames of hottest sommer day.

90.

Stella thinke not that I by verse seeke fame,
Who seeke, who hope, who love, who live but thee;
Thine eyes my pride, thy lips mine history:
If thou praise not, all other praise is shame.

---

3. *she:* another woman
4. *present pay:* immediate reward
8. *cates:* dainties; *pray:* prey
3. *wont:* accustomed
5. *long-staid:* long-delayed

Nor so ambitious am I, as to frame   5
A nest for my yong praise in Lawrell tree:
In truth I sweare, I wish not there should be
Graved in mine Epitaph a Poets name:
Ne if I would, could I just title make,
That any laud to me thereof should grow,   10
Without my plumes from others wings I take.
For nothing from my wit or will doth flow,
Since all my words thy beauty doth endite,
And love doth hold my hand, and makes me write.

91.

Stella, while now by honours cruell might,
I am from you, light of my life mis-led,
And that faire you my Sunne, thus overspred,
With absence Vaile, I live in Sorowes night.
If this darke place yet shew like candle light,   5
Some beauties peece as amber colourd hed,
Milke hands, rose cheeks, or lips more sweet, more red,
Or seeing gets blacke, but in blacknesse bright.
They please I do confesse, they please mine eyes,
But why? because of you they models be,   10
Models such be wood-globes of glistring skies.
Deere, therefore be not jealous over me,
If you heare that they seeme my hart to move,
Not them o no, but you in them I love.

92.

Be your words made (good Sir) of Indian ware,
That you allow me them by so small rate?

---

6. *Lawrell:* the poet's crown
8. *Graved:* Engraved
9. *Ne:* Nor; *could I:* 1598 reads *I could*
10. *laud:* praise
11. *Without:* Unless
8. *gets:* jets, bits of a black substance (her eyes)
11. *wood-globes:* wooden celestial globes on which the stars were painted
1. *made . . . ware:* as valuable . . . as Indian merchandise
2. *allow . . . rate:* give me only a few of them

Or do you cutted Spartanes imitate,
Or do you meane my tender eares to spare?
That to my questions you so totall are, 5
When I demaund of *Phenix Stellas* state,
You say forsooth, you left her well of late,
O God, thinke you that satisfies my care?
I would know whether she did sit or walke,
How cloth'd, how waited on, sighd she or smilde, 10
Whereof, with whom, how often did she talke,
With what pastime, times journey she beguilde,
If her lips daignd to sweeten my poore name,
Say all, and all, well sayd, still say the same.

Tenth song

O deare life, when shall it be,
That mine eyes thine eyes may see?
And in them thy mind discover,
Whether absence have had force
Thy remembrance to divorce, 5
From the image of thy lover?

Or if I me self find not,
After parting ought forgot,
Nor debard from beauties treasure,
Let no tongue aspire to tell, 10
In what high joyes I shall dwell,
Only thought aymes at the pleasure.

Thought therefore I will send thee,
To take up the place for me;

---

3. *cutted:* taciturn or laconic. The austerity of the Spartans was traditional.
5. *totall:* brief (in your answers)
6. *Phenix:* the mythical Egyptian bird, a symbol of rebirth; Astrophil would like to believe that Stella will come to life again for him
9. *did:* 1598 omits this word
6. *thy:* 1598 reads *the*
7. *me:* my
8. *ought:* anything

Long I will not after tary,   15
There unseene thou maist be bold,
Those faire wonders to behold,
Which in them my hopes do cary.

Thought see thou no place forbeare,
Enter bravely every where,   20
Seaze on all to her belonging;
But if thou wouldst garded be,
Fearing her beames, take with thee
Strength of liking, rage of longing.

Thinke of that most gratefull time,   25
When my leaping hart will clime,
In my lips to have his biding,
There those roses for to kisse,
Which do breath a sugred blisse,
Opening rubies, pearles deviding.   30

Thinke of my most Princely power,
When I blessed shall devower,
With my greedy licorous sences,
Beauty, musicke, sweetnesse, love
While she doth against me prove   35
Her strong darts, but weake defences.

Thinke, thinke of those dalyings,
When with Dovelike murmurings,
With glad moning passed anguish,
We change eyes, and hart for hart,   40
Each to other do depart,
Joying till joy makes us languish.

O my thought my thoughts surcease,
Thy delights my woes increase,

33. *licorous:* intoxicated, but also lecherous
35. *prove:* test
39. *moning passed:* moaning which surpasses
41. *depart:* give, divide
43. *my thought:* 1598 inverts these two words; the line means that thoughts themselves are brought to an end by thought

My life melts with too much thinking;   45
Thinke no more but die in me,
Till thou shalt revived be,
At her lips my Nectar drinking.

93.

O fate, o fault, o curse, child of my blisse,
What sobs can give words grace my griefe to show?
What inke is blacke inough to paint my wo?
Through me, wretch me, even *Stella* vexed is.
Yet truth (if Caitifs breath may call thee) this   5
Witnesse with me, that my foule stumbling so,
From carelesnesse did in no maner grow,
But wit confus'd with too much care did misse.
And do I then my selfe this vaine scuse give?
I have (live I and know this) harmed thee,   10
Tho worlds quite me, shall I me selfe forgive?
Only with paines my paines thus eased be,
That all thy hurts in my harts wracke I reede;
I cry thy sighs; my deere, thy teares I bleede.

94.

Griefe find the words, for thou hast made my braine
So darke with misty vapors, which arise
From out thy heavy mould, that inbent eyes
Can scarce discerne the shape of mine owne paine.
Do thou then (for thou canst) do thou complaine,   5
For my poore soule, which now that sicknesse tries,
Which even to sence, sence of it selfe denies,
Though harbengers of death lodge there his traine.

---

4. *vexed is*: suffers pain
5. *Caitifs*: Wretch's
7. *carelesnesse*: lack of care or love
8. *misse*: make a mistake
9. *scuse*: excuse
11. *quite*: acquit
3. *inbent eyes*: eyes turned inward
6. *tries*: experiences

486

Or if thy love of plaint yet mine forbeares,
As of a caitife worthy so to die,   10
Yet waile thy selfe, and waile with causefull teares,
That though in wretchednesse thy life doth lie,
Yet growest more wretched then thy nature beares,
By being placed in such a wretch as I.

95.

Yet sighs, deere sighs, indeede true friends you are,
That do not leave your lest friend at the wurst,
But as you with my breast I oft have nurst,
So gratefull now you waite upon my care.
Faint coward joy no longer tarry dare,   5
Seeing hope yeeld when this wo strake him furst:
Delight protests he is not for the accurst,
Though oft himselfe my mate in armes he sware.
Nay sorrow comes with such maine rage, that he
Kils his owne children, teares, finding that they   10
By love were made apt to consort with me.
Only true sighs, you do not go away,
Thanke may you have for such a thankfull part,
Thanke-worthiest yet when you shall breake my hart.

96.

Thought with good cause thou likest so well the night,
Since kind or chance gives both one liverie,
Both sadly blacke, both blackly darkned be,
Night bard from Sun, thou from thy owne Sun light;
Silence in both displaies his sullen might,   5
Slow heavinesse in both holds one degree,
That full of doubts, thou of perplexity;
Thy teares expresse nights native moisture right.

2. *lest:* least; 1598 reads *left*
6. *strake:* struck
8. *my . . . sware:* he swore he was my companion in arms; 1598 reads *arme* for *armes*
2. *kind:* nature
6. *holds one degree:* has equal rank

In both a mazefull solitarinesse:
In night of sprites the gastly powers do stur,   10
In thee or sprites or sprited gastlinesse:
But but (alas) nights side the ods hath fur,
For that at length yet doth invite some rest,
Thou though still tired, yet still doost it detest.

97.

Dian that faine would cheare her friend the Night,
Shewes her oft at the full her fairest face,
Bringing with her those starry Nimphs, whose chace
From heavenly standing hits each mortall wight.
But ah poore Night in love with *Phœbus* light,   5
And endlesly dispairing of his grace,
Her selfe (to shew no other joy hath place)
Silent and sad in mourning weedes doth dight:
Even so (alas) a Lady *Dians* peere,
With choise delights and rarest company,   10
Would faine drive cloudes from out my heavy cheere.
But wo is me, though joy it selfe were she,
She could not shew my blind braine waies of joy,
While I dispaire my Sunnes sight to enjoy.

98.

Ah bed, the field where joyes peace some do see,
The field where all my thoughts to warre be traind,
How is thy grace by my strange fortune staind!
How thy lee shores by my sighes stormed be!
With sweete soft shades thou oft invitest me   5

---

10. *do:* 1598 reads *to*
11. *sprited:* caused by spirits
12. *fur:* far
1. *Dian:* the moon, and the chaste goddess of the hunt
3. *chace:* hunting
4. *standing:* shooting position; *wight:* creature
5. *Phœbus:* the sun's
8. *weedes:* garments; *dight:* dress
1. *field:* battlefield

To steale some rest, but wretch I am constraind,
(Spurd with loves spur, though gald and shortly raind
With cares hard hand) to turne and tosse in thee.
While the blacke horrors of the silent night,
Paint woes blacke face so lively to my sight,   10
That tedious leasure markes each wrinckled line:
But when *Aurora* leades out *Phœbus* daunce,
Mine eyes then only winke, for spite perchance,
That wormes should have their Sun, and I want mine.

99.

When far spent night perswades each mortall eye,
To whom nor art nor nature graunteth light,
To lay his then marke wanting shafts of sight,
Clos'd with their quivers in sleeps armory;
With windowes ope then most my mind doth lie,   5
Viewing the shape of darknesse and delight,
Takes in that sad hue, which with th'inward night,
Of his mazde powers keepes perfit harmony:
But when birds charme, and that sweete aire, which is
Mornes messenger, with rose enameld skies   10
Cals each wight to salute the floure of blisse;
In tombe of lids then buried are mine eyes,
Forst by their Lord, who is asham'd to find
Such light in sense, with such a darkned mind.

100.

O teares, no teares, but raine from beauties skies,
Making those Lillies and those Roses grow,

7. *gald:* galled, 1598 reads *gold; shortly raind:* tightly held in check
10. *lively:* lifelike
11. *markes:* 1598 reads *makes*
13. *winke:* close
3. *his:* its. The antecedent is "eye" in l. 1. *marke wanting:* lacking a target
at which they can be aimed
5. *windowes ope:* eyelids open; *lie:* deceive me
8. *mazde:* confused
9. *charme:* morning song. Cf. Milton, *Paradise Lost*, IV, 642: "With
Charm of earliest Birds."

Which ay most faire, now more then most faire show,
While gracefull pitty beauty beautifies.
O honied sighs, which from that breast do rise,   5
Whose pants do make unspilling creame to flow,
Wing'd with whose breath, so pleasing *Zephires* blow,
As can refresh the hell where my soule fries.
O plaints conserv'd in such a surged phraise,
That eloquence it selfe envies your praise,   10
While sobd out words a perfect Musike give.
Such teares, sighs, plaints, no sorrow is, but joy:
Or if such heavenly signes must prove annoy,
All mirth farewell, let me in sorrow live.

101.

Stella is sicke, and in that sicke bed lies
Sweetnesse, which breathes and pants as oft as she:
And grace, sicke too, such fine conclusions tries,
That sickenesse brags it selfe best graced to be.
Beauty is sicke, but sicke in so faire guise,   5
That in that palenesse beauties white we see,
And joy, which is inseperate from those eyes:
Stella now learnes (strange case) to weepe in thee.
Love moves thy paine, and like a faithful page
As thy lookes sturre, comes up and downe to make   10
All folkes prest at thy will thy paine to asswage,
Nature with care sweates for her darlings sake,
Knowing worlds passe, ere she enough can find
Of such heaven stuffe, to cloath so heavenly a mind.

---

3. *ay:* ever
9. *surged:* Ringler emends to *sugred* (sugared)
13. *prove annoy:* turn out to be painful
3. *such . . . tries:* engages in such a fine test of strength
7. *inseperate:* inseparable
9. *Love . . . paine:* Your pain arouses Love; *Love* is the subject of *comes* in the next line (Ringler)
11. *folkes prest:* servants ready
14. *heaven stuffe:* heavenly material

102.

Where be those Roses gone, which sweetned so our eyes?
Where those red cheeks, which oft with faire encrease did frame
The height of honor in the kindly badge of shame?
Who hath the crimson weeds stolne from my morning skies?
How doth the colour vade of those vermillion dies,　　　5
Which Nature selfe did make, and selfe engraind the same?
I would know by what right this palenesse overcame
That hue, whose force my hart still unto thraldome ties?
Galleins adoptive sonnes, who by a beaten way
Their judgements hackney on, the fault on sicknesse lay,　　10
But feeling proofe makes me say they mistake it furre:
It is but love which makes his paper perfit white,
To write therein more fresh the story of delight,
While beauties reddest inke Venus for him doth sturre.

103.

O happie Tems, that didst my *Stella* beare,
I saw thy selfe with many a smiling line
Upon thy cheerefull face, joyes livery weare:
While those faire planets on thy streames did shine.
The bote for joy could not to daunce forebeare,　　　5
While wanton winds with beauties so devine
Ravisht, staid not, till in her golden haire
They did themselves (o sweetest prison) twine.
And faine those Æols youth there would their stay
Have made, but forst by Nature still to flie,　　10
First did with puffing kisse those lockes display:
She so discheveld, blusht; from window I

---

3. *kindly*: natural. A blush is normally taken to be a sign of shame.
5. *vade*: fade
9. *Galleins*: Galen, Greek physician of the second century A.D. Sidney considers those doctors who still follow his methods to be old-fashioned.
11. *feeling proofe*: my own emotional experience; *furre*: far
1. *Tems*: Thames
4. *faire planets*: i.e., Stella's eyes
9. *Æols youth*: sons of Aeolus, the god of the wind

With sight thereof cride out; o faire disgrace,
Let honor selfe to thee graunt highest place.

104.

Envious wits what hath bene mine offence,
That with such poysonous care my lookes you marke,
That to each word, nay sigh of mine you harke,
As grudging me my sorrowes eloquence?
Ah, is it not enough, that I am thence,   5
Thence, so farre thence, that scarcely any sparke
Of comfort dare come to this dungeon darke,
Where rigours exile lockes up all my sense?
But if I by a happy window passe,
If I but stars upon mine armour beare,   10
Sicke, thirsty, glad (though but of empty glasse:)
Your morall notes straight my hid meaning teare,
From out my ribs, and puffing proves that I
Do *Stella* love, fooles, who doth it deny?

Eleventh song

Who is it that this darke night,
Underneath my window playneth?
It is one who from thy sight,
Being (ah) exild, disdayneth
Every other vulgar light.   5

Why alas, and are you he?
Be not yet those fancies changed?
Deere when you find change in me,
Though from me you be estranged,
Let my chaunge to ruine be.   10

---

14. *honor:* honor's
8. *rigours:* probably a contracted form of "rigorous"
9. *happy:* fortunate (because it is Stella's)
11. (*though . . . glasse*): the parenthetical words refer back to the empty window of l. 9
12. *morall notes:* moralizing interpretations
1–2. The first two lines of each stanza in this song are spoken by Stella.

Well in absence this will dy,
Leave to see, and leave to wonder:
Absence sure will helpe, if I
Can learne, how my selfe to sunder
From what in my hart doth ly.   15

But time will these thoughts remove:
Time doth worke what no man knoweth.
Time doth as the subject prove,
With time still the affection groweth
In the faithfull Turtle dove.   20

What if you new beauties see,
Will not they stir new affection?
I will thinke they pictures be,
(Image like of Saints perfection)
Poorely counterfeting thee.   25

But your reasons purest light,
Bids you leave such minds to nourish?
Deere, do reason no such spite,
Never doth thy beauty florish
More, then in my reasons sight.   30

But the wrongs love beares, will make
Love at length leave undertaking;
No the more fooles it do shake,
In a ground of so firme making,
Deeper still they drive the stake.   35

Peace, I thinke that some give eare:
Come no more, least I get anger.

---

12. *Leave:* Cease
18. *Time . . . prove:* Time works according to the nature of the subject influenced by it
23. *they:* 1598 reads *thy*
27. *minds:* ideas, thoughts
37. *least . . . anger:* lest I become angry

Blisse, I will blisse forbeare,
Fearing (sweete) you to endanger,
But my soule shall harbour thee.   40

Well, be gone, be gone I say,
Lest that *Argus* eyes perceive you,
O unjust fortunes sway,
Which can make me thus to leave you,
And from lowts to run away.   45

105.

Unhappie sight, and hath she vanisht by
So neere, in so good time so free a place?
Dead glasse doost thou thy object so imbrace,
As what my hart still sees thou canst not spie?
I sweare by her I love and lacke, that I   5
Was not in fault, who bent thy dazling race
Onely unto the heav'n of *Stellas* face,
Counting but dust what in the way did lie.
But cease mine eyes, your teares do witnesse well,
That you guiltlesse thereof, your Nectar mist: 10
Curst be the page from whence the bad torch fell,
Curst be the night which did your strife resist,
Curst be the Cochman which did drive so fast,
With no worse curse then absence makes me tast.

106.

O absent presence *Stella* is not here;
False flattering hope, that with so faire a face,

---

40. *thee:* Ringler emends to *there*
42. *Argus:* the mythical giant with one hundred eyes, who guarded Zeus' heifer, Io
43. *unjust:* Ringler emends to *unjustest*
3. *Dead glasse:* the window through which Stella could perhaps have been seen. Cf. "empty glasse" in no. 104, l. 11.
6. *dazling race:* "the flickering course of the beams of sight" (Ringler)
11. *page:* servant (bearing the torch)

Bare me in hand, that in this Orphane place,
Stella, I say my *Stella,* should appeare.
What saist thou now, where is that dainty cheere,   5
Thou toldst mine eyes should helpe their famist case?
But thou art gone now that selfe felt disgrace,
Doth make me most to wish thy comfort neere.
But heere I do store of faire Ladies meete,
Who may with charme of conversation sweete,   10
Make in my heavy mould new thoughts to grow:
Sure they prevaile as much with me, as he
That bad his friend but then new maim'd, to be
Mery with him, and not thinke of his woe.

107.

Stella since thou so right a Princesse art
Of all the powers which life bestowes on me,
That ere by them ought undertaken be,
They first resort unto that soveraigne part;
Sweete for a while give respite to my hart,   5
Which pants as though it still should leape to thee:
And on my thoughts give thy Lieftenancy
To this great cause, which needs both use and art.
And as a Queene, who from her presence sends
Whom she imployes, dismisse from thee my wit,   10
Till it have wrought what thy owne will attends.
On servants shame oft Maisters blame doth sit;
O let not fooles in me thy workes reprove,
And scorning say, see what it is to love.

---

3. *Bare . . . hand:* Deceived me
5. *cheere:* food
6. *famist:* famished
9. *store:* a good supply
11. *mould:* body
3. *ere:* before; *ought:* anything
7. *Lieftenancy:* deputized authority

108.

When sorrow (using mine owne fiers might)
Melts downe his lead into my boyling brest,
Through that darke fornace to my hart opprest,
There shines a joy from thee my only light;
But soone as thought of thee breeds my delight,　　　5
And my yong soule flutters to thee his nest,
Most rude dispaire my daily unbidden guest,
Clips streight my wings, streight wraps me in his night,
And makes me then bow downe my head, and say,
Ah what doth *Phœbus* gold that wretch availe,　　　10
Whom iron doores do keepe from use of day?
So strangely (alas) thy works in me prevaile,
That in my woes for thee thou art my joy,
And in my joyes for thee my only annoy.

The end of Astrophel and Stella.

---

10. *Phœbus:* the sun's

CHRISTOPHER MARLOWE

1564–93

1.

The passionate Sheepheard to his love

Come live with mee, and be my love,
And we will all the pleasures prove,
That Vallies, groves, hills and fieldes,
Woods, or steepie mountaine yeeldes.

And wee will sit upon the Rocks,   5
Seeing the Sheepheards feede theyr flocks
By shallow Rivers, to whose falls
Melodious byrds sings Madrigalls.

And I will make thee beds of Roses,
And a thousand fragrant poesies,   10
A cap of flowers, and a kirtle,
Imbroydred all with leaves of Mirtle.

A gowne made of the finest wooll,
Which from our pretty Lambes we pull,
Fayre lined slippers for the cold,   15
With buckles of the purest gold.

A belt of straw and Ivie buds,
With Corall clasps and Amber studs,

---

2. *prove:* test, try out
10. *poesies:* posies, wreaths of flowers
11. *kirtle:* light inner garment

And if these pleasures may thee move,
Come live with mee, and be my love.   20

The Sheepheards Swaines shall daunce & sing
For thy delight each May-morning.
If these delights thy minde may move,
Then live with mee, and be my love.

2.

Hero and Leander

On *Hellespont* guiltie of True-loves blood,
In view and opposit two citties stood,
Seaborders, disjoin'd by *Neptunes* might:
The one *Abydos*, the other Sestos hight.
At *Sestos*, *Hero* dwelt; *Hero* the faire,   5
Whom young *Apollo* courted for her haire,
And offred as a dower his burning throne,
Where she should sit for men to gaze upon.
The outside of her garments were of lawne,
The lining, purple silke, with guilt starres drawne,   10
Her wide sleeves greene, and bordered with a grove,
Where *Venus* in her naked glory strove,
To please the carelesse and disdainfull eies,
Of proud *Adonis* that before her lies.
Her kirtle blew, whereon was many a staine,   15
Made with the blood of wretched Lovers slaine.

1ff. For Chapman's additions to Marlowe's poem, see the Commentary
and below, note to l. 485.
3. *Seaborders:* the border between the cities is the sea; many editors emend
to "Sea-borderers"
4. *hight:* was called
6. *Apollo . . . haire:* Apollo the sun god was famous for his radiant locks,
but his courting of Hero is Marlowe's own invention
7. *burning throne:* the sun
10. *guilt:* gilded; the stars were sewn (*drawne*) onto the lining of her robe
12–14. *Where . . . lies:* Maclure notes the parallel with Shakespeare's
Venus and Adonis, l. 241, "At this Adonis smiles as in disdain"
15. *kirtle:* inner gown, petticoat

Upon her head she ware a myrtle wreath,
From whence her vaile reacht to the ground beneath.
Her vaile was artificiall flowers and leaves,
Whose workmanship both man and beast deceaves.   20
Many would praise the sweet smell as she past,
When t'was the odour which her breath foorth cast,
And there for honie, bees have fought in vaine,
And beat from thence, have lighted there againe.
About her necke hung chaines of peble stone,   25
Which lightned by her necke, like Diamonds shone.
She ware no gloves, for neither sunne nor wind
Would burne or parch her hands, but to her mind,
Or warme or coole them, for they tooke delite
To play upon those hands, they were so white.   30
Buskins of shels all silvered, used she,
And brancht with blushing corall to the knee;
Where sparrowes pearcht, of hollow pearle and gold,
Such as the world would woonder to behold:
Those with sweet water oft her handmaid fils,   35
Which as shee went would cherupe through the bils.
Some say, for her the fairest *Cupid* pyn'd,
And looking in her face, was strooken blind.
But this is true, so like was one the other,
As he imagyn'd *Hero* was his mother.   40
And oftentimes into her bosome flew,
About her nakcd necke his bare armes threw.
And laid his childish head upon her brest,
And with still panting rockt, there tooke his rest.
So lovely faire was *Hero, Venus* Nun,   45
As nature wept, thinking she was undone;
Because she tooke more from her than she left,
And of such wondrous beautie her bereft:

---

17. *ware:* wore
26. *lightned:* brightened
28. *but . . . mind:* unless she chose
29. *Or:* Either to
31. *Buskins:* Knee boots
32. *brancht . . . corall:* the coral formed a branchlike pattern
38. *strooken:* struck
44. *still:* continuous
47. *she . . . she:* both pronouns refer to Hero

Therefore in signe her treasure suffred wracke,
Since *Heroes* time, hath halfe the world been blacke.　　50
Amorous *Leander*, beautifull and yoong,
(Whose tragedie divine *Musæus* soong)
Dwelt at *Abidus*, since him, dwelt there none,
For whom succeeding times make greater mone.
His dangling tresses that were never shorne,　　55
Had they beene cut, and unto *Colchos* borne,
Would have allu'rd the vent'rous youth of *Greece*,
To hazard more, than for the golden Fleece.
Faire *Cinthia* wisht, his armes might be her spheare,
Greefe makes her pale, because she mooves not there.　　60
His bodie was as straight as *Circes* wand,
Jove might have sipt out *Nectar* from his hand.
Even as delicious meat is to the tast,
So was his necke in touching, and surpast
The white of *Pelops* shoulder, I could tell ye,　　65
How smooth his brest was, & how white his bellie,
And whose immortall fingars did imprint,
That heavenly path, with many a curious dint,
That runs along his backe, but my rude pen,
Can hardly blazon foorth the loves of men.　　70
Much lesse of powerfull gods, let it suffise,
That my slacke muse, sings of *Leanders* eies.

---

50. *blacke*: i.e., dark-skinned
52. *Musæus*: the Greek poet (fifth century A.D., but thought to be contemporary with Homer) whose *Hero and Leander*, in Latin translation, was Marlowe's source
58. *golden Fleece*: the Argonauts, led by Jason, retrieved the golden fleece from King Aeetes of Colchis
59. *Cinthia*: the moon; *spheare*: orbit
61. *Circes*: the witch whose magic, in the *Odyssey*, transformed men into animals
62. *Jove . . . hand*: Leander is like Ganymede, Jupiter's cupbearer
65. *Pelops*: whose father Tantalus had him cooked and served at a banquet of the gods. He was restored to life and the part of his shoulder which had been eaten was replaced with ivory. See Ovid, *Metamorphoses*, VI, for the story.
68. *curious dint*: exquisite indentation (referring to his backbone)
70. *hardly*: 1598 misprints *hardiy*
72. *slacke*: loose, weak

Those orient cheekes and lippes, exceeding his
That leapt into the water for a kis
Of his owne shadow, and despising many,   75
Died ere he could enjoy the love of any.
Had wilde *Hippolitus, Leander* seene,
Enamoured of his beautie had he beene,
His presence made the rudest paisant melt,
That in the vast uplandish countrie dwelt,   80
The barbarous *Thratian* soldier moov'd with nought,
Was moov'd with him, and for his favour fought.
Some swore he was a maid in mans attire,
For in his lookes were all that men desire,
A pleasant smiling cheeke, a speaking eye,   85
A brow for love to banquet roiallye,
And such as knew he was a man would say,
Leander, thou art made for amorous play:
Why art thou not in love, and lov'd of all?
Though thou be faire, yet be not thine owne thrall.   90
    The men of wealthie *Sestos,* everie yeare,
(For his sake whom their goddesse held so deare,
Rose-cheekt *Adonis*) kept a solemne feast,
Thither resorted many a wandring guest,
To meet their loves; such as had none at all,   95
Came lovers home, from this great festivall.
For everie street like to a Firmament
Glistered with breathing stars, who where they went,
Frighted the melancholie earth, which deem'd,
Eternall heaven to burne, for so it seem'd,   100

73–76. *his . . . any:* alluding to the story of Narcissus
73. *orient:* brightly shining
75. *shadow:* reflection
77. *Hippolitus:* who preferred hunting to love and was accordingly disliked
by Venus
79. *paisant:* peasant
80. *uplandish:* rustic
81. *Thratian:* The Thracians were noted for their ferocity; *nought:* naught
86. *roiallye:* royally
90. *thine owne thrall:* a slave to yourself
92. *goddesse:* Venus
97. *Firmament:* sky
98. *who:* which

As if another *Phaeton* had got
The guidance of the sunnes rich chariot.
But far above, the loveliest *Hero* shin'd,
And stole away th'inchaunted gazers mind,
For like Sea-nimphs inveigling harmony,   105
So was her beautie to the standers by.
Nor that night-wandring pale and watrie starre,
(When yawning dragons draw her thirling carre,
From *Latmus* mount up to the glomie skie,
Where crown'd with blazing light and majestie,   110
She proudly sits) more over-rules the flood,
Than she the hearts of those that neere her stood.
Even as, when gawdie Nymphs pursue the chace,
Wretched *Ixions* shaggie footed race, .
Incenst with savage heat, gallop amaine,   115
From steepe Pine-bearing mountains to the plaine:
So ran the people foorth to gaze upon her,
And all that view'd her, were enamour'd on her.
And as in furie of a dreadfull fight,
Their fellowes being slaine or put to flight,   120
Poore soldiers stand with fear of death strooken,
So at her presence all surpris'd and tooken,
Await the sentence of her scornefull eies:
He whom she favours lives, the other dies.
There might you see one sigh, another rage,   125
And some (their violent passions to asswage)
Compile sharpe satyrs, but alas too late,
For faithfull love will never turne to hate.

---

101. *Phaeton:* Phaethon, whom Zeus struck down with a thunderbolt after
he lost control of the sun's chariot
107. *starre:* the moon
108. *yawning:* opening wide their mouths (to devour); *thirling carre:* spin-
ning chariot
109. *Latmus:* Mount Latmos was the seat of Cynthia, goddess of the moon
111. *over-rules:* reigns over; *flood:* tides
113. *gawdie:* the unnatural "gaudiness" of the nymphs who take part in the
hunt (*chace*) is perhaps related to the artificiality of Hero's costume de-
scribed earlier (ll. 9ff.)
114. *Ixions . . . race:* the centaurs, sons of Ixion, who was punished for lov-
ing Hera by being bound upon a wheel of fire
115. *amaine:* in full force
118. *on:* of
121. *strooken:* stricken
127. *Compile sharpe satyrs:* write sharply critical satires

And many seeing great princes were denied,
Pyn'd as they went, and thinking on her died.   130
On this feast day, O cursed day and hower,
Went *Hero* thorow *Sestos*, from her tower
To *Venus* temple, were unhappilye,
As after chaunc'd, they did each other spye.
So faire a church as this, had *Venus* none,   135
The wals were of discoloured *Jasper* stone,
Wherein was *Proteus* carved, and o'rehead,
A livelie vine of greene sea agget spread;
Where by one hand, light headed *Bacchus* hoong,
And with the other, wine from grapes out wroong.   140
Of Christall shining faire, the pavement was,
The towne of *Sestos*, cal'd it *Venus* glasse,
There might you see the gods in sundrie shapes,
Committing headdie ryots, incest, rapes:
For know, that underneath this radiant floure,   145
Was *Danaes* statue in a brazen tower,
Jove, slylie stealing from his sisters bed,
To dallie with *Idalian Ganimed:*
And for his love *Europa*, bellowing loud,
And tumbling with the Rainbow in a cloud,   150

---

132. *thorow:* through
133. *were:* where
134. *spye:* 1598 has a comma, not a period, after this word
135. *So . . . none:* This was the most beautiful of all the temples devoted to Venus
136. *discoloured:* multi-colored
137. *Proteus:* a sea god who could assume various forms and shapes
138. *livelie:* lifelike; *agget:* agate (colored green like the sea)
139. *Bacchus:* the god of wine
144. *headdie:* hurried on with passion
145. *underneath . . . floure:* i.e., depicted on the surface of this lower floor
146. *Danaes:* Jupiter came to Danae in a golden shower
147. *sisters:* Juno's
148. *Idalian Ganimed:* perhaps because Jove is said to have carried him off from Mount Ida to be his cupbearer
149. *Europa:* Jupiter took the form of a bull for this escapade
150. *And . . . cloud:* Jove as the rain god

Blood-quaffing *Mars*, heaving the yron net,
Which limping *Vulcan* and his *Cyclops* set:
Love kindling fire, to burne such townes as *Troy*,
Sylvanus weeping for the lovely boy
That now is turn'd into a *Cypres* tree,   155
Under whose shade the Wood-gods love to bee.
And in the midst a silver altar stood,
There *Hero* sacrificing turtles blood,
Vaild to the ground, vailing her eie-lids close,
And modestly they opened as she rose: 160
Thence flew Loves arrow with the golden head,
And thus *Leander* was enamoured.
Stone still he stood, and evermore he gazed,
Till with the fire that from his count'nance blazed,
Relenting *Heroes* gentle heart was strooke,   165
Such force and vertue hath an amorous looke.
   It lies not in our power to love, or hate,
For will in us is over-rul'd by fate.
When two are stript long ere the course begin,
We wish that one should loose, the other win.   170
And one especiallie doe we affect,
Of two gold Ingots like in each respect,
The reason no man knowes, let it suffise,
What we behold is censur'd by our eies.
Where both deliberat, the love is slight,   175
Who ever lov'd, that lov'd not at first sight?
   He kneel'd, but unto her devoutly praid;
Chast *Hero* to her selfe thus softly said:

151–52. Mars struggling to escape from the net thrown over himself and
Venus by the latter's husband, Vulcan
154. *Sylvanus:* a forest god, who loved the youth Cyparissus. Most of the
stories alluded to in ll. 146–56 are to be found in Ovid's *Metamorphoses.*
158. *turtles:* turtledoves'
159. *Vaild:* Bowing reverently; *vailing:* veiling
165. *strooke:* struck
166. *vertue:* strength
169. *course:* race
170. *loose:* lose
171. *affect:* prefer
174. *censur'd by:* subject to the judgment of
175. *both deliberat:* each party deliberates

Were I the saint hee worships, I would heare him,
And as shee spake those words, came somewhat nere him.   180
He started up, she blusht as one asham'd;
Wherewith *Leander* much more was inflam'd.
He toucht her hand, in touching it she trembled,
Love deepely grounded, hardly is dissembled,
These lovers parled by the touch of hands,   185
True love is mute, and oft amazed stands,
Thus while dum signs their yeelding harts entangled,
The aire with sparkes of living fire was spangled,
And night deepe drencht in mystie *Acheron,*
Heav'd up her head, and halfe the world upon,   190
Breath'd darkenesse forth (darke night is *Cupids* day)
And now begins *Leander* to display
Loves holy fire, with words, with sighs and teares,
Which like sweet musicke entred *Heroes* eares,
And yet at everie word shee turn'd aside,   195
And alwaies cut him off as he replide,
At last, like to a bold sharpe Sophister,
With chearefull hope thus he accosted her.
    Faire creature, let me speake without offence,
I would my rude words had the influence,   200
To lead thy thoughts, as thy faire lookes doe mine,
Then shouldst thou bee his prisoner who is thine.
Be not unkind and faire, mishapen stuffe
Are of behaviour boisterous and ruffe.
O shun me not, but heare me ere you goe,   205
God knowes I cannot force love, as you doe.
My words shall be as spotlesse as my youth,
Full of simplicitie and naked truth.
This sacrifice (whose sweet perfume descending,
From *Venus* altar to your footsteps bending)   210
Doth testifie that you exceed her farre,
To whom you offer, and whose Nunne you are,

---

184. *grounded:* based; *hardly:* with difficulty
185. *parled:* conversed
189. *Acheron:* one of the four rivers in the classical hell. 1598 adds the
marginal note, "A periphrasis [i.e., paraphrastic description] of night."
197. *Sophister:* one who reasons speciously
203. *mishapen stuffe:* ungainly persons

Why should you worship her, her you surpasse,
As much as sparkling Diamonds flaring glasse.
A Diamond set in lead his worth retaines,   215
A heavenly Nimph, belov'd of humane swaines,
Receives no blemish, but oft-times more grace,
Which makes me hope, although I am but base,
Base in respect of thee, divine and pure,
Dutifull service may thy love procure,   220
And I in dutie will excell all other,
As thou in beautie doest exceed loves mother.
Nor heaven, nor thou, were made to gaze upon,
As heaven preserves all things, so save thou one.
A stately builded ship, well rig'd and tall,   225
The Ocean maketh more majesticall:
Why vowest thou then to live in *Sestos* here,
Who on Loves seas more glorious wouldst appeare?
Like untun'd golden strings all women are,
Which long time lie untoucht, will harshly jarre.   230
Vessels of Brasse oft handled, brightly shine,
What difference betwixt the richest mine
And basest mold, but use? for both not us'de,
Are of like worth. Then treasure is abus'de,
When misers keepe it; being put to lone,   235
In time it will returne us two for one.
Rich robes, themselves and others do adorne,
Neither themselves nor others, if not worne.
Who builds a pallace and rams up the gate,
Shall see it ruinous and desolate.   240
Ah simple *Hero*, learne thy selfe to cherish,
Lone women like to emptie houses perish.

---

214. *flaring:* flashy
222. *loves mother:* Venus
223. *gaze upon:* i.e., only to look at
224. *one:* Leander himself
230. *long . . . untoucht:* i.e., if they lie untouched for a long time
233. *mold:* earth
235. *lone:* loan
239. *rams:* blocks

Lesse sinnes the poore rich man that starves himselfe,
In heaping up a masse of drossie pelfe,
Than such as you: his golden earth remains,   245
Which after his disceasse, some other gains.
But this faire jem, sweet, in the losse alone,
When you fleet hence, can be bequeath'd to none.
Or if it could, downe from th'enameld skie,
All heaven would come to claime this legacie,   250
And with intestine broiles the world destroy,
And quite confound natures sweet harmony.
Well therefore by the gods decreed it is,
We humane creatures should enjoy that blisse.
One is no number, mayds are nothing then,   255
Without the sweet societie of men.
Wilt thou live single still? one shalt thou bee,
Though never-singling *Hymen* couple thee.
Wild savages, that drinke of running springs,
Thinke water farre excels all earthly things: 260
But they that dayly tast neat wine, despise it.
Virginitie, albeit some highly prise it,
Compar'd with marriage, had you tried them both,
Differs as much, as wine and water doth.
Base boullion for the stampes sake we allow,   265
Even so for mens impression do we you.
By which alone, our reverend fathers say,
Women receave perfection everie way.
This idoll which you terme *Virginitie*,
Is neither essence subject to the eie,   270

---

244. *drossie pelfe*: "filthy lucre"
247. *jem*: gem
251. *intestine broiles*: civil wars
255. *One . . . number*: a maxim from Aristotle (*Metaphysics*, 1080a)
257. *still*: always
258. *never-singling Hymen*: the god of marriage, who never separates what he joins
261. *neat*: strong, uncut
265. *Base . . . allow*: We allow money (bullion) that is inferior to pass for real currency because of the imprint upon it; *impression* in the next line is to be taken both literally and figuratively
267. *our . . . say*: another Aristotelian maxim, taken over by the scholastic philosophers
270. *essence*: something that exists (a philosophical term)

No, nor to any one exterior sence,
Nor hath it any place of residence,
Nor is't of earth or mold celestiall,
Or capable of any forme at all.
Of that which hath no being, doe not boast,   275
Things that are not at all, are never lost.
Men foolishly doe call it vertuous,
What vertue is it, that is borne with us?
Much lesse can honour bee ascrib'd thereto,
Honour is purchac'd by the deedes wee do.   280
Beleeve me *Hero*, honour is not wone,
Untill some honourable deed be done.
Seeke you for chastitie, immortall fame,
And know that some have wrong'd *Dianas* name?
Whose name is it, if she be false or not,   285
So she be faire, but some vile toongs will blot?
But you are faire (aye me) so wondrous faire,
So yoong, so gentle, and so debonaire,
As *Greece* will thinke, if thus you live alone,
Some one or other keepes you as his owne.   290
Then *Hero* hate me not, nor from me flie,
To follow swiftly blasting infamie.
Perhaps, thy sacred Priesthood makes thee loath,
Tell me, to whom mad'st thou that heedlesse oath?
    To *Venus*, answered shee, and as shee spake,   295
Foorth from those two tralucent cesternes brake,
A streame of liquid pearle, which downe her face
Made milk-white paths, wheron the gods might trace
To *Joves* high court. Hee thus replide: The rites
In which Loves beauteous Empresse most delites,   300
Are banquets, Dorick musicke, midnight revell,
Plaies, maskes, and all that stern age counteth evill.
Thee as a holy Idiot doth she scorne,
For thou in vowing chastitie, hast sworne

---

273. *mold:* form, shape
284. *Dianas:* the goddess of chastity
296. *tralucent cesternes:* translucent cisterns or pools
298. *trace:* walk
301. *Dorick:* solemn, majestic
302. *maskes:* masques

To rob her name and honour, and thereby 305
Commit'st a sinne far worse than perjurie.
Even sacrilege against her Dietie,
Through regular and formall puritie.
To expiat which sinne, kisse and shake hands,
Such sacrifice as this, *Venus* demands. 310
    Thereat she smild, and did denie him so,
As put thereby, yet might he hope for mo.
Which makes him quickly re-enforce his speech,
And her in humble manner thus beseech.
    Though neither gods nor men may thee deserve, 315
Yet for her sake whom you have vow'd to serve,
Abandon fruitlesse cold Virginitie,
The gentle queene of Loves sole enemie.
Then shall you most resemble *Venus* Nun,
When *Venus* sweet rites are perform'd and done, 320
Flint-brested *Pallas* joies in single life,
But *Pallas* and your mistresse are at strife.
Love *Hero* then, and be not tirannous,
But heale the heart, that thou hast wounded thus,
Nor staine thy youthfull years with avarice, 325
Faire fooles delight, to be accounted nice.
The richest corne dies, if it be not reapt,
Beautie alone is lost, too warily kept.
These arguments he us'de, and many more,
Wherewith she yeelded, that was woon before, 330
Heroes lookes yeelded, but her words made warre,
Women are woon when they begin to jarre.
Thus having swallow'd *Cupids* golden hooke,
The more she striv'd, the deeper was she strooke.

---

312. *put:* turned back; *mo:* more
321. *Pallas:* Minerva, goddess of wisdom; *joies:* joys
325. *avarice:* stinginess
326. *nice:* coy
327. *corne:* wheat
328. *alone:* without aid
329. *arguments:* 1598 misprints *argumsnts*
332. *jarre:* quarrel

510

Yet evilly faining anger, strove she still,   335
And would be rhought to graunt against her will.
So having paus'd a while, at last shee said:
Who taught thee Rhethoricke to deceive a maid?
Aye me, such words as these should I abhor,
And yet I like them for the Orator.   340
   With that *Leander* stoopt, to have imbrac'd her,
But from his spreading armes away she cast her,
And thus bespake him. Gentle youth forbeare
To touch the sacred garments which I weare.
   Upon a rocke, and underneath a hill,   345
Far from the towne (where all is whist and still,
Save that the sea playing on yellow sand,
Sends foorth a ratling murmure to the land,
Whose sound allures the golden *Morpheus,*
In silence of the night to visite us.)   350
My turret stands, and there God knowes I play
With V*enus* swannes and sparrowes all the day,
A dwarfish beldame beares me companie,
That hops about the chamber where I lie,
And spends the night (that might be better spend)   355
In vaine discourse, and apish merriment.
Come thither; As she spake this, her toong tript,
For unawares (*Come thither*) from her slipt,
And sodainly her former colour chang'd,
And here and there her eies through anger rang'd.   360
And like a planet, mooving severall waies,
At one selfe instant, she poore soule assaies,
Loving, not to love at all, and everie part,
Strove to resist the motions of her hart.

-----

335. *evilly:* poorly
336. *rhought:* most editors emend to "thought," but "wrought," in this
spelling, may be the word intended here
346. *whist:* quiet
349. *Morpheus:* the god of sleep
353. *dwarfish beldame:* dwarflike old woman
356. *apish:* apelike, silly
361. *And . . . waies:* the Ptolemaic system conceived of each planet as
moving in its own orbit and, at the same time, being moved about by
forces exerted from other planets
362. *selfe instant:* and the same moment

And hands so pure, so innocent, nay such,   365
As might have made heaven stoope to have a touch,
Did she uphold to Venus, and againe,
Vow'd spotlesse chastitie, but all in vaine,
Cupid beats downe her praiers with his wings,
Her vowes above the emptie aire he flings: 370
All deepe enrag'd, his sinowie bow he bent,
And shot a shaft that burning from him went,
Wherewith she strooken, look'd so dolefully,
As made Love sigh, to see his tirannie.
And as she wept, her teares to pearle he turn'd,   375
And wound them on his arme, and for her mourn'd.
Then towards the pallace of the destinies,
Laden with languishment and griefe he flies.
And to those sterne nymphs humblie made request,
Both might enjoy ech other, and be blest.   380
But with a ghastly dreadfull countenaunce,
Threatning a thousand deaths at everie glaunce,
They answered Love, nor would vouchsafe so much
As one poore word, their hate to him was such.
Harken a while, and I will tell you why: 385
Heavens winged herrald, *Jove-borne Mercury*,
The selfe-same day that he asleepe had layd
Inchaunted *Argus*, spied a countrie mayd,
Whose carelesse haire, in stead of pearle t'adorne it,
Glist'red with deaw, as one that seem'd to skorne it: 390
Her breath as fragrant as the morning rose,
Her mind pure, and her toong untaught to glose.
Yet prowd she was, (for loftie pride that dwels
In tow'red courts, is oft in sheapheards cels.)
And too too well the faire vermilion knew,   395
And silver tincture of her cheekes, that drew
The love of everie swaine: On her, this god
Enamoured was, and with his snakie rod,

---

371. *sinowie:* sinewy
377. *destinies:* Fates
390. *it:* pearl
392. *glose:* deceive, flatter
394. *cels:* huts
398. *snakie rod:* the caduceus of Mercury

Did charme her nimble feet, and made her stay,
The while upon a hillocke downe he lay, 400
And sweetly on his pipe began to play,
And with smooth speech, her fancie to assay,
Till in his twining armes he lockt her fast,
And then he woo'd with kisses, and at last,
As sheap-heards do, her on the ground hee layd, 405
And tumbling in the grasse, he often strayd,
Beyond the bounds of shame, in being bold
To eie those parts, which no eie should behold.
And like an insolent commaunding lover,
Boasting his parentage, would needs discover 410
The way to new *Elisium:* but she,
Whose only dower was her chastitie,
Having striv'ne in vaine, was now about to crie,
And crave the helpe of sheap-heards that were nie.
Herewith he stayd his furie, and began 415
To give her leave to rise, away she ran,
After went *Mercurie,* who us'd such cunning,
As she to heare his tale, left off her running.
Maids are not woon by brutish force and might,
But speeches full of pleasure and delight. 420
And knowing *Hermes* courted her, was glad
That she such lovelinesse and beautie had
As could provoke his liking, yet was mute,
And neither would denie, nor graunt his sute.
Still vowed he love, she wanting no excuse 425
To feed him with delaies, as women use:
Or thirsting after immortalitie,
All women are ambitious naturallie,
Impos'd upon her lover such a taske,
As he ought not performe, nor yet she aske. 430
A draught of flowing *Nectar,* she requested,
Wherewith the king of Gods and men is feasted.

---

402. *her . . . assay:* i.e., as we might say "to make her fancy him"
410. *Boasting his parentage:* Mercury was Jupiter's son; *discover:* reveal
411. *Elisium:* paradise
414. *nie:* nearby
425. *wanting:* lacking

He readie to accomplish what she wil'd,
Stole some from *Hebe* (*Hebe, Joves* cup fil'd,)
And gave it to his simple rustike love,
Which being knowne (as what is hid from *Jove*) 435
He inly storm'd, and waxt more furious,
Than for the fire filcht by *Prometheus*;
And thrusts him down from heaven, he wandring here,
In mournfull tearmes, with sad and heavie cheare 440
Complaind to *Cupid, Cupid* for his sake.
To be reveng'd on *Jove*, did undertake,
And those on whom heaven, earth, and hell relies,
I mean the Adamantine Destinies,
He wounds with love, and forst them equallie, 445
To dote upon deceitfull *Mercurie.*
They offred him the deadly fatall knife,
That sheares the slender threads of humane life,
At his faire feathered feet, the engins layd,
Which th'earth from ougly *Chaos* den up-wayd: 450
These he regarded not, but did intreat,
That Jove, usurper of his fathers seat,
Might presently be banisht into hell,
And aged *Saturne* in *Olympus* dwell.
They granted what he crav'd, and once againe, 455
Saturne and *Ops*, began their golden raigne.
Murder, rape, warre, lust and trecherie,
Were with *Jove* clos'd in *Stigian* Emprie.
But long this blessed time continued not,
As soone as he his wished purpose got; 460
He recklesse of his promise, did despise
The love of th'everlasting Destinies.
They seeing it, both Love and him abhor'd,
And *Jupiter* unto his place restor'd.

---

439. *him:* Mercury
440. *mournfull tearmes:* a sad state; *cheare:* countenance
449. *engins:* instruments
450. *up-wayd:* carried up
452. *fathers:* Saturn, Jove's father
453. *presently:* immediately
456. *Ops:* Saturn's wife
458. *Stigian Emprie:* the empire of hell, in which the river Styx ran

514

And but that Learning, in despight of Fate,   465
Will mount aloft, and enter heaven gate,
And to the seat of *Jove* it selfe advaunce,
Hermes had slept in hell with ignoraunce.
Yet as a punishment they added this,
That he and Povertie should alwaies kis.   470
And to this day is everie scholler poore,
Grosse gold, from them runs headlong to the boore.
Likewise the angrie sisters thus deluded,
To venge themselves on *Hermes*, have concluded
That *Midas* brood shall sit in Honors chaire,   475
To which the *Muses* sonnes are only heire:
And fruitfull wits that in aspiring are,
Shall discontent, run into regions farre;
And few great lords in vertuous deeds shall joy,
But be surpris'd with every garish toy.   480
And still inrich the loftie servile clowne,
Who with incroching guile, keepes learning downe.
Then muse not, *Cupids* sute no better sped,
Seeing in their loves, the Fates were injured.

By this, sad *Hero*, with love unacquainted,   485
Viewing *Leanders* face, fell downe and fainted.
He kist her, and breath'd life into her lips,
Wherewith as one displeas'd, away she trips.
Yet as she went, full often look'd behind,
And many poore excuses did she find,   490
To linger by the way, and once she stayd,
And would have turn'd againe, but was afrayd,

465. *Learning:* Hermes (Mercury) was also the god of learning and scholarship; *in . . . of:* despite
472. *boore:* boor
474. *venge:* revenge
475. *Midas brood:* those who, like King Midas, have the golden touch
477. *in aspiring:* in a state of aspiration, "on the way up." Most editors emend to *inaspiring* and take the word to mean "unambitious."
480. *surpris'd:* captivated
481. *loftie . . . clowne:* proud (but actually base) fool
483. *sped:* succeeded
485. Chapman begins what he calls the "second sestiad" of Marlowe's poem with this line.

In offring parlie, to be counted light.
So on she goes, and in her idle flight,
Her painted fanne of curled plumes let fall,   515
Thinking to traine *Leander* therewithall.
He being a novice, knew not what she meant,
But stayd, and after her a letter sent.
Which joyfull *Hero* answerd in such sort,
As he had hope to scale the beauteous fort,   500
Wherein the liberall graces lock'd their wealth,
And therefore to her tower he got by stealth.
Wide open stood the doore, hee need not clime,
And she her selfe before the pointed time,
Had spread the boord, with roses strowed the roome,   505
And oft look't out, and mus'd he did not come.
At last he came, O who can tell the greeting,
These greedie lovers had, at their first meeting.
He askt, she gave, and nothing was denied,
Both to each other quickly were affied.   510
Looke how their hands, so were their hearts united,
And what he did, she willingly requited.
(Sweet are the kisses, the imbracements sweet,
When like desires and affections meet,
For from the earth to heaven, is *Cupid* rais'd,   515
Where fancie is in equall ballance pais'd)
Yet she this rashnesse sodainly repented,
And turn'd aside, and to her selfe lamented.
As if her name and honour had beene wrong'd,
By being possest of him for whom she long'd: 520
I, and shee wisht, albeit not from her hart,
That he would leave her turret and depart.

---

493. *parlie:* to stop and speak; *light:* wanton
494. *idle:* unthinking, heedless
496. *traine:* entice
504. *pointed:* appointed
505. *boord:* table; *strowed:* strewn
510. *affied:* betrothed
515–16. *For . . . pais'd:* Earth becomes like heaven when two lovers love
each other equally; *pais'd:* poised
521. *I:* Aye

The mirthfull God of amorous pleasure smil'd,
To see how he this captive Nymph beguil'd.
For hitherto hee did but fan the fire,   525
And kept it downe that it might mount the hier.
Now waxt she jealous, least his love abated,
Fearing, her owne thoughts made her to be hated.
Therefore unto him hastily she goes,
And like light *Salmacis*, her body throes   530
Upon his bosome, where with yeelding eyes,
She offers up her selfe a sacrifice,
To slake his anger, if he were displeas'd,
O what god would not therewith be appeas'd?
Like *Æsops* cocke, this jewell he enjoyed,   535
And as a brother with his sister toyed,
Supposing nothing else was to be done,
Now he her favour and good will had wone.
But know you not that creatures wanting sence,
By nature have a mutuall appetence,   540
And wanting organs to advaunce a step,
Mov'd by Loves force, unto ech other lep?
Much more in subjects having intellect,
Some hidden influence breeds like effect.
Albeit *Leander* rude in love, and raw,   545
Long dallying with *Hero*, nothing saw
That might delight him more, yet he suspected
Some amorous rites or other were neglected.
Therefore unto his bodie, hirs he clung,
She, fearing on the rushes to be flung,   550

---

526. *hier:* higher
527. *jealous:* afraid
530. *light Salmacis:* a wanton nymph who made love to Hermaphroditus.
Cf. Ovid, *Metamorphoses*, IV, 285ff. *throes:* throws
535. *Æsop's cocke:* who found a precious jewel in his barnyard, but cast it
away because it wasn't a barleycorn. As Maclure notes, the simile is am-
biguous in its context.
539. *creatures . . . sence:* inanimate objects
540. *mutuall appetence:* desire for each other
542. *lep:* leap—as if by magnetic attraction
545. *rude:* unexperienced
549. *unto . . . clung:* he clasped her body to his
550. *rushes:* a common floor covering in Elizabethan times

Striv'd with redoubled strength, the more she strived,
The more a gentle pleasing heat revived,
Which taught him all that elder lovers know,
And now the same gan so to scorch and glow,
As in plaine termes (yet cunningly) he crav'd it, 555
Love alwaies makes those eloquent that have it.
Shee, with a kind of graunting, put him by it,
And ever as he thought himselfe most nigh it,
Like to the tree of *Tantalus* she fled,
And seeming lavish, sav'de her maydenhead. 560
Ne're king more sought to keepe his diademe;
Than *Hero* this inestimable gemme.
Above our life we love a stedfast friend,
Yet when a token of great worth we send,
We often kisse it, often looke thereon, 565
And stay the messenger that would be gon:
No marvell then, though *Hero* would not yeeld
So soone to part from that she deerely held.
Jewels being lost are found againe, this never,
T'is lost but once, and once lost, lost for ever. 570
Now had the morne espy'de her lovers steeds,
Whereat she starts, puts on her purple weeds,
And red for anger that he stayd so long,
All headlong throwes her selfe the clouds among,
And now *Leander* fearing to be mist, 575
Imbrast her sodainly, tooke leave, and kist,
Long was he taking leave, and loath to go,
And kist againe, as lovers use to do,
Sad *Hero* wroong him by the hand, and wept,
Saying, let your vowes and promises be kept. 580

---

551. *Striv'd:* Strove
554. *gan:* began
555. *cunningly:* artfully
557. *put . . . it:* kept him away from it
559. *Tantalus:* who grasped, in hell, for the fruit of a tree which he was never able to reach
571. *lovers steeds:* Apollo's horses, who draw his chariot
572. *she:* Aurora, the dawn; *weeds:* garments
578. *use:* are accustomed
579. *wroong:* wrung

Then standing at the doore, she turnd about,
As loath to see *Leander* going out.
And now the sunne that through th'orizon peepes,
As pittying these lovers, downeward creepes.
So that in silence of the cloudie night,   585
Though it was morning, did he take his flight.
But what the secret trustie night conceal'd,
Leanders amorous habit soone reveal'd,
With *Cupids* myrtle was his bonet crownd,
About his armes the purple riband wound,   590
Wherewith she wreath'd her largely spreading heare,
Nor could the youth abstaine, but he must weare
The sacred ring wherewith she was endow'd,
When first religious chastitie she vow'd:
Which made his love through *Sestos* to bee knowne,   595
And thence unto *Abydus* sooner blowne,
Than he could saile, for incorporeal Fame,
Whose waight consists in nothing but her name,
Is swifter than the wind, whose tardie plumes,
Are reeking water, and dull earthlie fumes.   600
Home when he came, he seem'd not to be there,
But like exiled aire thrust from his sphere,
Set in a forren place, and straight from thence,
Alcides like, by mightie violence,
He would have chac'd away the swelling maine,   605
That him from her unjustly did detaine.
Like as the sunne in a Dyameter,
Fires and inflames objects remooved farre,

---

583. *th'orizon:* the horizon
588. *habit:* way of dressing
590. *riband:* ribbon
591. *she:* Hero; *largely:* loosely, widely
597. *Fame:* rumor
600. *reeking:* smoking, in a vaporlike way
602. *exiled . . . sphere:* air displaced from the sphere (in the Ptolemaic system) of the earth. A pun on "heir" is possible here.
603. *forren:* foreign
604. *Alcides:* Hercules
605. *maine:* sea
607. *in a Dyameter:* shining directly downward

And heateth kindly, shining lat'rally;
So beautie, sweetly quickens when t'is ny,   610
But being separated and remooved,
Burnes where it cherisht, murders where it loved.
Therefore even as an Index to a booke,
So to his mind was yoong *Leanders* looke.
O none but gods have power their love to hide,   615
Affection by the count'nance is describe.
The light of hidden fire it selfe discovers,
And love that is conceal'd, betraies poore lovers.
His secret flame apparantly was seene,
Leanders Father knew where hee had beene,   620
And for the same mildly rebuk't his sonne,
Thinking to quench the sparckles new begonne.
But love resisted once, growes passionate,
And nothing more than counsaile, lovers hate.
For as a hote prowd horse highly disdaines,   625
To have his head control'd, but breakes the raines,
Spits foorth the ringled bit, and with his hoves,
Checkes the submissive ground: so hee that loves,
The more he is restrain'd, the woorse he fares,
What is it now, but mad *Leander* dares?   630
O *Hero, Hero,* thus he cry'de full oft,
And then he got him to a rocke aloft.
Where having spy'de her tower, long star'd he on't,
And pray'd the narrow toyling *Hellespont,*
To part in twaine, that hee might come and go,   635
But still the rising billowes answered no.
With that hee stript him to the yv'rie skin,
And crying, Love I come, leapt lively in.

---

609. *heateth . . . lat'rally:* warms them naturally when it shines obliquely
upon them
610. *ny:* near
619. *apparantly:* plainly
627. *ringled:* with rings (on each end of the bit)
628. *Checkes:* Stamps on
630. *What . . . dares?:* What won't mad Leander do now?
634. *toyling:* aroused, agitated
638. *lively:* quickly

520

Whereat the saphir visag'd god grew prowd,
And made his capring *Triton* sound alowd, 640
Imagining, that *Ganimed* displeas'd,
Had left the heavens, therefore on him hee seaz'd.
Leander striv'd, the waves about him wound,
And puld him to the bottome, where the ground
Was strewd with pearle, and in low corrall groves, 645
Sweet singing Meremaids, sported with their loves
On heapes of heavie gold, and tooke great pleasure,
To spurne in carelesse sort, the shipwracke treasure.
For here the stately azure pallace stood,
Where kingly *Neptune* and his traine abode, 650
The lustie god imbrast him, cald him love,
And swore he never should returne to Jove.
But when he knew it was not *Ganimed*,
For underwater he was almost dead,
He heav'd him up, and looking on his face, 655
Beat downe the bold waves with his triple mace,
Which mounted up, intending to have kist him,
And fell in drops like teares, because they mist him.
Leander being up, began to swim,
And looking backe, saw *Neptune* follow him. 660
Whereat agast, the poore soule gan to crie,
O let mee visite *Hero* ere I die.
The god put *Helles* bracelet on his arme,
And swore the sea should never doe him harme.
He clapt his plumpe cheekes, with his tresses playd, 665
And smiling wantonly, his love bewrayed.
He watcht his armes, and as they opend wide,
At every stroke, betwixt them would he slide,

---

639. *saphir . . . god:* Neptune, with his green face
640. *capring Triton:* the capering son of Neptune who blows on a shell.
For Ganymede, see above, line 148 n.
648. *sort:* way; *shipwracke:* shipwrecked
650. *traine:* retinue
655. *heav'd:* lifted
663. *Helles:* the daughter of Athamas and Nephele, drowned in the
Hellespont, which was named after her. Some versions of the story say that
Neptune rescued her and that she had a son by him.
666. *bewrayed:* revealed

And steale a kisse, and then run out and daunce,
And as he turnd, cast many a lustfull glaunce, 670
And threw him gawdie toies to please his eie,
And dive into the water, and there prie
Upon his brest, his thighs, and everie lim,
And up againe, and close beside him swim.
And talke of love: *Leander* made replie, 675
You are deceav'd, I am no woman I,
Thereat smilde *Neptune*, and then told a tale,
How that a sheapheard sitting in a vale,
Playd with a boy so faire and kind,
As for his love, both earth and heaven pyn'd; 680
That of the cooling river durst not drinke,
Least water-nymphs should pull him from the brinke.
And when hee sported in the fragrant lawnes,
Gote-footed Satyrs, and up-staring Fawnes,
Would steale him thence. Ere halfe this tale was done, 685
Aye me, *Leander* cryde, th'enamoured sunne,
That now should shine on *Thetis* glasie bower,
Descends upon my radiant *Heroes* tower.
O that these tardie armes of mine were wings,
And as he spake, upon the waves he springs. 690
Neptune was angrie that hee gave no eare,
And in his heart revenging malice bare:
He flung at him his mace, but as it went,
He cald it in, for love made him repent.
The mace returning backe, his owne hand hit, 695
As meaning to be veng'd for darting it.
When this fresh bleeding wound *Leander* viewd,
His colour went and came, as if he rewd
The greefe which *Neptune* felt. In gentle brests,
Relenting thoughts, remorse and pittie rests. 700

---

671. *toies:* toys, perhaps ornaments like the bracelet
684. *up-staring Fawnes:* the Fauni were forest gods; the epithet, if not an error for "up-starting" (springing-up), may mean "looking up at the shepherd's boy"
687. *Thetis:* a sea nymph
692. *bare:* bore
696. *As . . . it:* As if it intended to revenge itself on Neptune for throwing it
698. *rewd:* rued

And who have hard hearts, and obdurat minds,
But vicious, harebraind, and illit'rat hinds?
The god seeing him with pittie to be moved,
Thereon concluded that he was beloved.
(Love is too full of faith, too credulous,   705
With follie and false hope deluding us.)
Wherefore *Leanders* fancie to surprize,
To the rich *Ocean* for gifts he flies.
'Tis wisedome to give much, a gift prevailes,
When deepe perswading Oratorie failes.   710
By this *Leander* being nere the land,
Cast downe his wearie feet, and felt the sand.
Breathlesse albeit he were, he rested not,
Till to the solitarie tower he got.
And knockt and cald, at which celestiall noise,   715
The longing heart of *Hero* much more joies
Then nymphs & sheapheards, when the timbrell rings,
Or crooked Dolphin when the sailer sings;
She stayd not for her robes, but straight arose,
And drunke with gladnesse, to the dore she goes. 720
Where seeing a naked man, she scriecht for feare,
Such sights as this, to tender maids are rare.
And ran into the darke her selfe to hide,
Rich jewels in the darke are soonest spide.
Unto her was he led, or rather drawne,   725
By those white limmes, which sparckled through the lawne.
The neerer that he came, the more she fled,
And seeking refuge, slipt into her bed.
Whereon *Leander* sitting, thus began,
Through numming cold, all feeble, faint and wan: 730
    If not for love, yet love for pittie sake,
Me in thy bed and maiden bosome take,

---

702. *hinds:* rude rustics
707. *surprize:* capture
717. *timbrell:* tambourine
718. *crooked Dolphin:* the musician Arion was saved from drowning by a dolphin; *crooked* (curved) refers to the fish's shape as it leaps from the water
721. *scriecht:* shrieked
726. *lawne:* her light, filmy garment

At least vouchsafe these armes some little roome,
Who hoping to imbrace thee, cherely swome.
This head was beat with manie a churlish billow,   735
And therefore let it rest upon thy pillow.
Herewith afrighted *Hero* shrunke away,
And in her luke-warme place *Leander* lay.
Whose lively heat like fire from heaven fet,
Would animate grosse clay, and higher set   740
The drooping thoughts of base declining soules,
Then drerie *Mars*, carowsing *Nectar* boules.
His hands he cast upon her like a snare,
She overcome with shame and sallow feare,
Like chast *Diana*, when *Acteon* spyde her,   745
Being sodainly betraide, dyv'd downe to hide her.
And as her silver body downeward went,
With both her hands she made the bed a tent,
And in her owne mind thought her selfe secure,
O'recast with dim and darksome coverture.   750
And now she lets him whisper in her eare,
Flatter, intreat, promise, protest and sweare,
Yet ever as he greedily assayd
To touch those dainties, she the *Harpey* playd,
And every lim did as a soldier stout,   755
Defend the fort, and keep the foe-man out.
For though the rising yv'rie mount he scal'd,
Which is with azure circling lines empal'd,
Much like a globe, (a globe may I tearme this,
By which love sailes to regions full of blis,)   760
Yet there with *Sysiphus* he toyld in vaine,
Till gentle parlie did the truce obtaine.

---

734. *cherely swome:* happily swam
737. *Herewith afrighted:* Frightened by these words
739. *lively:* vigorous; *fet:* fetched
742. *drerie:* bloody; *Nectar boules:* bowls of nectar
744. *sallow:* of a sickly yellow color
750. *coverture:* covering
754. *Harpey:* in Virgil's *Aeneid* (III, 225ff.) the monstrous Harpies snatch away a banquet from the Trojan sailors
758. *empal'd:* ornamented
761. *Sysiphus:* Sisyphus was condemned to roll a stone up a hill in hell; however much he tried, it always rolled down again

She trembling strove, this strife of hers (like that
Which made the world) another world begat,
Of unknowne joy. Treason was in her thought,   765
And cunningly to yeeld her selfe she sought.
Seeming not woon, yet woon she was at length,
In such warres women use but halfe their strength.
Leander now like Thebian *Hercules*,
Entred the orchard of *Th'esperides*.   770
Whose fruit none rightly can describe, but hee
That puls or shakes it from the golden tree:
Wherein *Leander* on her quivering brest,
Breathlesse spoke some thing, and sigh'd out the rest;
Which so prevail'd, as he with small ado,   775
Inclos'd her in his armes and kist her to.
And everie kisse to her was as a charme,
And to *Leander* as a fresh alarme.
So that the truce was broke, and she alas,
(Poore sillie maiden) at his mercie was.   780
Love is not ful of pittie (as men say)
But deaffe and cruell, where he meanes to pray.
Even as a bird, which in our hands we wring,
Foorth plungeth, and oft flutters with her wing.
And now she wisht this night were never done,   785
And sigh'd to thinke upon th'approching sunne,
For much it greev'd her that the bright day-light,
Should know the pleasure of this blessed night.
And then like *Mars* and *Ericine* displayd,
Both in each others armes chaind as they layd.   790

763-72. The order of the lines followed here is that of the original 1598
edition. Most modern editors rearrange the sequence so that lines 763-72
follow lines 773-84. The 1598 order can, however, be defended, especially
if one gives full weight to the possible contemporary meanings of *truce* in
lines 762 and 779. A pun on "trouse" (drawers, or knee breeches), the
singular of the later "trousers," is perhaps intended. The word could also
mean "bushwood."
770. *Th'esperides*: the gardens of the Hesperides. It was Hercules' task to
steal their golden fruit.
775. *small ado*: little trouble
778. *alarme*: call to arms
782. *pray*: prey
783. *wring*: hold
789. *Ericine*: Venus, who had a shrine on Mount Eryx. For her escapade
with Mars, see above, lines 151-52.

Againe she knew not how to frame her looke,
Or speake to him who in a moment tooke,
That which so long so charily she kept,
And faine by stealth away she would have crept,
And to some corner secretly have gone,   795
Leaving *Leander* in the bed alone.
But as her naked feet were whipping out,
He on the suddaine cling'd her so about,
That Meremaid-like unto the floore she slid,
One halfe appear'd the other halfe was hid.   800
Thus neere the bed she blushing stood upright,
And from her countenance behold ye might,
A kind of twilight breake, which through the heare,
As from an orient cloud, glymse here and there.
And round about the chamber this false morne,   805
Brought foorth the day before the day was borne.
So *Heroes* ruddie cheeke, *Hero* betrayd,
And her all naked to his sight displayd.
Whence his admiring eyes more pleasure tooke,
Than *Dis*, on heapes of gold fixing his looke.   810
By this *Apollos* golden harpe began,
To sound foorth musicke to the *Ocean*,
Which watchfull *Hesperus* no sooner heard,
But he the day bright-bearing Car prepar'd.
And ran before, as Harbenger of light,   815
And with his flaring beames mockt ougly night,
Till she o'recome with anguish, shame, and rage,
Dang'd downe to hell her loathsome carriage.
          Desunt nonnulla.

---

798. *cling'd:* clasped
803. *heare:* hair
804. *orient cloud:* an early-morning cloud; *glymse:* gleams, glimmers. Some
editors emend to *glimpsed.*
810. *Dis:* the god of riches
813. *Hesperus:* Venus, as the evening star: apparently an error by Marlowe
for Lucifer, the morning star
814. *day . . . Car:* the chariot of the dawn, which brings brightness
818. *Dang'd:* Hurled
819. *Desunt nonnulla:* "Some things are lacking." Obviously a comment by
the printer of 1598, Edward Blunt.

THOMAS CAMPION

1567–1620

From A Booke of Ayres (1601)

1.

My sweetest Lesbia, let us live and love,
And, though the sager sort our deedes reprove,
Let us not way them: heav'ns great lampes doe dive
Into their west, and strait againe revive,
But, soone as once set is our little light,   5
Then must we sleepe one ever-during night.

If all would lead their lives in love like mee,
Then bloudie swords and armour should not be,
No drum nor trumpet peaceful sleepes should move,
Unles alar'me came from the campe of love: 10
But fooles do live, and wast their little light,
And seeke with paine their ever-during night.

When timely death my life and fortune ends,
Let not my hearse be vext with mourning friends,
But let all lovers, rich in triumph, come,   15
And with sweet pastimes grace my happie tombe;
And, Lesbia, close up thou my little light,
And crowne with love my ever-during night.

---

1. *Lesbia:* this lyric is based on Catullus, V, "Vivamus, mea Lesbia, atque amemus"
3. *way:* weigh, consider
6. *ever-during:* everlasting

2.

I care not for these Ladies
That must be woode and praide,
Give me kind Amarillis
The wanton countrey maide;
Nature art disdaineth,   5
Her beautie is her owne;
    Her when we court and kisse,
    She cries, forsooth, let go:
    But when we come where comfort is,
    She never will say no.   10

If I love Amarillis,
She gives me fruit and flowers,
But if we love these Ladies,
We must give golden showers;
Give them gold that sell love,   15
Give me the Nutbrowne lasse,
    Who when we court and kisse,
    She cries, forsooth, let go:
    But when we come where comfort is,
    She never will say no.   20

These Ladies must have pillowes,
And beds by strangers wrought,
Give me a Bower of willowes,
Of mosse and leaves unbought,
And fresh Amarillis,   25
With milke and honie fed,
    Who when we court and kisse,
    She cries, forsooth, let go:
    But when we come where comfort is,
    She never will say no.   30

---

2. *woode and praide*: wooed and begged

3.

Followe thy faire sunne, unhappy shaddowe:
Though thou be blacke as night,
And she made all of light,
Yet follow thy faire sunne, unhappie shaddowe.

Follow her whose light thy light depriveth: 5
Though here thou liv'st disgrac't,
And she in heaven is plac't,
Yet follow her whose light the world reviveth.

Follow those pure beames whose beautie burneth,
That so have scorched thee,   10
As thou still blacke must bee,
Til her kind beames thy black to brightnes turneth.

Follow her while yet her glorie shineth:
There comes a luckles night,
That will dim all her light;   15
And this the black unhappie shade devineth.

Follow still since so thy fates ordained:
The Sunne must have his shade,
Till both at once doe fade,
The Sun still prov'd, the shadow still disdained.   20

4.

When to her lute Corrina sings,
Her voice revives the leaden stringes,
And doth in highest noates appeare
As any challeng'd eccho cleere;
But when she doth of mourning speake,   5
Ev'n with her sighes the strings do breake.

20. *prov'd:* approved
2. *leaden:* heavy
4. *challeng'd:* aroused

And, as her lute doth live or die,
Led by her passion, so must I:
For when of pleasure she doth sing,
My thoughts enjoy a sodaine spring;   10
But if she doth of sorrow speake,
Ev'n from my hart the strings doe breake.

5.

Follow your Saint, follow with accents sweet,
Haste you, sad noates, fall at her flying feete;
There, wrapt in cloud of sorrowe, pitie move,
And tell the ravisher of my soule I perish for her love.
But if she scorns my never-ceasing paine,   5
Then burst with sighing in her sight, and nere returne againe.

All that I soong still to her praise did tend,
Still she was first, still she my songs did end.
Yet she my love and Musicke both doeth flie,
The Musicke that her Eccho is, and beauties simpathie;   10
Then let my Noates pursue her scornefull flight:
It shall suffice that they were breath'd, and dyed, for her delight.

6.

Thou art not faire, for all thy red and white,
For all those rosie ornaments in thee;
Thou art not sweet, though made of meer delight,
Nor faire nor sweet, unlesse thou pitie mee.
I will not sooth thy fancies: thou shalt prove   5
That beauty is no beautie without love.

Yet love not me, nor seeke thou to allure
My thoughts with beautie, were it more devine;
Thy smiles and kisses I cannot endure,
I'le not be wrapt up in those armes of thine.   10

---

7. *still*: always
5. *prove*: discover

Now shew it, if thou be a woman right:
Embrace, and kisse, and love me, in despight.

7.

Blame not my cheeks, though pale with love they be;
The kindly heate unto my heart is flowne,
To cherish it that is dismaid by thee,
Who art so cruell and unsteedfast growne:
For nature, cald for by distressed harts,   5
Neglects and quite forsakes the outward partes.

But they whose cheekes with careles blood are stain'd
Nurse not one sparke of love within their harts,
And, when they woe, they speake with passion fain'd,
For their fat love lyes in their outward parts: 10
But in their brests, where love his court should hold,
Poore Cupid sits and blowes his nailes for cold.

8.

The man of life upright,
    Whose guiltlesse hart is free
From all dishonest deedes,
    Or thought of vanitie,

The man whose silent dayes   5
    In harmeles joyes are spent,
Whome hopes cannot delude,
    Nor sorrow discontent,

That man needes neither towers
    Nor armour for defence,   10
Nor secret vautes to flie
    From thunders violence.

---

2. *kindly*: natural
1. *The . . . upright*: a paraphrase of Horace's famous "Integer vitae"
(*Odes*, I, 22)
11. *vautes to flie*: vaults to flee to

Hee onely can behold
   With unafrighted eyes
The horrours of the deepe,   15
   And terrours of the Skies.

Thus, scorning all the cares
   That fate, or fortune brings,
He makes the heav'n his booke,
   His wisedome heev'nly things,   20

Good thoughts his onely friendes,
   His wealth a well-spent age,
The earth his sober Inne,
   And quiet Pilgrimage.

9.

Harke, al you ladies that do sleep:
   The fayry queen Proserpina
Bids you awake and pitie them that weep;
   You may doe in the darke
What the day doth forbid:
   Feare not the dogs that barke,   5
      Night will have all hid.

But if you let your lovers mone,
   The Fairie Queene Proserpina
Will send abroad her Fairies ev'rie one,   10
   That shall pinch blacke and blew
Your white hands, and faire armes,
   That did not kindly rue
      Your Paramours harmes.

In Myrtle Arbours on the downes,   15
   The Fairie Queene Proserpina,
This night by moone-shine leading merrie rounds,
   Holds a watch with sweet love;

---

13. *rue:* take pity on
17. *rounds:* dances in a ring

Downe the dale, up the hill,
  No plaints or groanes may move   20
     Their holy vigill.

All you that will hold watch with love,
  The Fairie Queene Prosperpina
Will make you fairer then Diones dove;
  Roses red, Lillies white,   25
And the cleare damaske hue,
  Shall on your cheekes alight:
     Love will adorne you.

All you that love, or lov'd before,
  The Fairie Queene Proserpina   30
Bids you encrease that loving humour more:
  They that yet have not fed
On delight amorous,
  She vowes that they shall lead
     Apes in Avernus.   35

10.

When thou must home to shades of under ground,
And there ariv'd, a newe admired guest,
The beauteous spirits do ingirt thee round,
White Iope, blith Hellen, and the rest,
To heare the stories of thy finisht love,   5
From that smoothe toong whose musicke hell can move:

Then wilt thou speake of banqueting delights,
Of masks and revels which sweete youth did make,
Of Turnies and great challenges of knights,
And all these triumphes for thy beauties sake: 10

---

24. *Diones dove:* Dione was the mother of Venus, to whom the dove was sacred. An earlier printing of this poem read *Dianas.*
26. *damaske:* pink
35. *Apes in Avernus:* "to lead apes in hell" was a proverbial punishment for old maids
4. *Iope:* mentioned by Propertius (II, 28, 51), whose poem serves as Campion's source
9. *Turnies:* Tournaments

When thou hast told these honours done to thee,
Then tell, O tell, how thou didst murther me.

From *Two Bookes of Ayres* (c. 1613)

11.

Author of light, revive my dying spright,
Redeeme it from the snares of all-confounding night.
    Lord, light me to thy blessed way:
For, blinde with worldly vaine desires, I wander as a stray.
    Sunne and Moone, Starres and underlights I see,   5
But all their glorious beames are mists and darknes, being
    compar'd to thee.

Fountaine of health, my soules deepe wounds recure,
Sweet showres of pitty raine, wash my uncleannesse pure.
    One drop of thy desired grace
The faint and fading hart can raise, and in joyes bosome
    place.   10
    Sinne and Death, Hell and tempting Fiends may rage;
But God his owne will guard, and their sharp paines and griefe
    in time asswage.

12.

To Musicke bent is my retyred minde,
And faine would I some song of pleasure sing:
But in vaine joyes no comfort now I finde:
From heav'nly thoughts all true delight doth spring.
Thy power, O God, thy mercies to record   5
Will sweeten ev'ry note, and ev'ry word.

---

1. *spright:* spirit
5. *underlights:* lesser lights
7. *recure:* remedy
5–6. *Thy . . . word:* i.e., every note and word will be sweetened if they
record God's power and mercies

All earthly pompe or beauty to expresse,
Is but to carve in snow, on waves to write.
Celestiall things, though men conceive them lesse,
Yet fullest are they in themselves of light: 10
Such beames they yeeld as know no meanes to dye:
Such heate they cast as lifts the Spirit high.

13.

Tune thy Musicke to thy hart,
Sing thy joy with thankes, and so thy sorrow:
  Though Devotion needes not Art,
Sometime of the poore the rich may borrow.

Strive not yet for curious wayes: 5
Concord pleaseth more, the lesse 'tis strained;
  Zeale affects not outward prayse,
Onely strives to shew a love unfained.

Love can wondrous things effect,
Sweetest Sacrifice, all wrath appeasing;   10
  Love the highest doth respect,
Love alone to him is ever pleasing.

14.

Come, chearfull day, part of my life, to mee:
For, while thou view'st me with thy fading light,
Part of my life doth still depart with thee,
And I still onward haste to my last night.
  Times fatall wings doe ever forward flye,   5
  Soe ev'ry day we live, a day wee dye.

But, O yee nights ordain'd for barren rest,
How are my dayes depriv'd of life in you,
When heavy sleepe my soule hath dispossest,
By fayned death life sweetly to renew!   10

---

5. *curious:* elaborate, artful
7. *affects:* desires

Part of my life, in that, you life denye:
So ev'ry day we live, a day wee dye.

15.

Jacke and *Jone*, they thinke no ill,
But loving live, and merry still;
Doe their weeke dayes worke, and pray
Devotely on the holy day;
Skip and trip it on the greene,   5
And help to chuse the Summer Queene;
Lash out, at a Country Feast,
Their silver penny with the best.

Well can they judge of nappy Ale,
And tell at large a Winter tale;   10
Climbe up to the Apple loft,
And turne the Crabs till they be soft.
Tib is all the fathers joy,
And little *Tom* the mothers boy.
All their pleasure is content;   15
And care, to pay their yearely rent.

Jone can call by name her Cowes,
And decke her windowes with greene boughs;
Shee can wreathes and tuttyes make,
And trimme with plums a Bridall Cake.   20
Jacke knowes what brings gaine or losse,
And his long Flaile can stoutly tosse;
Make the hedge, which others breake,
And ever thinkes what he doth speake.

Now, you Courtly Dames and Knights,   25
That study onely strange delights,

---

2. *still:* always
7. *Lash:* Fling
9. *nappy:* strong
12. *Crabs:* crab apples
19. *tuttyes:* nosegays
23. *others breake:* i.e., the nobility, who break the hedges while hunting

Though you scorne the home-spun gray,
And revell in your rich array;
Though your tongues dissemble deepe,
And can your heads from danger keepe;   30
Yet, for all your pompe and traine,
Securer lives the silly Swaine.

16.

Harden now thy tyred hart with more then flinty rage;
Ne'er let her false teares henceforth thy constant griefe asswage.
Once true happy dayes thou saw'st, when shee stood firme and
    kinde,
Both as one then liv'd, and held one eare, one tongue, one
    minde.
But now those bright houres be fled, and never may
    returne: 5
What then remaines, but her untruths to mourne?

Silly Tray-tresse, who shall now thy carelesse tresses place?
Who thy pretty talke supply? whose eare thy musicke grace?
Who shall thy bright eyes admire? what lips triumph with
    thine?
Day by day who'll visit thee and say, th' art onely mine?   10
Such a time there was, God wot, but such shall never be:
Too oft, I feare, thou wilt remember me.

17.

Give beauty all her right,
Shee's not to one forme tyed;
Each shape yeelds faire delight,
Where her perfections bide.
Hellen, I grant, might pleasing be;   5
And *Ros'mond* was as sweet as shee.

---

1. *Harden now*: based on Catullus, VIII, 11–18, "sed obstinata mente
perfer, obdura etc."
7. *Tray-tresse*: Traitoress, with a pun on "tresses"
11. *wot*: knows
6. *Ros'mond*: Rosamond Clifford, the mistress of Henry II. As "the fair
Rosamond" she became a heroine for Elizabethan poets.

Some the quicke eye commends,
Some smelling lips and red;
Pale lookes have many friends,
Through sacred sweetnesse bred.
Medowes have flowres that pleasure move,
Though Roses are the flowres of love.

Free beauty is not bound
To one unmoved clime:
She visits ev'ry ground,
And favours ev'ry time.
Let the old loves with mine compare,
My sov'raigne is as sweet, and fayre.

18.

Though your strangenesse frets my hart,
Yet may not I complaine:
You perswade me, 'tis but Art,
That secret love must faine.
If another you affect,
'Tis but a shew t' avoid suspect.
Is this faire excusing? O no, all is abusing.

Your wisht sight if I desire,
Suspitions you pretend;
Causelesse you your selfe retire,
While I in vaine attend.
This a Lover whets, you say,
Still made more eager by delay.
Is this faire excusing? O no, all is abusing.

When another holds your hand,
You sweare I hold your hart:
When my Rivals close doe stand
And I sit farre apart,

---

8. *smelling:* sweetly smelling
5. *affect:* favor
6. *suspect:* suspicion

I am neerer yet then they,
Hid in your bosome, as you say.   20
Is this faire excusing? O no, all is abusing.

Would my Rival then I were,
Some els your secret friend:
So much lesser should I feare,
And not so much attend.   25
They enjoy you, ev'ry one,
Yet I must seeme your friend alone.
Is this faire excusing? O no, all is abusing.

19.

A secret love or two, I must confesse,
    I kindly welcome for change in close playing:
Yet my deare husband I love ne'erthelesse,
    His desires, whole or halfe, quickly allaying,
At all times ready to offer redresse.   5
    His owne he never wants, but hath it duely,
    Yet twits me, I keepe not touch with him truly.

The more a spring is drawne, the more it flowes;
    No Lampe lesse light retaines by lighting others:
Is hee a looser his losse that ne're knowes?   10
    Or is he wealthy that wast treasure smothers?
My churle vowes no man shall sent his sweet Rose:
    His owne enough and more I give him duely,
    Yet still he twits mee, I keepe not touch truly.

Wise Archers beare more then one shaft to field, 15
    The Venturer loads not with one ware his shipping:

---

19. *then:* than
23. *Some:* Someone; *friend:* lover
2. *close:* secret. This poem recalls the Prologue of Chaucer's Wife of Bath
7. *keepe not touch:* don't live up to my part of the bargain
12. *sent:* scent
16. *Venturer:* speculative merchant

Should Warriers learne but one weapon to weilde?
   Or thrive faire plants ere the worse for the slipping?
One dish cloyes, many fresh appetite yeeld:
     Mine owne Ile use, and his he shall have duely,   20
     Judge then what debter can keepe touch more truly.

From *The Third and Fourth Booke of Ayres* (c. 1617)

20.

Were my hart as some mens are, thy errours would not move
    me:
But thy faults I curious finde, and speake because I love thee;
Patience is a thing divine and farre, I grant, above mee.

Foes sometimes befriend us more, our blacker deedes
    objecting,
Then th' obsequious bosome guest, with false respect
    affecting:
Friendship is the glasse of Truth, our hidden staines detecting. 5

While I use of eyes enjoy, and inward light of reason,
Thy observer will I be, and censor, but in season:
Hidden mischiefe to conceale in State and Love is treason.

21.

Breake now my heart and dye! Oh no, she may relent.
Let my despaire prevayle! Oh stay, hope is not spent.
Should she now fixe one smile on thee, where were despaire?
    The losse is but easie which smiles can repayre.
    A stranger would please thee, if she were as fayre.   5

Her must I love or none, so sweet none breathes as shee;
The more is my despayre, alas, shee loves not mee:

---

18. *ere:* ever; *slipping:* cutting, taking slips from
1. *errours:* transgressions
2. *curious:* strange
8. *observer:* follower

But cannot time make way for love through ribs of steele?
    The Grecian, inchanted all parts but the heelc,
    At last a shaft daunted, which his hart did feele.   10

22.

Now winter nights enlarge
    The number of their houres,
And clouds their stormes discharge
    Upon the ayrie towres;
Let now the chimneys blaze   5
    And cups o'erflow with wine,
Let well-tun'd words amaze
    With harmonie divine.
Now yellow waxen lights
    Shall waite on hunny Love,   10
While youthfull Revels, Masks, and Courtly sights,
    Sleepes leaden spels remove.

This time doth well dispence
    With lovers long discourse;
Much speech hath some defence,   15
    Though beauty no remorse.
All doe not all things well:
    Some measures comely tread,
Some knotted Ridles tell,
    Some Poems smoothly read.   20
The Summer hath his joyes,
    And Winter his delights;
Though Love and all his pleasures are but toyes,
    They shorten tedious nights.

23.

Shall I come, sweet Love, to thee,
    When the ev'ning beames are set?

---

9. *Grecian:* Achilles, who was magically protected in all parts but the heel,
which Paris' arrow pierced
10. *hunny:* honey
13–14. *dispence With:* allow

Shall I not excluded be?
>> Will you finde no fained lett?
>>> Let me not, for pitty, more,
>>> Tell the long houres at your dore.

Who can tell what theefe or foe,
>> In the covert of the night,
For his prey, will worke my woe,
>> Or through wicked foule despight:
>>> So may I dye unredrest,
>>> Ere my long love be possest.

But, to let such dangers passe,
>> Which a lovers thoughts disdaine,
'Tis enough in such a place
>> To attend loves joyes in vaine.
>>> Doe not mocke me in thy bed,
>>> While these cold nights freeze me dead.

24.

>> Be thou then my beauty named,
Since thy will is to be mine:
>> For by that am I enflamed,
Which on all alike doth shine.
>>> Others may the light admire,
>>> I onely truely feele the fire.

>> But, if lofty titles move thee,
Challenge then a Sov'raignes place:
>> Say I honour when I love thee,
Let me call thy kindnesse grace.
>>> State and Love things divers bee,
>>> Yet will we teach them to agree.

---

4. *lett*: hindrance
6. *Tell*: Count
8. *Challenge*: Claim

Or, if this be not sufficing,
Be thou stil'd my Goddesse then:
   I will love thee sacrificing,   15
In thine honour Hymnes Ile pen.
      To be thine, what canst thou more?
      Ile love thee, serve thee, and adore.

25.

Never love unlesse you can
Beare with all the faults of man:
Men sometimes will jealous bee
Though but little cause they see,
   And hang the head, as discontent,   5
   And speake what straight they will repent.

Men that but one Saint adore
Make a shew of love to more:
Beauty must be scorn'd in none,
Though but truely serv'd in one: 10
   For what is courtship, but disguise?
   True hearts may have dissembling eyes.

Men, when their affaires require,
Must a while themselves retire:
Sometimes hunt, and sometimes hawke,   15
And not ever sit and talke.
   If these, and such like, you can beare,
   Then like, and love, and never feare.

26.

   Shall I then hope when faith is fled?
Can I seeke love when hope is gone?
   Or can I live when Love is dead?
Poorely hee lives, that can love none.
      Her vowes are broke, and I am free;   5
      Shee lost her faith in loosing mee.

---

17. *what . . . more?*: what more can you want?

544

When I compare mine owne events,
When I weigh others like annoy,
   All doe but heape up discontents
That on a beauty build their joy.   10
      Thus I of all complaine, since shee
      All faith hath lost in loosing mee.

So my deare freedome have I gain'd
Through her unkindnesse and disgrace;
   Yet could I ever live enchain'd,
As shee my service did embrace.   15
      But shee is chang'd, and I am free:
      Faith failing her, Love dyed in mee.

27.

There is a Garden in her face,
Where Roses and white Lillies grow;
   A heav'nly paradice is that place,
Wherein all pleasant fruits doe flow.
      There Cherries grow, which none may buy   5
      Till Cherry ripe themselves doe cry.

Those Cherries fayrely doe enclose
Of Orient Pearle a double row,
   Which when her lovely laughter showes,
They looke like Rose-buds fill'd with snow.   10
      Yet them nor Peere nor Prince can buy,
      Till Cherry ripe themselves doe cry.

Her Eyes like Angels watch them still;
Her Browes like bended bowes doe stand,
   Threatning with piercing frownes to kill   15
All that attempt with eye or hand

7. *events:* fate
16. *As:* As long as
6. *Cherry ripe:* the cry of the London street vendors; *cry:* both "cry out" and "offer for sale"
13. *watch:* guard

Those sacred Cherries to come high,
Till Cherry ripe themselves doe cry.

28.

Are you what your faire lookes expresse?
    Oh then be kinde:
From law of Nature they digresse
    Whose forme sutes not their minde:
  Fairenesse seene in th' outward shape   5
  Is but th' inward beauties Ape.

Eyes that of earth are mortall made,
    What can they view?
All's but a colour or a shade,
    And neyther alwayes true.   10
  Reasons sight, that is eterne,
  Ev'n the substance can discerne.

Soule is the Man; for who will so
    The body name?
And to that power all grace we owe   15
    That deckes our living frame.
  What, or how, had housen bin,
  But for them that dwell therein?

Love in the bosome is begot,
    Not in the eyes;   20
No beauty makes the eye more hot,
    Her flames the spright surprise:
  Let our loving mindes then meete,
  For pure meetings are most sweet.

---

3. *digresse:* swerve
6. *Ape:* mimic
17. *had housen bin:* were houses for
22. *spright:* soul

29.

I must complain, yet doe enjoy my Love;
She is too faire, too rich in lovely parts:
Thence is my grief, for Nature, while she strove
With all her graces and divinest Arts
    To form her too too beautifull of hue,   5
    Shee had no leasure left to make her true.

Should I, agriev'd, then wish shee were lesse fayre?
That were repugnant to mine owne desires:
Shee is admir'd, new lovers still repayre;
That kindles daily loves forgetfull fires.   10
    Rest, jealous thoughts, and thus resolve at last:
    Shee hath more beauty then becomes the chast.

From *Observations* (1602)

30.

Raving warre, begot
In the thirstye sands
Of the *Lybian* Iles,
Wasts our emptye fields;
What the greedye rage   5
Of fell wintrye stormes
Could not turne to spoile,
Fierce *Bellona* now
Hath laid desolate,
Voyd of fruit, or hope.   10
Th' eger thriftye hinde,
Whose rude toyle reviv'd
Our skie-blasted earth,

---

10. *That:* i.e., jealousy of the new lovers
1. *Raving warre:* Campion offers this poem as an example of "Iambick
dimeter . . . a peece of a *Chorus* in a Tragedy"
8. *Bellona:* goddess of war
11. *hinde:* farm laborer

Himselfe is but earth,
Left a skorne to fate   15
Through seditious armes:
And that soile, alive
Which he duly nurst,
Which him duly fed,
Dead his body feeds: 20
Yet not all the glebe
His tuffe hands manur'd
Now one turfe affords
His poore funerall.
Thus still needy lives,   25
Thus still needy dyes
Th' unknowne multitude.

An Elegye

31.

Constant to none, but ever false to me,
    Traiter still to love through thy faint desires,
Not hope of pittie now nor vaine redresse
    Turns my griefs to teares, and renu'd laments.
Too well thy empty vowes, and hollow thoughts   5
    Witnes both thy wrongs, and remorseles hart.
Rue not my sorrow, but blush at my name;
    Let thy bloudy cheeks guilty thoughts betray.
My flames did truly burne, thine made a shew,
    As fires painted are which no heate retayne,   10
Or as the glossy *Pirop* faines to blaze,
    But, toucht, cold appeares, and an earthy stone.
True cullours deck thy cheeks, false foiles thy brest,
    Frailer then thy light beawty is thy minde.

---

21. *glebe:* soil
22. *tuffe:* tough
Title: offered as an example of "Elegeick" verse, in imitation of classical elegaics.
11. *Pirop:* red bronze

None canst thou long refuse, nor long affect,   15
    But turn'st feare with hopes, sorrow with delight,
Delaying, and deluding ev'ry way
    Those whose eyes are once with thy beawty chain'd.
Thrice happy man that entring first thy love
    Can so guide the straight raynes of his desires,   20
That both he can regard thee, and refraine:
    If grac't, firme he stands, if not, easely falls.

32.

    Rose-cheekt *Lawra*, come,
Sing thou smoothly with thy beawties
Silent musick, either other
        Sweetely gracing.
    Lovely formes do flowe   5
From concent devinely framed;
Heav'n is musick, and thy beawties
        Birth is heavenly.
    These dull notes we sing
Discords neede for helps to grace them;   10
Only beawty purely loving
        Knowes no discord:
    But still mooves delight,
Like cleare springs renu'd by flowing,
Ever perfect, ever in them-
        selves eternall.   15

---

15. *affect:* favor
16. *turn'st:* alternate
1. *Rose-cheekt:* offered as an example of "The English Sappick"
6. *concent:* agreement, harmony

From Richard Alison's *An Howres Recreation in Musicke* (1606)

33.

What if a day, or a month, or a yeare
Crown thy delights with a thousand sweet contentings?
Cannot a chance of a night or an howre
Crosse thy desires with as many sad tormentings?
    Fortune, honor, beauty, youth   5
    Are but blossoms dying;
    Wanton pleasure, doating love,
    Are but shadowes flying.
    All our joyes are but toyes,
    Idle thoughts deceiving;   10
    None have power of an howre
    In their lives bereaving.

Earthes but a point to the world, and a man
Is but a point to the worlds compared centure:
Shall then a point of a point be so vaine   15
As to triumph in a seely points adventure?
    All is hassard that we have,
    There is nothing biding;
    Dayes of pleasure are like streames
    Through faire meadowes gliding.   20
    Weale and woe, time doth goe,
    Time is never turning:
    Secret fates guide our states,
    Both in mirth and mourning.

For a full discussion of the authorship of this poem, usually attributed to Campion, see Davis' edition, p. 507.
12. *bereaving*: vanishing
14. *centure*: center
16. *in . . . adventure*: in the chance of a single point
21. *Weale*: Happiness
22. *turning*: i.e., turning back

THE SONNETEERS

THOMAS WATSON

c. 1557–92

From *Hekatompathia* (1582)

1.

This passion is all framed in manner of a dialogue,
wherein the Author talketh with his owne heart,
beeing nowe through the commandement and
force of love separated from his bodie miracu-
louslie, and against nature, to follow his mistres,   5
in hope, by long attendance upon her, to pur-
chase in the end her love and favour, and by that
meanes to make him selfe all one with her owne
hearte.

Speake gentle heart, where is thy dwelling place?   10
With her, whose birth the heavens themselves have blest.
What dost thou there? Somtimes behold her face,
And lodge sometimes within her cristall brest:
        She cold, thou hot, how can you then agree?
        Not nature now, but love doth governe me.   15
With her wilt thou remaine, and let mee die?
If I returne, wee both shall die for griefe:
If still thou staye, what good shall growe thereby?
Ile move her heart to purchase thy reliefe:
        What if her heart be hard, and stop his eares?   20
        Ile sigh aloud, and make him soft with teares:

Title: Watson's sequence of one hundred "sonnets" has as its subtitle "Or
Passionate Centurie of Love." Each of the eighteen-line poems is accom-
panied by an introductory commentary. The poems selected here are
numbers 3 and 14 in the original. In 1593 Watson's *Tears of Fancie,* an-
other sequence, was published. The best modern edition of *Hekatompathia*
is that of S. K. Heninger, Jr. (Scholars' Facsimiles and Reprints, Gaines-
ville, Fla., 1964).
20. *his:* its

554

If that prevaile, wilte thou returne from thence?
Not I alone, her heart shall come with mee:
Then will you both live under my defence?
So long as life will let us both agree: 25
   Why then dispaire, goe packe thee hence away,
   I live in hope to have a golden daie.

2.

The Authour still pursuing his invention upon the
song of his Mistres, in the last staffe of this sonnet
he falleth into this fiction: that whilest he greed-
elie laied open his eares to the hearing of his
Ladies voice, as one more then halfe in a doubt,   5
that *Apollo* him selfe had beene at hand, Love e-
spiyng a time of advantage, transformed him selfe
into the substance of aier, and so deceitfullie
entered into him with his owne great goodwill
and desire, and nowe by mayne force still hol-   10
deth his possession.

Some that reporte great *Alexanders* life,
They say, that harmonie so mov'd his mind,
That oft he roase from meat to warlike strife
At sounde of Trumpe, or noyse of battle kind,   15
   And then, that musickes force of softer vaine
   Caus'd him returne from strokes to meat againe.
And as for me, I thinke it nothing strange,
That musick having birth from heav'ns above,
By divers tunes can make the minde to change: 20
For I my selfe in hearing my sweete Love,
   By vertue of her song both tasted griefe,
   And such delight, as yeelded some reliefe.
When first I gan to give attentive eare,
Thinking *Apolloes* voice did haunte the place,   25
I little thought my Lady had beene there:
But whilest mine eares lay open in this case,
   Transform'd to ayre Love entred with my will,
   And nowe perforce doth keepe possession still.

---

2. *staffe*: i.e., six-line stanza

THOMAS LODGE

c. 1558–1625

From *PHILLIS, Honoured with Pastorall Sonnets,
Elegies, and amourous delights* (1593)

1.

Devoide of reason, thrale to foolish ire,
I walke and chase a savage fairie still,
Now neere the flood, straight on the mounting hill,
Now midst the woodes of youth, and vaine desire:
For leash I beare a cord of carefull griefe,   5
For brach I lead an over forward minde,
My houndes are thoughtes, and rage dispairing blind,
Paine, crueltie, and care without reliefe:
But they perceiving that my swift pursute,
My flying fairie cannot overtake,   10
With open mouthes their pray on me do make,
Like hungrie houndes that lately lost their suite.
And full of furie on their maister feede,
To hasten on my haplesse death with speede.

2.

I would in rich and golden coloured raine,
With tempting showers in pleasant sort discend,

1ff. A great many of the sonnets in Lodge's collection are translations from
the French. The two poems given here (numbers 31 and 34 in the original)
are versions of Ronsard, *Amours*, I, 120 and I, 20; *thrale*: thrall
6. *brach*: female hunting dog
12. *suite*: scent, quarry
1. *raine*: Zeus wooed Danae by changing himself into a shower of gold. He
carried off Europa by appearing to her in the form of a white bull (line 5).
For another sonnet on this theme, see below, Barnes, No. 1.

Into faire *Phillis* lappe (my lovely friend)
When sleepe hir sence with slomber doth restraine.
I would be chaunged to a milk-white Bull,   5
When midst the gladsome fieldes she should appeare,
By pleasant finenes to surprise my deere,
Whilest from their stalkes, she pleasant flowers did pull:
I were content to wearie out my paine,
To bee *Narsissus* so she were a spring   10
To drowne in hir those woes my heart do wring:
And more I wish transformed to remaine:
That whilest I thus in pleasures lappe did lye,
I might refresh desire, which else would die.

GILES FLETCHER THE ELDER
1546–1611

From *Licia* (1593)

1.

I wish sometimes, although a worthlesse thing,
Spurd by ambition, glad for to aspyre,
My selfe a Monarch, or some mightie King:
And then my thoughtes doe wish for to be hyer.
But when I view what windes the Cedars tosse, 5
What stormes men feele that covet for renowne,
I blame my selfe that I have wisht my losse,
And scorne a kingdome, though it give a crowne.
A' Licia thou, the wonder of my thought,
My heartes content, procurer of my blisse, 10
For whome a crowne, I doe esteme as nought,
And Asias wealth, too meane to buy a kisse;
    Kisse me sweete love, this favour doe for me:
    Then Crownes and Kingdomes shall I scorne for thee.

2.

In tyme the strong and statelie turrets fall,
In tyme the Rose, and silver Lillies die,
In tyme the Monarchs captives are and thrall,
In tyme the sea, and rivers are made drie:

1ff. The sonnets selected from *Licia* are numbers 12, 28, and 47 in the
original edition. The best modern edition of Fletcher's works is that of
Lloyd E. Berry, *The English Works of Giles Fletcher the Elder* (Madison,
Wisconsin, University of Wisconsin Press, 1964).
9. A': Ah

The hardest flint, in tyme doth melt asunder,   5
Still living fame, in tyme doth fade away,
The mountaines proud, we see in tyme come under,
And earth for age, we see in tyme decay:
The sunne in tyme, forgets for to retire,
From out the east, where he was woont to rise,   10
The basest thoughtes, we see in time aspire,
And greedie minds, in tyme do wealth dispise,
    Thus all (sweet faire) in tyme must have an end:
    Except thy beautie, vertues, and thy friend.

3.

Lyke Memnons rocke toucht, with the rising Sunne,
Which yeelds a sownd, and ecchoes foorth a voice:
But when its drownde, in westerne seas is dunne,
And drousie lyke, leaves off to make a noise.
So I (my love) inlightned with your shyne,   5
A Poets skill within my soule I shroud,
Not rude lyke that, which finer wittes declyne,
But such as Muses to the best allowde.
But when your figure, and your shape is gone,
I speechlesse am, lyke as I was before: 10
Or if I write, my verse is fill'd with moane,
And blurd with teares, by falling in such store.
    Then muse not (Licia) if my Muse be slacke,
    For when I wrote, I did thy beautie lacke.

---

1. *Memnons rocke*: the statue of Amenophis III at Thebes was called that
of Memnon, an Ethiopian prince who fought with Priam at Troy. It is
said to have produced a musical murmur when touched by the rising sun.
3. *its*: i.e., "the sun is"; *dunne*: dark

BARNABE BARNES

c. 1569–1609

From *Parthenophil and Parthenope* (1593)

1.

Jove for Europaes love tooke shape of Bull,
And for Calisto playde Dianaes parte
And in a golden shower, he filled full
The lappe of Danae with coelestiall arte,
Would I were chang'd but to my mistresse gloves,   5
That those white lovely fingers I might hide,
That I might kisse those hands, which mine hart loves
Or else that cheane of pearle, her neckes vaine pride,
Made proude with her neckes vaines, that I might folde
About that lovely necke, and her pappes tickle,   10
Or her to compasse like a belt of golde,
Or that sweet wine, which downe her throate doth trickle,
To kisse her lippes, and lye next at her hart,
Runne through her vaynes, and passe by pleasures part.

2.

Ah sweet content, where is thy mylde abode?
Is it with shepheardes and light-harted swaynes?
Which sing upon the downes and pype abroade
Tending their flockes and cattell on the playnes?

---

1 ff. The sonnets selected are numbers 63 and 66 in the original edition.
Barnes also published a sequence of religious sonnets (A *Divine Century of
Spiritual Sonnets*) in 1595.
2. *Calisto:* Callisto, one of Diana's nymphs. Wooed by Jupiter, she became
the mother of Arcas, the legendary ancestor of the Arcadians.
8. *cheane:* chain

Ah sweet content, where doest thou safely rest?   5
In heaven, with Angels which the prayses sing
Of him that made and rules at his behest
The mindes, and harts of every living thing?
Ah sweet content, where doth thine harbour hold,
Is it in Churches, with Religious men,   10
Which please the goddes with prayers manifold,
And in their studies meditate it then.
Whether thou doest in heaven, or earth appeare,
Be where thou wilt, thou will not harbour here.

HENRY CONSTABLE

1562–1613

From *Diana* (1594)

1.

Deere to my soule, then leave me not forsaken,
Flie not, my hart within thy bosome sleepeth:
Even from my selfe and sense I have betaken
Mee unto thee, for whom my spirit weepeth.
And on the shoare of that salt tearie sea,   5
Couch'd in a bed of unseene seeming pleasure,
Where, in imaginarie thoughts thy faire selfe lay,
But being wakt, robd of my lives best treasure,
I call the heavens, ayre, earth, & seas, to heare
My love, my trueth, and black disdaind estate: 10
Beating the rocks with bellowings of dispaire,
Which stil with plaints my words reverberate.
Sighing, alas, what shall become of me?
Whilst Eccho cryes, what shal become of me.

2.

Whilst Eccho cryes, what shall become of mee,
And desolate my desolations pitty,
Thou in thy beauties charrack sitt'st to see
My tragick down-fall, and my funerall ditty.

1ff. Constable's sequence, first published in 1592, is organized in eight
"decades." The sonnets given here are the eighth and ninth of the fifth
decade and the second of the sixth decade in the 1594 edition. The modern
scholarly edition is that of Joan Grundy (Liverpool, Liverpool University
Press, 1960).
12. *my . . . reverberate:* echo back my words. This sonnet is linked to the
next, as the last line of no. 1 becomes the first line of no. 2.
3. *charrack:* galleon

No Tymbrell, but hart thou play'st upon,   5
Whose strings are stretch'd unto the hiest key,
The dyapazon love, love is the unison,
In love, my life and labours wast away.
Onely regardlesse, to the world thou leav'st mee,
Whilst slaine-hopes, turning from the feast of sorrow,   10
Unto Dispaire (their King) which nere deceives me,
Captives my hart, whose blacke night hates the morrow.
And hee, in ruth of my distressed cry,
Plants mee a weeping starre within mine eye.

3.

To live in hell, and heaven to behold,
To welcome life, and die a living death,
To sweat with heate, and yet be freezing cold,
To graspe at starres, and lye the earth beneath;
To tread a Maze that never shall have end,   5
To burne in sighes, and starve in daily teares,
To clime a hill, and never to discend,
Gyants to kill, and quake at childish feares;
To pyne for foode, and watch Thesperian tree,
To thirst for drinke, and Nectar still to draw,   10
To live accurst, whom men hold blest to be,
And weepe those wrongs which never creature saw,
If this be love, if love in these be founded,
My hart is love, for these in it are grounded.

---

5. *Tymbrell:* musical instrument like the tambourine
7. *dyapazon:* the interval and consonance of a musical octave; *unison:* the combination of musical parts at the same pitch or in octaves
11. *nere:* never
6. *starve:* die slowly
9. *Thesperian tree:* which bore the golden apples guarded by the Hesperides and the dragon Ladon

WILLIAM PERCY

1575–1648

From *Coelia* (1594)

1.

Relent, my deere, yet unkind *Coelia,*
At length relent, and give my sorrowes end,
So shall I keepe my long wisht holyday,
And set a trophey on a froward frend,
Nor tributes, nor imposts, nor other duties,   5
Demaund I will as lawfull conqueror;
Duties, tributes, imposts unto thy beauties,
My selfe will pay, as yeelded servitor.
Then quicke relent, thy selfe surrender us:
Brave sir and why, quoth she, must I relent?   10
Relent, cry'd I, thy selfe doth conquer us,
When eftsoons with my propper instrument,
She cut me off, ay me, and answered,
You cannot conquer and be conquered.

2.

It shall be sayd I dy'de for *Coelia;*
Then quicke thou grieslie man of *Erebus,*
Transport me hence unto *Proserpina,*
To be adjudg'd as wilfull amor'us:
To be hong up within the liquid aire,   5

1ff. Percy's sequence, from which numbers 17 and 19 are selected here, contains only twenty sonnets.
12. *eftsoons:* soon afterward
2. *grieslie:* ugly; *man of Erebus:* Charon, the ferryman of hell
3. *Proserpina:* daughter of Ceres, carried off by Pluto and made his queen

For all the sighs which I in vaine have wafted,
To be through *Lethes* waters clensed faire,
For those darke clouds which have my lookes 'or'ecasted,
To be condemd to everlasting fire,
Because at *Cupids* fire I wilful brent me,   10
And to be clad for deadly dumps in mire:
Among so manie plagues which shall torment me,
One solace I shall find when I am over,
It will be knowne I dy'de a constant lover.

---

10. *brent:* burned
11. *dumps:* fits of depression

ANONYMOUS

From *Zepheria* (1594)

1.

When we in kind embracements had agre'd
To keepe a royall banquet on our lips,
How soone have we another feast decreed?
And how at parting have we mourn'd by fits?
Eftsoones in absence have we wayld much more,5
Till those voyd houres of intermission
Were spent, that we might revell as before,
How have we bribed time for expedition?
And when remitted to our former love-playes,
How have we (overweening in delight)10
Accus'd the father Sexten of the dayes?
That then with Eagles wings he tooke his flight.
But now (old man) flye on, as swift as thought,
Sith eyes from love and hope from heart is wrought.

1ff. The sonnet selected is number 26 in the anonymous original edition.
Each of its forty poems is called a "Canzon."
9. *remitted:* sent back
11. *father . . . dayes:* i.e., Father Time

BARTHOLOMEW GRIFFIN

fl. 1596

From *Fidessa* (1596)

1.

Care-charmer sleepe, sweet ease in restles miserie,
The captives libertie, and his freedomes song:
Balme of the brused heart, mans chiefe felicitie,
Brother of quiet death, when life is too too long.
A Comedie it is, and now an Historie,   5
What is not sleepe unto the feeble minde?
It easeth him that toyles, and him that's sorrie:
It makes the deaffe to heare, to see the blinde.
Ungentle sleepe, thou helpest all but me,
For when I sleepe my soule is vexed most: 10
It is *Fidessa* that doth master thee,
If she approach (alas) thy power is lost.
But here she is: see how he runnes amaine,
I feare at night he will not come againe.

2.

Flye to her heart, hover about her heart,
With daintie kisses mollifie her heart:
Pierce with thy arrowes her obdurate heart,
With sweet allurements ever move her heart.
At midday and at midnight touch her heart,   5
Be lurking closely, nestle about her heart:
With power, (thou art a god) command her heart,

1ff. The sonnets selected are numbers 15, 23, 35, and 39 in the original
edition.

Kindle thy coales of love about her heart,
Yea even into thy selfe transforme her heart.
Ah she must love, be sure thou have her heart,   10
And I must dye, if thou have not her heart.
Thy bed (if thou rest well) must be her heart:
He hath the best part sure that hath the heart:
What have I not, if I have but her heart?

3.

I have not spent the Aprill of my time,
The sweet of youth in plotting in the aire:
But doe at first adventure seeke to clime,
Whil'st flowers of blooming yeares are greene and faire.
I am no leaving of al-withering age,   5
I have not suffred many winter lowres:
I feele no storme, unlesse my Love doe rage,
And then in griefe I spend both daies and houres.
This yet doth comfort that my flower lasted,
Untill it did approach my Sunne too neere: 10
And then (alas) untimely was it blasted,
So soone as once thy beautie did appeare.
But after all, my comfort rests in this,
That for thy sake my youth decaied is.

4.

My Ladies haire is threeds of beaten gold,
Her front the purest Christall eye hath seene:
Her eyes the brightest starres the heavens hold.
Her cheekes red Roses, such as seld have been:
Her pretie lips of red vermilion dye,   5
Her hand of yvorie the purest white:
Her blush Aurora, or the morning skye,
Her breast displaies two silver fountaines bright,

---

3. *first adventure:* the first chance I have
6. *lowres:* dark moments
2. *front:* forehead
4. *seld:* seldom, rarely

The Spheares her voyce, her grace the Graces three,
Her bodie is the Saint that I adore,   10
Her smiles and favours sweet as honey bee,
Her feete faire *Thetis* praiseth evermore.
But ah the worst and last is yet behind,
For of a Gryphon she doth beare the mind.

---

12. *Thetis:* one of the Nereids, the mother of Achilles
14. *Gryphon:* Griffin puns on his own name

RICHARD LYNCHE

fl. 1596–1601

From *Diella* (1596)

1.

What sugred termes, what all-perswading arte,
What sweet mellifluous words, what wounding lookes
Love usd for his admittance to my hart?
Such eloquence was never read in bookes;
He promisd pleasure, rest, and endlesse joy,   5
Fruition of the fairest shee alive,
His pleasure paine, rest trouble, joy annoy,
Have I since found, which me of bliss deprive;
The Trojan horse thus have I now let in,
Wherein inclosd these armed men were plac'd,   10
Bright eyes, faire cheekes, sweet lips, & milk white skin
These foes my life have overthrown & raz'd.
Faire outward shewes, prove inwardly the worst,
Love looketh faire, but Lovers are accurst.

2.

But thou my deere sweet-sounding Lute be still,
Repose thy troubled strings upon this mosse,
Thou hast full often easd me gainst my will,
Lye down in peace, thy spoile were my great losse,
Ile speake inough of her, (too cruell) hart,   5
Enough to moove the stonie Rocks to ruth,

1ff. The sonnets selected are numbers 4 and 16 in the original edition.
6. *Fruition:* Enjoyment
4. *spoile:* destruction

And cause these trees weepe tears to heare my smart
Though (cruell she) will not once way my truth.
Her face is of the purest white and red,
Her eyes are christall, and her haire is gold,   10
The world for shape with garlands crown her head,
And yet a Tygresse hart dwells in this mold:
But I must love her (Tigresse) too too much,
Forc'd must I love, because I finde none such.

---

8. *way:* weigh, consider
12. *mold:* form, body

WILLIAM SMITH

fl. 1596

From *Chloris* (1596)

1.

TO THE MOST EXCELLENT
and learned Shepheard
Collin Cloute.

Collin my deere and most entire beloved,
My muse audatious stoupes hir pitch to thee,
Desiring that thy patience be not moved
By these rude lines, written heere you see,
Faine would my muse whom cruell love hath wronged,   5
Shroud hir love labors under thy protection,
And I my selfe with ardent zeale have longed,
That thou mightst knowe to thee my true affection.
Therefore good *Collin*, graciously accept
A few sad sonnets, which my muse hath framed,   10
Though they but newly from the shell are crept,
Suffer them not by envie to be blamed.
But underneath the shadow of thy wings
Give warmth to these yong-hatched orphan things.

1ff. The linked sonnets of No. 1 are dedicatory poems introducing *Chloris*.
No. 2 is the twenty-ninth poem of the sequence. "Collin Cloute" is, of
course, Edmund Spenser.

Give warmth to these yong-hatched orphan things,
Which chill with cold to thee for succour creepe,
They of my studie are the budding springs,
Longer I cannot them in silence keepe.
They will be gadding sore against my minde.   15
But curteous shepheard, if they run astray
Conduct them, that they may the path way finde,
And teach them how, the meane observe they may.
Thou shalt them ken by their discording notes,
Their weedes are plaine, such as poore shepheards weare,   20
Unshapen, torne and ragged are their cotes,
Yet foorth they wandring are devoid of feare.
They wich have tasted of the muses spring,
I hope will smile upon the tunes they sing.

2.

Some in their harts their Mistris colours bears,
Some hath hir gloves, some other hath hir garters,
Some in a bracelet wears hir golden hears,
And some with kisses seale their loving charters.
But I which never favor reaped yet,   5
Nor hath one pleasant looke from hir faire brow,
Content my selfe in silent shade to sit
In hope at length my cares to overplow.
Meane while mine eies shall feede on hir faire face,
My sighs shall tell to hir my sad designes,   10
My painefull pen shall ever sue for grace
To helpe my hart, which languishing now pines.
    And I will triumph still amidst my woe
    Till mercy shall my sorrowes overflowe.

---

19. *ken:* know; *discording:* discordant
20. *weedes:* clothing

RICHARD BARNFIELD

1574–1627

From *Poems: In divers humors* (1598)

1.

If Musique and sweet Poetrie agree,
As they must needes (the Sister and the Brother)
Then must the Love be great, twixt thee and mee,
Because thou lov'st the one, and I the other.
Dowland to thee is deare; whose heavenly tuch   5
Upon the Lute, doeth ravish humaine sense:
Spenser to mee; whose deepe Conceit is such,
As passing all Conceit, needs no defence.
Thou lov'st to heare the sweete melodious sound,
That Phoebus Lute (the Queene of Musique) makes: 10
And I in deepe Delight am chiefly drownd,
When as himselfe to singing he betakes.
One God is God of Both (as Poets faigne)
One Knight loves Both, and Both in thee remaine.

1ff. The sonnet is the first of a group of poems entitled "Poems: In divers humors," which appeared in 1598 as part of *The Encomium of Lady Pecunia.* For Barnfield's works see the edition by Montague Summers (London, The Fortune Press, 1936). The sonnet has the subtitle "To his friend Maister R. L. In praise of Musique and Poetrie."
5. *Dowland:* John Dowland (1563–1626), the famous Elizabethan lutist
7. *Conceit:* imagination
13. *One God:* Apollo, the patron of both music and poetry

SAMUEL DANIEL
1562–1619

From *Delia* (1592)

1.

If so it hap, this of-spring of my care,
These fatall Antheames, lamentable Songs:
Come to their view, who like afflicted are;
Let them sigh for their owne, and mone my wrongs.
But untoucht hearts, with unaffected eie,   5
Approach not to behold my heavinesse:
Cleer-sighted you, soone note what is awrie,
Whilst blinded soules mine errours never gesse.
You blinded soules whom youth and errour leade,
You out-cast Eaglets, dazeled with your sunne: 10
Doe you, and none but you my sorrowes reade,
You best can judge the wrongs that she hath done.
That she hath done, the motive of my paine;
Who whilst I love, doth kill me with disdaine.

1ff. *Delia* first appeared in 1592. The texts presented here, taken from the
1623 edition, often revise the readings of earlier editions. The numbers of
the poems, in the 1592 text, are 3, 4, 6, 9, 30, 45, 46, and 48. See the edi-
tion by A. C. Sprague (Cambridge, Mass., Harvard University Press, 1930).
2. *lamentable:* 1592 reads *sad and mornefull*
4. *sigh for:* 1592 reads *yet sigh*
6. *my heavinesse:* 1592 reads *so great distresse*
8. *soules:* 1592 reads *ones*
11. *Doe:* 1592 reads *Ah*

2.

These plaintive Verse, the Postes of my desire,
Which haste for succour to her slow regard,
Beare not report of any slender fire,
Forging a griefe to winne a fames reward.
Nor are my passions limnd for outward hew,   5
For that no colours can depaint my sorrowes:
Delia her selfe, and all the world may view
Best in my face, where cares hath tild deepe forrowes.
No Bayes I seeke to decke my mourning brow,
O cleer-eyde Rector of the holy Hill: 10
My humble accents beare the Olive bough,
Of intercession but to move her will.
These lines I use, t'unburthen mine owne hart;
My love affects no fame, nor steemes of Art.

3.

Faire is my Love, and cruell as she's faire;
Her brow-shades frownes, although her eyes are sunny;
Her smiles are lightning, though her pride despaire;
And her disdaines are Gall: her favours Hunny.
A modest Maide, deckt with a blush of honor,   5
Whose feete doe tread greene paths of youth and love,
The wonder of all eyes that looke upon her:
Sacred on earth, design'd a Saint above.
Chastitie and Beautie, which were deadly foes,
Live reconciled friends within her brow: 10
And had she pitty to conjoyne with those,
Then who had heard the plaints I utter now.
O had she not beene faire, and thus unkinde,
My Muse had slept, and none had knowne my minde.

---

1. *Postes:* couriers
5. *limnd:* drawn, painted
8. *where:* 1592 reads *how*
11. *beare:* 1592 reads *crave*
12. *intercession . . . will:* 1592 reads *her milde pittie and relenting will*
14. *steemes:* esteems

4.

If this be love, to drawe a wearie breath,
Paint on floods, till the shore crie to th'aire:
With downeward lookes, still reading on the earth;
These sad memorials of my loves dispaire:
If this be love, to warre against my soule,   5
Lie downe to waile, rise up to sigh and grieve:
The never-resting stone of Care to roule,
Still to complaine my griefes, whilst none relieve.
If this be love to cloathe me with darke thoughts,
Haunting untrodden paths to waile apart;   10
My pleasures horror, Musicke tragicke notes,
Teares in mine eyes, and sorrow at my hart.
If this be love, to live a living death,
Then doe I love and draw this wearie breath.

5.

I once may see when yeares shall wreck my wrong,
When golden haires shall chaunge to silver wier:
And those bright raies, that kindle all this fier,
Shall faile in force, their working not so strong.
Then beauty (now the burthen of my song)   5
Whose glorious blaze the world doth so admire,
Must yeeld up all to tyrant Times desire;
Then fade those flowers which deckt her pride so long.
When, if she grieve to gaze her in her glasse,
Which then presents her winter-withered hew,   10
Goe you my verse, go tell her what she was;
For what she was, she best shall find in you.
Your firy heate lets not her glory passe,
But (Phænix-like) shall make her live anew.

---

1. *wreck:* avenge

6.

Care-charmer Sleepe, sonne of the sable night,
Brother to death, in silent darknes borne:
Relieve my languish, and restore the light,
With darke forgetting of my cares returne.
And let the day be time enough to mourne,   5
The shipwracke of my ill adventred youth:
Let waking eyes suffice to waile their scorne,
Without the torment of the nights untruth.
Cease dreames, th'Images of day desires,
To modell forth the passions of the morrow: 10
Never let rising Sunne approve you liers,
To adde more griefe to aggravate my sorrow.
Still let me sleepe, imbracing clouds in vaine;
And never wake to feele the dayes disdayne.

7.

Let others sing of Knights and Palladines,
In aged accents, and untimely words:
Paint shadowes in imaginary lines,
Which well the reach of their high wits records;
But I must sing of thee, and those faire eies,   5
Autentique shall my verse in time to come,
When yet th'unborne shall say, Lo where she lies,
Whose beauty made him speake that else was dombe.
These are the Arkes, the Trophies I erect,
That fortifie thy name against old age,   10
And these thy sacred vertues must protect,
Against the darke and times consuming rage.
Though th'error of my youth in them appeare,
Suffice, they shew I liv'd and lov'd thee deere.

---

6. *adventred:* chanced
11. *approve you:* prove you tò be
6. *Autentique:* Authenticate
13. *in them appeare:* 1592 reads *they shall discover*
14. *lov'd thee deere:* 1592 reads *was thy lover*

8.

None other fame mine unambitious Muse,
Affected ever but t'eternize thee:
All other honors doe my hopes refuse,
Which meaner priz'd and momentary bee.
For God forbid I should my Papers blot,   5
With mercenary lines, with servile Pen:
Praising vertues in them that have them not,
Basely attending on the hopes of men.
No, no, my Verse respects nor *Thames* nor *Theaters*,
Nor seekes it to be knowne unto the Great: 10
But *Avon* poore in fame, and poore in waters,
Shall have my Song, where *Delia* hath her seat.
Avon shall be my *Thames*, and she my Song,
No other prouder Brookes shall heare my wrong.

MICHAEL DRAYTON
1563–1631

From *Idea* (1594)

1.

To the Reader of these Sonnets
Into these Loves, who but for Passion lookes,
At this first sight, here let him lay them by,
And seeke else-where, in turning other Bookes,
Which better may his labour satisfie.
No farre-fetch'd Sigh shall ever wound my Brest,   5
Love from mine Eye a teare shall never wring,
Nor in *Ah-mees* my whyning Sonnets drest,
(A Libertine) fantastickly I sing:
My Verse is the true image of my Mind,
Ever in motion, still desiring change;   10
And as thus to Varietie inclin'd,
So in all Humors sportively I range:
My muse is rightly of the English straine,
That cannot long one fashion intertaine.

2.

How many paltry, foolish, painted things,
That now in Coaches trouble ev'ry street,
Shall be forgotten, whom no Poet sings,
Ere they be well wrap'd in their winding Sheet?

Title: Idea first appeared in 1593 and was subsequently revised by Drayton in later editions. The texts presented here, after the dedicatory "To the Reader," are numbers 6, 8, 14, 15, 20, 21, 37, 44, and 61 in the final 1619 edition. The best edition of Drayton's works is that of J. W. Hebel (5 vols., Oxford, Oxford University Press, 1931–41).

Where I to thee Eternitie shall give,   5
When nothing else remayneth of these dayes,
And Queenes hereafter shall be glad to live
Upon the almes of thy superfluous prayse;
Virgins and Matrons reading these my Rimes,
Shall be so much delighted with thy story,   10
That they shall grieve, they liv'd not in these Times,
To have seene thee, their Sexes onely glory:
So shalt thou flye above the vulgar Throng,
Still to survive in my immortall Song.

3.

There's nothing grieves me, but that Age should haste,
That in my dayes I may not see thee old,
That where those two cleare sparkling Eyes are plac'd,
Onely two Loope-holes, then I might behold.
That lovely, arched, yvorie, pollish'd Brow,   5
Defac'd with Wrinkles, that I might but see;
Thy daintie Hayre, so curl'd, and crisped now,
Like grizzled Mosse upon some aged Tree;
Thy Cheeke, now flush with Roses, sunke, and leane,
Thy Lips, with age, as any Wafer thinne,   10
The Pearly Teeth out of thy Head so cleane,
That when thou feed'st, thy Nose shall touch thy Chinne:
These Lines that now thou scorn'st, which should delight thee,
Then would I make thee read, but to despight thee.

4.

If he, from Heav'n that filch'd that living Fire,
Condemn'd by Jove to endlesse Torment bee,
I greatly marvell, how you still goe free,
That farre beyond Prometheus did aspire:
The Fire he stole, although of Heav'nly kind,   5
Which from above he craftily did take,
Of livelesse Clods, us living Men to make,
He did bestow in temper of the Mind.

---

1. *he:* Prometheus
7. *livelesse:* without life, dead

But you broke into Heav'ns immortall store,
Where Vertue, Honour, Wit, and Beautie lay;   10
Which taking thence, you have escap'd away,
Yet stand as free as ere you did before:
Yet old Prometheus punish'd for his Rape.
Thus poore Theeves suffer, when the greater scape.

5.

His Remedie for Love

Since to obtaine thee, nothing me will sted,
I have a Med'cine that shall cure my Love,
The powder of her Heart dry'd, when she is dead,
That Gold nor Honour ne'r had pow'r to move;
Mix'd with her Teares, that ne'r her true-Love crost,   5
Nor at Fifteene ne'r long'd to be a Bride,
Boyl'd with her Sighes, in giving up the Ghost,
That for her late deceased Husband dy'd;
Into the same then let a Woman breathe,
That being chid, did never word replie,   10
With one thrice-marry'd's Pray'rs, that did bequeath
A Legacie to stale Virginitie.
If this Receit have not the pow'r to winne me,
Little Ile say, but thinke the Devill's in me.

6.

An evill spirit your beautie haunts Me still,
Where with (alas) I have beene long possest,
Which ceaseth not to tempt Me to each Ill,
Nor gives Me once, but one poore minutes rest:
In Me it speakes, whether I Sleepe or Wake,   5
And when by Meanes, to drive it out I try,

Title: The title appears as a marginal gloss in the 1619 edition.
1. *sted:* aid, help

With greater Torments, then it Me doth take,
And tortures Me in most extremity;
Before my Face, it layes downe my Despaires,
And hastes Me on unto a sudden Death;   10
Now tempting Me, to drowne my Selfe in teares,
And then in sighing, to give up my breath;
Thus am I still provok'd, to every Evill,
By this good wicked Spirit, sweet Angell Devill.

7.

A witlesse Gallant, a young Wench that woo'd,
(Yet his dull Spirit her not one jot could move)
Intreated me, as e'r I wish'd his good,
To write him but one Sonnet to his love:
When I, as fast as e'r my Penne could trot,   5
Powr'd out what first from quicke Invention came;
Nor never stood one word thereof to blot,
Much like his Wit, that was to use the same:
But with my Verses he his Mistress wonne,
Who doted on the Dolt beyond all measure.   10
But see, for you to Heav'n for Phraze I runne,
And ransacke all Apollos golden Treasure;
Yet by my Froth, this Foole his Love obtaines,
And I lose you, for all my Wit and Paines.

8.

Deare, why should you command me to my Rest,
When now the Night doth summon all to sleepe?
Me thinkes this Time becommeth Lovers best;
Night was ordayn'd, together Friends to keepe:
How happy are all other living Things,   5
Which though the Day dis-joyne by sev'rall flight,
The quiet Ev'ning yet together brings,
And each returnes unto his Love at Night?
O, Thou that art so courteous else to all,
Why should'st thou, Night, abuse me onely thus,   10

---

3. *e'r*: ever

That ev'ry Creature to his kind do'st call,
And yet 'tis thou do'st onely sever us?
Well could I wish, it would be ever Day,
If when Night comes, you bid me goe away.

9.

Whilst thus my Pen strives to eternize thee,
Age rules my Lines with Wrinkles in my Face,
Where, in the Map of all my Miserie,
Is model'd out the World of my Disgrace;
Whilst in despite of tyrannizing Times,   5
Medea-like, I make thee young againe,
Proudly thou scorn'st my World-out-wearing Rimes,
And murther'st Vertue with thy coy disdaine:
And though in youth, my Youth untimely perish,
To keepe Thee from Oblivion and the Grave,   10
Ensuing Ages yet my Rimes shall cherish,
Where I entomb'd, my better part shall save;
And though this Earthly Body fade and die,
My Name shall mount upon Eternitie.

10.

Since ther's no helpe, Come let us kisse and part,
Nay, I have done: You get no more of Me,
And I am glad, yea glad with all my heart,
That thus so cleanly, I my Selfe can free,
Shake hands for ever, Cancell all our Vowes,   5
And when We meet at any time againe,
Be it not seene in either of our Browes,
That We one jot of former Love reteyne;
Now at the last gaspe, of Loves latest Breath,
When his Pulse fayling, Passion speechlesse lies,   10
When Faith is kneeling by his bed of Death,
And Innocence is closing up his Eyes,
Now if thou would'st, when all have given him over,
From Death to Life, thou might'st him yet recover.

---

6. *Medea-like:* the Greek sorceress Medea restored the youth of Jason's father Aeson

FULKE GREVILLE, LORD BROOKE
1554–1628

From *Caelica* (1580–1600)

1.

Caelica, I overnight was finely used,
Lodg'd in the midst of paradise, your Heart:
Kind thoughts had charge I might not be refused,
Of every fruit and flower I had part.
But curious Knowledge, blowne with busie flame,   5
The sweetest fruits had downe in shadowes hidden,
And for it found mine eyes had seene the same,
I from my paradise was straight forbidden.
Where that Curre, Rumor, runnes in every place,
Barking with Care, begotten out of feare;   10
And glassy Honour, tender of Disgrace,
Stands *Ceraphin* to see I come not there;
While that fine soyle, which all these joyes did yeeld,
By broken fence is prov'd a common field.

2.

The *nurse-life* Wheat within his greene huske growing,
Flatters our hope and tickles our desire,

Title: Caelica was apparently written between 1580 and 1600 but was not published until 1633, five years after Greville's death. The texts presented here are numbers 37, 39, 63, 85, 86, 99, and 102 in the 1633 edition. For Greville's works, see the edition by Geoffrey Bullough (2 vols., Edinburgh, Oliver and Boyd, 1939).
12. *Ceraphin:* Seraphim, the angels who were set as guards over paradise after the fall of Adam and Eve
1. *nurse-life:* life-fostering

Natures true riches in sweet beauties shewing,
Which set all hearts, with labours love, on fire.
No lesse faire is the Wheat when golden eare 5
Showes unto hope the joyes of neare enjoying:
Faire and sweet is the bud, more sweet and faire
The Rose, which proves that time is not destroying.
Caelica, your youth, the morning of delight,
Enamel'd o're with beauties white and red, 10
All sense and thoughts did to beleefe invite,
That Love and Glorie there are brought to bed;
And your ripe yeeres love-noone (he goes no higher)
Turnes all the spirits of Man into desire.

3.

Caelica, when I did see you every day,
I saw so many worths so well united,
As in this union while but one did play,
All others eyes both wondred and delighted:
Whence I conceav'd you of some heavenly mould, 5
Since Love, and Vertue, noble Fame and Pleasure,
Containe in one no earthly metall could,
Such enemies are flesh, and blood to measure.
And since my fall, though I now onely see
Your backe, while all the world beholds your face, 10
This shadow still shewes miracles to me,
And still I thinke your heart a heavenly place:
For what before was fil'd by me alone,
I now discerne hath roome for every one.

4.

Love is the Peace, whereto all thoughts doe strive,
Done and begun with all our powers in one:
The first and last in us that is alive,
End of the good, and therewith pleas'd alone.
Perfections spirit, Goddesse of the Minde, 5
Passed through hope, desire, griefe and feare,

A simple Goodnesse in the flesh refin'd,
Which of the joyes to come doth witnesse beare.
Constant, because it sees no cause to varie,
A Quintessence of Passions overthrowne,   10
Rais'd above all that change of objects carry,
A Nature by no other nature knowne:
For Glorie's of eternitie a frame,
That by all bodies else obscures her name.

5.

The Earth with thunder torne, with fire blasted,
With waters drowned, with windie palsey shaken
Cannot for this with heaven be distasted,
Since thunder, raine and winds from earth are taken:
Man torne with Love, with inward furies blasted,   5
Drown'd with despaire, with fleshly lustings shaken,
Cannot for this with heaven be distasted,
Love, furie, lustings out of man are taken.
Then Man, endure thy selfe, those clouds will vanish;
Life is a Top which whipping Sorrow driveth;   10
Wisdome must beare what our flesh cannot banish,
The humble leade, the stubborne bootlesse striveth:
   Or Man, forsake thy selfe, to heaven turne thee,
   Her flames enlighten Nature, never burne thee.

6.

In Night when colours all to blacke are cast,
Distinction lost, or gone downe with the light;
The eye a watch to inward senses plac'd,
Not seeing, yet still having power of sight,
Gives vaine *Alarums* to the inward sense,   5
Where feare stirr'd up with witty tyranny,
Confounds all powers, and thorough selfe-offence,
Doth forge and raise impossibility:
Such as in thicke depriving darkenesse,

3. *distasted:* offended
7. *thorough selfe-offence:* through self-injury

Proper reflections of the errour be,   10
And images of selfe-confusednesse,
Which hurt imaginations onely see;
And from this nothing seene, tels newes of devils,
Which but expressions be of inward evils.

7.

O false and treacherous *Probability*,
Enemy of truth, and friend to wickednesse;
With whose bleare eyes opinion learnes to see
Truths feeble party here, and barrennesse.
When thou hast thus misled Humanity,   5
And lost obedience in the pride of wit,
With reason dar'st thou judge the Deity,
And in thy flesh make bold to fashion it.
Vaine thought, the word of Power a riddle is,
And till the vayles be rent, the flesh newborne,   10
Reveales no wonders of that inward blisse,
Which but where faith is, every where findes scorne;
Who therfore censures God with fleshly sp'rit,
As well in time may wrap up infinite.

BIBLIOGRAPHY

The following general works on sixteenth-century poetry can be profitably consulted:

PAUL J. ALPERS, ed., *Elizabethan Poetry, Modern Essays in Criticism*, Oxford, Oxford University Press, 1967.

JOHN M. BERDAN, *Early Tudor Poetry 1485–1547*, New York, Macmillan, 1920.

JOHN RUSSELL BROWN and BERNARD HARRIS, eds., *Elizabethan Poetry*, Stratford-Upon-Avon Studies, 2, London, Edward Arnold, 1960.

DOUGLAS BUSH, *Mythology and the Renaissance Tradition*, New York, W. W. Norton, 1963.

MAURICE EVANS, *English Poetry in the Sixteenth Century*, London, Hutchinson's University Library, 1955.

E. H. FELLOWES, *English Madrigal Verse, 1588–1632*, 3rd. Edition revised, Oxford, Clarendon Press, 1968.

CATHERINE ING, *Elizabethan Lyrics*, London, Chatto and Windus, 1951.

C. S. LEWIS, *English Literature in the Sixteenth Century Excluding Drama*, Oxford, Clarendon Press, 1954.

JOHN L. LIEVSAY, *The Sixteenth Century: Skelton Through Hooker*, New York, Goldentree Bibliographies, Appleton, Century and Crofts, 1968.

H. A. MASON, *Humanism and Poetry in the Early Tudor Period*, London, Routledge and Kegan Paul, 1959.

DOUGLAS L. PETERSON, *The English Lyric from Wyatt to Donne*, Princeton, Princeton University Press, 1967.

VERÉ L. RUBEL, *Poetic Diction in the English Renaissance from Skelton Through Spenser*, London, Oxford University Press, 1941.

G. GREGORY SMITH, *Elizabethan Critical Essays*, 2 vols., Oxford, Oxford University Press, 1904.

HALLETT SMITH, *Elizabethan Poetry*, Ann Arbor, University of Michigan Press, 1968.

JOHN STEVENS, *Music and Poetry in the Early Tudor Court*, London, Methuen, 1961.

ELIZABETH J. SWEETING, *Early Tudor Criticism*, Oxford, Blackwell, 1940.

JOHN THOMPSON, *The Founding of English Metre*, New York, Columbia University Press, 1961.

ROSEMOND TUVE, *Elizabethan and Metaphysical Imagery: Renaissance Poetic and Twentieth-Century Critics*, Chicago, Chicago University Press, 1947.

YVOR WINTERS, "The Sixteenth-Century Lyric in England: a Critical and Historical Interpretation," *Poetry*, 53–54 (1939), 258–72, 320–35. Reprinted in Alpers, *Elizabethan Poetry*.

COMMENTARY

JOHN SKELTON

LIFE   Born about 1460, Skelton received the degree of laureate from Oxford in 1490 and from Cambridge in 1493. He was ordained a priest in 1498 and about that time became tutor to the young prince Henry (later King Henry VIII). By 1502 he had received the rectory of Diss, which he held until at least 1511. Skelton spent much time at the court during the first two decades of the century, but he fell into disfavor after his satires against Wolsey (*Colin Clout, Why Come Ye Not to Court, Speke Parrot*) in the early 1520s. His morality play, *Magnificence,* was probably written about 1515–16. Although he apparently made his peace with Wolsey before his death in 1529, he is said to have died in sanctuary at Westminster.

EDITIONS   A new scholarly edition of Skelton's poetry is being prepared for the Clarendon Press by Robert S. Kinsman and Edmund Reiss. This will replace A. Dyce's 1843 edition (London, Thomas Rodd, 2 vols.). A useful selection is Kinsman's *John Skelton, Poems* (Oxford, Clarendon Press, 1969). See also the edition, partially modernized, by Philip Henderson (London, J. M. Dent, 1931; fourth edition, 1964).

TEXT   The selections given here are based upon various sixteenth-century printings of Skelton's poems. The texts have been checked against the Dyce and Kinsman editions. For bibliographical descriptions of the early editions see Robert S. Kinsman and Theodore Yonge, *John Skelton: Canon and Census* (New York, Renaissance Society of America, 1967).

STUDIES   Nan C. Carpenter, *John Skelton,* New York, Twayne Publishers, 1967.

H. L. R. Edwards, *Skelton: the Life and Times of an Early Tudor Poet,* London, Jonathan Cape, 1949.

Stanley Eugene Fish, *John Skelton's Poetry,* New Haven and London, Yale University Press, 1965.

I. A. Gordon, *Skelton, Poet Laureate,* Melbourne, Melbourne University Press, 1943.

A. R. Heiserman, *Skelton and Satire*, Chicago, Chicago University Press, 1961.

L. J. Lloyd, *Skelton: a Sketch of His Life and Writings*, Oxford, Blackwell, 1939.

William Nelson, *John Skelton, Laureate*, New York, Columbia University Press, 1939.

Maurice Pollet, *John Skelton*, Paris, Didier, 1962; English translation by John Warrington, London, J. M. Dent, 1971.

SIR THOMAS MORE

LIFE   More was born in London in 1477 and received his early education at St. Anthony's School. After two years as a page in the household of Cardinal Morton (1490–92), he matriculated at Oxford, leaving two years later to begin his legal studies at the inns of court. His English poetry dates from his early years. Appointed Under-Sheriff of London in 1510, More had already joined the international circle of humanists; his position in it was secured by the publication of *Utopia* in 1516 and of his Latin poems in 1518. He entered the royal service in 1517, becoming Under-Treasurer in 1522 and Chancellor of the Duchy of Lancaster in 1525. In 1529, upon Wolsey's fall, he was made Lord Chancellor, holding that position until his resignation in May of 1532. In April 1534, More was imprisoned for his refusal to take the oath accompanying the Act of Succession. Tried for treason on July 1, 1535, he was executed on July 6.

EDITION   The standard edition of More's works is the *Yale Edition of the Works of St. Thomas More*, Executive Editor, R. S. Sylvester, 16 volumes, New Haven, Yale University Press, 1963—. Volumes so far published are *The History of Richard III* (1963); *Utopia* (1965); *Responsio ad Lutherum* (1969), and *The Confutation of Tyndale's Answer* (1973).

TEXT   The texts of More's poems presented here are based on the 1557 edition of his *English Works* as edited for the Yale *Complete Works*.

STUDIES T. E. Bridgett, *The Life of Blessed Thomas More,* London, Burns and Oates, 1891.

R. W. Chambers, *Thomas More,* London, Jonathan Cape, 1935.

R. W. Gibson and J. Max Patrick, *St. Thomas More: a Preliminary Bibliography of His Works to 1750,* New Haven, Yale University Press, 1961.

G. M. Marc' hadour, *Thomas More ou la sage folie,* Paris, Seghers, 1971.

E. E. Reynolds, *The Field Is Won,* London, Burns and Oates, 1968.

R. S. Sylvester, ed., *St. Thomas More: Action and Contemplation,* New Haven, Yale University Press, 1972.

R. S. Sylvester and D. P. Hardings, eds., *Two Early Tudor Lives* (Roper's *Life of More* and Cavendish's *Life of Wolsey*), New Haven, Yale University Press, 1962.

THOMAS WYATT

LIFE Wyatt was born at Allington, Kent, in 1503. Educated at St. John's College, Cambridge, he married Elizabeth Brooke in 1520. His service at court included embassies to France in 1526, to Italy in 1527, to Spain in 1537, and to Paris and Flanders in 1539–40. In 1528, he published his translation of Plutarch, the *Quyete of Mynde.* Wyatt's position at court, despite a series of royal appointments, was never secure. He was imprisoned for brawling in 1534 and again, on suspicion of treason, after the fall of Anne Boleyn in 1536. In 1541, he was acquitted of charges made against him by Edmund Bonner. After the trial, he retired to his country estate, where he died in 1542.

EDITIONS *Collected Poems of Sir Thomas Wyatt,* ed. Kenneth Muir and Patricia Thomson, Liverpool, Liverpool University Press, 1969. The standard edition of *Tottel's Miscellany* (1557) is that of Hyder E. Rollins, 2 vols., revised edition, Cambridge, Mass., Harvard University Press, 1965.

TEXT The texts presented here are those established by Richard C. Harrier in preparation for his forthcoming edition of Wyatt.

All readings have been collated against the Muir-Thomson edition (abbreviated as *MT* in the notes to each poem).

STUDIES   Sergio Baldi, *La Poesia di Sir Thomas Wyatt*, Florence, Felice Le Monnier, 1953.

Otto Hietsch, *Die Petrarcaübersetzungen Sir Thomas Wyatts; eine sprachvergleichende Studie*, Vienna, Wilhelm Braunmüller, 1960.

Kenneth Muir, *Life and Letters of Sir Thomas Wyatt*, Liverpool, Liverpool University Press, 1963.

Hallett Smith, "The Art of Sir Thomas Wyatt," *Huntington Library Quarterly*, 9 (1946), 323–55.

Raymond Southall, *The Courtly Maker: An Essay on the Poetry of Wyatt and His Contemporaries*, Oxford, 1964.

Patricia Thomson, *Sir Thomas Wyatt and His Background*, Stanford, Stanford University Press, 1964.

E. M. W. Tillyard, *The Poetry of Sir Thomas Wyatt: A Selection and a Study*, London, Chatto and Windus, 1949.

HENRY HOWARD, EARL OF SURREY

LIFE   Born in 1517, Surrey was the son of Thomas Howard, third Duke of Norfolk (1473–1555). He was a close friend, from boyhood, of Henry, Duke of Richmond (d. 1536), the bastard son of Henry VIII. Surrey married Frances Vere, daughter of the Earl of Oxford, in 1532. He was imprisoned at Windsor in 1537 on suspicion of sympathy with the Pilgrimage of Grace rebels and again, in the Fleet, in 1542–43. During military service in France in 1544, he was wounded at the siege of Montreuil. Suspected of treason in late 1546, he was imprisoned with his father in the Tower, and executed in early 1547, shortly before the death of Henry VIII.

EDITIONS   *The Poems of Henry Howard, Earl of Surrey*, ed. Frederick M. Padelford, revised ed., Seattle, University of Washington Press, 1928.

Poems, ed. Emrys Jones, Oxford, Clarendon Press, 1963.

TEXT   The texts presented here are those established by Charles

W. Eckert in his unpublished Ph.D. dissertation, "The Poetry of Henry Howard, Earl of Surrey," Washington University (St. Louis), 1960.

STUDIES Edwin R. Casady, *Henry Howard, Earl of Surrey*, New York, Modern Language Association of America, 1938.

Ivy L. Mumford, "Italian Aspects of Surrey's Lyrics," *English Miscellany*, 16 (1965), 19–36.

Florence H. Ridley, ed., *The* Aeneid *of Henry Howard, Earl of Surrey*, Berkeley, University of California Press, 1963.

THOMAS SACKVILLE

LIFE Sackville, born in 1536, was educated at both Oxford and Cambridge before becoming a barrister at the Inner Temple. He helped to plan the *Mirror for Magistrates* in the late 1550s and collaborated with Thomas Norton to produce the first English blank verse tragedy, *Gorboduc*, which was acted in 1561. Sackville was knighted in 1567 and thereafter became a prominent statesman of Elizabeth's reign, serving as Privy Councilor, commissioner at state trials, ambassador, and Lord Treasurer (from 1599). In 1586 he announced the sentence of death to Mary Queen of Scots and, as Lord High Steward, he presided at the trial of Essex in 1601. Sackville was created Earl of Dorset in 1604, four years before his death.

EDITION A *Mirror for Magistrates*, ed. Lily B. Campbell, Cambridge, Cambridge University Press, 1938.

TEXT The text is that of the 1563 edition of the *Mirror*, in which Sackville's "Induction" and "Complaint of Buckingham" first appeared. Sackville's dedicatory sonnet to *The Courtier* is taken from the 1561 edition of Hoby's translation.

STUDIES Paul Bacquet, *Thomas Sackville, L'Homme et L'Oeuvre*, Geneva, Droz, 1966.

Donald A. Davie, "Sixteenth-Century Poetry and the Common Reader: the Case of Thomas Sackville," *Essays in Criticism*, 4 (1954), 117–27.

Marguerite Hearsey, ed., *The Complaint of Henry, Duke of Buckingham*, New Haven, Yale University Press, 1936.

J. Swart, *Thomas Sackville: A Study in Sixteenth-Century Poetry*, Groningen, Academisch Proefschrift, 1949.

GEORGE GASCOIGNE

LIFE Born in 1539, Gascoigne received his education at Cambridge and the inns of court. His early translations, *Jocasta* (from Euripides) and *The Supposes* (from Ariosto) were acted at Gray's Inn in 1566. Despite serving twice in Parliament, Gascoigne met with little success in his efforts to advance at court. Imprisoned for debt in 1570, he volunteered two years later for service with the army in the Low Countries. *A Hundreth Sundrie Flowres* appeared in 1573; it was reissued, much revised, as *The Posies* in 1575. In his last years, Gascoigne seems to have undergone a moral conversion that led him to produce a number of didactic works. He died in 1577.

EDITIONS *The Complete Works of George Gascoigne*, ed. John W. Cunliffe, 2 vols., Cambridge, Cambridge University Press, 1907–10.

A Hundreth Sundrie Flowres, ed. C. T. Prouty, Columbia, Missouri, Missouri University Press, 1942.

TEXT The texts of Gascoigne's Dedicatory Epistle of the poems and of *Certayne notes of Instruction* are taken from *The Posies of George Gascoigne*, 1575. *The Steele Glas* is edited from the 1576 edition.

STUDIES C. T. Prouty, *George Gascoigne, Elizabethan Courtier, Soldier, and Poet*, New York, Columbia University Press, 1942.

D. T. Starnes, "Gascoigne's *The Complaint of Philomene*," *Texas Studies in English*, 26 (1947), 26–41.

Thomas B. Stroup and H. Ward Jackson, "Gascoigne's *Steele Glas* and 'The Bidding of the Bedes,'" *Studies in Philology*, 58 (1961), 52–60.

SIR WALTER RALEIGH

LIFE　Raleigh (or Ralegh) was born in Devonshire in 1552. After service with the army on the Continent, he settled in London about 1575. Rapidly rising in royal favor, he became Elizabeth's best-known courtier before his fall from grace (after his marriage to Elizabeth Throckmorton) in 1592. Raleigh's voyages of exploration began in 1578 and included journeys to Guiana in 1595 and again in 1617. He was kept in prison by King James from 1603, when he was found guilty of treason, until 1616, when he was released to sail on the last Guiana voyage. Arrested upon his return, he was executed on October 29, 1618.

EDITIONS　*The Works of Sir Walter Raleigh*, ed. William Oldys and Thomas Birch, 8 vols., Oxford, 1829, reprinted, New York, Burt Franklin, 1965. A new edition of Raleigh's works is being undertaken by Pierre Lefranc.
The Poems of Sir Walter Raleigh, ed. Agnes M. C. Latham, London, Routledge and Kegan Paul, 1951.

TEXT　Raleigh's poems were never published in collected form during his lifetime. The texts presented here are based on contemporary miscellanies (*The Phoenix Nest*, 1593; *England's Helicon*, 1600; Francis Davison's *A Poetical Rapsodie*, 1602) and manuscripts.

STUDIES　Muriel C. Bradbrook, *The School of Night: A Study in the Literary Relationships of Sir Walter Raleigh*, Cambridge, Cambridge University Press, 1936.
Stephen Greenblatt, *Sir Walter Raleigh: Renaissance Man and His Roles*, New Haven, Yale University Press, 1973.
Margaret Irwin, *That Great Lucifer: A Portrait of Sir Walter Ralegh*, New York, Harcourt, Brace, 1960.
Pierre Lefranc, *Sir Walter Ralegh Écrivain*, Laval, Armand Colin, 1968.
Walter Oakeshott, *The Queen and the Poet*, London, Faber and Faber, 1960.
Willard M. Wallace, *Sir Walter Raleigh*, Princeton, Princeton University Press, 1959.

EDMUND SPENSER

LIFE Spenser was born in London in 1552, and educated at the Merchant Taylors' School, where the headmaster was Richard Mulcaster, and at Pembroke Hall, Cambridge (B.A. 1573; M.A. 1576). *The Shepheardes Calender*, which heralded a new era in English poetry, was published in 1579. From 1580 until near the end of his life, Spenser served the government in Ireland, his stay there interrupted only by visits to London in 1589 and 1595–96 to supervise the publication of *The Faerie Queene* (Books I–III, 1590, and Books I–VI, 1596). In 1594 he married Elizabeth Boyle, whose courtship he celebrated in the *Amoretti* and *Epithalamion* (published together in 1595). The *Prothalamion* appeared in 1596. In October 1598, Spenser's castle at Kilcolman was burned by the Irish and the poet was forced to flee to London. He died, in distress, if not completely destitute, in January 1599.

EDITIONS *The Works of Edmund Spenser, a Variorum Edition*, ed. Edwin A. Greenlaw, F. M. Padelford, C. G. Osgood, and others, 10 vols., Baltimore, Johns Hopkins University Press, 1932–49.
The Complete Poetical Works of Edmund Spenser, ed. R. E. Neil Dodge, Cambridge, Mass., Houghton Mifflin, 1908.

TEXT The texts of the *Amoretti* and *Epithalamion* are taken from the first edition of 1595, that of the *Prothalamion* from the edition of 1596.

STUDIES Harry Berger, "Spenser's 'Prothalamion': An Interpretation," *Essays in Criticism*, 15 (1965), 363–80.
B. E. C. Davies, *Edmund Spenser: A Critical Study*, Cambridge, Cambridge University Press, 1933.
Robert Ellrodt, *Neoplatonism in the Poetry of Spenser*, Geneva, Droz, 1960.
Thomas M. Greene, "Spenser and the Epithalamic Convention," *Comparative Literature*, 9 (1957), 215–28.
A. Kent Hieatt, *Short Time's Endless Monument*, New York, Columbia University Press, 1960.

William Nelson, ed., *Form and Convention in the Poetry of Edmund Spenser*, New York, Columbia University Press, 1961.

William Nelson, *The Poetry of Edmund Spenser, a Study*, New York, Columbia University Press, 1963.

W. L. Renwick, *Edmund Spenser: An Essay on Renaissance Poetry*, London, Edward Arnold, 1925.

J. Norton Smith, "Spenser's 'Prothalamion': A New Genre," *Review of English Studies*, New Series, 10 (1959), 173–78.

W. B. C. Watkins, *Shakespeare and Spenser*, Princeton, Princeton University Press, 1950.

SIR PHILIP SIDNEY

LIFE Born in 1554, Sidney was educated at Shrewsbury School and Christ Church, Oxford. From 1572 to 1575 he traveled in France, Germany, Austria, Italy, and Poland and in 1577 he went abroad again as a diplomatic emissary to the Elector Palatine. By 1578 he had already achieved fame as the foremost courtier of England, if not of Europe. In 1580 Sidney incurred some royal disfavor by his opposition to the proposed marriage between Elizabeth and the Duke of Anjou. The first version of the *Arcadia* (the *Old Arcadia*) was completed in the summer of 1580; Sidney's revisions of it into the *New Arcadia* (first published in 1590) occurred at intervals between 1580 and 1584. The best date for the composition of *Astrophil and Stella* is the summer of 1582. Knighted in 1583, Sidney married Frances Walsingham in the autumn of that year. He was recalled to court in 1585 and made governor of Flushing. Sidney died at Arnheim, from the effects of a wound received while leading troops to the relief of Zutphen, on October 17, 1586.

EDITIONS *The Complete Works of Sir Philip Sidney*, ed. Albert Feuillerat, 4 vols., Cambridge, Cambridge University Press, 1917–26.

The Poems of Sir Philip Sidney, ed. William A. Ringler, Jr., Oxford, Clarendon Press, 1962.

Astrophel and Stella, ed. Max Putzel, New York, Doubleday, 1967.

TEXT The text of *Astrophil and Stella* presented here is based on the 1598 edition of the *Countess of Pembroke's Arcadia . . . with sundry new additions.*

STUDIES John Buxton, *Sir Philip Sidney and the English Renaissance,* second ed., New York, St. Martin's Press, 1964.

John F. Danby, *Poets on Fortune's Hill: Studies in Sidney, Shakespeare, Beaumont and Fletcher,* London, Faber and Faber, 1952.

Vanna Gentili, ed., *Astrophil and Stella,* Biblioteca Italiana di Testi Inglesi, 10, Bari, Adriatica Editrice, 1965.

David Kalstone, *Sidney's Poetry: Contexts and Interpretations,* Cambridge, Mass., Harvard University Press, 1965.

Franco Marenco, "Astrophil and Stella," *Filologia e Letteratura,* 13 (1967).

R. L. Montgomery, *Symmetry and Sense, the Poetry of Sir Philip Sidney,* Austin, Texas, University of Texas Press, 1961.

Kenneth O. Myrick, *Sir Philip Sidney as a Literary Craftsman,* Cambridge, Mass., Harvard University Press, 1935.

James M. Osborn, *Young Philip Sidney, 1572–1577,* New Haven, Yale University Press, 1972,

Theodore Spencer, "The Poetry of Sir Philip Sidney," *English Literary History,* 12 (1945), 251–78.

Jack Stillinger, "The Biographical Problem of Astrophel and Stella," *Journal of English and Germanic Philology,* 59 (1960), 617–39.

Malcolm W. Wallace, *The Life of Sir Philip Sidney,* Cambridge, Cambridge University Press, 1915.

Mona Wilson, *Sir Philip Sidney,* London, Duckworth, 1931.

Richard B. Young, "English Petrarke: A Study of Sidney's Astrophel and Stella," in *Three Studies in the Renaissance: Sidney, Jonson, Milton,* New Haven, Yale University Press, 1958.

CHRISTOPHER MARLOWE

LIFE Marlowe was born at Canterbury in 1564. He attended Corpus Christi College, Cambridge, but by June 1587, he had already been employed by the government in some kind of secret service. From 1587 until his death in 1593, he lived in London and it was during this period that the great plays were written and produced. Marlowe led a wild life, often brawling; shortly before his death, he was accused of atheism by his onetime friend, the playwright Thomas Kyd. He was killed in a tavern fight on May 30, 1593.

EDITIONS *Works*, ed. C. F. Tucker Brooke, Oxford, Clarendon Press, 1910.

Marlowe's Poems, ed. L. C. Martin, London and New York, Methuen, 1931.

The Poems, ed. Millar Maclure, London, Methuen, 1968.

Hero and Leander, A Facsimile of the First Edition, 1598, ed. L. L. Martz, Washington and New York (The Folger Library Facsimiles), 1972.

For Chapman's continuation of *Hero and Leander*, see *The Poems of George Chapman*, ed. Phyllis B. Bartlett, New York, Modern Language Association, 1941. Chapman divides Marlowe's poem into two "sestiads" and adds four sestiads of his own.

TEXT The text of *Hero and Leander* is that of the first 1598 edition, from the unique copy in the Folger Shakespeare Library. "The Passionate Sheepheard to his love" is taken from *England's Helicon*, 1600.

STUDIES Muriel C. Bradbrook, "Hero and Leander," *Scrutiny*, 2 (1933), 59–64.

Paul M. Cubeta, "Marlowe's Poet in Hero and Leander," *College English*, 26 (1965), 500–5.

R. S. Forsythe, " 'The Passionate Shepherd' and English Poetry," *Publications of the Modern Language Association*, 40 (1925), 692–742.

Russell Fraser, "The Art of Hero and Leander," *Journal of English and Germanic Philology*, 57 (1958), 743–54.

S. K. Heninger, Jr., "The Passionate Shepherd and the Philosophic Nymph," *Renaissance Papers 1962*, (Durham, N.C., Duke University Press, 1963), 63–70.

C. S. Lewis, *Hero and Leander*, British Academy Lecture, London, 1952.

J. B. Steane, *Marlowe: A Critical Study*, Cambridge, Cambridge University Press, 1964.

THOMAS CAMPION

LIFE Born in 1567, Campion was both law student and physician as well as musician and poet. He spent three years at Peterhouse, Cambridge, apparently without taking a degree. His first poems were published in 1591 and his important *Observations in the Art of English Poesie* (answered by Samuel Daniel's *A Defence of Ryme*, 1603) appeared in 1602. From 1602 until 1605, Campion was on the Continent. In the latter year he received the degree of M.D. from the University of Caen. In 1615 Campion was examined and found innocent in the notorious case of Sir Thomas Overbury. His *Books of Airs*, four in all, were published in 1600, 1613, and 1617. He died in London on March 1, 1620.

EDITION *The Works of Thomas Campion*, ed. Walter R. Davis, New York, Doubleday, 1967.

TEXT The texts presented here are those established by Professor Davis for his edition.

STUDIES G. L. Hendrickson, "Elizabethan Quantitative Hexameters," *Philological Quarterly*, 28 (1949), 237–60.

Miles M. Kastendieck, *England's Musical Poet, Thomas Campion*, New York, Oxford University Press, 1938.

Catherine W. Peltz, "Thomas Campion, An Elizabethan Neo-Classicist," *Modern Language Quarterly*, 11 (1950), 3–6.

R. W. Short, "The Metrical Theory and Practice of Thomas Campion," *Publications of the Modern Language Association*, 59 (1944), 1003–18.

G. D. Willcock, "Passing Pitefull Hexameters: A Study of Quantity and Accent in English Renaissance Verse," *Modern Language Review*, 29 (1934), 1–19.

The following collections and studies on the Elizabethan sonnet may be profitably consulted.

THOMAS CROSLAND, *The English Sonnet,* London, M. Secker, 1917.

MARTHA F. CROWE, *Elizabethan Sonnet Cycles,* 4 vols., London, Kegan Paul, Trench, Trübner, 1896–98.

LISLE C. JOHN, *The Elizabethan Sonnet Sequences,* New York, Columbia University Press, 1938.

SIDNEY LEE, *Elizabethan Sonnets,* 2 vols., New York, E. P. Dutton, 1904.

J. W. LEVER, *The Elizabethan Love Sonnet,* London, Methuen, 1956.

JANET G. SCOTT, *Les Sonnets Élisabéthains,* Paris, H. Champion, 1929.

INDEX

Ye learned sisters which have oftentimes, 392

Ye learned sisters which have oftentimes, 392
Ye old mule, that thinck your self so fayre, 138
Ye tradefull Merchants that with weary toyle, 350
Yet sighs, deere sighs, indeede true friends you are, 486
You that do search for everie purling spring, 425
You that have spent the silent night, 253
You that in love finde lucke and habundance, 153
You that with allegories curious frame, 432
Your words my friend (right healthfull caustiks) blame, 429
Youre ugly tokyn, 91
Ys yt possyble, 156

Zepheria, 565